An Evangelical Mind

Nathanael Burwash and the Methodist Tradition in Canada, 1839–1918

MARGUERITE VAN DIE

D0075261

WITHDRAWN FROM
M.C.S. LIBRARY

E. P. B. C. LIBRARY

McGill-Queen's University Press
Kingston, Montreal, London

© McGill–Queen's University Press 1989
ISBN 0-7735-0695-0

Legal deposit second quarter 1989
Bibliothèque nationale du Québec

∞

Printed in Canada on acid-free paper

This book has been published with the help of a grant
from the Canadian Federation for the Humanities, using
funds provided by the Social Sciences and Humanities
Research Council of Canada.

Canadian Cataloguing in Publication Data
Van Die, Marguerite
  An evangelical mind
  (McGill-Queen's Studies in the History of Religion; 3)
  Includes index.
  Bibliography: p.
  ISBN 0-7735-0695-0
  1. Burwash, N. (Nathanael), 1839–1918.
  2. Methodist Episcopal Church—Canada—History.
  3. Canada—Church history.
  4. Methodists—Canada—
  Biography. I. Title. II. Series.
  BX8495.B89V37 1989   287.6320924   C89-090032-0

To the memory of my father, Willem Van Die (1914–1987)

Contents

Acknowledgments

Throughout the research and writing of this book I have received generous assistance from many people. Ever since this study began as a doctoral dissertation, I have benefited from the valuable insight and constructive criticism offered by Richard Allen, formerly of McMaster University, my thesis supervisor. I am especially grateful for his willingness to combine that role with a demanding schedule as a member of the Ontario Legislature. I appreciate the permission for this arrangement and the encouragement and financial support given by the Department of History at the University of Western Ontario. Additional financial support for research was given by the Social Sciences and Humanities Research Council of Canada and the Government of Ontario, while a grant from the Advisory Research Committee of Queen's University has helped defray the costs of preparing the manuscript in its final form.

The competent assistance and excellent resources available at the Weldon Library, University of Western Ontario, the E.J. Pratt Library at Victoria University, and the United Church of Canada Archives in Toronto made research a pleasure. At the United Church of Canada Archives I was especially fortunate to be able to avail myself of the services of Glenn Lucas and Neil Semple, whose intimate familiarity with the Archives' valuable resources in Canadian Methodism greatly facilitated and enlivened my research.

For the more difficult task of maintaining morale during the long period of writing, I owe a debt of thanks to many people, but in particular to Katherine Ridout, Pamela Hutchins-Orr, and my colleagues and students at Queen's Theological College, Kingston. Katherine Ridout also kindly drew on her familiarity with the Burwash Papers and subjected the manuscript in one of its early stages to an informed reading. Hugh Moorhouse, A.B. McKillop, and my colleague George

Rawlyk also read the manuscript, offering advice and encouraging me to seek publication.

A sincere thanks is due to those who provided clerical assistance, to Eileen Fleming and to Dorothy Schweder of Queen's Theological College, whose help went beyond the call of duty, and to Jackie Doherty, whose cheerful and efficient assistance under pressure brought the manuscript through its final stages. At McGill-Queen's University Press, Donald Akenson, Rosalind Malcolm, Diane Duttle, and Joan McGilvray provided sound editorial advice and helped me over the hurdles of publication. The manuscript has benefited greatly from Freya Godard's painstaking copy-editing. Finally, I wish to express my appreciation to my family, who patiently endured the times of frustration which accompanied the progress of this book and who encouraged me to persevere. To my father especially, whose interest sustained me but who did not live to see the manuscript in its final form, I owe deep gratitude.

Nathanael Burwash and twin sons, William Arthur and Richard Clarke, both of whom died in 1889. (UCA)

The Burwash family, ca. 1890. (*Left to right*) Back row: Adam Proctor, Edward Moore Jackson, Lachlin Taylor. Front row: Chancellor and Mrs Burwash, Nathanael Alfred. (UCA)

Chancellor Burwash.
(N. Burwash, *History
of Victoria College*
[Toronto: Victoria
College Press 1927],
frontispiece)

Victoria University.
Pen drawing by Willem
Hart. (Courtesy of the
artist)

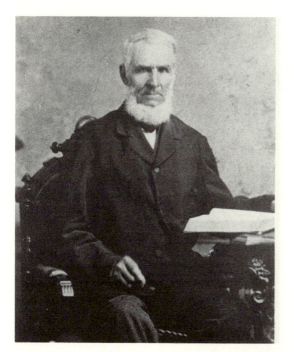

Adam Burwash, father
of Nathanael Burwash.
(United Church of
Canada Archives
[UCA], Toronto)

Anne Taylor Burwash,
mother of Nathanael
Burwash. (UCA)

Nathanael Burwash in 1866, aged 27, just before beginning his duties as professor of natural science at Victoria College

Samuel Sobieski Nelles, principal of Victoria College/University, 1850-87. (UCA)

Nathanael Burwash, ca. 1873, shortly after his appointment as dean of Theology. (UCA)

Margaret Proctor Burwash and her daughter Anne Eliza Taylor, who died in 1874. (UCA)

Chancellor and Mrs Burwash with the Koro family in Tokyo, Japan, in 1913. (UCA)

An Evangelical Mind

Introduction

Secluded behind one of Toronto's busiest commercial districts, its collegiate Gothic strangely incongruous in the contemporary architectural landscape, stands Burwash Hall, the men's residence of Victoria University. Completed in 1913, Burwash Hall represented the collaboration of two staunch Methodists, Nathanael Burwash, Victoria's president and chancellor from 1887 to 1913, and Chester Massey, whose father's estate funded the building. Its first dean of men was Chester's son Vincent, who, fresh from Oxford, tried with only a modicum of success to impart a measure of Old World gentility to the hall's boisterous residents.[1]

To Nathanael Burwash the completion of Burwash Hall and this valiant attempt to elevate colonial manners were part of a greater vision, the integration of his denomination, Canadian Methodism, into the mainstream of the nation. It was largely due to his efforts that Victoria University in 1892 had made the transition from an independent Methodist institution in Cobourg to a federated college of the provincial University of Toronto. Burwash hoped that through this new alliance Canadian Methodists would be able to co-operate with other religious denominations to provide moral and intellectual leadership to a young and developing nation. Today a number of buildings continue to testify to his vision, for by 1913 the Victoria campus included, in addition to Burwash Hall, a large brown freestone academic building, a women's residence, Annesley Hall, and the Birge-Carnegie Library. Of Nathanael Burwash himself, however, very little is known.

Born on 25 July 1839 in the province of Lower Canada, Nathanael was the eldest son of Adam Burwash and Anne Taylor, both devout Methodists. In 1844 the family moved to take up a farm in Baltimore, Upper

Canada, a hamlet close to Cobourg, home of Victoria College, Methodism's institution of higher learning in central Canada. Here young Burwash entered in 1852 as a preparatory student, graduating with a BA in 1859. Although he had expressed some inclination towards the study of law, he finally opted first for education and, after a year as a tutor at Victoria, for the ministry. From that point his career was set: theology and education became his lifelong interests. After six years in the Methodist ministry, from 1861 to 1866, he was asked to return to Victoria as an instructor in the natural sciences. He assumed his duties early in 1867 after a few months' preparatory work at the Sheffield School of Science at Yale.

In 1868 he married Margaret Proctor, daughter of Edward Proctor, registrar for Lambton County. Before her marriage Margaret had attended the Wesleyan Female College in Hamilton and had spent one year as preceptress at the female branch of the Wesleyan Academy in Sackville, New Brunswick. A quiet, strong minded-woman, she shared her husband's interest in education and expended much time and effort on behalf of Victoria's women students.[2] Of their twelve children, only four, Edward Moore Jackson, Lachlin Taylor, Nathanael Alfred, and Adam Proctor, survived beyond adolescence. Though Edward entered the ministry, his primary academic interest was geology, in which he completed a Ph D at the University of Chicago in 1911. This interest was shared by his brother Lachlin, who worked for some time as an inspector of mines for the Dominion Department of the Interior, and who achieved a certain amount of fame as one of the searchers for the 1845 Franklin expedition.[3] Both brothers contributed to substantial scholary publications on various aspects of Canadian geology.[4]

For their father, however, geology remained an avocation. Although he did teach the sciences from 1867 to 1873, he did so on condition that he be allowed to teach theology should the opportunity arise to establish a theological faculty at Victoria. With this goal in mind, he received a BD from the Methodist Episcopal seminary, the Garrett Biblical Institute in Evanston, Illinois, and an STD (Doctor of Sacred Theology) in 1876. In 1873 his wishes were met, and he was appointed dean of theology at Victoria and in that capacity took a leading role in upgrading the theological training of the Methodist ministry. As an administrator, professor, fund raiser, and secretary of the Educational Society of the Methodist Church from 1874 to 1886, he had a demanding schedule. Nevertheless, he was also able to write a surprising amount, most of which quickly became required reading for the Methodist ministry: *Wesley's Doctrinal Standards, Part I, The Sermons* (1881, 1902, 1909); *A Handbook of the Epistle of St. Paul to the Romans* (1887); *Inductive Studies in Theology* (1896); and a *Manual of*

Christian Theology on the Inductive Method (1900). Known for "an intelligent wise conservatism" in matters of doctrine and at the same time for a liberal attitude towards contemporary biblical scholarship, Burwash was primarily responsible for the acceptance of the teaching of the higher criticism in the theological institutions of the Methodist Church in Canada.

Theology, however, was only part of his larger concern to maintain the relevance and influence of religion in the changing social and intellectual world of late Victorian Canada. For this reason Burwash became one of the leading advocates of university federation in the 1880s. Appointed president and chancellor of Victoria University in 1887, he was successful both in achieving federation and in insisting that its terms continued to be met. Moreover, his long years of work on the University of Toronto Senate and the Ontario Educational Council allowed him to exert great influence on Ontario's educational system. In 1902 he was elected to the Royal Society of Canada, to which he contributed a number of papers, and in 1906 he became a sectional president. His primary interest lay in moral and educational organizations, and he was a charter member of the Canadian Methodist Historical Society, a member of the Canadian Society of Authors, and a director of the Canadian Peace and Arbitration Society and the Methodist Social Union, to mention only a few. Historically minded, he wrote a number of books devoted to university federation and to Methodism in central Canada: *Egerton Ryerson* in the Makers of Canada series, a *History of Victoria College*, published posthumously in 1927, and the first three chapters of *The History of the University of Toronto and Its Colleges 1827–1906*.

As an educator and the denomination's only theologian of any stature, Burwash was highly visible in the Methodist Church of Canada, and his voice carried considerable weight. Besides serving for years as secretary of the Educational Society, he was appointed to many church committees and in 1889 was elected president of the Bay of Quinte Conference, which in 1913, in appreciation for his years of service to the church, established a Burwash Memorial Lectureship. When church union negotiations began between the Presbyterian, Congregational, and Methodist Churches in 1902, he was appointed president of the subcommittee on doctrine. In that capacity he had a decisive influence on the doctrinal statement for the proposed United Church. After retiring as chancellor in 1913 he still taught church history at Victoria and practical theology at the Methodist National Training School, an institution established for instructing and training women for missionary and social work. In addition speaking engagements continued to keep him in touch with Methodists throughout Canada, and in 1913, at the request of graduates of Victoria serving as missionaries in Japan, he and his wife were able to make an extended tour of the Methodist missions of that country. He died on 30 March 1918 after a brief illness.

Given his long and varied career, it is surprising that Burwash has received so little scholary attention, other than to illustrate various aspects of intellectual history in Canada. As a professor in the natural sciences who had to come to grips with the writings of Charles Darwin, his response to evolutionary science has attracted some interest.[5] So too has his part in the controversy within Canadian Methodism from 1890 to 1910 over the teaching of the higher criticism.[6] An ardent Loyalist and imperialist who spoke on a number of occasions on "the great moral fact of the white man's burden," he has been briefly acknowledged and set within the wider context of Canadian imperialist thought by Carl Berger in *A Sense of Power*.[7] And as an earnest young Canadian who in his first visit to Paris in 1868 was proudly guided by "one little text, the admonition of the aged apostle Paul to Timothy ... 'Keep thyself pure,' " he deserves his place in A.B. McKillop's *A Disciplined Intelligence*, as an illustration of the continuity and prominence of the moral dimension in Anglo-Canadian thought.[8] Finally, in his capacity as a university administrator he has attracted some notice, though not always of the most favourable kind. As chancellor of Victoria University, federated with what he considered to be Canada's national university, he was not averse to interfering in the affairs of other universities, be it faculty appointments at Mount Allison or requests for public funding by Queen's University.[9] Both his administrative competence and his pivotal position in university federation have been recognized more favourably by C.B. Sissons in his *History of Victoria University* and to a lesser extent in various writings devoted to the history of the University of Toronto.[10]

However, it is not primarily as an imperialist, a nationalist or an administrator that contemporaries appear to have remembered him, but as a Methodist. To Sir Wilfrid Laurier he was reputedly "the head and front of Methodism."[11] To Maurice Hutton, principal of University College, he was "our Nathanael without guile."[12] His colleague and successor as dean of theology, F.H. Wallace, eulogized him as a "saint of God" and quickly added, "And yet he was no mystic in any quietistic sense. He proved his faith by his work. He had definite aims and he could labor and fight for them."[13] In 1936 in celebration of Victoria's first centenary, four Burwash Memorial Lectures were delivered, devoted to a nostalgic reconstruction of the past. By then Methodism had terminated its identity as a denomination, but Nathanael Burwash continued to be remembered fondly as "an evangelical mystic, in other words a Methodist."[14] Later scholarship has agreed, and in the one very brief assessment which has been made of Burwash's theology, Thomas Langford has observed, "Sensitive to the rising scientific ethos, he attempted to maintain central ligaments of the Wesleyan tradition and present them to his era."[15]

It is in that capacity, as someone who consciously tried to live and express the Wesleyan tradition in the late nineteenth century, that Burwash is of significance to those interested in understanding Canada's intellectual and religious heritage. His life span, 1839–1918, covers a period in western Christianity that historians have generally associated with a decline, or at best a profound re-orientation, of religious belief and practice. Intellectual historians like A.B. McKillop and Ramsay Cook, for example, have noted a decrease in the personal faith of a number of educated young Canadians as they came to terms with the critical thought of the late Victorian period.[16] Thus McKillop chose to conclude his analysis of the effect of scientific inquiry and British idealism on religious faith with a chapter entitled "The Sadness and Joy of Knowledge." Cook, who examined the nature and effect of social criticism, observed in a similar vein that "the religious crisis provoked by Darwinian science and the historical criticism of the Bible led religious people to attempt to salvage Christianity by transforming it into an essentially social religion."[17]

These studies are only part of a larger body of historical literature devoted to a critical analysis on the nineteenth-century Canadian intellectual tradition.[18] But though the philosophical background has received considerable attention, little is known of the theological assumptions which guided educated Canadians. Did the distinctive doctrines of the various denominations, for example, help determine the way in which intellectuals met such new influences as Darwinian thought and the higher criticism, or influence their receptivity to British idealism? To what extent did religious experience affect individual belief in post-Darwinian Canada? This is especially relevant in the case of those raised in the Methodist tradition, where experience and belief were inextricably connected. Because we know little about the nature of Methodist theology in Canada, it has been impossible to give an informed answer to such questions.

The studies of Canadian Methodism that do exist, however, are in general agreement with the conclusion that, as elsewhere, Methodists experienced far-reaching changes in belief and practice during the period under examination. Historians have spoken of "an eclipse of revivalism," a "decline of revival," and of the transformation "from a select body of converts into a far-reaching urban, social institution."[19] In *Church and Sect in Canada*, a pioneering study, that explained religious change in terms of underlying social conditions, S.D. Clark concluded that by the middle of the nineteenth century Methodism had already begun to lose its vitality. As the otherworldliness and fervour of the sect began to give way to a socially conservative church, by the time of church union in 1925 Methodism had largely succumbed to "the growing dominance of secular values associated with Politics and Big Business." The main causes of this decline were the accommodation with the teachings of Darwinian science and biblical criticism, a reliance upon a university-educated ministry, and the increased affluence of Methodists.[20] These arguments have been repeated in various forms by a number of other historians, and since each of these developments involved Burwash directly, they will be examined in some detail in this study.

At the outset, however, one point should be made that has escaped the notice of scholars who have concluded that Canadian Methodism changed significantly during the nineteenth century. Such a change necessarily had to take place within the limits imposed by the doctrinal standards of the Methodist Church. As a result of Wesley's provisions for the Methodist societies after his death, these standards, consisting of his first fifty-two sermons and his *Notes on the New Testament* could not be altered in any way and were binding on anyone who preached or performed any act of public worship on Methodist property.

Safeguarded initially in a Deed of Declaration, and later in a Model Deed of the Wesleyan Methodist Church of Canada, the doctrinal standards were finally made inviolable by the terms of the 1883 Basis of Union, which was enacted by Parliament the following year.[21] As one Methodist minister, W.I. Shaw, professor of theology at the Wesleyan Theological College in Montreal commented, "We have locked ourselves in and then thrown away the key.[22] Such "imprisonment," however, should not be understood as total confinement, for it was also recognized that the doctrinal standards were open to different interpretations and that disagreements had to be settled "by the prevalent spirit of the different Churches." As the denomination's leading theologian and editor of one of the doctrinal standards used by all students in the Methodist ministry, Wesley's *Standard Sermons*, Burwash had an important influence on that spirit.

In order to understand that spirit, it is necessary to view Methodism in Canada, not simply as a separate denomination, but as an expression of a wider movement, the evangelical revival of the eighteenth and nineteenth centuries. Unfortunately, as George A. Rawlyk has recently observed, "there has been ... little serious attempt made to explore the often fascinating connection between evangelical religion and evolving Canadian culture."[23] Quite the contrary holds true for Britain and, to an even greater extent, for the United States, where the pervasiveness and importance of evangelicalism in the Victorian period have received due recognition. Leonard I. Sweet has remarked, "It would be as difficult to unscramble a mixed omelette as to separate Evangelicalism from nineteenth-century American culture."[24] Such research as has been done in Canada, in particular an introductory overview by Goldwin French, "The Evangelical Creed in Canada," points to a similar conclusion.[25] According to French the effects of evangelical Protestantism on Canada have been both profound and enduring: "The work of Hugh MacLennan, E.J. Pratt and Northrop Frye are the logical and characteristic outcome of the dilemmas and values built into our cultural history by the power of the evangelical churches."[26]

While not professing to shed light on the country's literary heritage, this book too will continue to probe the nature and influence of nineteenth-century evangelicalism in Canada by exploring the life and thought of one of its most influential exponents. Today, the term "evangelicalism" has unfortunately become synonymous with a resurgent conservative Protestantism, a definition that distorts its nineteenth-century meaning.[27] In the Victorian period, however, the name "evangelical" was appropriated by such mainline denominations as the Methodists and the Baptists and in varying degrees Presbyterians, Congregationalists, and members of the Church of England. Evangelicals shared a strong conviction of the importance of individual salvation through repentance and conversion and the acceptance of a disciplined life that reflected a spiritual transformation. Their authority for their views on the sinfulness of the human condition and for outlining the plan of salvation were the Scriptures, which they viewed as recording the real, historical character of God's saving work. Whereas evangelicals might differ about details and emphasis, they were united in this concern with biblical, experiential, and "vital" religion and formed a fellowship that was both trans-denominational and trans-Atlantic.[28]

They also saw themselves sharing a common heritage and considered their emphasis on conversion and a life of holiness under the direction of the Holy Spirit to be a faithful reflection of the spirituality of the New Testament churches. Historians, on the other hand, have generally emphasized the Puritan ancestry of evangelicalism in the English-speaking world and the impact in the mid-eighteenth century of the Great Awakening in the American colonies and the Methodist revival in Great Britain.[29]

With its concern for individual salvation, evangelicalism emphasized the theological position developed by John Wesley in the eighteenth century. "Our main doctrines," Wesley had insisted, "which include all the rest, are three – that of repentance, of faith, and of holiness. The first of these we account, as it were, the porch of religion; the next, the door; the third religion itself. These three doctrines he considered to be the essence of "the true, the scriptural, experimental religion."[30]

Though Wesley spared no effort in preaching, explaining, and applying these doctrines, little is known about the value placed upon them by his Methodist followers in Victorian Canada. No Canadian was probably as familiar with Wesley's writings as Nathanael Burwash, and therefore an examination of his writing can help determine to what extent Wesley's evangelical doctrines continued to direct the decisions of Methodists in Canada as they came into contact with the intellectual and structural changes of the late nineteenth century.

In order to answer such a question, it is necessary to examine briefly the way in which evangelicals turned belief into action. Religion for them expressed itself in a complete transformation of life, not simply the paying of lip service to a series of dogmas. Because of this total commitment, evangelicalism found a natural partner in revivalism. "Revivalism," one historian has correctly concluded, "is merely a proselytical tool of evangelism," and in order to emphasize the partnership he has used the term evangelical revivalism to describe the movement that began with Wesley and others in the eighteenth century.[31] Such proselytizing can take many forms, and revivalism should not be identified simply with the emotionalism that often accompanied the impassioned preaching of repentance and conversion. Nor should it be equated with periodic evangelistic assaults intended to revive flagging commitment. To evangelicals the need to "refresh" the faith was constant, and the means available were many and extended well beyond the pulpit. Moreover, Wesley had considered the world his parish, and later evangelicals too shared a zeal to spread the gospel and "win the world for Christ." Second only to their desire for the transformation of the individual was their desire to "spread scriptural holiness" and Christianize the nation. To do this they had at their disposal a wide array of voluntary associations and parachurch institutions. These included missions, Bible and tract societies, publishing houses, Sunday schools, and temperance and other moral reform organizations, as well as seminaries and colleges. Religious faith and practice, therefore, not only affected the lives of individuals but also found expression in institutions established to ensure the continuity and permanence of the revival.[32]

Students of revivalism in the United States have been able to refine and deepen their understanding of this intimate relationship between religious belief and its cultural expression. By building on the pioneer research of Perry Miller, they have examined religious revival as part of a larger process of cultural reorganization or awakening.[33] William G. McLoughlin has summarized this relationship: "Awakenings – the most vital and yet most mysterious of all folk arts – are periods of cultural revitalization that begin in a general crisis of beliefs and values and extend over a period of a generation or so, during which time a profound reorientation in beliefs and values takes place. Revivals alter the lives of individuals; awakenings alter the world view of a whole people"[34] McLoughlin's correlation between revivalism and cultural awakening has proved helpful in determining the extent of evangelical continuity in Canadian Methodism during Burwash's lifetime. In this period of almost eighty years, the denomination made crucial decisions concerning the religious nurture of Methodist children, established its own institution of higher education in central Canada, began to train its ministry in the college classroom, accepted university federation in Toronto, and entered into church union negotiations with the Presbyterians and Congregationalists. Burwash was intimately involved in all of these developments, and his position on each was directly affected by his understanding of the nature of evangelical revivalism. Thus, in order to reconstruct Burwash's intellectual and religious formation and the ideals which motivated him, I have derived insight from American research into the connection between revivalism and awakening. At the same time, studies of the religious dimensions of nineteenth-century British and American higher education have helped me to integrate Canadian developments into the mainstream of trans-Atlantic evangelicalism.

In acknowledging this debt, I should at the same time make it clear that I have attempted to avoid what John W. Grant has termed "the subtle temptation to write into Canadian Church history assumptions derived from the study of other countries." Nevertheless Grant has also drawn attention to "an equivocal tradition that is distinctly Canadian," which began when the Nova Scotia educator Thomas McCulloch decided to model his theological seminary in 1803 on both the Log Colleges of American Presbyterianism and the University of Edinburgh.[35] This book, dealing as it does with the American as well as the British influences that shaped Burwash's thought and action, is part of that equivocal tradition. As such, it has also drawn upon the small but respectable body of historical literature by John Moir and others who have begun to examine the American influence on nineteenth-century Canadian religion.[36]

The structure of this study combines a thematic with a chronological approach. The research was shaped by two basic questions. In the first place, to ascertain to what extent late nineteenth-century Canadian Methodism maintained Wesley's evangelical doctrines, it was necessary to examine the authority of Wesley's thought for the denomination's leading educator and theologian. The first four chapters, therefore, probe successively into Wesley's four central evangelical doctrines and their influence on Burwash's life and thought: repentance, conversion and the witness of the Spirit, Christian perfection or sanctification, and the importance of the Scriptures for salvation. Secondly, in order to understand more clearly how social and intellectual changes affected religious faith during this period, I have examined in detail six significant issues involving Burwash, Canadian Methodism, and in certain instances, society at large: (1) childhood religious education, (2) the claims of reason and religion in the college curriculum of the 1850s and the effect of Darwinian science after 1859, (3) the increased affluence of the laity, (4) theological education and the teaching of the higher criticism, (5) university federation, and (6) church union and the termination of Methodism as a separate denomination. Though the intent was not to write a detailed biography, I have followed a chronological approach to the extent that each issue is examined within the context of a different period of Burwash's life. Other biographical detail, however, has been introduced only if relevant to the issue under examination.

After such complexity, the main conclusions are really quite simple. It will be noted that during the period in question, contrary to what has generally been assumed, John Wesley's theology continued to be considered authoritative by both Burwash and the Methodist Church. At the same time, this doctrinal conservatism was accompanied by an openness to social change, for the spirit in which Wesley's thought was interpreted (with one exception) reflected the cultural optimism of the Victorian period. Convinced of the power of revivalism to transform culture and "make Christianity at home in the world," Burwash consistently sought to apply the old evangelical teachings to new institutions and scientific thought. This simultaneous affirmation of Wesley's thought and cultural change gave a dynamism to Canadian Methodism that, though fascinating, has also led to misinterpretation.

Because historians have failed to recognize the continued authority of Wesley's thought, this dynamism has been seen as part of a decline of religious belief. Usually the focus has therefore been on the growth of religious doubt and scepticism. The present analysis is a reminder that for many individuals an informed faith, based on evangelical experience, was also a valid way to deal with such apparent threats to Christianity as Darwinian evolution and the higher criticism. And, where historians of Methodism in Canada have discerned a discontinuity with the beliefs and practices of an earlier period, this study will draw attention to evangelical continuity.

Continuity, however, does not necessarily mean permanence. It will also be noted that by its very desire to transform and Christianize culture, late-nineteenth-century evangelicalism in Canada had to undergo change, for it had become inextricably connected to, and in the end vitiated by, culture. And so, ultimately this book points to the irony that by the early decades of the twentieth century, evangelical Christianity had been undermined perhaps more by the compelling vision of men and women of faith than by the destructive seeds of religious doubt.

CHAPTER ONE

The Making of a Methodist: Mothers and the Perpetuation of Revival

Shortly before his death in March 1918, Nathanael Burwash set his pen to presenting in final form the autobiographical sketches and essays that had intermittently occupied him for the previous decade.[1] The purpose of the manuscript, which bore the information if uninspired title "Life and Labours of Nathanael Burwash," was unmistakably didactic; in fact, according to its author's own guidelines admission many years earlier, "the serious aim of biography must always be the instruction of those just entering life."[2] The thought was not unusual for his age. One scholar familiar with Victorian religious biographies has observed, "The biographer himself reads the evidence of the life as if it were a novel and God were the novelist ... the finished biography is more accurately compared to literary criticism; it is a report upon an obscure but momentous work of art."[3]

It is not surprising then that Burwash's "Life" was intended to be part of a greater corpus of literature, for Canadian Methodist historical writing to a large extent already consisted of ministerial biographies.[4] The uncontested dean of an earlier generation of practitioners of this genre had been John Carroll, who in 1867 had issued the first of a five-volume series under the eloquent title *Case and his Cotemporaries: The Canadian itinerant's memorial: Constituting a biographical history of Methodism in Canada.*[5] Using the Methodist circuit rider Elder William Case as a pivotal figure, Carroll had intended to capture for a younger generation the excitement of religious revivalism as it had swept central Canada during the first half of the nineteenth century. Inherent in this "heroic age" of Methodism with its documentation of lives plucked from the ways of sin lay a dramatic appeal that Carroll used to full advantage. Thus, while chronicling the conversion of that venerable patriarch William Case, he had been able to confide subtly to his reader, "We have learned pretty directly that William's youth was characterized by "wildness," and that his amiable heart and handsome person exposed him to some dangers from which he did not wholly escape."[6]

William Case died in 1855, when Nathanael Burwash, a member of the second generation of Canadian Methodists, was sixteen years old. Whereas William's youth had been characterized by a discreet wildness, Natnanael Burwash admitted in 1909 before an audience of young Methodists, "I cannot remember a time when I did not desire above all things to be a true child of God."[7] Such virtue is rarely revivalist material. However it is precisely the lives of this next generation of Canadian Methodists that provide insight into the nature of revivalism during the second half of the nineteenth century. Here the existing research contains some significant analysis. Students of revivalist movements like Ernst Troeltsch, Richard Niebuhr, and in Canada, S.D. Clark have concluded that by its nature revivalism is of short duration.[8] According to Niebuhr, "as with ethics, so with doctrine, so also with the administration of religion. An official clergy, theologically educated and schooled in the refinements of ritual takes the place of lay leadership; easily imported creeds are substituted for the difficult enthusiasms of the pioneers; children are born into the group and infant baptism or dedication becomes once more a means of grace. So the sect becomes a church."[9] Another scholar, applying Niebuhr's analysis to Canada, but with a more positive interpretation, has viewed this process as the inevitable result of urbanization. He concludes that from 1854 to 1884 the Methodist Church was "transformed from a select body of converts into a far reaching social institution."[10]

Nathanael Burwash was born in 1839, at a time when Methodism in Canada was consciously making the transition from a movement of recently converted adults to a religion of the family. During this time also, it was beginning to grope about for its own ecclesiastical arrangements appropriate to Canada. What has not been fully recognized by the proponents of the sect-church typology is that the circumstances of Methodism in Canada were unique. Not one but two ecclesiastical systems presented themselves as models.[11] To the south, Methodists had been organized by Wesley since 1784 into the Methodist Episcopal Church, source of central Canada's earliest exposure to Methodism. At the same time, by 1839, the direction of Canadian Methodism lay in the hands of the parent British Wesleyan Conference, which had separated from the Church of England only after Wesley's death.[12]

The question of membership for the second generation of Canadian Methodists had both ecclesiastical and theological significance. Would children automatically become members through baptism and thus be born into the community, to be retained through religious nurture? Or would they, like their parents, be required to follow the condition that John Wesley had instituted for society membership and "show a desire to flee from the wrath to come"? Repentance on the part of a child assumed a sinful nature, and so any study of Methodism in the second half of the nineteenth century must inevitably include an examination of the prevalent attitude to the moral nature of the child, as well as an analysis of the evangelical doctrine of the atonement.[13]

These very issues would become a preoccupation in Nathanael Burwash's life and thought as he tried to deal as a theologian with the nature and persistence of the central evangelical doctrines and practices of Methodism. Given his pivotal role in guiding the thought and practice of the Canadian Methodist ministry, he would be in a unique position to exert influence in this area. Thus the account of his own religious formation, which he began to spell out shortly before his death, calls for examination, for its didactic intent was obvious and can best be understood in relation to the official decisions and arrangements adopted by his denomination. That account, as may be expected with any issue relating to nineteenth-century English Canada, begins with the fact of the British connection.

FAMILY BACKGROUND

"I was born in July 1839 within the bounds of the old Ottawa Circuit, the fourth circuit formed in Canadian Methodism." Most people link their birth with a family name or a geographic location, but Nathanael Burwash characteristically chose to introduce himself in connection with one of the oldest Methodist circuits of central Canada, which in 1839 had already been burned over three times by the fires of religious revivalism.[14] Friends of the family knew that the Burwash name could claim a direct connection to a certain "Sir Bartholomew Berghersh, a great Baron of England" whose marvellous exploits during the time of Edward III were recounted in Froissart's *Chronicles*, as well as to a number of medieval bishops entombed in Lincoln Cathedral. In his autobiography, however, Burwash acknowledged true kinship only with a more concrete ancestor, Nathanael Burwash, "the first of that name in America."[15]

This first Nathanael, who was born in England in 1743, had settled in what is now Vermont shortly before the outbreak of the American Revolution and married a woman whose family unfortunately turned out to be strongly pro-patriot. In 1802, after leading a "life of persecution" because of his Loyalism and receiving a sizeable inheritance following the death of his mother in England, Burwash moved with his wife and their six children to British North America. There he took up a thousand-acre tract near St Andrew's, forty-five miles northwest of Montreal. Unfortunately, he was soon confronted with family tragedy when his wife, unbalanced by homesickness, abandoned her family and died as she tried to find her way back on foot to her native home.

Despite this calamity, loyalty to the British crown became a tradition in the Burwash family, again often at a cost. During the war of 1812 a son died in combat at Crysler's farm, during the 1837 rebellion a grandson, Adam, junior, enlisted in the British army, and in 1866, during that third great test of British loyalty, the Fenian raids, Adam's son, the second Nathanael, then a young Methodist preacher in Hamilton, offered his services as chaplain. And in 1918 he in turn in the final year of his life, saw two of his four sons serving overseas in France, with a third convalescing at home from wounds received in active service.[16] That the British connection was not a light matter in the Burwash family tradition is a point to be noted. Whereas historians of religion in the American colonies have conjectured that revivalism provided a central impulse for republicanism, this was not necessarily the case in Canada. Nathanael Burwash never neglected an opportunity to demonstrate the Loyalist roots of Canadian Methodism. In so doing he was simply following the example of an earlier generation whose most notable representative had been Egerton Ryerson.[17]

However, loyalty to England's crown did not mean loyalty to her established church. While the first Nathanael and his family had been stalwart members of the Church of England, in the course of a revival on the Ottawa circuit in 1826, one of his sons had joined the Methodist society, accompanied by his wife and older children, including Adam, junior, the father of Nathanael Burwash. Methodist circuit riders had been active in the region since 1800, and although they had a slight head start over the Anglicans, the Presbyterians, and the Baptists, the War of 1812 had been disruptive and Methodist membership had declined. It was only in 1826 that the cause of Methodism on the Ottawa circuit began to flourish, and between 1826 and 1836, thanks to a number of revivals, society membership increased from 40 to 667.[18]

British immigration to Lower Canada peaked during these years, and among those who were converted in the 1836 revival on the Ottawa circuit were John Taylor, a schoolteacher and recent immigrant from Scotland, his wife Anna McLean, and their three sons and daughters.[19] Although he had been an elder, precentor, and clerk of session in the Church of Scotland, Taylor decided to attend the Methodist services when he found only a Scottish secessional church in his new home at St Andrew's, Quebec. His children had required some persuasion, for the Taylors had a scholarly bent and were critical of the lack of education among the Methodist itinerants. However, shortly after his conversion the eldest son, Lachlin, abandoned his earlier prejudice and entered the Methodist ministry, where he achieved considerable prominence, first as agent of the Upper Canada Bible Society and later as secretary for the British and Foreign Bible Society. In that capacity the extensive knowledge he acquired of Manitoba and the northwest led to a request by the Canadian government to act as an immigration recruitment agent in Great Britain.[20] Taylor's eldest daughter, Anne, like her father a school teacher, spent a short time in the household of Franklin Metcalf, a prominent retired Methodist preacher, and in 1838 married Adam Burwash junior, who had just been released from military service.[21] Their first child, Nathanael, was born at St Andrew's on 25 July 1839.

THE CANADIAN METHODIST MILIEU

The year 1839, the centenary of John Wesley's formation of the first Methodist society (and also the year of Nathanael Burwash's birth) marked a milestone in the history of international Methodism. In celebration, Methodists throughout Britain, Ireland, the United States, and British North America solemnly arranged to assemble simultaneously at an agreed time on October 25 to acknowledge "through worship and a pecuniary contribution ... the advantages conferred upon us, upon the Church, and upon the world, by the glorious revival of religion, of which the revered and ever-memorable John Wesley was the divinely selected and qualified instrument."[22]

For Canadian Methodists this international commemoration also marked the beginning of a period of internal consolidation. Not unlike the family of the first Nathanael Burwash, they too had had to contend for a time with conflicting loyalties. However, the large influx of British immigrants to central Canada during the 1820s and 1830s determined that Methodism in British North America would be oriented to the British Wesleyan rather than to the American Methodist Episcopal tradition. In 1833 the two groups had joined forces, and the 1935 revival on the Ottawa circuit had taken place under the combined efforts of a former Methodist Episcopal preacher, Asahel Hurlburt, and a British Wesleyan, Stephen Brownell.[23] Although the union had collapsed by 1840, it was reconstructed in 1847, this time permanently but with a separate Methodist Episcopal Church continuing in existence until 1884.[24]

While Methodism in central Canada did, therefore, have two parent traditions, it was also aware of the need to forge its own identity. In

1831 George Ryerson, writing to his younger brother Egerton after attending the British Wesleyan Conference in Bristol, had tried to distinguish Canadian Methodism from the British and American expression as "independent of either – agreeing in *faith*, in *religious discipline*, in *name* and *doctrine* and *unity* of *spirit* – but different in some ecclesiastical arrangements rendered necessary from local circumstances."[25] This distinction did not always find ready acceptance in the eyes of the parent British Wesleyan Conference. Under the leadership of Jabez Bunting, British Wesleyanism in the 1830s and 1840s was highly conservative, and Canadian experimentation with "ecclesiastical arrangements" during these years called forth a sharp rebuke and a reminder in 1834 that "it is not prudent to be frequently altering our modes of proceeding. The founder of Methodism said, 'Do not mend our rules, but keep them.' In your part of the world, it is of peculiar importance that the grand object of all our people, next to the salvation of their souls, should be the salvation of the people around them."[26]

There was one group especially whose salvation was of concern to both the parent and Canadian Conference during these troubled years, and which would influence the ecclesiastical arrangements that were ultimately adopted. Increasingly, as witnessed by the conversion of the Burwash and Taylor families, children and young people were turning Methodism into a family religion. Every effort was made, therefore, to impress upon ministers and parents the need to instruct the second generation in the basic principles of Methodism and to bring them to conversion. In 1836, for example, the year the Taylor family was converted, the annual address of the British Conference to the members of the Wesleyan Methodist Church in Canada, reminded parents: "More is necessary to eradicate the natural evil propensities of your children, and to establish them in the way that is good, than amiable manners, a moral exterior, or even polite education; rest not until, in the heart of each individual of your families a genuine work of the Spirit of grace is hopefully wrought."[27]

With this second generation of Methodists lay the future of religious revivalism in Canada. John Wesley himself, in a sermon on the duties of parents to provide religious instruction for their children, had asked, "What will the consequence be, if they adopt not this resolution? if family religion be neglected? – if care be not taken of the rising generation? Will not the present revival of religion in a short time die away?" Methodists in Canada shared Wesley's anxiety, and in their *Discipline*, a book of laws and practices adopted in 1833, following the American example, they reprinted Wesley's own detailed advice to his preachers on how to provide for "the rising generation."[28]

CHILDHOOD RELIGIOUS
TRAINING

The household of Adam Burwash and Anne Taylor shared the Conference's desire to transmit religion to "the rising generation." Wesley's *Sermons* formed part of the literature in their home, and as Nathanael took pains to demonstrate in his autobiography, his parents worked single-mindedly to provide their sons with moral and religious training in the home. After Nathanael they had had five more sons, John, Adam, Lachlin, Stephen, and Samuel Thomas. The last three were born in Baltimore, Upper Canada, where Adam Burwash had taken up a farm in 1844 following the example of Anne's parents, the Taylors. During the first years at Baltimore there was as yet no Sunday school, and all early religious training took place in the home.[29]

From the day of their marriage a tradition of family prayer in the morning and evening was established. Both parents were remembered by their eldest son as "praying people," and as a young boy he had often come across his father in his "prayer closet," the granary in the barn, praying out loud for his sons, for the church, and since he was an enthusiastic advocate of experiential religion, "for the revival of power." His mother, faithful to the decorum expected of her sex, "in the quiet of her bedchamber whispered prayers to God." Whenever her sons faced anything unusual or had to go on a journey, it was to her room that they were sent to pray, first with her, and as they grew older, on their own.

Whereas Adam Burwash's chief concern for his sons was their conversion, Anne Taylor, who had been trained as a school teacher, emphasized "the ethical" aspect of religion. To do this, there were a number of methods at her disposal. During the early years at Baltimore there had been no Sunday evening service, and neighbouring Methodists were accustomed to hold cottage prayer meetings in various homes. Adam Burwash was a constant attendant and active participant at these services, but his wife remained at home. Sunday evening was her time for religious instruction with the children. In later years this "Sunday evening service" became one of her son's most treasured memories and invariably received mention in his sermons and addresses on Christian nurture. He recalled it in minute detail in his autobiography – his mother seated before the fire, his two-year-old brother John on her knee, and on a stool at her feet, five-year-old Nathanael.

Their mother began by giving them a verse from Scripture to repeat (for neither child could yet read), and then, drawing on her own training in the Church of Scotland, she taught them from the Shorter Catechism, asking the questions and supplying the answers they were to repeat. Next she sang a hymn, such as "On Jordan's Stormy Banks I Stand," whose strong visual imagery appealed to a child's imagination. It is probably from those Sunday evenings that Burwash's own later interest in liturgical music can be dated, as well as his preference for teaching "viva voce" without the use of texts.[30]

This part of the "service," however, was only a preliminary. Raised on the theology of the Shorter Catechism, Anne Taylor saw God, not as "an indefinite ideal of kindness and good nature, but a holy God before whom sin was an awful thing." At the same time she also looked back to her own Methodist experience of conversion and thus stressed the need to repent and seek forgiveness. Accordingly, the climax to the Sunday evening service was the sermon and exhortation:

Then came the talk about *sin* and its awful consequences, about heaven and its beauty and glory, about God and his all-seeing eye, knowing all that we do and looking at the very thoughts of our hearts. Then the exhortation, pleading with us to avoid sin and to do right, and to seek God's forgiveness. Finally this, as her own heart became full and her voice trembled with emotion, melted into prayer until we too were melted and wept with her and she pleaded with God to bless her children and forgive their sins.[31]

The instructing, exhorting mother and the contrite, sobbing children were of course a replay of the well-known revival service. The major components were unchanged, but the actors had shifted roles, the mother taking the place of the revivalist preacher and the infants that of the awakened, penitent sinners. And so, evangelical revivalism entered into the experience of infants as well as adults, not through the preaching of an itinerant evangelist, but through the exhortations of a godly mother. And a mother, unlike a preacher, had the advantage of ubiquity and even omniscience in the eyes of her young children.

There was, therefore, no danger of backsliding in the Burwash household. Until the conscience of the child was fully trained, Anne Taylor, through constant watchfulness, acted as a conscience for her sons. "She detected the seeds of sin in the passions of childhood and strove to check them at the first building of their growth," Burwash approvingly recalled. Since Nathanael as an adult acquired a reputation for saintliness and his brother John was often commended for his unwavering moral stance, it may be assumed that Anne Taylor either did her work remarkably well or had extremely malleable material at her disposal.[32] In either case, she was most certainly facilitated by her eldest son's pedestrian imagination. As a young minister, for example, the list of childhood sins Burwash was able to display before his congregation went no further than tormenting birds, destroying property, knocking down other children, playing games of chance, and the only sin with which he may have identified personally – turning play into "idolatry" by neglecting other, more serious matters.[33] The list, as well as the lack of creativity, may be considered a tribute to the thoroughness with which Anne Taylor had performed her task. To quote her son, "thus were laid deep moral foundations. Conscience was awakened, never again to become torpid."[34]

Such moral training demanded total devotion and scrupulous attention, and a mother's duties extended far beyond the infancy of the child. When Anne Taylor died in 1886, a local minister noted pointedly that "for more than forty years, she consecrated herself to one work – the training of her children for Christ." Equipped with a "peculiarly sensitive disposition," (shared, it may be added, by her eldest son, who all his life had to cope with nervous strain and physical exhaustion), she had refrained from taking a prominent part in the social life of the community, for, it was emphasized, her task as mother had left her "but few hours to spare for society." As recorded in her obituary, her final words to her sons, two of whom by 1886 were well-known Methodist educators, were "Tell them all to live good lives."

But moral goodness was not the only distinguishing mark of Methodist piety. At the age of seven, young Burwash became more aware of the place of religion in the lives of the men of his immediate circle, his father, and the Methodist preachers who conducted special revival services, called protracted meetings, at the little Baltimore schoolhouse. Whereas his mother had emphasized the "ethical" aspect of religion, his father was especially attracted to the experiential, or "mystical," element in Methodism. "The doctrine of knowledge of forgiveness of sins," Burwash recalled, was particularly prominent in his father's life. On many occasions, walking with his father to church, he would hear him asking a neighbour who had met up with them, "Brother, do you know your sins forgiven this morning?"

Under his mother's training young Burwash had realized that he was a sinner who had to ask for forgiveness. Now, at the age of seven, he became aware that he should also actually know his sins to be forgiven. Having overheard a local minister describe the purpose and form of a revival meeting, he decided to accompany his father and at the end of the meeting went forward to the penitent bench. Other than the usual repentance, he experienced nothing. His anxiety increased, his inability to receive the knowledge of forgiveness became confused with his fear of death, and from the age of seven to thirteen, young Nathanael, at least by his own later account, lived a miserable moral existence, penitent and awakened but unforgiven. The way to conversion for a godly child appeared at least as arduous as for the hardened sinner. Not until his first year at college, when he was thirteen, during a protracted meeting conducted by a fellow student, was he finally able to lay claim to the coveted knowledge of sins forgiven.[35]

When conversion did take place, he recognized in it the influence of his mother's Christian training. First, there was a very direct connection. At the age of ten, shortly after he had once again unsuccessfully ventured forth at a protracted meeting, his mother had fallen ill and almost died. Beside themselves with grief, Nathanael and his brother John had been unable to stay in her room and had rushed to the barn to pray, where shortly thereafter, an aunt came to them with the news that the fever had miraculously broken. Later Burwash realized that this answer to prayer had been a sign of God's forgiveness, antedating his conscious knowledge of three years later. When that experience finally did take place, he was again aware of the part played by his mother in preparing him to receive this assurance of divine grace: "I did not call this faith. I did not call it conversion. It was not decision merely, for during at least six years before, if not under the exhortations of a noble godly mother even before that first kneeling at the penitent bench in the old schoolhouse, I desired to be a Christian and had virtually made my choice, and for all these years had been seeking it with varying degrees of earnestness."[36]

His remarks bring to light one important difference between conversion as experienced by adults and by children raised in a revivalist tradition. For the adult, conversion often marked a radical disjunction with the past, and its basic stages – conviction of sin, repentance, justification, and assurance – could be swift and searing; for the child, the first two stages were part of childhood formation, intimately connected, if not confused, with memories of parental love and concern. To this effect, Phillip Greven, in a penetrating study of an earlier generation of evangelical children in seventeenth- and eighteenth-century America, has suggested that for children brought up in this religious tradition, the new birth was not a rejection but an acceptance of their formative years in infancy and early childhood: "Evangelicals did not remember their own earliest experiences, and few ever reported their earliest memories, yet their actions, their beliefs, and their temperaments reveal, as nothing else could, that their earliest and most formative experiences still shaped and influenced their lives throughout youth and adulthood."[37]

For Burwash, the mature theologian and educator, this meant acknowledging openly and frequently the role played by his mother in his religious formation and, by extension, in the formation of every Methodist. Thus it was axiomatic that "the mother makes the boy," and that "out of the godly, prayerful, faithful home come the deepest springs of religious life."[38] As an educator he was even able to offer a "scientific" explanation for the close correlation which he perceived between the faith of mothers and their children. Women, he argued, were by nature endowed with special Christian moral virtues such as patience, fortitude, and intuition, and these equipped them better than men to provide moral training to a child. During infancy children were not yet in a position to make moral decisions and thus had to live vicariously through their mother. In this way, with time and practice, the mother's moral virtues became those of the child.[39] In the case of mothers and sons (and Burwash's own career and family circumstances tended to overlook the existence of daughters), these same moral virtues when practised by a dutiful son were known as "moral manliness." As he often emphasized, "a strong clear imperative conscience is the *sine qua non* of true manhood."[40] Although in the end conversion was the work of the Spirit, it was the mother who had played the dominant role in forming the conscience and thus in laying the foundations for conversion.

Burwash was not alone in acknowledging that mothers were vital in the formation of a young Methodist. John Wesley himself, after his conversion at Aldersgate, considered the religious training to which Susanna Annesley had subjected her large brood of children to be a model for all Methodist parents.[41] Following Wesley's example, Canadian Methodists of Burwash's generation took every opportunity to extoll the virtues of the "Mother of Methodism."[42] John Potts, a prominent Toronto minister, reminded the female readers of the *Canadian Methodist Magazine* in 1891, "Every Christian wife and mother throughout Methodism should make the life and character of Susanna Wesley a constant study, and the good effect would be manifest upon the discipline of our famlies, the welfare of our children, and the piety of our Churches."[43]

Methodist mothers generally appeared to be assured of a favourable press, and there was no short supply of grateful sons who acknowledged their influence. "Remember your mother's prayers for you," Hart Massey impressed upon Victoria University's students in 1892 when they were leaving the quiet town of Cobourg to embark on academic life in worldly Toronto.[44] "Two influences have profoundly affected my life, my mother's life teaching and example, and the ministry of the Methodist Church," confessed Joseph Flavelle in 1906, and rare are the memoirs of a Methodist that do not pay tribute to the formative influence of a pious mother.[45] In fact, Nathanael Burwash extolled the virtues of no fewer than four prominent Canadian Methodist women and mothers in biographical sketches for the *Canadian Methodist Magazine*.[46] The model of the mother as minister was especially prominent in one of these, a description of the exemplary training which Anna Vincent Massey had given to her sons, Vincent and Raymond (and which remarkably resembled his own). The Christian nurture provided by the mother in the home, Burwash concluded, transcended any contribution to true piety made by the church or the Sunday school. Indeed, "the permanence and strength of religion in the world in the next generation depends more upon this than upon either the pulpit or the revival service."[47]

The statement serves as a reminder that even when the camp meetings and the protracted meetings became infrequent, as they did by the 1870s, this need not be interpreted as a sign of the decline of religious revivalism. As the pastoral addresses of the 1830s and 1840s had emphasized, Canadian Methodism was becoming a family religion. Its future, therefore, lay not in the first place in the hands of itinerant evangelists, preachers, and Sunday school teachers, but in the Christian training provided by the mother in the home. And, as Phillip Greven, Peter Gregg Slater, and other students of early childhood religious training have demonstrated, this tradition predated Methodism, going back to the Puritan period, and transcended denominational lines.[48]

However, these same historians have also suggested that by the late 1840s – the very time when Anne Taylor was impressing upon her young sons their sinfulness and need for forgiveness – the theology on which revivalism and evangelical child training had been based was being called into question.[49] Indeed, according to one writer, "the 1820s and 30s were the last period in which the evangelical complexities of original sin as relating to infants, and the doctrinal arguments for and against their damnation, could summon any interest from the general populace."[50] During these decades the belief in the innate depravity of the child began to give way to a Romantic, sentimental understanding of childhood that depicted the infant as a "sweet angel," an innocent creature, pure at birth, and thus considerably closer than adults to God. Directly related to this shift in theology was a new, more liberal understanding of the other essential doctrine of religious revivalism, the atonement. Christ's death on the cross, formerly understood as a sign of God's righteousness with its effect dependent on human repentance and divine forgiveness, was now interpreted as an expression of God's unconditional gift of love to all humankind.[51]

The reasons given for this declining interest in infant depravity and the new sentimentalization of childhood vary, but the causes cited most often are the growing influence of educators like Rousseau, Pestalozzi, and Froebel, a decline in infant mortality, and the mother's replacement of the father as the dominant parent in child rearing.[52] Related to this last point is the suggestion that the theological shift represented an

unconscious effort by ministers as well as women to justify their existence in a society that was increasingly coming to view them as mar-
ginal.[53] Whatever the causes, historians agree that the shift in attitude
and in theology was a response to changes in society.

Scholarship on this issue, it should be noted, has concentrated almost
exclusively on the work of Congregationalist theologians writing in the
Calvinist tradition of Jonathan Edwards. Canadian Methodists are
simply assumed to have followed suit in re-evaluating the theological
assumptions of revivalism. According to one study, "Canada could not
help but share the romantic insistence that children were the special
objects of God's favour and, of necessity, the true recipients of parental
affection."[54] If this was indeed the case, the implications for Methodism
in Canada were far-reaching. In the first place, such a view of the child
negated the principles on which the exhortations concerning family religion in the 1830s had been based. Moreover, conditions for church
membership, also a concern of the period, would also be affected. For
as one historian has asked, if the soul came into the world already
prepared and converted, "why delay or complicate admission into a
church society which could only benefit by the presence of young
Christians?"[55]

THE MORAL STATUS OF
THE METHODIST CHILD

Theology

For Methodists, the questioning of the moral status of the child was
complicated by the rather thorny legacy left by John Wesley.[56] It is true
that Wesley had safeguarded Methodist doctrine by inserting his *Standard Sermons* and *Notes on the New Testament* into the Trust Deed of
every Methodist chapel. And in the ecclesiastical arrangements he provided for the American Methodists, he did make clear provisions for
the continuation of infant baptism. However, when it came to defining
the nature of that baptism he left a number of confusing instructions.
On the one hand, he had been taught as a member of the Church of
England to regard baptism as the washing away of original sin. On the
other hand, he also insisted that the work begun in baptism should
result in repentance, faith, and obedience. Thus, on the question of
infant baptism, as one theologian has recently pointed out, "a tension
ran through Wesley's thought."[57] It was left to Wesley's followers to
resolve that tension in the nineteenth century. They did this not only in
a society that by the 1840s was re-evaluating the moral nature of childhood, but also as Protestants reacting to the Anglo-Catholic move-

ment. In response to the latter, they thought it imperative to rid Wesley's remarks on baptism of any hint of baptismal regeneration.[58] Moreover, since Methodism had originated as a collection of religious societies within the Church of England, it was necessary to make permanent ecclesiastical arrangements once it became a separate church. This included establishing the condition for membership for the children of believers and ensuring that "the rising generation" would retain the faith of their parents.

As an adult, Nathanael Burwash would contribute in a significant way to all three of these issues – the need to clarify Wesley's teaching on infant baptism, to make arrangements for the religious instruction of children, and to provide for their formal acceptance into church membership. Moreover, as an educator and theologian, he was also aware of the wider cultural milieu in which these issues were being resolved, for he was well acquainted with the growing body of scholarship re-evaluating the moral condition of the child and the doctrine of the atonement.[59]

Thanks to the sound instruction of his mother, indications of the position he would take on these issues were already visible early in his career. Already at the age of sixteen as an elementary school teacher, Burwash displayed a marked interest in the religious and moral training of children. Later, during his short interlude in the active ministry in the 1860s, he was especially appreciated by his congregations for his effective work with children. His limited collection of books at that time contained the writings of two Congregationalist theologians, Timothy Dwight (1757–1817) and Horace Bushnell (1807–76), both considered leading figures in the transition to the Romantic understanding of childhood. While Timothy Dwight's thought was still firmly rooted in the theological tradition of his famous grandfather, Jonathan Edwards, he did place a new emphasis on the receptivity of the child to Christian nurture and on the special gifts of the mother for this task. Given his own childhood training, Burwash found the five volumes of Dwight's *Theology* a valuable mine for his sermons on Christian nurture. At the same time, he was careful to warn parents to distinguish the "enlightening, quickening and restraining influence of the Holy Spirit from purity of nature."[60]

Of the writings of Horace Bushnell he was much more critical. Bushnell, whose influential *Views on Christian Nurture* appeared in 1847, has been considered "a Romantic-Calvinist," a hybrid. Though he still believed that the child was born with a sinful nature, he also argued that proper moral training could entirely eliminate the need for conversion. "The child is to be trained, not for conversion at some advanced age, but [is] expected to *"grow up a Christian* ... God offers grace to make it possible."[61] Burwash's own childhood training had clearly shaped his Christian character, but he disagreed with Bushnell that conversion could be entirely eliminated, and he issued a strong warning to that effect to his congregation: "It is far, very very far from being enough for you to teach your children morality however exact: you would not trust to morality for your own salvation. How can you then for theirs? Let your great aim be not simply to have them moral but by the help of God to have them converted."[62] In the journal he kept during his first years in the ministry, he was gratified to record that a sizeable number of children "weeping for their sins" had come forward during a protracted meeting and were now organizing a special prayer group at school during recess for the conversion of their classmates.[63] Three years later, in 1864, as part of the general interest in Christian nurture, the denominational *Christian Guardian* printed a new Wesleyan catechism for children. The columns were cut out by Burwash, pasted into a notebook, and used as a manual to instruct the children of his Toronto congregation. The method of instruction he adopted was that of his mother many years earlier, and one of the definitions his young pupils were expected to repeat was that of the "new birth ... that great change which God works in the soul, when he raises it from the death of sin to the life of righteousness."[64]

However, while the 1864 catechism might teach the need for the new birth, that same year the *Christian Guardian* began to publish views on Christian nurture that undermined the need for the conversion of the child. Although very similar to those of Horace Bushnell, they came, not from the Congregationalist, but from the American Methodist tradition, and they went beyond Bushnell on the matter of the sinful nature of the child. In 1842 F.G. Hibbard, a Methodist Episcopal minister in the Genesee Conference, had published a lengthy treatise intended to refute the teachings of the Baptists on adult baptism and to expunge any vestiges of sacramentarianism or baptismal regeneration from Wesley's writing. It was Hibbard's contention that all children baptized in infancy were at the same time born again. Linking his view to the atonement, he argued that children were in a state of innocence at birth as a result of Christ's death. Therefore, the main concern of the church was not conversion but Christian nurture to keep children in their initial condition of innocence.[65] Hibbard's views were printed with approval in the *Christian Guardian* in 1864, as were the similar teachings of another American Methodist, Robert Olin.[66]

The stress with both Hibbard and Olin, however, lay less on the child's innocence than on the duty of parents and church to provide Christian nurture. For Canadian Methodists this duty had been an annual refrain in official denominational pronouncements since the

1830s, and the editor of the *Christian Guardian* heartily endorsed the heightened awareness created by Olin and Hibbard, pointing out that "Unless childhood is nurtured and trained, with the utmost solicitude and by all available means, the religion of Christ can never become universal, or permanently deep, fruitful, and progressive."[67]

For some ministers this commitment to the nurture of children also included the theological re-evaluation of the nature of the atonement and the moral condition of childhood.[68] The most forceful defence of this view came a little later, in 1876, from the pen of Henry Flesher Bland, a highly respected minister of the Montreal Conference. As one who had come to question the authenticity of his own youthful conversion, Bland preferred to concentrate on providing sound Christian instruction rather than on encouraging what often appeared to be superficial conversions.[69]

In a sermon, published in the *Sunday School Banner* under the title "Universal Childhood drawn to Christ," in which he cited Scripture as well as Hibbard and Wesley as sources, Bland made a strong plea for the innocence and irresponsibility of the child because of the unconditional benefits of Christ's atonement. Since children were by birth pure, he argued, there was no need for them to undergo a conversion or rebirth to become fit for the kingdom of God.[70] Such an understanding of the innocence of the child by virtue of the atonement brought him into direct conflict with Nathanael Burwash, who in 1881 read before the ministerial association of the Cobourg District an essay entitled "The Moral Condition of Childhood."[71] When printed later in the *Christian Guardian*, the essay called forth a spirited debate and a re-issue by Bland of his earlier sermon, accompanied by a critique of Burwash's stand.[72]

By 1884 Burwash had been dean of theology at Victoria College for almost a decade and could already point to two theological publications: a lecture before the Victoria College Union entitled *The Nature, Genesis, and Results of Sin*, and an annotated edition of Wesley's sermons, entitled *Wesley's Doctrinal Standards, Part I*. The latter work was part of his continuing attempt to formulate for his students a systematic theology that remained true to the evangelical nature of Wesley's practical religion while drawing out the full implications of his thought.[73] In keeping with other Methodist theologians, in particular North Americans like Nathan Bangs, Wilbur Fisk, and Daniel Whedon, Burwash referred to this theology as Arminian.[74] Though Arminianism and Calvinism agreed on the individual's sinful condition, he was especially concerned to draw a clear distinction between the Arminian emphasis on moral responsibility and Calvinist "necessitarian" teaching. Central to this distinction was a correct understanding of the atonement, and though his first major publication on the doctrines of sin and the atonement would not appear until 1896, the main contours were already firmly in place in his essay "The Moral Condition of Childhood."[75]

No question, he began, was of greater importance to the church than a correct understanding of the moral status of its children and the means required to promote their eternal well-being. By drawing extensively on Scripture, on the articles on original sin in the Anglican Thirty-Nine Articles, and the Methodist Twenty-Five Articles, and on Wesley's writings, he underscored the destructive effects of the sin of Adam on the entire human race, child as well as adult. Original sin, he warned, "is not, even in the child, a *mere nominal* or *theoretical matter*, but a terrible power ready to wake up into life." All therefore deserved divine wrath, and no one could escape this dire moral condition except through the atonement of Christ.

Fortunately, when it came to the atonement, Arminian theology offered a much brighter prospect than Calvinism. Whereas the latter taught that Christ had died only for the elect, the Arminian teaching of John Wesley, clearly expressed in the fifth standard sermon, proclaimed that because of the atonement God had made a new covenant with the entire human race, permitting all who repented and believed to be saved. Hope, therefore, was offered to all, but there was a condition: salvation was dependent on individual repentance and faith.[76]

Here Burwash differed significantly from the view of the atonement held by his Methodist colleagues Hibbard and Bland. They had argued that the benefits of the atonement were unconditional, enabling the child to enter life in an already regenerated state. In Burwash's eyes, such a position not only advocated the error of "absolute universalism or unconditional election," but also misinterpreted John Wesley by confusing universal grace with individual regeneration. He did concede, since they too had quoted Wesley, that Wesley had not always understood the full implications of his preaching and had at times continued to betray vestiges of Church of England sacramentarianism when he had spoken of having sinned away the grace of his baptism, thereby implying that the sacrament had a regenerative power. "But all this belonged not to the Methodist Arminian theology which he was founding but to the churchism which he was leaving behind, Burwash insisted. "And the whole evangelical Christianity of our day has taken up the central idea of his theology, that the new birth is the conscious crisis of religious experience preceded by repentance, conditioned upon faith, wrought by the Word and Spirit of God, and completed in the full assurance of Sonship."[77] To depart from these basic doctrines and to fail to apply them to children, as well as to adults, would change the work of the church "to a process of *education*, as distinguished from the work of *evangelization*."[78]

Arminian theology, therefore, according to Burwash, logically entailed that the moment the child began to show the effects of original sin, with *"the first pang of conscience* arising from the first awakening of inborn sin," he or she was to be taught the Scriptural way of salvation, which consisted of "conscious repentance, faith, and the new birth of the Spirit." Methodism's understanding of the new birth, he emphasized, had been its great contribution to modern theology.[79]

The reaction to Burwash's essay varied; some of the readers of the *Christian Guardian* found his stand offensive.[80] One angry letter to the editor exclaimed that in such a theology "irresponsible infants are little else than germs of depravity, destined to blossom into sinners at the very outset of their conscious moral life. They are sinful and capable only of sin."[81] Henry Flesher Bland's laconic response was, "A somewhat poor lookout for those who die in infancy, idiocy, and heathenism, none of whom can experience the new birth in the way conditioned by the Essayist."[82] His colleague in the Montreal Conference, W.I. Shaw, professor at the Wesleyan Theological College in Montreal, agreed. In a digest of the Methodist doctrinal standards issued in 1895, Shaw maintained that "the gospel call to 'repent and be converted' is meant for responsible adults, and becomes impiously grotesque when addressed to infants."[83]

The Child's Relationship to the Church

There the matter might have rested, for both sides had justified their stand by quoting Wesley and, as Methodists, had worked out their thought within the doctrinal standards. However, the question of the moral status of the child was also of direct and vital relevance to the organizational structures of Methodism. These, unlike doctrine, had not been fixed at Wesley's death, nor were they uniform. The General Conference of the Methodist Episcopal Church in the United States, for example, in 1856 endorsed the position advanced earlier by F.G. Hibbard that all children were members of the kingdom of God because of the unconditional benefits of the atonement, and were therefore entitled to baptism. Moreover, while the Conference gave specific direction for the nurture and instruction of children before they would be received into full membership, there was no specification or implication that repentance or the "desire to flee from the wrath to come," was a precondition.[84]

The Wesleyan Methodists in Canada, on the other hand, despite the warning in the 1830s from the British parent conference against "ecclesiastical innovation," took considerably longer to settle their organizational structures. They displayed a remarkable proclivity for unions, which continued until 1925, when the main Methodist tradition ceased its existence as a separate denomination. During this lengthy unsettled period, the moral status of the Canadian Methodist child can best be called ambivalent, and his or her relationship to the church remained in a state of flux.

As early as 1854 Egerton Ryerson, in a heated controversy, had advocated that baptized children should be accepted as full church members after receiving catechetical instruction, the practice that was adopted two years later by the Americans. Though unsuccessful, Ryerson's stand did have the effect that greater provision began to be made for the instruction of children.[85] These were years when the Wesleyan Methodist Church in Canada was expressing a growing self-awareness and making a concerted effort to integrate its children into the fabric of church life. In 1864 it issued a new edition of the *Discipline* under the editorship of John Douse. A British Wesleyan from Yorkshire, Douse had considerable influence as district chairman on shaping Nathanael Burwash's understanding of church polity when the latter was a young probationer in Belleville.[86] The new *Discipline* retained the theological definition of infant baptism formulated by the American Conference, but it deviated from the American church by admitting baptized children as probationers for full membership only after they had given "evidence of a desire to flee from the wrath to come, and to be saved from their sins."[87]

Repentance as a precondition for the membership of children was, however, short-lived and was again dropped with the Methodist union of 1874. Nevertheless, after both the 1874 and 1883 unions, ambiguities remained in the moral status of the Methodist child. Though the need for repentance was no longer explicit, the catechisms as well as certain sections of the rite for the administration of infant baptism continued to describe the child's depraved condition in most unequivocal language, as "self-willed, and, but for the grace of God, inclined only to evil."[88]

Such inconsistency did not go unchallenged. Not surprisingly, in light of his views on the distinctive doctrines of Methodism, Nathanael Burwash considered it imperative to clarify once and for all the relationship of baptized children to the church and to emphasize that a clear experience of sin and repentance continued to be essential elements of a saving faith. He did so by turning not to the American but to the British Wesleyan example. In 1897 he had been instrumental in preparing with the general superintendent, Albert Carman, and others a new catechism for the Methodist Church, in which an entire section had been devoted to "the conditional benefits of the atonement."[89] Three years later at the General Conference of 1902 and at the very time when church union negotiations with the Presbyterians and Congregationalists had seriously begun, a committee was formed to re-examine the relation of baptized children to the church and to introduce any necessary changes into the Methodist ritual, including the form for the administration of infant baptism. At the time of the 1883 union a similar committee had been established, chaired by Henry Flesher Bland. Bland had died in 1898, and this time it was his younger colleague, Nathanael Burwash, whose name appeared first on the list of committee members.[90]

When the committee issued its report in 1906, there was little doubt whose hand had directed it, for in 1904 Burwash had already described the guidelines for the revision in a detailed article, submitted to the *Canadian Methodist Magazine*. At that time he had expressed strong reservations about what he considered significant modifications of Wesley's teaching on the relationship between baptism and the new birth made to the ritual since Wesley's death by the American General Conference and adopted with some variations in Canada. At the same time he approvingly drew attention to an 1882 revision of the Wesleyan Methodist ritual in England, based on the *Book of Common Prayer*. Applauding its "conservative spirit," it was, in his opinion "the most successful Methodist revision which has yet been made."[91]

Two years later, in 1906, in the preamble to the report of the commission on ritual, the Canadian committee also pointed out the conservative spirit which had guided its revisions. However, though the suggested amendments were conservative, they were highly significant and represented a change in the condition upon which children were accepted into full church membership. As always, the minister was reminded of his responsibility to provide religious instruction for the children of the church. But this time the 1864 precondition for membership was re-introduced, for children were to be brought "to true repentance and decision for Christ, and to the exercise of saving faith" before being publicly received into church membership. And in the definition of baptism, which up to this point had followed the American position, there was now a difference. A clear distinction was made between baptism and rebirth, and children by baptism were no longer "members" but "heirs of the Kingdom of God."[92] Here a term was used that repeated a point Burwash had emphasized in his 1881 essay: "The Church takes children in, not because they have salvation already, but because they *need it*, and have a *right to it* by God's covenant mercy under which they have been born."[93]

There was little discussion on the report, which was passed easily. Not all, it should be noted, agreed with its tenor, and at least one member of the Conference did express a preference for more "up to date" views and as a strong believer in childhood innocence protested about the continuation in the baptismal form of references to "the old Adam" in a new-born infant. At that point Nathanael Burwash put an end to the debate by reminding his progressive colleague that "there was one of the most fundamental and essential doctrines of Methodism, the doctrine that every man must be born again. All came into the world with a life that must be regenerated."[94] And so, totally in defiance of all Romantic sensibility concerning infancy, the Canadian Methodist child, at least officially, entered the twentieth century, unequivocally depraved, morally responsible, and in need of the new birth.

CONCLUSION

Exactly seventy years earlier in 1836, in the annual address of Conference, the members of the Wesleyan Methodist Church in Canada had been reminded in a very similar manner that the salvation of their children was to be achieved, not through Christian nurture, but through their conversion. For a denomination that historians have generally considered to be especially responsive to the changes of nineteenth-century Canadian society, this reaffirmation of old doctrines and practices seems reactionary and strangely out of character. In 1906 Canadian Methodists, who even by 1884 were considered by one historian to have made the transition from a body of converts to a "mature social institution," were reimposing a condition of membership usually seen as appropriate to a religious society or sect. Moreover, though Richard Niebuhr has asserted that "doctrines and practice change with the mutations of social structure, not vice versa," Methodism in Canada in 1906 was officially subscribing to a view of the moral nature of the child that was oddly at variance with that presumably held by society at large.[95]

Part of this apparent hesitance to adapt doctrine and practice to social change can be attributed to the peculiar doctrinal and ecclesiastical provisions John Wesley made for his Methodist followers. When it came to re-evaluating the moral nature of children and defining their relationship to the church, Methodists had to work within a different framework than, for example, Congregationalists. Part of it can also be attributed to their special circumstances as Methodists in Canada, with two ecclesiastical traditions on which to draw, and the opportunities for re-evaluation provided by a succession of church unions.

But the main reason for the 1906 decision on the moral nature of children and their relationship to the church lies in the nature of evangelical revivalism itself. It is here that Burwash's contribution to the debate on the moral nature of the child is especially relevant.

Religious revivalism was not simply the manifestation of a certain type of religious behaviour, a "seemingly hysterical, enthusiastic conversion" at camp and revival meetings, as has often been supposed.[96] Had it been limited to this, it would probably indeed have passed away with the disappearance of the unsettling conditions of frontier life. Burwash's account of his own childhood religious training is a reminder that revivalism could be as much an element of home life as of the more public services of the camp meeting, chapel, and church. Rooted in evangelical theology, the basic beliefs of revivalism could be summarized in a few central doctrines. As Burwash's childhood training demonstrates, "Evangelicalism was never really a theological system so much as a way of life. It did not present itself to its adherents as a logical set of beliefs but rather as a series of vivid and compelling personal experiences."[97]

By its nature, therefore, evangelical revivalism became integrated into the very pattern of an individual's life. In a penetrating analytical essay, *Revivals, Awakenings and Reform*, William F. McLoughlin has explored this simple observation more fully by linking the religious revival to the wider cultural concept of a revitalization movement or awakening, as described in the anthropological research of Anthony F.C. Wallace.[98] If we accept this hypothesis, the story of Nathanael Burwash's family quite rightly began with the cultural disorientation of the first Nathaneal after the American Revolution and with the immigration of his maternal grandparents, the Taylors. From there it extended to the conversion of his parents, who in turn, drawing on their own recent religious experience and their earlier childhood training, with single-minded concentration tried to direct and shape the values and faith of their children. And in this way, what began as a revival, that is, a re-orientation of religious beliefs, by the time of the second generation had taken the form of an awakening, a cultural revitalization.

For young Burwash, therefore, unlike those converted as adults, revivalism was not a matter of re-orienting earlier beliefs. Thanks to his mother's training, there was only one way of looking at reality. And so, though he did concede in the account of his childhood religious training, written in 1918, that "modern theology would doubtless say that in this there was too much of the law and too little of the gospel of love," he immediately dismissed the thought. "But looking back now through the experience of more than seventy years, I do not think she was wrong," he mused. "Sin was there by the fallen nature, and conscious conviction of its presence must precede and prepare the way for its cure by the power of redeeming love."[99]

However, while his childhood religious training may account for his unwillingness, or more accurately, his inability, to change his views on the moral nature of the child, there is another, more profound reason for his intransigence and perhaps that of his generation. When religious revivalism is set within the wider context of an awakening or cultural reorientation, childhood formation is part of the much larger complex of values, beliefs, and practices that give shape to an individual's life. As Clifford Geertz has written, "In religious belief and practice a group's ethos is rendered intellectually reasonable by being shown to represent a way of life ideally adapted to the actual state of affairs the world view describes, while the world view is rendered emotionally convincing by being presented as an image of an actual state of affairs."[100] Though subsequent chapters of this study will explore more fully this relationship between religious belief or doctrine and perception of reality, this concept is also of direct relevance to understanding the debate in Canadian Methodism concerning the moral nature of the child.

What really was the issue in this debate? An earlier study has assumed that it was a controversy centred on infant depravity, with Burwash defending an outmoded viewpoint, arguing "in a social vacuum" with a theological precision that was "irrelevant and overly harsh for Victorian Canada." Bland, on the other hand, it is suggested, championed a more optimistic and merciful interpretation, "which seemed to be more appropriate for the experiences of the age."[101] Burwash's intricate, laboured logic does indeed leave him open to the charge of theological precision. But that theological precision, it must be emphasized, was not in the first place directed to the doctrine of infant depravity. The full title of his 1881 essay in its published form was "The Relation of Children to the Fall, the Atonement, and the Church," and his principal aim in the controversy with Bland was to explain, defend, and maintain the Arminian understanding of the atonement.

To a nineteenth-century Methodist the doctrine of the atonement was not merely a theological statement but, in a deeper sense, a cultural concept by which to understand human experience.[102] Arminian theology did emphasize God's universal grace in the atonement, but it also stressed the need for individual repentance and reconciliation. The heart of Methodist piety, as Burwash never grew tired of pointing out, lay in this conversion experience, in "the act of freewill, by which man cooperated with God in the work of salvation."[103] Unlike in Calvinism, the individual was not a helpless victim, a "sinner in the hands of an angry God," to use Jonathan Edward's familiar phrase, but a morally responsible agent, able to co-operate with God in the great work of salvation. "Moral responsibility," Burwash argued in the opening sentence of his study of the atonement published in 1896, "is a fact most clearly revealed both in universal human consciousness and in the Holy Scriptures."[104] It took only a little logic to show that the entire human race was linked together by a natural law "of race responsibility": "It is the foundation of all the altruistic virtues. Every man under it becomes his brother's keeper. Individual responsibility without it could not attain its most God-like development. If it made the fall possible, it also made possible salvation. If it has entailed a long heritage of ills, it has raised up a countless army of workers with Christ, in saving others even by dying themselves."[105]

Seen in this light, the thought of those who opted for childhood innocence had far-reaching implications. By making the effect of the atonement universal and unconditional and by removing the distinction between grace and regeneration, these writers were not only undermining Methodism's essential teaching of the need for repentance and conversion, but they were also threatening the natural law that held society together.[106] Co-operation would give way to individualism, moral responsibility to irresponsibility.

The essential first step in forming a child's moral consciousness consisted in imparting an awareness of sin. As a result the doctrine of infant depravity, when correctly related to the doctrine of the atonement, was worth defending, not only in 1881, but again in the midst of church union negotiations in 1906. And that is why Nathanael Burwash, educator and theologian, sat down only a few months before his death in 1918 to write a detailed account of his own religious training at the hand of Anne Taylor, seventy years earlier. The reason was obvious. Though much had gone into the making of Canadian Methodism – the work of the Spirit, the American Revolution, British immigration, the writings and institutions left behind by John Wesley, and the decisions of annual conferences – in the end, thanks to Burwash's understanding of the atonement, it was a mother who would continue to make a young Methodist and to provide society with its moral foundations.

CHAPTER TWO

The College Student: Reason and Religion

I would gladly give away all I am, and all I ever may become, all the years, every one of them, which may be given me to live, but for one week of my old child's faith, to go back to calm and peace again, and then to die in hope.

J.A. Froude, *The Nemesis of Faith*

Nathanael Burwash, unlike some of his contemporaries whose "honest doubt" led them away from the religion in which they had been raised, spent his life as a preacher, educator, and theologian reaffirming the faith of his childhood.[1] As he frequently acknowledged in his later years, two formative influences had shaped his life and thought: his mother and his years as an undergraduate at Victoria College, Cobourg.[2] However, while these influences would shape his theology, they had not shaped the questions to which that theology addressed itself. Here Burwash was not that different from J.A. Froude, who also had been forced to come to grips with intellectual problems that his parents had never known. For Burwash the questions would not come until after his graduation in 1859. When they did, they marked the mood of an entire era. At the end of that era, as Owen Chadwick has wryly observed, even "schoolboys decided not to have faith because Science, whatever that was, disproved Religion, whatever that was."[3]

Thanks to his years at Victoria College, young Burwash had no difficulty in defining science and religion. As a student his mind had been shaped by the empiricism of the Common Sense philosophers, and as a young Methodist converted during a college revival he knew the essential nature of religion as well to be intensely experiential. After he graduated, in an age of increased religious doubt, he called upon the arsenal of this earlier intellectual and spiritual education to expound a theology that used the inductive method of science but whose foundations lay in the vital experience of religion. In this way Nathanael Burwash was able not only to keep both science and religion, but also to insist that the two, if properly defined, were essential for ensuring the continued vitality of Canadian Methodism in a time of religious and intellectual unrest.

Such confidence in the compatibility between reason and faith, especially on the part of a Methodist theologian, should not be accepted without examination, for it runs counter to general opinion. Since the days when John Wesley tried to convince his opponents that his followers were not uneducated religious enthusiasts, there had been a lingering suspicion that Methodism and reason were mutually exclusive.[4] And, greatly to the chagrin of Wesley's loyal supporters in British North America, that prejudice also found root in the new world. In the words of the Anglican divine, John Strachan, the Methodist ministry could be dismissed as "numbers of uneducated itinerant preachers, who leaving their steady employment, betake themselves to preaching the gospel from idleness or a zeal without knowledge."[5]

Whereas John Strachan made no claims to objectivity when judging the intellectual formation of Methodists, the same cannot be said for twentieth-century scholars. And yet the view that "zeal" and "knowledge" are incompatible has endured. The Canadian Methodist educator, Egerton Ryerson, for example, emerges in an analysis of Victorian critical thought, A.B. McKillop's *A Disciplined Intelligence*, as having a highly ambivalent attitude towards "the relationship between the intellectual and the moral faculties, between scientific inquiry and the 'piety of feeling' which for him constituted the essence of the educational experience." Thus at Victoria College when Ryerson was principal, McKillop observes, though much was said in favour of a liberal education, that education was "above all to be pervaded by the study of theology."[6]

Another historian has concluded his history of early-nineteenth-century Methodism in Upper Canada with an observation in a similar vein, pointing out that by the 1840s a growing emphasis upon "the precepts of science and philosophy rather than upon the dogmas of religion ... provided an increasing threat to the naive empirical teachings of Methodism."[7] One writer's study of secularization is often another's analysis of progress and modernization, and in a second study of Canadian Methodism this same effect of education upon religion has been applauded. Not only did it lead to "a more demanding and critical audience and a more sensitive church hierarchy," but it resulted in a redefinition of the concept of spiritual renewal. "Gradual growth in grace, within an evolutionary framework, appeared at least as legitimate and more rational than the seemingly hysterical, enthusiastic conversion."[8]

Though none of these studies lays claim to an extensive analysis of

Methodist theology to support such observations, substantial evidence is indeed available for the American Methodist experience. In a detailed analysis, significantly entitled *Theological Transition in American Methodism: 1790–1935*, Robert Chiles has detected a profound shift in Methodist doctrine in the century and a half after Wesley's death away from revelation and religious experience to an increased emphasis on reason, natural theology, and philosophical demonstration. To Chiles the major influences in this redefinition of doctrine were the writings of the eighteenth-century Christian apologists Joseh Butler and William Paley and the teachings of the Common Sense Realism, or Scottish Philosophy, of Thomas Reid and Dugald Stewart. Until the 1870s these were the standard fare at American and Canadian colleges and figured prominently on the reading list of Methodist probationers for the ministry.[9]

Against this backdrop the story of Nathanael Burwash's years at Victoria College is well worth examining. Stretching over nine years, his college experience included three years (1852–5) as a preparatory school student, one year as an elementary school teacher, three years (1856–9) as an undergraduate, and a final year as a tutor in mathematics before he entered the Methodist ministry in 1860. During this time he was not only exposed to the writings of Butler and Paley and the Scottish Philosophers, but he also displayed a marked proclivity for scientific investigation and rational demonstration. Moreover, it was to his first year in college that he dated his conversion, that central experience of Methodist piety and the principal cause of the charges of religious enthusiasm and irrational behaviour directed at Methodists. A year later he took part in a college revival that affected most of Victoria's students, some of whom, like Albert Carman, W.H. Withrow, Alexander Sutherland, John Potts, Edward B. Ryckman, William Kerr, William Dean, and Byron M. Britton would have a decisive influence on the fortunes of their denomination and its educational work. An examination of the relationship between reason and faith in a college education of the 1850s will therefore provide insight not only into the thought of Nathanael Burwash, but also into the nature of revivalism in Canada in the second half of the nineteenth century.

THE IMPACT OF THE SECOND GREAT AWAKENING

When young Burwash registered at Victoria College in October 1852, the school had already been in existence for twenty-six years, first as the Upper Canada Academy, and after 1841 as a degree-granting institution under its present name. As early as 1830, when it had become apparent that Upper Canada's one institution of higher learning, King's College, would be "a school of sectarian views" under what Methodists considered to be the baneful influence of the Anglican archdeacon John Strachan, the Methodist Conference in Canada had considered the feasibility of establishing its own "seminary of learning." Neither sectarian nor elitist, but proudly utilitarian, theirs was to be "a Seminary of Education, where youth may be trained in the knowledge and obedience of God, and at the same time be instructed in the various branches of human learning, which the present state of society renders essentially necessary, in order to respectability and usefulness, and for the proper and successful discharge of the duties of the different stations of life to which Providence may call them."[10]

In the royal charter, obtained in October 1836, these aims were again spelled out in the general description of the institution as "an Academy for the General Education of Youth in the various branches of Literature and Science on Christian principles." Though the school was to be managed by a board appointed by the annual meeting of the Wesleyan Methodist Church in Upper Canada and funded by the denomination, there were to be no religious tests for faculty and students: "All students shall be free to embrace and pursue any religious creed and attend any place of worship which their parents and guardians may direct."[11] This commitment to a common Christianity remained unchanged in 1841, when the Academy's charter was revised, and it was also the basis of the new college curriculum, an "English and Liberal Education," which Egerton Ryerson outlined in detail in his inaugural address in 1841 as Victoria's first principal.

That curriculum was virtually unchanged when young Burwash entered in 1852, and it remained essentially intact until the 1870s, when greater room was made for theology and the sciences. Since it has already been the focus of scholarly interest, there will be no need to repeat an analysis of its component parts.[12] It should be noted, however, that Victoria and her curriculum were in no way unique but part of the larger scene of American evangelical higher education.

The immediate forerunner of the Upper Canada Academy had been Cazenovia Seminary in New York, which until 1836 had registered a large number of Methodist students from Upper Canada and continued to supply some of the faculty for the new Canadian institution. Until the 1860s, when it began to draw on its own graduates, Victoria looked to American Methodist colleges for its instructors. Moreover, the curriculum that Egerton Ryerson had described in 1841 was, with the exception of its greater emphasis on English literature and the physical sciences, a faithful copy of the standard American college curriculum as outlined in the "Yale Report on the Classics," published in 1828.[13]

As early as 1830 Egerton Ryerson had drawn the attention of the readers of the *Christian Guardian* to the "salutary influence" of Methodist colleges in the United States and had suggested them as a model for the proposed academy.[14] These colleges were part of a larger American phenomenon, the religious revival movement of the first decades of the nineteenth century commonly referred to as the Second Great Awakening (1800–30). This movement, which some historians consider to have originated in 1801 in the Yale College revival under the earnest preaching of President Timothy Dwight, cut across denominational lines. However, observers have noted the prominent role played by Methodists in establishing the many educational institutions which followed in its wake and which were intended to implement the ideals of evangelical Christianity.[15] Often established, like the Upper Canada Academy, in a frontier setting, these colleges were committed to providing an advanced practical and utilitarian education to young people of all social and religious backgrounds.[16]

Behind this egalitarianism, however, was a profound concern on the part of college educators that a rapidly developing, progressive society stood in danger of losing its religious and moral underpinnings. Largely led by moderate Calvinists, evangelical educators tried to steer between the excesses of religious enthusiasm and the destructive effects of the rationalism and scepticism of the Enlightenment. By means of the college curriculum they tried instead to establish a semi-official culture which insisted that piety and learning went hand in hand. Moralistic, flexible, activist, and increasingly untheological, this curriculum was intended to meet the needs of an expanding and changing society. As a result, though educators assimilated some of the values of the eighteenth-century Enlightenment, including the importance of reason, they did so selectively, making a careful distinction between the proper use of reason, and rationalism, which they equated with religious scepticism. At the same time, they were generally optimistic that through the proper use of reason, the individual would be led to see the truths of the Christian religion and practise these in his daily life so that society might progress in an orderly fashion.

To implement this vision, they were able to turn to the writings of eighteenth-century Christian apologists like William Paley and Samuel Butler, and to the easily comprehensible, empiricist philosophy of Scottish Realism, or Common Sense, which made room for social and scientific progress and at the same time affirmed unchanging moral principles.[17] They also had at their disposal the standard, highly structured college curriculum of the 1828 Yale Report, adopted in 1841 at Victoria. Like the writings of Common Sense, this curriculum accommodated both reason and revelation and has been aptly summarized by one historian, Stow Persons, under the title, "Protestant scholasticism":

Protestant scholasticism represented a synthesis of seventeenth-century religious ideas with those of the Enlightenment. Its fundamental proposition was the assertion that reality is an orderly and intelligible structure. Facts were apprehended by the physical senses, and their relationships were established by the use of the reasoning faculty. When broadly understood by a mature and well-informed intelligence, these facts, whether of nature or of human life, were clear proof of the existence of the deity and His providence.[18]

In this nineteenth-century revision of the Enlightenment, which Henry May has called the "Didactic Enlightenment," reason was called upon, not to question revelation, but to support it.[19]

This was the general background to Egerton Ryerson's liberal education, and this synthesis of religious and Enlightenment ideas was even more marked in the thought of Samuel Nelles, the man who was Victoria's principal from 1850 to 1887. More than anyone else, he exerted a profound influence on Burwash, first as an undergraduate, and after 1867 as his colleague.[20] Earmarked for the position of principal in 1836 by Egerton Ryerson while still an undergraduate at the Wesleyan University in Middletown, Connecticut, Nelles had received most of his higher education in American Methodist institutions. But for two years, 1842–4, he had been one of Victoria's first three undergraduates, leaving when Ryerson exchanged his position of principal for that of Assistant Minister of Education. Even as a student Nelles had already espoused Enlightenment values. At the college's first Annual Exhibition in 1843 in a speech, "The Spirit of Inquiry," he had made an ardent plea for the freedom of the mind to investigate all matters for itself. Defending reason before an assembled audience of parents and college supporters, he had forcefully argued, "Bigotry and Superstition and Tyranny have marshalled their thousand hosts to check her progress and put forth all their venom to quench her very existence in the human soul."[21] Six years later, still true to the spirit of this undergraduate address, he recorded in his diary the decision to undertake "a radical scrutiny of my religion. I can no longer trust myself blindly in those notions imbibed from others. I will try for myself. I erect my own Reason as umpire in the great trial."[22]

The appeal to reason, however, did not lead Samuel Nelles to a loss of faith. As his students remarked and the journals he kept at various points in his life confirm, he remained unaffectedly devout. The use of reason did lead him to deplore the ravages of superstition, bigotry, and dogmatism upon true religion, and these in turn also became the enemies of his students, in particular of Nathanael Burwash.[23] For young Burwash, who was in danger of becoming somewhat of a religious zealot, Samuel Nelles was an ideal model.[24] Extremely well-read and able to draw on an unusual variety of literary and philosophical sources with which to illustrate his regular Saturday afternoon talks to his students, Nelles managed to alleviate seriousness and profundity with wit. And when he was unable to maintain his usual detachment and found the unenlightened intrusion of some of his fellow Methodists into the affairs of Victoria College a little too oppressive, he fled to his books. These included such favourite writers as Jeremy Taylor, Joseph Butler, William Channing, and John Wesley, whose "liberal spirit" and "Broad Churchism" he so often missed in Wesley's followers.[25]

REASON IN THE LIFE OF A YOUNG METHODIST

To young Nathanael Burwash, exposure to college and Nelles's benign influence marked an "epoch" in his life. Looking back on his classroom work in his autobiography, he saw it as a transition, "the passage from the childlife of seeing, hearing and becoming acquainted with the things and facts to a new life of reasoned thought about those facts," and he concluded, "The pleasure of that experience returns with its remembrance to this day."[26]

The nature of that "reasoned thought" will become more apparent when one examines the course in moral philosophy that he took as an "extra" during his second year. His exposure to this course, which was normally reserved for the final year of undergraduate work, was somewhat premature, but the text, Francis Wayland's *Elements of Moral Science*, could be safely handled by students of all ages. Wayland, a Baptist minister and president of Brown University, explained in the preface that it was his intention "to state the moral law, and the reason for it, in as few and as comprehensive terms as possible." He added that he considered it much more desirable to state what was true than to "point out what was exploded, discuss what was doubtful, or disprove what was false."

Highly exhortative, moral philosophy employed a recitation method consisting of questions and prescribed answers. In this way it avoided any mere "speculation" on the part of the student and tried to approximate the method of the physical sciences by "objectively" examining "the motives and rules of human actions." As a result, it relied heavily on introspection, a favourite technique for young evangelicals who, like Burwash, had been taught the importance of right motives from early childhood.

The transition from early childhood training to the use of reason at college was therefore simple. It was primarily a matter of realizing that what up to this point had been termed his "conscience" was really the "moral faculty." Acting as "the judiciary branch of the moral life," the moral faculty enabled the individual to choose between right and wrong. This placed a heavy emphasis on education, for though it was possible to learn part of one's duty simply by the "light of nature" or natural religion, full knowledge could only be acquired by the "additional light" of revealed religion. This, of necessity, had to be taught, and thus Wayland's chapters dealt with such signposts of evangelical orthodoxy as "observance of the Sabbath," "general duty of chastity," and "benevolence to the unhappy." Burwash detected the limitations of Wayland when he later referred to the text as "a system of Christian ethics rather than an ethical philosophy."[27] In a detailed study of nineteenth-century texts in moral philosophy, *The Instructed Conscience*, D.H. Meyer has supported this evaluation by showing a direct correlation between Wayland's teaching and the central beliefs and ideals of the time.[28] Samuel Nelles, too, succinctly stated the relationship of Wayland's concerns to the life of the mind for Methodists with the dictum "Moral purity does more than all things else to expand and invigorate the mind."[29]

The course in mental philosophy also taught by Nelles was closely related to moral philosophy but taken at a more suitable time (Burwash's second-last year as an undergraduate). The text, *Mental Philosophy*, by an American Methodist, Thomas Upham, was really a treatise on psychology rather than metaphysics and was especially recommended for its defence of the empiricism of John Locke, as modified by the Scottish Realists, against the Kantian idealism that had begun to worry evangelical educators.[30] The school of Scottish Common Sense Realism, best known in North America through the writings of Thomas Reid (1710-96) and his student Dugald Stewart (1753-1828), constituted the orthodox philosophy of evangelicals and appeared to ensure that in a rapidly changing world religion and morality were unassailable.[31] Thus, when Samuel Nelles lectured on the thought of Stewart, a sound, moderate Calvinist, he was able to tell his students that although Stewart was not a theologian, he was "friendly to Christianity" and his high moral tone inspired the reader with a love of virtue.[32]

Like John Locke, the Scottish Realists were empiricists. But whereas Locke had suggested that the individual can only come to know things outside his own subjective experience through the medium of mental phantasms called "ideas," they argued that knowledge begins not with ideas but with judgmental perceptions which form "the common sense of mankind." Confident that this "common sense" was unassailable, and at times confusing what is habitually taken for granted with what is really known (as their critics pointed out), the Scottish Realists, through simplified texts like Upham's *Mental Philosophy*, provided students with a restatement and defence of the first truths of philosophy without in any way appearing to undermine the truths of revealed religion.[33]

Young Burwash, who in his final year at college would record in his diary, "O how fatal a spirit of speculation and a desire for riches are to true piety," took eagerly to this course in mental philosophy.[34] Although some of the psychological insight he gained through the course found expression in highly stilted Byronesque verse, mental discipline prevailed and Upham's lessons led to a scholarly discourse on the subject "beauty," delivered to the Victoria College Literary Society in January 1859.

Stating his firm refusal to take his audience on a beguiling study of beauty in the ideal sense, he promised to take the more scientific approach of tracing the emotions of the mind to the objects that cause them. As he reminded his long-suffering listeners on the forty-fourth page of his discourse, such a procedure was "least liable to error. We may be mistaken in the qualities of external objects but we cannot be mistaken in our consciousness of experiencing certain states of mind or entertaining certain thoughts."[35] And that was the lesson of Common Sense.

If mental philosophy was an early interest, natural science was even more so. He was fascinated with the new study of electricity, magnetism, and electromagnetism, but like many of his generation he settled on geology as a lasting avocation.[36] It provided the occasion for another equally lengthy discourse, "The Coincidences of the Geological with the Mosaic Account of Creation," delivered in 1858, again to the Literary Association. This time his source (to the point of plagiarism) was the highly popular *Footprints of the Creator* (1847) by the Scottish Free Church minister, Hugh Miller. The moral tone of the address was high, and with Miller he insisted that any conflict between the discoveries of science and divine revelation was impossible, since "truth ... is immutable and always consistent with itself."[37]

In making such a statement young Burwash was merely echoing one of the basic principles on which his college curriculum was based, the harmony between human reason and divine revelation. Behind that curriculum the principle lay a trust in the objective tangibility of the Newtonian world and the belief that it was possible for the mind to apprehend the divinely created, harmonious structure of the universe. As T.D. Bozeman has argued, it was primarily the writings of the Scottish Realists that created this receptivity to empiricism among American Protestants. At the same time it also gave them a common language, and terms like "trust in the senses," "mind," "matter," the "sublime," and above all "truth" would continue to mark the thought and writing of those who, like Burwash, had been schooled in the tradition.[38]

As his discourses to the Literary Association had revealed, young Burwash's excessive penchant for reasoned demonstration was held thoroughly in check by the authority of revelation. Accordingly, in the final year of his studies he eagerly followed the course in which these two inclinations received their fullest attention, the Evidences of Christianity. Since the college curriculum had in large part represented the response of evangelical educators to the deism of the Enlightenment, the assigned reading usually included two of the best-known pieces of eighteenth-century apologetic literature, William Paley's *Natural Theology or Evidences of the Existence and Attributes of Deity Collected from the Appearance of Nature* (1802) and Joseph Butler's *Analogy of Religion*.[39] The latter never failed to delight Samuel Nelles, as it had John Wesley at an earlier date, and Paley's *Natural Theology* more than once evoked from Nelles the contented exclamation in his journal, "It is a happy world after all."[40]

Burwash not only shared their pleasure but indoctrinated himself with a double dose of Christian apologetics, choosing to read in addition Leslie's *Short and Easy Method with the Deists* and Lyttleton's *Conversion of St. Paul*. Looking back on his reading in the *Evidences* many years later, he reflected on how well they had served their purpose: "The objections of the sceptics as there set forth seemed to me to be all satisfactorily answered and the faith of my childhood fully confirmed."[41] Indeed, in every course of the curriculum faith had not only not been undermined, but wherever possible it had been affirmed and defended by reason. At Victoria College in the 1850s the aspirations of what Henry May has called the "Didactic Enlightenment" had been fully met. Young Burwash would graduate in 1859, fully convinced of the truth of revealed religion and, thanks to his familiarity with the *Evidences* and his awareness of the moral law, fully equipped to take on the enemy who lurked outside the college, "the scoffer, the blasphemer, and the sceptic."[42] As May has observed, "Though Revelation was nowhere contradicted and always eventually sustained, it was a matter of honor to arrive at the correct conclusions only through methods of reasoning which would – or so the teachers insisted – carry conviction to any honest infidel."[43]

RELIGION IN THE LIFE OF A
YOUNG METHODIST

To a Methodist, the arsenal called to the defence of religion was not itself religion. "Religion," Samuel Nelles reminded his students, "is the light of the soul and the strength of the soul."[44] John Wesley called it "the life of God in the soul of man" or more fully, "righteousness, the image of God stamped on the heart, the love of God and man, accompanied with the peace that passeth all understanding, and joy in the Holy Ghost."[45] And though Wesley made no small claims for the achievement of reason, he was also quick to insist that reason "is utterly incapable of giving either faith, or hope or love; and consequently of producing either real virtue, or substantial happiness. Expect these from a higher source, even from the Father of the Spirits of all flesh."[46] Samuel Nelles was fully in agreement, for notwithstanding his task as educator, he noted in his journal, "The young divine needs Greek and Hebrew and logic and History and Geography but he needs more than all these, a deep growth of grace in his own heart. He must look to his inner life."[47]

Thus, at Victoria there was also the "inner life." In the first place, there were the institutions intended to promote this life: the class meeting, church services, and protracted meeting, for while religion was in the first place the work of the Spirit, every human effort was expended to facilitate that work. At the opening of the college Nelles and the superintendent of Cobourg Circuit called a meeting of all students who were already church members. They enrolled their names and assigned them to Methodist classes, either at the college or in town under the leadership of professors; most students preferred the latter. Those who were not members but of Methodist background were required to attend the Methodist church in Cobourg twice every Sunday, where their attendance was duly recorded.[48]

Though to some these regulations were oppressive, for Nathanael Burwash this new religious environment marked a turning point. It ended the spiritual anxiety, which had been plaguing him since the age of seven, that unlike adult Methodists, he had no certain knowledge that his sins were forgiven.[49] It was not until his first year at college, in December 1852, during a protracted meeting conducted by George McRitchie, one of his fellow students preparing for the ministry, that he finally obtained a measure of relief. Under McRitchie's exhortations to the unconverted to seek the pardoning mercy of God, "all the convictions of past years came back with renewed power. And yet I seemed powerless to go to that alter of prayer. I stood in a pew trembling from head to foot and my whole soul seemed to cry out 'God be merciful to me a sinner,' when in a moment like a flash of light, I saw that God was declared to be gracious and merciful through Christ forgiving transgression and sin, and I began to claim that mercy as mine."[50] In Wesleyan spirituality this was the great crisis of religious life and the beginning of the new birth, known as "justification by faith," when the penitent sinner trusted totally in the atonement of Christ for complete forgiveness. John Wesley had himself described "the change which God works in the heart through faith in Christ" in very similar terms and had insisted that this experience was the one essential condition for salvation.[51]

To Wesley, however, who had felt his heart strangely warmed at Aldersgate in 1738, an assurance of forgiveness always accompanied justifying faith. This doctrine of a direct assurance by the Holy Spirit aroused no little controversy, for it left Wesley and his followers open to accusations of religious enthusiasm, and its manifestation at revivals often took the form of excessive emotionalism.[52] To John Strachan, writing in 1806, Canadian Methodists overstepped every law of religious decorum: "They will bawl twenty of them at once, tumble on the ground, laugh, sing, jump and stamp, and this they call the working of the spirit."[53]

John Wesley, to whom "all irrational religion is false religion," shared this disapproval and went to considerable lengths to explain the nature of assurance.[54] Commonly referred to as "the witness of the Spirit," the description was extended over two of Wesley's Standard Sermons, for its nature was complex. In the first place, there was the witness of God's Spirit to the pardoned sinner, and this Wesley described, not without some hesitation, as "an inward impression on the soul, whereby the Spirit of God directly witnesses to my spirit, that I am a child of God; that Jesus Christ hath loved me, and given himself for me; and that all my sins are blotted out, and even I, am reconciled to God."[55] This witness of the Spirit, however, was always accompanied by the witness of the individual's own spirit, which expressed itself in a feeling of "love, joy, peace, long suffering, gentleness, goodness, fidelity, meekness, temperance," also referred to as a good conscience.[56] Since a conscious sense of God's presence could not possibly co-exist with a conscious consent to sin, those who had experienced the new birth were constantly called upon to exercise their will and refrain from sin. "Let none," Wesley insisted, "ever presume to rest in any supposed testimony of the Spirit, which is separate from the fruit of it."[57]

In later years this exposition of classical Wesleyan spirituality would figure prominently in Burwash's annotated edition of the *Standard Sermons*. In his class lectures, too, he adhered firmly to the authorized version, but his own conversion in 1852 had fallen somewhat short of the standard model. If the few instances when he referred to his conversion are pieced together, it would appear that he fully accepted the atonement at the 1852 protracted meeting but did not at that time receive the witness of the Spirit. Thus, outside of his immediate family, he kept his experience to himself and at times questioned whether it indeed meant that he had been "born again."[58] This state of limbo ended dramatically during the following college year, 1853-4, the year of the great college revival.

That October a number of young men who had been converted the previous summer during the revivals conducted in Toronto, Hamilton, Belleville, Kingston, and Montreal by an American evangelist, James Caughey, enrolled at Victoria to prepare for the ministry. To the fourteen-year-old Burwash these older students were moral giants, "men whose manly moral character as well as their intellectual ability, though they were not yet advanced scholars commanded respect." Numbering fewer than a dozen, in a largely unconverted student body ten times the size, they began to attempt the conversion of their classmates through private prayer, personal discussions, and weekly prayer meetings. A few of these men happened to live in the same boarding house as Burwash, and although he had told no one of his recent conversion, he was paid the supreme compliment of being asked to join in their evangelization efforts.[59]

Their work did not proceed without opposition. Although the college curriculum, in particular the course in moral philosophy, made every effort to instill in students a love of virtue and a proper respect for the moral faculty, theory did not always yield practical results. In actual fact, Victoria's students were on the whole a poor reflection of the moral universe depicted in the writings of the Rev. Francis Wayland. In the past there had been other college revivals, one in 1838 shortly after the opening of the Upper Canada Academy, and again in 1843-4 when Egerton Ryerson had been principal of the college.[60] After Ryerson's departure, however, discipline had deteriorated. His temporary replacement, "the saintly Dr Wilson" would later be remembered, in the words of one graduate, as "designed by nature to adorn the classic shades of Parnassus, rather than to shine as the guide and governor of a body of tempestuous youths."[61] Wilson's successor, the Rev. Alexander MacNab, proved to be equally weak and had abruptly terminated his brief but intense contact with Methodist youth by unceremoniously leaving his denomination for the Church of England.[62] Accordingly, Samuel Nelles had found a turbulent student body largely composed of younger academy students awaiting him when he assumed his duties in 1850. One of his express aims had been to improve the moral tone of the college, and for this purpose he had urged the Methodist Conference to send more of its probationers for the ministry to Victoria.[63] The Caughey converts were the result.

In the autumn of 1853 this group, assisted by young Burwash, found their earnest concern with the moral and spiritual welfare of the student body to be the cause of general levity and sometimes obstruction. Burwash later vividly recalled one prayer meeting in the college that ended in chaos when a large number of students, whose souls were at that moment the object of anxious prayer, invaded the room. Turning it into total darkness, they hurled marbles and sticks of pine kindling at the tallow candles, which were its only light, and in the ensuing melee caused a blackboard to crash down on the back of one of the earnest evangelists. The experience was probably the closest approximation of Christian martyrdom in Victorian Canada and it, too, bore fruit.

Suddenly in January, after a protracted meeting in Cobourg, the rowdiness came to an end, and a revival swept through the college:

Deep seriousness began to prevail and before long scores of students began to decide for a better life. The work spread with great power. The ordinary work of the students was almost completely suspended. Instead of the usual lectures, the professors were holding meetings for deeply distressed inquiries. At almost any hour of the day the voice of prayer might be heard from some student's room, where two or three earnest souls, often boys of fourteen, had met for prayer.[64]

One of these fourteen-year-old boys was, of course, Nathanael Burwash, for whom the revival resulted in his first active involvement in evangelistic work. Whereas he had previously been too shy to speak about his own religious experience, he now began to conduct prayer meetings in his lodgings in emulation of his older models. It was also during this revival that his own earlier conversion was finally confirmed, and in May 1854 he became a member of the Wesleyan Methodist Church in Canada. As he later reflected, "To me this revival was as the perfecting of my conversion for it gave me the full assurance of my adoption, courage to make a public profession of what God had done for my soul and strength to take up my cross and take part in all Christian work."[65] The revival marked the beginning of an evangelistic career for others as well. One of Burwash's housemates, Albert Carman, who was six years his senior and a "serious, earnest young man within a year of graduation," was converted at that time, and later occupied the position of General Superintendent of the Methodist Church for many years.[66]

EVALUATION: REASON AND
RELIGION IN TRANSITION

In the opinion of Nathanael Burwash, the revival marked a turning point for the hard-pressed Nelles and the faculty and brought a permanent end to the college's disciplinary turmoil. Reflecting in his *History of Victoria College*, where the 1853–4 revival was given due attention, Burwash made his own biases perfectly clear, "What it meant for the College is seen in this fact that every undergraduate was converted, and from that time forward the students who led the College in sholarship and ability stood for orderly and Christian conduct. This became a tradition perpetuated from generation to generation."[67] If this assessment is indeed accurate, it would have to be concluded that, thanks to the revival, the goal of the course in moral philosophy had finally been met. Lasting morality was the result, not of reason, but of religion.

But was it? Burwash's assessment of the radical change in student behaviour is open to question. While the rather cryptic minutes of Victoria's faculty meetings from the 1850s to 1913 (the year when Burwash's own tenure as chancellor ended) do slowly begin to show a decreased preoccupation with students' misdemeanours, reminiscences of college pranks printed in the student journal, *Acta Victoriana*, leave no illusions about sainthood.[68] On the contrary (as some students were gratified to note), Burwash's own saintliness as a professor and chancellor tended to colour his view of the students' behaviour. At least once, for example, a disciplinary case was allowed readmission to the college, following earnest assurances by his friends that they were praying for his conversion.[69] It is safe to assume that the reasons for any change in the students' behaviour during Burwash's undergraduate days had best be sought elsewhere than simply in the beneficent effects of religion.

Historians who have studied the institutions of higher learning founded as a result of the Second Great Awakening have observed that "seasons of revival" such as that experienced at Victoria in 1853–4 were common.[70] But they have also noted that little connection appeared to exist between the students' religious experience and the course of study they followed at college. Whereas courses based on Common Sense philosophy taught the students the intellectual foundations of religion, college revivals were intended to win their hearts.

To heal this split between faith and reason became the preoccupation of a number of college presidents, most notably Noah Porter at Yale. First as professor from 1849–71 and thereafter until 1886 as president, Porter revised the old curriculum of the 1828 Yale Report in order to place less emphasis on mental discipline and more on Christian nurture.

Increasingly the college came to be depicted as a Christian community. Such a concept was further encouraged by fatherly baccalaureate addresses, the example of "godly professors," and a proliferation of student societies whose primary purpose was character formation. These reforms were emulated elsewhere, and recent scholarship has suggested that between the two traditional types of institutions of higher education in the nineteenth century, the school of mental discipline and the modern secular university, there existed a transitional type, the Christian college.[71]

At Victoria in the 1850s a similar transition was already clearly underway. Besides Ryerson's revision of the curriculum to make more room for English literature and the natural sciences, a change in atmosphere had been introduced when Samuel Nelles became principal in 1850. Examples of this were the latter's Saturday afternoon talks (known as "latest advices"), his enthusiasm for literature, his desire to improve the behaviour of the student body by asking the Methodist Conference to send more ministerial candidates to the college, and his encouragement of student participation in societies like the Literary Association. Moreover, the makeup of the student body was also changing. The year 1853-4 had opened with a large increase in the number of younger students entering the preparatory school. Many of these, in Burwash's recollection, came from backgrounds similar to his own and, like young Burwash, they soon fell under the spell of Samuel Nelles.[72]

One of their principal's best-known traits was his strong dislike of sectarianism and fanaticism, and he took every opportunity to point out to the students the need to integrate religious revivalism into the wider field of Christian ethics. In 1857, for example, in an address to the student body on his favourite theme, the relationship between learning and religion, he expressed the view that "the Creator has united them very closely together, and they are never dissevered except to the serious disadvantage both of learning and religion." Religion without learning easily became "superstition and fanaticism," and learning without the moral base provided by religion grew "proud, shallow and unprofitable," or degenerated into "the handmaid of lust, of sensual indulgence."[73]

This conscious combination of reason and faith, reflected in the college's atmosphere and in the temperament of its principal, probably accounts for the change Burwash perceived in student behaviour. In a different way young Burwash also had been affected by the dual emphasis on reason and faith. Though he had had to wait seven anxious years, first for conversion and then for full assurance, there had been much in his childhood religious training and college education that enabled him to analyse more fully the experience of the new birth, once it did take place, and to be able afterwards to enter intelligently into Wesley's detailed exposition. Anne Taylor's emphasis on moral training, on the need to repent from sin and to exercise the will, made the "fruits of the Spirit" a recognizable and desirable goal and, in fact, little different from the way of life he had been taught since childhood. Moreover, the course in moral philosophy, which he happened to be taking during the year he was converted, allowed him to link his new religious experience to the more general concept of the moral law, thereby divesting conversion of some of its behavioural peculiarities.

Commenting many years later on Wesley's description of the new birth and the fruits of the Spirit, Burwash chose to describe Methodism as "peculiarly ethical Christianity," since "all moral law enters, not as an ornamental addition but as an essential element of true Christian experience."[74] He would also be highly critical of a religious revivalism that emphasized experience for its own sake: '[Too many people] wreck their holiness of life upon this rock. They imagine that, ecstatic experience gained, the whole work is forever done. They forget that the experience becomes character and holy life *only through the will*."[75]

In his later memories of the 1853–4 college revival, it was especially this awareness of the moral law and of the importance of the will that he remarked in the behaviour of his fellow students. As the effects of the revival came to be felt outside the college walls, Burwash saw a new period beginning in Methodist spiritual life. In his opinion this new expression of Methodist spirituality, "less emotional, but more free from some of the defects which attach to a religion purely founded on feeling," also led to greater co-operation with other evangelical denominations. In 1860 a new interest in foreign missions brought together members from Anglican, Presbyterian, Baptist, Congregational, and Methodist churches in a week of prayer meetings in Cobourg, followed by a revival:

But this was not the old Methodist revival with its penitent bench and its shoutings of "Hallelujah!" The spirit was indeed there and some old Methodists could scarcely restrain themselves, but the quieter spirit won the day, and a new type of evangelism had its birth, a type more congenial to an age in which the education of the entire population was creating a life less impulsive and emotional than that of the early days of our country.[76]

But was this "quieter spirit" also a confirmation of the fact that education had undermined the experiential nature of evangelical Christianity? In the case of Calvinism, extensive historical research has indeed demonstrated a re-evaluation after the Second Great Awakening, particularly as a result of the Common Sense philosophy taught in the college curriculum. The special emphasis which Common Sense gave to the moral sense as a rational faculty undermined not only the doctrine of infant depravity, but also election. More applicable to Methodism was the re-evaluation of the function of divine grace in conversion. As D.H. Meyer has noted, "ethical theory, to be universally appplicable, could neither discriminate between the regenerate and the unregenerate nor tolerate the uncertainty of divine election. And the new moral psychology, in its precise description of man's moral nature, could not take account of the unpredictable and arbitrary intrusions of God's grace."[77]

The influence of moral philosophy on American Methodism was profound, for the teaching of the Common Sense philosophy on human freedom and moral perfectibility found a receptive attitude among theologians. However, Robert Chiles and others have argued that this acceptance resulted in a redefinition of the role of the Spirit in salvation. Theologians like Miner Raymond (1811–97) and John Miley (1813–95), offered a revised interpretation of the atonement that emphasized God's moral nature rather than God's gracious forgiveness. For Miley, moreover, who followed a tradition which had begun earlier with the influential Methodist theologian, Richard Watson (1781–1833), empirical evidence of salvation in the form of the witness of the Spirit became less important than it had been with Wesley.[78]

Here Nathanael Burwash provides an interesting contrast. Educated in the same tradition of Common Sense philosophy, and briefly a student of Miner Raymond's at the Garrett Biblical Institute in 1871, he differed from his American colleagues in a number of significant ways.[79] As a ministerial candidate he had studied Watson's *Theological Institutes*, but in later life he was highly critical of Watson's emphasis on prophecy and miracles as a defence of Christianity, to the neglect of the internal evidence of the Spirit, "the very thing in which Wesley insisted!"[80] Moreover, in his interpretation of the atonement, Burwash consciously maintained a tension between divine grace and human responsibility. In so doing he followed the medieval theologian Anselm's concept of Christ's atonement as a "propitiation," that is, as a reason for God to forgive sin or, to use Wesley's term, a ransom.[81] Finally, the witness of the Spirit became one of the most prominent themes of his preaching in his lectures in practical theology and in the ideal he presented to his students in the class meetings he conducted for fifty years at Victoria College.[82] In fact, it can be argued that Nathanael Burwash considered it his special duty as a theologian and preacher to maintain a prominent place for the work of the Spirit in Canadian Methodism.[83]

In so doing he ran counter to the theological transition that was taking place. Beginning in the 1860s, he began to detect more and more signs of "the rationalizing, or rather the reduction to an intellectual process or programme of the work of the Spirit in the inner religious life." This took place through new theories of the atonement or at the level of popular religion, through the influence of the teachings of the Plymouth Brethren, who while they insisted on conversion, ignored the importance of the "fruits of the Spirit." Moreover, there were indications in the revivalism of the second half of the century that penitent sinners were no longer being instructed in the "necessity of moving forward to the full assurance of sins forgiven and the marks of the new birth."[84]

Too many conversions appeared to be superficial or temporary, and one of the main reasons he published his annotated edition of Wesley's *Standard Sermons* in 1881 was to counteract this tendency.[85] While he pointed out in his discussion of the two sermons on the witness of the Spirit that Wesley did not consider assurance to be necessary for final salvation, he also emphasized, following Wesley, that inward and outward holiness could not be attained without it.[86] Burwash's edition of the *Standard Sermons* became mandatory reading for all ministerial students after 1883, but his campaign did not stop here. In 1910, as chairman of the Committee on Evangelism, he was successful in having the General Conference of the Methodist Church pass a report which unequivocally reminded ministers that "in all our efforts for salvation of souls, we emphasize the importance of a clear and definite experience of the witness of the Holy Ghost; and that we urge young Christians never to rest short of this."[87]

"The witness of the Holy Spirit" was also the title of his last recorded lecture, delivered on 21 February 1917 to the deaconesses of the Methodist National Training School. No other subject, he said, had been more fully emphasized in the apostolic age of the church. And the recovery of the work of the Spirit, as witnessed in the new birth, was the great distinguishing mark of the religious revival movement begun by John Wesley.[88] He considered this emphasis on the witness of the Spirit as part of the conversion experience to have been characteristic of Methodist piety during his college years, a period he nostalgically referred to in his old age as Primitive Methodism.[89]

But why did he put such emphasis on a doctrine which in the past had been directly responsible for the accusations of excessive emotionalism levelled against the followers of John Wesley, and which he himself appears to have experienced only imperfectly? The reason is simple, and it links Nathanael Burwash, not to the revivalism of the camp meetings of the early nineteenth century, but to the new involvement of

Canadian Methodism in higher education. The change began in the year of his graduation from Victoria College. That year, 1859, marked a turning point in the history of western science and religion, with the publication of Charles Darwin's *Origin of Species*, followed in 1860 by the series of studies in biblical criticism known as the *Essays and Reviews*. As the implications of these writings began to penetrate the colleges, no educated Christian would ever again be able to take the two basic tenets of the old college curriculum as self-evident: that nature contained the clear signs of a benevolent Creator and that this God had provided additional, completely reliable information about himself in the Scriptures.[90] As Burwash would later reflect, neither the natural theology of William Paley, nor the system of Christian ethics expounded by Francis Wayland was adequate to "reach the difficulties arising from the incoming of positivism, agnosticism, transcendental-ism, and other forms of doubt just beginning to find their way into our Canadian intellectual life."[91]

Some found refuge in what A.B. McKillop has termed "the secret of Hegel." Hegelian idealism, as taught by devout Christians like John Watson, professor of philosophy at Queen's College, Kingston, did not capitulate to evolutionary science, but rather offered a new understand-ing of the universe that encompassed evolution even as it retained man's fundamental moral nature and the essential beliefs of the Chris-tian faith. But in spite of the intent to safeguard the faith, the result was that by the end of the nineteenth century, for many of those schooled in idealist philosophy the sacred had largely come to be expressed in secular terms, as the concepts and language of philosophy undermined and changed the meaning of the traditional beliefs of Christianity. As a result, McKillop has noted "the deeply ironic legacy of the idealists upon Protestantism in Canada."[92]

Unlike the Canadian intellectuals of the post-1859 era who are the subject of McKillop's study, neither Samuel Nelles nor Burwash be-lieved that the answer to the challenge posed to revealed religion by science lay in philosophical idealism. While sympathetic to the "new spiritual philosophy" of T.H. Green, John and Edward Caird, and their Canadian disciple, John Watson, Nelles and Burwash also expressed reservations. Fellow Methodists like Albert Carman were even more outspoken in their critique.[93] By the 1870s, even though Nelles was teaching the thought of Immanuel Kant to his classes in philosophy, he always used a supplementary text, which in 1878 was Gregory Smith's *Character of Christian Morality*. Nelle's objection to the philosophy of Kant and to that of the British idealist, T.H. Green – that they made the standard or end of morality lie not in a personal God but in humanity – was familiar in evangelical circles and was shared by Burwash.[94]

The latter, who as a student had rallied reason to the defence of revealed religion, willingly admitted that philosophical idealism did appear to place religion "upon a new and firm rational foundation." However, here also lay the "subtle" danger it presented to revealed religion, for "in doing this it silently assumes that this is the one and only foundation upon which religious faith can be built and that all religious truth must be received by the methods of philosophy."[95] His own approach to the use of reason differed significantly, as he demonstrated in an 1878 public lecture, "The Genesis, Nature, and Results of Sin." Illustrating the harmony between the truth obtained through biblical exegesis and that obtained through reason, he tried to "help the faltering faith of some to see that the path of reason lies parallel to that of true faith."[96] Reason could be used in support of faith, and it might be called upon to give added certainty, but it could never replace faith.

TRUE CERTAINTY IN RELIGION: A CRISIS AND A RESPONSE

There was a simple reason why reason could not replace faith in the changed intellectual environment of the post-1859 era. To Burwash, religion was still the work of the Spirit, and thus true certainty in religion did not rest in reason but in the old Methodist experience of the witness of the Spirit. As he explained in the preface of his *Manual of Christian Theology on the Inductive Method*, published in 1900 and the product of thirty years of lecturing to ministerial students, true certainty in religion could only be found in "the inner assurance of faith."[97] Thus any true and lasting theology had to proceed by the inductive method, beginning with living faith as its foundation, but tested by the Word, reason, and conscience.[98] This was the answer of an avid student of natural science and Common Sense philosophy to the problem faced by revealed religion in the period after Darwin and the *Essays and Reviews*. But for Burwash as a Methodist it was also the only answer.

Here Burwash's personal experience helps to explain why, unlike some of his colleagues in the American Methodist tradition, he placed such emphasis on the work of the Spirit. In 1862, when he was a young college graduate and a recent probationer in the Methodist ministry stationed in Belleville, Nathanael Burwash had for one brief but intense moment undergone the great Victorian crisis of faith. Its memory influenced him for the rest of his career, and this experience explained in part his hostility to rationalism and his untiring emphasis on the witness of the Spirit. As a young minister he had taken great pride in his college education, still a novelty for the period and an asset at a time when religious scepticism was beginning to make inroads among some of the younger members of his congregation. Primarily young professionals, these individuals did not confine their reading of periodical literature to the *Christian Guardian*, and by way of book reviews were coming into contact with the new literature that was beginning to unsettle religious faith. To this group Burwash had continued to proclaim confidently from the pulpit that "not a single one of the teachings of the Bible can be proved irrational or inconsistent by the most radical reformer of philosophy and public opinion."

Since his listeners did not appear convinced, Burwash decided to confront their leader, a young man he respected highly. It was at that time that he became aware of two books which were the cause of their scepticism, Theodore Parker's *Ten Sermons on the Absolute Religion* and the recently published first volume on the Pentateuch by Bishop Colenso. Asked if he would read these books, Burwash consented without hesitation, certain that he would be able to refute any arguments they might contain against revealed religion, for had he not "studied Paley and Butler and Horne and read many other volumes on the Evidences?"

Unfortunately, the armour of a college education did not prove adequate to the combined onslaught of Parker and Colenso. The effect produced by Colenso will be examined in a later chapter, but Theodore Parker's transcendentalism alone or, as Burwash phrased it, "pantheistic philosophy," was enough to shatter his defences and completely undermine his faith. As he later recalled, "here was a new field and a new method, a method which challenged you on the fundamental basis of philosophy." It seemed to him that Parker's description of the Christian religion appealed entirely to sentiment and to the moral faculty and left no room for what to a Methodist was the essence of true religion, the regenerative work of the Spirit. In his perplexity, however, it was the latter which became the one source of certainty left to him as he struggled with the issues raised by his reading. He described his crisis of faith as follows:

I read the books and sometimes seemed to feel all certain ground sinking from under my feet. Then I would put down the books and on my knees seek anew that light and certainty which God had aforetime given me when I saw that He is His holiness, His goodness, His truth and His love was the most certain thing in all the universe, and so I returned to the battle, confident that in some way the difficulties must be unravelled and the truth made clear. My faith in God and Christ and salvation from sin was fixed and unshaken but in some way I must solve these problems.[99]

Confronted by transcendentalism and the higher criticism, Anne Taylor's religious training and Wesley's insistence on the internal evidence of the Spirit had withstood the test.

Four years later, in June 1866, while stationed in Hamilton he became even more convinced of the importance of assurance in the life of a Christian. The occasion was the unexpected Fenian invasion at Ridge-way, and in an outburst of patriotism the twenty-six-year old Burwash volunteered his services as chaplain to the 13th Militia Battalion. In later years the event made an exciting story for his sons and students and resulted in his being gazetted an honorary lieutenant-colonel in the Canadian Militia in 1912. But it also had theological significance. The first victim of the battle had been a Methodist Sunday school teacher who, as he lay dying in Burwash's arms had pleaded for and received "brighter evidence." To Burwash, the theologian, this incident under-scored the possibility and necessity of assurance in a vital religious experience, and it became a favourite illustration in his lectures on the witness of the Spirit.[100]

Nevertheless, simply to insist on the need and availability of such evidence was not enough. For someone like Burwash who had been schooled in the principles of the "Didactic Enlightenment," reason and religion were mutually supportive. Even though this had not appeared to be the case in his 1862 crisis of faith, no student trained by Samuel Nelles could fall back on dogmatism (as Burwash was briefly tempted to). Given the ability of the mind to know truth and the complete harmony of all truth, there was no alternative but to engage in one's own humble "search for truth."

That search took over thirty years, but by 1900 its end was publicly heralded. That year, in a lengthy address to the students of the University of Michigan and in the second chapter of his *Manual of Christian Theology*, which appeared shortly after, he demonstrated how the mind could come to know religious truth. As his eldest son perceptively noted, commenting after his father's death on the 1859 discourse on beauty, "the basis of ultimate certainty here laid down was one of the lasting acquirements of his mind, and appears in a slightly amplified form as the foundation of the inductive theology of forty years later."[101] The amplifications, however, were significant. Certainty as a state of mind, Burwash argued in 1900, was obtained through seven different means: the use of the five senses, self-consciousness, pure reason apprehending necessary truth, the moral intuition which "yields conviction of the right," the aesthetic intuition, the religious intuition (the basis of faith), and finally, spiritual consciousness. The last, spiritual conscious-ness, which combined the religious intuition with the moral intuition, might be questioned by many, he conceded, but "the truly spiritual man will both understand it and recognize its validity." It provided the individual with more than a strong faith in the existence of God, for it was a deep religious communion, characterized by "a direct sense of the Divine presence ... an immediate personal consciousness of God which fills the soul with reverential and adoring love and joy."[102] Thus, in the age after Darwin and the *Essays and Reviews*, true certainty in religion was still simply what it had always been in the language of theology, the witness of the Spirit. And for the students at the University of Michigan, where the address had been entitled "Intuitive Certainty in Religion" and based on the text, 1 John 4:10, "He that believeth on the Son of God hath the witness in himself," there was a final exhortation, "Have you received this intuition?"[103]

For a student who had received the assurance of pardon during a college revival in 1854 and who was also an ardent devotee of experimental science and trained in moral philosophy, the answer to the problem of true certainty in religion had in the end been simple. When philosophical theory failed to express the facts of religious experience correctly, the theory had only to be revised. Those revisions, it should be noted, were neither very original nor extensive. John Wesley himself, while attempting to describe the witness of the believer's own spirit or conscience, had briefly considered using the new term of moral sense for conscience, following the example of Frances Hutcheson, one of the precursors of Common Sense.[104]

Added to the influence of Wesley was the writing of another nineteenth-century evangelical, James McCosh, who had been a minister in the Free Church of Scotland and president of Princeton College from 1864 to 1894, where his pride in college revivals rivalled that of his Canadian colleague, Nathanael Burwash. In 1866 McCosh's *Intuitions of the Mind Inductively Investigated* had already helped Samuel Nelles prevent what he considered to be an increasing rift between religion and morality.[105] For Burwash, who felt free to amend McCosh according to his own experience of religious and moral certainty, the concept of intuitive knowledge, which was apprehended by the mind without the aid of a reasoning process, was the corrective to the defects of his college course in metaphysics.[106]

Finally in the 1880s there had appeared the writings of Borden Parker Bowne, a Methodist philosopher of international reputation, teaching at Boston University. Bowne's philosophy, known as personalism, stressed personality as the fundamental reality and was intended to combat the materialism and naturalism of a scientific environment. Burwash's own philosophy was rooted in an earlier period, but he eagerly incorporated Bowne's defence of theism into his lectures. Following Bowne, he emphasized that the centre of all ethics was not the self or humanity, but a personal God, "a loving father in whom we live, move and have our being."[107]

Burwash's efforts to integrate the experiential religion of John Wesley into a metaphysical system would have a decisive effect on his own receptivity to the scientific and biblical scholarship of the late nineteenth century, and would in turn determine the attitude of his students in the Methodist ministry. If certainty in religion and morality was intuitive, and if the highest degree of religious certainty lay in that special experience of Wesleyan spirituality known as the witness of the Spirit, then all other areas of knowledge could be safely investigated. Therefore, as far as Burwash was concerned, education had not at all replaced the old-fashioned Wesleyan conversion. On the contrary, in an age where knowledge was endlessly expanding and the old certainties were in danger of disappearing, the witness of the Spirit was even more vital to the Christian scholar of 1900 than it had been to a young college student trained in the 1850s.

CONCLUSION

When revivalistic movements are seen as part of a larger cultural awakening, the efforts by Samuel Nelles and Nathanael Burwash to harmonize reason and religion acquire added significance. Donald G. Mathews has drawn attention to the importance of the Second Great Awakening as an organizing process and social movement. Essential to such an understanding is the realization that the measure of the success of the Awakening lay not in the length of the various periods of enthusiasm (even though ministers of the time might think so) but in the number of new churches and institutions organized which could persist when the enthusiasm died down.[108]

One such institution of course, was Victoria College, where thanks to Nelles, later assisted by Burwash, religion became integrated into the curriculum and the life of the college community. But Victoria was only the first of an increasing number of Methodist organs involved in education and transmitting the revivalism of an earlier period into the changed cultural milieu of the second half of the century. A striking feature of these educational activities and institutions is that almost all were headed by ministers who had been part of Victoria's student body in the 1850s. Not all had completed the four years required for graduation, but as ministerial students all had been exposed to the core of the college curriculum, for Upham, Wayland, Paley, and Butler were also standard texts for probationers in the ministry.[109]

Their appetite for work and their energy were remarkable. For four decades William H. Withrow was the editor of the influential *Canadian Methodist Magazine* and of a number of Sunday school periodicals, besides writing a prodigious number of historical and biographical volumes. Alexander Sutherland made the Board of Missions his special preserve, while John Potts displayed his reputed financial wizardry in a number of national church activities before taking on the position of secretary of the Education Society in 1892. Before becoming general superintendent in 1883, Albert Carman, too, had been a teacher in mathematics and later principal of Albert College, the Methodist Episcopal Church's institution of higher learning in Belleville.[110] Marked by longevity, this group, by the first decades of the twentieth century, had come to be referred to as "the Old Guard of Canadian Methodism."

William McLoughlin, using the anthropological research of Anthony Wallace, has emphasized the importance in an awakening of certain key individuals who articulate and consolidate the aspirations of those who have experienced the religious conversion of the revival. "Such people," he argues, "have never repudiated the older world views entirely; instead they have claimed merely to shed new light on them, that is to look upon old truths from a new perspective."[111] Canadian Methodism's Old Guard lacked unanimity on a number of important questions. However, one issue on which they were in complete agreement was that the new light of learning they had first encountered in their college studies (and which was also responsible for their promotion) was to be retained as an essential attribute of Canadian Methodism. Outlining the distinctive features of Wesleyan theology, Alexander Sutherland drew attention to "the encouragements and facilities which it affords for the most liberal mental culture."[112] W.H. Withrow agreed, and informed readers of the *Canadian Methodist Magazine*, "No church has done more to develop, often among unpropitious circumstances, high literary culture and profound learning."[113]

There was one other issue on which they were unanimous and which revealed their continued ability to use the lessons of the past to shed light on new circumstances. When negotiations for union with the Presbyterian and Congregational denominations began in 1902, the group lent the movement its active support, notwithstanding ongoing disagreement on other issues. For Nathanael Burwash the roots of church union could be detected in the distant past, in the college revival of 1853–4 when a more restrained experience of conversion had facilitated co-operation with members of other evangelical denominations in union revivals. There may have been some basis to this, for the curriculum of the 1850s was standard in Christian colleges (it was not until the 1870s that amendments began to be made at Victoria).[114] Thus the ideals of the "Didactic Enlightenment," especially a disdain for sectarianism and an emphasis on the moral faculty over sentiment, were capable of influencing the thought of a generation of devout students who had been trained in the various denominational colleges established in central and eastern Canada in the 1840s.

A college education was only one of a number of factors leading to a more restrained expression of revivalism. Methodist pulpit preaching was also undergoing a change in style and tone. One person who was instrumental in bringing this about was the American revivalist James Caughey, whose quiet manner and rather scholarly approach appeared to find a much greater appeal among Canadian and British Wesleyan Methodists than among his own countrymen.[115] Caughey's preaching had led directly to the 1853–4 college revival, and his preaching style found strong reinforcement in the Canadian pulpit from 1868 to 1872 through the example of Morley Punshon, past president of the British Wesleyan Conference. The 1850s, therefore, were a period of transition, not simply at Victoria College, but within the denomination generally, as the enthusiasm of the revival began to find more sober and lasting forms of expression.

The laity, too, were affected. The lessons of the classroom integrating reason and religion could be carried into the workplace or the law office as well as into the pulpit. In the competitive society of late Victorian Canada, students like Hart Massey, William Kerr, and Byron Britton could see their own hard-won economic and social advancement to be but a confirmation of the moral lessons of the Rev. Francis Wayland.[116] Nor did success have to take place at the expense of experiential religion. As a student of John Wesley's theology has noted, "the possibility of real personal change must appear quite lively to an empiricist who believes that character, no less than knowledge, is all the product of experience."[117] That hard work and religion went hand in hand even Samuel Nelles had reminded his students in 1854 with the words "both intellectually and morally man needs help, the help of heaven and the help of his fellows, but neither of these will avail without *self-help*."[118] Whether they were headed for business, farming, the professions, or for the ministry, his students would have understood.

In a variety of ways, therefore, the lessons of the college and the religion of the revival became mutually supportive in a new age. While the age was new and the lessons of reason were new, the faith that reason defended was still the old faith. On that point, Nathanael Burwash as his denomination's leading theologian was adamant. His method, to defend the witness of the Spirit with the new language of philosophy, to defend tradition with the tools of innovation, was the method of the old college curriculum. It would also be one of its ironies, for such an approach was potentially radical. However, thanks to the thoroughness of their instruction in the lessons of reason and religion, Burwash and the Old Guard did not foresee that in the end the new would undermine the old.

CHAPTER THREE

The Pastor: Preaching, Philanthropy, and Christian Perfection

Nathanael Burwash spent only six years, from 1860 to 1866, in the active ministry, but they were years he considered invaluable to his mature career as dean of theology and chancellor of Canada's largest Methodist university. Four of these years were a period of training; the first, or probationary year, was spent at Newburgh, in the Kingston district, followed by two years "on trial" at Belleville and a year in Toronto before he was ordained in 1864.[1] He stayed one additional year in Toronto and was then moved to Hamilton. In 1867, after a three-month period of study at Yale University and a half year of preparation for his new appointment as professor of natural science, he was transferred by Conference to Victoria College.

These six years are well documented, not only in the final chapters of his unfinished autobiography and a large collection of sermons and addresses, but also in four lengthy journals.[2] The detailed entries in the latter provide significant information on Burwash's spiritual condition during these years and reveal much about the relationship between a minister and his congregation in central Canada's growing towns and cities. For Burwash these were years of apprenticeship in the ministry, a time when indispensable lessons were learned through trial and error. But for students of religion in Canada these years also offer a clue to a neglected but crucial connection between evangelical piety and social reform in the second half of the nineteenth century. That link was provided by a revitalization of John Wesley's teaching of Christian perfection or holiness. Christian perfection informed not only Burwash's own spirituality and that of influential ministerial colleagues like Albert Carman, but also that of Methodism's leading lay members. This doctrine, which Canadian students of religious revivalism have only recently begun to investigate, has long been of interest to American scholars.[3] The latter have drawn attention to its importance in both

Methodism and Congregationalism in the aftermath of the Second Great Awakening.[4] It has been argued that the wave of social reform which followed owed a great deal to a zeal for perfection. In the opinion of one historian, Timothy L. Smith, this holiness movement, especially as it was associated with the Great Prayer Meeting Revival of 1857–8, was a direct prelude to the social gospel movement.[5]

Here Burwash's brief ministry offers a different example of a correlation between revivalism and social change. For Burwash, who already placed a great emphasis on assurance and on the fruits of the Spirit, Christian perfection became the goal of a mature religious life. As had been the case with the quieter experience of assurance which he saw emerging under the impact of education, this doctrine also served as a bridge to a less emotional expression of revivalism which nevertheless remained rooted in Wesley's teaching. Under Burwash's direction, the teaching of Christian perfection, with its emphasis on right motive, total consecration, and individual moral growth, became a means of alerting Methodism's new entrepreneurial class to their responsibilities as Christian stewards. Thus during a period of accelerated denominational growth, new financial resources were harnessed to meet Canadian Methodism's increased material needs. Throughout his many years as the denomination's leading educator and theologian, Burwash would continue to mine this doctrine creatively, for its basic optimism meshed well with the mood of the Victorian age.

FINDING A NICHE IN A GROWING DENOMINATION

Newburgh, Belleville, Toronto, and Hamilton were all unusually prestigious stations for a young man just entering the ministry, and undoubtedly they indicated both respect for the young Burwash's abilities and the care with which the Stationing Committee of the Wesleyan Methodist Church was placing her college-educated ministers, still a relatively scarce commodity at that time. During these years three matters of concern reappeared unfailingly in the church's annual pastoral address to the membership. First, there was a pressing need for facilities to educate the denomination's growing number of young people. Second, since these institutions required funding, there followed appeals to laymen to share the fruits of their labours. Third, one can detect a not unrelated anxiety that increased education and private wealth might lead to a decline in individual holiness. Even the British Conference joined in the admonition: "We must never forget that, while 'knowledge is power,' its light can only be secured by its absolute and constant submission to the guidance of Revelation. With augmented power, augmented iniquity will ever be associated, unless it be shaped and directed by the Spirit of Truth."[6]

Ministerial direction in the rapidly growing Methodist community was therefore crucial. Hence it is not surprising to find Nathanael Burwash, the son of devout Methodists, nephew to the well-known Lachlin Taylor, and reputedly of serious and scholarly nature, stationed in the four circuits that contained the bulk of the denomination's student population in central Canada. In Newburgh there was an academy where Nelles had been principal and sole instructor the year after his graduation in 1846; Belleville would become the home of the Ontario Business College in 1864 and already contained the Methodist Episcopal Academy, known after 1866 as Albert College; Toronto housed a large variety of institutions of higher learning, though none of Methodist persuasion, unless one considered the medical faculty of Victoria College, commonly referred to as the Rolph School.[7] And in Hamilton, the Wesleyan Female College had opened it doors in 1861 for "the higher education of the daughters of Ontario."

Burwash's speaking engagements to young audiences were consequently frequent. Judging by the titles of the addresses as well as the contents, they were both edifying and informative: "Schools and Schoolboys," in Belleville in 1862, "Reading," to the Juvenile Missionary Meeting in Toronto, and "Our Mission Field 1866," in Hamilton.[8] Less didactic and probably of greater interest, as the rumblings of Charles Darwin's *Origin of Species* began to penetrate even Belleville, was a lecture in 1861 on geology. Burwash, who was poorly prepared since he expected the usual crowd, was somewhat alarmed to find the room "filled to overflowing with the elites of the place." The speaker's treatment was not original, but it was orthodox, drawing heavily on Hugh Miller's *Testimony of the Rocks*. Unfortunately for science and orthodoxy the elites must have been disappointed, for the speaker later confessed that he "had little liberty in speaking & altogether made a poor affair of it & was glad to slip home & forget my weariness & mortification in sleep."[9] Subsequent lectures found him humbler and presumably better prepared.

The existence of educational institutions, of course, was directly related to population density and length of settlement, and without exception Burwash's circuits also fell within the oldest areas of central Canadian Methodism. As early as 1790 William Losee, the first Methodist missionary to be appointed for Canada west of the Maritimes, had visited and preached along the Bay of Quinte. Methodism in the area grew quickly, and by the time Burwash was appointed to Belleville the town could already boast two Wesleyan churches (Pinnacle Street and Bleecker Street) and a Methodist Episcopal church on Tabernacle Street. Toronto's first Methodist chapel dated to 1818; Hamilton had begun as part of the Ancaster circuit where William Case had preached in 1808. By 1860 these centres had acquired institutions and traditions of long standing, at least by the standards of the time. Yet, as Burwash later recollected, in Toronto national immigrant loyalties were only slowly becoming submerged into denominational identities in the early 1860s, even though Methodism's British and American branches in Canada had officially been united since 1847.[10] Toronto was also the institutional centre of this increasingly self-conscious Canadian Methodism, and Burwash was able to make valuable contacts while stationed there. Among these were Anson Green, the book steward, with whose Book Room he was repeatedly in arrears.[11] There was Wellington Jeffers, editor of the *Christian Guardian* from 1860 to 1866, who asked him to write a number of guest editorials, and John Williams, who after 1884 shared the general superintendency with Albert Carman.[12] And of course there was Egerton Ryerson, later to be the subject of Burwash's contribution to the *Makers of Canada* and who was then already "far advanced in his great work of establishing and organizing the Ontario School System."[13]

FORGING LINKS WITH PHILANTHROPISTS

Besides meeting the denomination's hierarchy and some of its young people, Burwash made other, very valuable, connections during these years in the ministry. Denominational awareness and increased involvement with education were closely connected with anothr phenomenon, the well-to-do Methodist layperson, whose years of hard work and careful management were beginning to yield results by the 1860s. Burwash met and became intimate with a number of wealthy laypeople in his various congregations. In Belleville he was a frequent guest at the home of Nathan Jones, prominent local merchant, church trustee, and organist. His wife, Jane Clement Jones, was one of the congregation's most active members as a class leader for the young women and Bible instructor for the single men. She soon became Burwash's special confidante and at her death in 1895 was honoured by an eight-page eulogy in the *Canadian Methodist Magazine*.[14] Her brother-in-law, Billa Flint, was a successful politician who went on to a Senate appointment in 1867. In Burwash's final year at Belleville, Flint donated land for a third Wesleyan church, located on Bridge Street, thereby giving the young minister his first experience in fund raising.[15]

In Toronto he made contacts which much later would lead to the federation of Victoria College with the University of Toronto. As a preacher assigned to the Toronto East circuit, Burwash assisted in services at the Adelaide Street and Yorkville churches, but his special responsibility was Berkeley Street. Here one of the original trustees was James Gooderham, second son of William Gooderham, owner of the profitable Gooderham and Worts distillery and by 1864 president of the Bank of Toronto. The eldest son, William, had also become associated with Berkeley Street shortly after its formation in 1857.[16] William inherited the bulk of the family estate and after some hesitation became a committed Methodist, "sanctifying" the distillery profits through his philanthropy to a large number of denominational causes.[17] Not least of these was Victoria College, which thanks to a bequest of $230,000 at William's death in 1888 (left on the condition that it move to Toronto), was able to complete the negotiations for federation within the University of Toronto.

In 1864 federation was still in the distant future. The contacts with Hamilton businessmen were, however, of more immediate personal benefit. During his ministry in Hamilton from 1865 to 1866, Burwash's address was the elegant home of Edward Jackson, Esq., on Maiden Lane. Edward and Lydia Jackson had been friends of Lachlin Taylor's and now offered to give lodging to his nephew.[18] The comfort and the hospitality of the Jackson home provided benefits to a young minister that were not normally affordable on a single man's annual salary of $180, supplemented by $260 for board.[19] A strong friendship developed with the Jacksons and the other resident at Maiden Lane, William E. Sanford, their recently widowed son-in-law and nephew. Burwash's tithe account for 1865–6 contained a number of small monetary gifts and loans from the Jacksons (always scrupulously tithed or repaid), and the studies he pursued at Yale in the autumn of 1866 were made possible through the generosity of Edward Jackson.[20] Jackson became, in Burwash's words, "the best friend I ever had," and his first publication, *Memorials of the Life of Edward and Lydia Jackson* in 1876, was a glowing tribute, dedicated to William Sanford "in remembrance of the pleasant days spent together in the happy home of Mr. & Mrs. Jackson."[21]

When Burwash joined the Jacksons in 1865, the Hamilton Tin Factory of Edward Jackson, his younger partner, Dennis Moore, *et al.*, had been in operation for over thirty years. Profits in the tinware business had permitted diversification, primarily into railways and banking for Jackson, and real estate for Moore. William E. Sanford had also prospered and was already becoming known as the "Wool King of Canada" as he began to capitalize on the public's growing demand for cheap ready-made clothing and the military's need for boots, shoes, and uniforms.[22]

All three were devout Methodists, active class leaders, and prominent donors to Methodist institutions, particularly Victoria College. In 1866, Edward Jackson, assisted by the new minister, led the largest fund-raising drive to that date for the erection of the new Centenary Church in Hamilton, thereby inaugurating at the same time a decade of lavish church construction. At an earlier date Jackson had been the driving force behind the Wesleyan Female College and was its president until his death in 1872.[23] It was at the college's graduation exercises in 1865 that Burwash first encountered his future wife, Margaret Proctor of Sarnia, that year's class valedictorian. One of Margaret Proctor's close friends and fellow graduates was Letty Massey, Hart Massey's youngest sister.[24] The Masseys would become even more generous to Victoria College than the Hamilton group. However, the first of the large donations came from Hamilton in 1872 and 1874, only seven years after Burwash left the pastorate. Shortly before he died, Edward Jackson had been persuaded by Lachlin Taylor to endow a chair in theology at Victoria.[25] Lydia Jackson, who died the following year, worked actively with other members of the Hamilton group to supplement the initial endowment of $10,000.[26] The chair became known as the Edward Jackson Chair of Theology, and its first appointee, was, of course, Nathanael Burwash.

From the halls of Victoria College in 1860 to the hearts (and pocketbooks) of Methodist entrepreneurs in a short six years may be highly commendable for a young Horatio Alger, but for Nathanael Burwash, candidate for the Methodist ministry, and later dean of theology, the phenomenon does require some explanation. William Hincks, a student of Burwash's at Victoria in the early 1870s, later became a prominent Methodist minister and speaker on social and economic issues. The one time he could not undestand his otherwise revered professor of theology was when the latter defended the denomination's wealthy businessmen against Hincks's assertion that their power would involve them in ethical difficulties. To a young social reformer like Hincks such uncritical support was inexplicable.[27]

What Hincks did not realize, however, was that those who in old age appeared to be obstructing moral progress had, in their own youth, seen themselves as champions of that very same cause. A closer examination of Burwash's piety and preaching during this early phase of his career may show to what extent he, like his student, had taken a critical attitude towards the establishment in the name of progress. At the same time, this may shed more light on his admiration for men like Edward Jackson.

THE YOUNG PREACHER

On those who knew Burwash in those days "he left the impression ... of being naturally something of an ascetic, which years modified."[28] A photograph of the period depicts a finely featured, rather melancholy face, framed by short dark hair. While undoubtedly he cut a dashing figure in the pulpit, members of his congregation at Bleecker Street, Belleville, did at times smile at their young minister's excessive zeal, only to be rebuked: "It is not zeal not enthusiasm but O it is this sight of death & hell it is this terrible experience with the charge of immortal souls that wring my heart – & would make me glad to die and see you all saved."[29]

A century earlier John Wesley had defined his own task and that of his assistants with the simple injunction "to devote ourselves entirely to God; denying ourselves, taking up our cross daily; steadily aiming at one thing, to save our souls and them that hear us."[30] No candidate for the ministry could have taken those words more seriously than Nathanael Burwash, striving for the souls of Canadian Methodists. Following another piece of advice from Wesley, he kept a daily journal during the first two years of his ministry. Its pages are replete with self-chastisement – "I have been too ostentatious even in my desire to serve God"[31] – and renewed covenants to "consecrate all to the service of Jesus ... Farewell forever all schemes of earthly joy & pleasure & ambition."[32]

Hard on himself, he was hard on others. In the privacy of his journal he questioned whatever did not live up to his high standards of Christian spirituality. The tea meeting, always a favourite social means of fund raising, was one of the institutions that came under his scrutiny. Thoroughly incensed at the "unspiritual" speeches of some of his own colleagues, discomfited at having to eat "bread buttered on both sides," appalled by the general lack of organization, he concluded that the overall results of such social gatherings were of questionable value. Although the meeting had succeeded in raising two hundred dollars, "on the other hand there are results in the opposite direction: fondness for pleasure & excitement & a seeking of delight in the creature & not the creator, which more than counterbalance and leave us in doubt as to the utility & desirability of such occasions."[33]

Equally suspect was the emotionalism he witnessed at revival meetings. Anson Green, a much older colleague, once expressed the view that the strength of Methodist preaching lay in its ability to arouse emotions: "Our doctrines as well as the emotional and earnest nature of our devotions are well calculated to heal the broken heart and soothe the soul in moments of anguish ... Men love to be excited – will be excited; and of all excitement, religious transports are the most healthy, the most elevating, and the most beneficial."[34] Young Burwash was not in full agreement. One of the most oft-recurring temptations in the journal was "the wish to be called a revivalist and successful preacher."[35] His sermons do not appear to have aroused strong emotional responses; there is even a recorded instance where his preaching actually deterred two young people who had planned to come forward as penitents.[36] He did manage to quell his own suspicions, aroused by a friend, that the emotionalism at revivals was really only "owing to a kind of mesmeric influence exercised by the speaker and the persons singing, etc."[37] But although convinced that it could be the work of the Holy Spirit, he was keen to distinguish between true, lasting piety and superficial sentiments.

Yearly revival meetings when special outside speakers took the rostrum provided occasions to analyse the phenomenon more objectively. Of one of these, a camp meeting at Sidney concession near Belleville in September 1861, he left a particularly detailed and highly revealing account. He kept his reactions until the trip home, where there was ample time to indulge in evaluation, for the heavily burdened pony took over three hours to make the six-mile trip. Those were days when attending a camp meeting still involved an entire move of household effects. Dishes, chairs, pots, pans, stoves and stovepipes, a bedstead and bunks, "and various other articles too numerous to mention," had somehow all found their way back onto the wagon. On top of this symbol of a vanishing past sat Nathanael Burwash, engaged in "profitable discussion" with his hostess for the meeting. In the fashion of a sermon, the conversation covered three points: "First, what are the best means of promoting the work of God? ... second, how much of the scenes we have just witnessed are lasting genuine experience and how much is mere excitement? ... and third, [since the journal was shared at select intervals with a female reader] what are the necessary qualifications for a minister's wife?"

As to the first, the conclusion was that although a revivalist might awaken a sinner, it was doubtful whether the preaching they had just heard "would ever so develop to a man the great plan of salvation in all its parts as to lead him on from repentance to the maturity of an intelligent Christian." With regard to the emotional reactions which had accompanied the preaching, Burwash had strong suspicions that not all they had seen was the work of the Spirit: "Some who said they were blest would laugh incessantly, others clap their hands and jump. It seemed to be the whole object of some was to work themselves in some of these states, and I was sometimes tempted to think that they succeeded without any special assistance."[38] Not sporadic revivalism, but the maturing of the intelligent Christian was to be the goal. The goal, as well as the means, came naturally to one who by his own admission was "a teacher rather than a successful evangelist."[39] First, the atmosphere of the tea meeting was elevated by combining it with a lecture. Holding forth on John Wesley and his work, Burwash was admirably able to join the evangelistic with the didactic: "The theme was evangelistic the form didactic."[40]

A shift in style also became evident in his preaching. His very first sermon had been an impromptu address as a lay preacher in Baltimore when the expected minister had failed to turn up. It had followed the pattern of his first public testimony in class meeting, describing the joy experienced upon the certain knowledge of forgiveness of sin.[41] During the first year at Newburgh he continued this method of preparing sermons, working from a brief outline on the pulpit, but "leaving the elaboration, especially in hortatory matter and detailed language of presentation ... to extemporaneous suggestion which sometimes extended to new excursions of thought on lateral branches of the general subject."[42] An examination of extant unpublished sermons by Canadian Methodist ministers of this period leads one to conclude that Burwash was merely following the accepted practice.[43] Anson Green, who had strong views on what constituted the special nature of Methodism, often expressed his disapproval of ministers' reading sermons. It was not Methodistic for it hampered the work of the Spirit: "No verbal accuracy can make up for the want of unction. There may be occasions when reading is pardonable – even advisable, but like angels' visits, they are few and far between."[44] In his journal Burwash tended to agree: "Let a man train his mind not to a nice selection of the words to round out a sentence but to clearness vigour & loftiness of thought & let those thoughts be expounded in plain, racy, common English just as it comes up in his own mind as his mother taught him (unless she taught him bad grammar or vulgar slang) & he will find his way to the hearts and thoughts of all men."[45]

Yet a short time later, at the urging and criticism of his friend William Dean, a Victoria graduate with a law practice in Belleville, he began to write out his sermons in a five-quire folio book. Fortunately, he did not give his congregation further grounds for amusement by ascending to the pulpit with this formidable tome in hand, but instead tried to recall the written version by means of a short outline. The first performance produced much perspiration and very little apparent unction, but he was persuaded to continue the practice. He soon found that he could regain his former facility of expression, as well as the highly desirable fervour, while at the same time adding greater fullness of thought and research.[46] The custom became a lifelong habit and helped shape the prodigious memory for which he later became renowned. His preaching style too was generally favourably received. Samuel Nelles, for example, who first heard his former student preach in Cobourg one Sunday evening in January 1867, noted approvingly in his journal: "Prof. Burwash preached for me. Spirit of bondage and adoption. 55 mins. Good sermon. Simple, practical, fervent, faithful. Style colloquial, delivery natural and easy ... May he never lose his freshness of spirit."[47]

In style and sermon preparation there may have been a shift from the old-time revivalist towards the theologian, but Wesley's *Standard Sermons* continued to be the basis for his preaching. Studying for the first year ministerial examinations had taught him to make detailed outlines, material that later became the basis for his textbook at Victoria, *Wesley's Doctrinal Standards, Part I.*[48] He backed up his reading of Wesley with careful exegetical Bible reading in Greek and Hebrew, as he searched for proof texts for every Wesleyan doctrine: "These two constituted by far the most satisfactory and profitable part of my studies. The Wesleyan doctrine furnished material for preaching. It was a theology which could be preached. It set forth the way of salvation in such a way as helped my own soul and gave light for the instruction of others."[49]

This "instruction of others" implied a thoroughness in dealing with the converted soul that eliminated any chance of backsliding. "The very first step in the work of man's salvation is his conscience, in the enlightening and awakening process ... producing conviction of sin," a Toronto congregation was reminded. Sin weakened the conscience, whereas religion, through the truth of the Bible and the work of the Holy Spirit, regenerated the individual and created a new heart and disposition.[50] Preaching was intended not only to awaken but also to ensure that the conscience continued in active operation. As a child, Burwash's conscience had been under the close care of his mother, who had become "a conscience for her children." He now saw himself occupying the same position for the younger members of his congregations.

In this endeavour he received able assistance from the class leaders. One incident during his Belleville ministry figured prominently in his reminiscences of the later years. Society membership in those days included two categories: full-fledged members who attended class meetings, and "hearers" or "adherents" who did not have to submit to the searching discipline of the class meetings. To the former belonged the young female contingent of the congregation, whose souls were ably shepherded in a class conducted by Mrs Nathan Jones. To the latter belonged a group of young men, "the society young men of the time," who managed to permit themselves some moral laxity, though not complete freedom from the watchful eye of Mrs Jones, as they were members of her Bible study class.

Since Mrs Jones later appeared in Burwash's biographical sketches as the epitome of the thorough class leader, it must have been with some trepidation that the young women allowed themselves to be led astray once a year. With the first sleighing weather, the young men would organize a party which included supper, but also some dancing. The ladies would be invited, presumably enjoyed themselves but, having broken the Methodist discipline, did not dare go back to Mrs Jones' class until the next revival service.

Determined to put an end to this routine backsliding, Burwash preached a sermon that apparently created something of a sensation. "Puritanical in doctrine and sharply severe in spirit," it did have the desired effect of cancelling the sleighing party for that year. It also led the young people to shun him for a while, because as he later confessed, his handling of the matter had been neither "very perfect nor very wise."[51] By the time he left Belleville a year later, there had been a reconciliation. The moral standards he preached, however, remained as high as ever, and the final words in his parting sermon were addressed to the young people in the congregation: "Many of you like myself are young. Life seems all to lie before – though what or how long its course God only knows. Be not satisfied simply to be negatively religious. Aim high. Be resolved that from the days of your youth you will exemplify the holy principles of our blessed Christianity."[52]

Moral excellence and Christian maturity were not only ideals to be held out to the young. The older members also were in need of guidance in their worldly pursuits. Although he could not here claim the benefit of a shared experience, Burwash was equally confident in giving moral direction to those entrusted with wealth. Scripture's teaching was plain, and 1 Timothy 6:10, "For the love of money is the root of all evil," became a favourite text. As he told a Hamilton congregation in 1865, what the text clearly taught was not that money itself was evil but that its misuse could lead to perdition.[53] In 1861 in a sermon that probably owed more to the insight gained from his college course in moral philosophy than to firsthand experience in the market-place, he had gone to great lengths to explain to the tradesmen and merchants among his listeners the criteria that were to determine the price of an article. Under the heading "How shall the Christian let his light shine?" he had reminded the congregation of the golden rule, which "at once prohibits anything like a hard bargain, taking advantage of the necessities or ignorance of our neighbour, or even wishing to obtain for what we are selling more than its real value." Real value was the market price for the product, for this price "prohibits all undue extolling of what we sell or depreciation of what we buy. At the same time it encourages, yea, requires the utmost industry and carefulness."

In this type of a *laissez-faire* economy it was therefore essential that those who possessed wealth and were engaged in buying and selling should also be aware of their responsibilities: "In property, as in everything else, the Christian looks upon himself as the steward of God & considers it his duty to increase his property."[54] Stewardship was the Christian answer to the accumulation of wealth, and the future recipient of private Methodist largesse did not shrink from quoting John Wesley's warning to the church to beware of making rich men necessary: "How easily ... wealth may come to be recognized as a power in the church of Christ & the rich man be placed in authority over the house of God because he can pay." A steward, however, was "faithful, diligent & wise," and always mindful of the fact that he was not managing his wealth for his own, selfish interests.[55]

Those who had such an attitude to wealth could be assured of happiness and also of progress: "Holy happiness, holy progress is God's law ... God has so constituted us as moral & religious beings that the true promotion of our happiness & progress is at the farthest possible removed from all selfishness."[56] This close correlation between moral and economic law ensured that Christian nations, like individuals, could expect to be successful. In 1863 Torontonians were given a brief lesson in economic history: "Under the pure influence of Christianity has the commerce of England & almost the entire commerce of the world in modern times grown up. The moral precepts of Christianity (equity, justice) have to a great extent become its rules of right. And the consciences of men quickened into life by the grace of God have proved strong to maintain the right despite all the demoralizing influences of avarice and speculation."[57]

Since virtue was accompanied by progress, there was little need to draw a sharp distinction between material and moral growth, and one could side with the progressive forces of the time without hesitation. "Progress is preeminently the watchword of the present age" was the hackneyed introduction to a lecture on education in Belleville given in 1862. What followed was of greater interest, for the young Burwash dared to prophesy the condition of the world at the time when he would be old and grey:

Railroads and telegraphs around the world. Steamplows running through the fields & steam carriages along the streets scaring the old fashioned horses away into the deserts. Labour reduced to pasttime and healthy exercise. Schools &

schoolhouses in every hamlet. Colleges in every county. Grogshops & distilleries & all the abodes of vice vanished from the land. And the Bible in every house & the Gospel preached to every son & daughter of Adam throughout the wide world.[58]

If any in the audience had been disposed to take a critical attitude, they might have remarked that material progress had preceded intellectual and moral progress in the speaker's grandiose vision. But visions of progress, although they might be gratifying to hear from a preacher, were not a novelty in mid-Victorian Canada. Those who had read Samuel Smiles' *Self-Help* and applauded its belief in individual discipline and technological progress would have only received a reinforcement of those teachings.[59] And those who, like the speaker, were schooled in the writings of the moral philosophers, knew that thanks to God's contrivance, all sectors of the economy were so interrelated as to be in ultimate harmony and that there was a necessary connection between a nation's morality and its prosperity.[60] Moreover, the businessman's ethic that Burwash was proclaiming from the pulpit appeared to be a faithful reflection of generally accepted values in Canadian society as described by Michael Bliss in *A Living Profit*.[61] And in his concern with moral character, there was little distinction between young Burwash and the Canadian intellectuals whose mental and moral horizons have been reconstructed by A.B. McKillop in *A Disciplined Intelligence*.[62]

It may be asked, therefore, whether Burwash's ministry in the established Methodist communities in Belleville, Toronto, and Hamilton constituted an accommodation of religious revivalism to the values and requirements of a young, progressive society.[63] His dislike of the emotionalism traditionally associated with revival services, his method of writing sermons, and his concern with Christian nurture might all be cited as additional proof. Almost all his efforts as a preacher were directed at people already in the church, where through the active co-operation of class leaders like Jane Clement Jones, the moral environment had become markedly different from frontier conditions. There the preaching of an earlier generation had been in large part aimed at the conversion of the "hardened sinner."[64] In the two years during which he wrote his journal (in Newburgh and Belleville) Burwash made only two references to this species; both were drunkards, and one was murdered before he had the chance to repent; the other Burwash considered to lack the strength of character to be able to give up his habit.[65] Indeed, there were times when the self-chastisement in the journal also included his lack of diligence in seeking out sinners "to become acquainted with them for the very purpose of saving their souls."[66] It was obviously easier to be the friend of pious Methodists like Edward Jackson than the friend of sinners.

Such a reading, however, contradicts Burwash's own view of his ministry and fails to take into account an important aspect of John Wesley's teaching, namely, the doctrine of Christian perfection. To ignore this would leave a study of Burwash's years in the ministry incomplete.

CHRISTIAN PERFECTION

In later life, whenever he looked back on his early years in the ministry, Burwash never failed to express his admiration for the piety he had encountered in his congregations. He pointed out its distinguishing characteristics, and left no doubt that this was the standard he saw to have shaped his ministry:

The Providence which directed the first three years of my probation to the "Bay Country" in which the primitive type of Canadian Methodism had been so effectively maintained has always been to me a cause of gratitude ... The theology of these men was the theology of the *Sermons* and *Christian Perfection* of Wesley, their type of religion was its embodiment in Christian experience, and their ideal for the church was a continuous revival with the conversion of sinners and the sanctification of believers through the Baptism of the Holy Spirit. The type and spirit of this religious environment shaped my preaching and became a powerful influence in all my after life.[67]

Written in his autobiography during the final months of his life, these words contain none of the criticism evident in the journal. The tone of filial respect was right and proper. To coin the titles of two works by John Carroll, it showed that the "stripling preacher" had received his training in "the school of the prophets." John Carroll, however, had done more for Canadian Methodism than write books on the ministry. During the year 1855-6 he had been superintendent of the Belleville circuit and had directly contributed to shaping the piety which Burwash so admired in later years. That winter Belleville had been the scene of a remarkable revival during which some five hundred new members joined the town's various churches. The existing members of the Wesleyan Methodist church had also been affected, and in Burwash's words the church leaders had been "lifted to a higher plane of Christian life."[68] Five years later the effects of that revival were still visible. As he later reflected,

I was soon in touch with a body of workers in the Church, the prayer meeting and the Sunday School who gathered round the minister and formed for him a religious atmosphere such as I had not known before. The subject of the higher spiritual life had been a favorite theme with them. Some of them had libraries of choice books on the subject to the use of which I was made welcome. All these things gave me a new start for my work and put me in a better position to make that work successful.[69]

This "higher spiritual life" to which Burwash was referring was John Wesley's doctrine of Christian perfection, also known as holiness, entire sanctification, or perfect love. To Wesley the new birth had been only the introduction to the Christian life, for those who knew themselves to be justified and regenerated would also grow in grace and holiness: "When we are born again, then our sanctification, our inward and outward holiness, begins; and thence forward we are gradually to 'grow up in Him who is our Head.' "[70]

Wesley's reading of Scripture had led him to conclude that those who were regenerated and who increased in holiness could at some point also reach an experience of "entire sanctification." Its recognizing mark was "to have a heart so all-flaming with the love of God as continually to offer up every thought, word, and work, as a spiritual sacrifice, acceptable unto God in Christ."[71] Wesley made it clear that this experience of perfect love did not imply dispensation from natural and divine law: "We willingly allow, and continually declare, there is no such perfection, in this life, as implies either a dispensation from doing good, and attending all the ordinances of God; or a freedom from ignorance, mistake, temptation, and a thousand infirmities connected with flesh and blood."[72] Nor was the experience ever absolute; it could be lost at a moment's transgression. However those who had once experienced it felt the need of Christ even stronger than before: "For our perfection is not like that of a tree, which flourishes by the sap delved from its own root, but ... like that of a branch, which, united to the vine bears fruit, but severed from it, it is dried up and withered."[73]

American historians, most notably Timothy Smith and John L. Peters, have traced a renewed interest in this doctrine in American Methodism beginning in the 1830s and extending well into the 1860s.[74] During the 1840s British Wesleyanism experienced a similar renewal of interest in the doctrine, and a subsequent revival in England and Ireland resulted in the highly impressive spiritual statistics, "rather under than over the truth," of 21,625 justified and 9,222 entirely sanctified. The American Methodist evangelist James Caughey had been the moving spirit in this, on one of the numerous occasions that religious developments in North America influenced Great Britain.[75]

Closely connected to Caughey in this trans-Atlantic holiness revival was an American woman of remarkable spirituality, Phoebe Palmer, author of seven books on Christian perfection, who with her husband, a New York physician, propagated her views by travelling and holding meetings. In her preaching and writing on Wesley's doctrine, Mrs Palmer tended to overstress somewhat its experiential nature, as indicated by her favourite terms, "the second blessing" and the "baptism of the spirit." She insisted that it was the duty of Christians to seek the experience and that those who did not were in danger of eternal damnation. In this she went beyond Wesley's teaching, and at one point, while conducting revivals in western New York and Ontario in 1856, thought her deepening religious awareness to have been an indication of a possible "third blessing."[76] A number of American Methodists, like the well-known Nathan Bangs, expressed concern and in 1857 accused her of over-emphasizing the importance of the individual's faith at the expense of the witness of the Holy Spirit.[77]

It was James Caughey who had conducted the Belleville revival in 1855 as well as similar revivals in the early 1850s in Kingston, Toronto, London, and Hamilton. The latter revival, it may be recalled, had exerted a considerable influence on a number of the students at Victoria College during Burwash's second year. By the 1850s the Palmers were also conducting camp meetings in rural central Ontario, and their combined efforts, coupled with the distribution of a Boston monthly, the *Guide to Holiness*, widely disseminated the teachings on holiness.[78] As early as the late 1830s, references to revivals had begun to distinguish between people who were justified and those who were entirely sanctified. From 1853 on, the annual pastoral address of the Wesleyan Methodist Church in Canada also made explicit reference to the duty of members to seek the experience of entire sanctification.[79] In 1860, for example, the year that Burwash entered the ministry, the admonition was a clear echo of the teachings of Mrs Palmer: "We feel that we cannot too strongly urge upon you to rest not short of a renewed nature as the basis of Christian character, the starting point for the attainment of entire sanctification, and the only ground of a spiritual hope that a blessed immortality will finally be reached."[80] Moreover, before being received on trial, ministerial candidates were expected to respond in the affirmative to the following questions: "Are you going on to perfection? Do you expect to be made perfect in love in this life? Are you groaning after it?"[81] That same year they had already become thoroughly familiar with Wesley's treatise, *A Plain Account of Christian Perfection*, which had been part of the reading course of the probationary year since 1844.[82]

This background of a renewed interest in Christian perfection in Canadian Methodist circles helps explain the soul-searching in Burwash's journal and his moral exhortations from the pulpit. His father, Adam, had shown a special interest in "entire sanctification," and in the 1850s the *Guide to Holiness* began to come to the Burwash home regularly. Nathanael recalled first hearing of the doctrine at the age of fourteen during a sermon at the Baltimore chapel. This exposure led him to secure a copy of Wesley's treatise on Christian perfection and later "the writings of Mrs. Palmer and many other Americans on the subject." Now, in the early years of his ministry, this reading began to influence him seriously. In his own words, "I was now twenty-three years of age and for seven years I had before me the conviction that a more perfect Christian life than I had hitherto attained was a possibility and still more a duty."[83] As D.C. Meyer has quite rightly pointed out, for those evangelicals familiar with the writings of the moral philosophers, sanctification was more than a devotional ideal, it was a moral imperative.[84] When that imperative is added to Mrs Palmer's teachings and Burwash's own ascetic inclinations, it is not surprising that as soon as the young minister came into contact with the spirituality of his Belleville congregation, his own attainment of entire sanctification became almost an obsession.[85] Only three months after moving to Belleville, he wrote in a detailed journal entry that his search had been rewarded: "Last night I think will be an era in my life. Call it entire sanctification, perfect love, baptism of the Spirit, or what I may. God has blessed me above all that I have ever felt before. Up to this time I often feared [?] to say that I was fully cleansed but now there is not a doubt. Temptation flies before the grace of God & I feel truly strong in the Lord & in the power of his might."[86] Unfortunately, a short four days later he also had to record that he had lost the assurance when, during an unguarded moment conversing with members of his congregation, he "joined further in the vivacity" than was consistent with his ministerial status.[87] Subsequent entries show that the search was resumed with the intensity of a new quest.[88]

In reading the account in his autobiography written long after the experience, one has the impression that, looking back, Burwash forgot the fits and starts of his spiritual condition and replaced the memory with a calmer, more Wesleyan view of his search for the more perfect Christian life. The intensity of the journal entries had a little too much of Mrs Palmer's teaching of which he had by then become quite critical.[89] What is clear is that his later references to his own experience of entire sanctification always give a date that is almost a year after the one recorded in his journal, at a time when the entries had unfortunately become sporadic. In these references, as in the brief testimony he gave at his ordination in 1864, he always explicitly mentioned the fact that he had received the experience while reading Wesley's writings on the subject. At these times he also stressed, not the spiritual power of the experience as he had done in the journal, but his deep sense of humility and his renewed dedication: "It was not that I had attained or had received the blessing of perfect love or entire consecration or any other name, it was only that I saw my God as I had never seen before and that humbled before Him I only wished to be what he would have me be."[90]

And he always took pains to link his own experience and renewed consecration to a similar consecration on the part of the congregation's class leaders. His own search for perfection had been the preparation for a revival which had all the marks of what he had missed in the much criticized camp meeting of the previous year. He had drawn up a special covenant for the sanctified class leaders whereby they promised to meet once a week to pray for the conversion of individual sinners and to do all they could to reach these people through quiet, personal conversation or letter.[91] The similarities to the 1854 college revival are, of course, obvious. In his journal there are references to the formation of this small "holiness band" (set against a less spiritual backdrop of dreams of personal heroism and visions of world conquest).[92] A manuscript copy of the covenant, as well as of a "Guide for Seekers of Holiness," are evidence that for the most part these recollections are accurate.[93] The covenant was apparently printed and distributed beyond the small number for which it was initially drawn up.[94] In Belleville the efforts had the desired effect, to the extent that twenty-five young people in the congregation, according to Burwash's account, were converted and began actively to support their minister in his efforts to raise the spiritual state of the church.[95]

He formed a similar holiness band the following year in Toronto, where the influence of James Caughey and Mrs Palmer had been so considerable that it could still be detected forty years later by William Hincks when he was stationed in the Queen Street Methodist Church in 1895.[96] In Hamilton the scheme was also briefly implemented as preparation for a revival in November 1865.[97] When Burwash attended Yale the next fall to study science, he was even able to take part in a similar movement, for regular weekly prayer meetings had already been established in a number of American cities.[98] One of the first recorded items in his daily agenda was a "meeting for seekers of holiness" that he attended at the Elm Street Methodist Episcopal Church in New Haven.[99]

THE APPLICATION

When one considers, therefore, the importance that Wesley's teaching on Christian perfection had come to have in the spirituality of North American Methodism by the 1860s, it is not surprising that in the two eulogies of laypeople with whom he became friends during his pastorate, Burwash chose to organize the biographical details around this doctrine. "Jane Clement Jones" appeared in the *Canadian Methodist Magazine* in July 1895, over thirty years after his ministry in Belleville. By then Christian perfection had become a point of controversy within international Methodism and threatened to fall into disrepute. Extravagant claims by a number of evangelists, including Burwash's own student, Ralph C. Horner, had made the teachings of Phoebe Palmer appear orthodox in comparison.[100] Time and theological considerations, therefore, played a part in ordering Burwash's recollections of Mrs Jones, just as they did when it came time to chronicle his own experiences in the pastorate.

In his eulogy of Mrs Jones he emphasized that her life had been shaped by the doctrine of entire sanctification as preached in the 1850s, and although that preaching had tended to overvalue faith at the expense of works, it had nevertheless "called true followers of Christ up to a far higher consecration and more perfect Christian life than they had ever attempted before. It brought a power, of living present joy and peace, of abiding indwelling of the Spirit, unknown before; and certainly John Wesley would have rejoiced over it with great joy." Thus the life he was describing had been marked by consecration, devotion, and duty to her husband, her family, and the family business, but above all to the social and intellectual needs of Methodism in Belleville and to the city's poor and ill after 1879, with the formation of a Woman's Christian Association. It was this active consecration to work that had saved Mrs Jones from "that mere subjectivity which has marred the Christian perfection of so many good men, and which in our day has fallen into fanaticism, bringing reproach upon the very name of holiness."[101] Written in 1895, these words were still an echo of the concerns of the young preacher who had reflected critically on the physical manifestations of a camp meeting in 1861.

The Memorials of Edward and Lydia Jackson was published in 1876, before the storm of controversy over Christian perfection broke out. However, the pattern imposed on the life of Jane Clement Jones was already clearly visible. Again didactic considerations were not overlooked, since "the serious aim of biography must always be the instruction of those who are just entering life."[102] Accordingly, the philanthropic activities of the Jacksons were extolled in great detail, for they were concrete evidence of the Christian stewardship to which Burwash had often exhorted his listener from the pulpit. The lives of Edward and Lydia Jackson were depicted as a true example of Christian perfection in the business world. As explained in the preface, the study was to be "the progressive picture of the inner life of a man," a demonstration that even in "the quiet industries of trade and agriculture ... the highest excellence of character may be developed."[103] The piety of the Jacksons was, therefore, described as one of steady, quiet progress marked only by one tragedy, the death of their only child, Mrs William E. Sanderson, in 1857. From that crisis, the parents had emerged with even greater dedication "to a higher grander Christian life than they had ever experienced before."[104] As with Jane Clement Jones, there was no explicit reference to an actual experience of Christian perfection, but the readers were left in no doubt that by their dedication and piety the Jacksons had reached the level of the fully sanctified Christian. Such perfection, of course, by its very nature defied accurate description. Describing the death of Edward Jackson, Burwash could only conclude that "our language must utterly fail to describe his grand Christian character. Taking him for all, he was the most perfect man we ever knew."[105]

Whether or not those who had done business with Edward Jackson would subscribe to this evaluation of the man, a lack of records must leave unanswered. If the life of the one Canadian Methodist entrepreneur of which we have a more complete record, Michael Bliss's *A Canadian Millionaire: The Life and Times of Sir Joseph Flavelle, Bart., 1858–1939*, may serve as a model, the doctrine of Christian perfection could act as a very conscious motive to philanthropy – even though society at large might be less impressed by motive than by effect.[106] To critics of wealth and power, like William Hincks, Burwash's veneration of the wealthy had seemed at best a trifle naive. But had he desired, the author of *The Memorials of Edward and Lydia Jackson* could have pointed to an impeccable source for his portrayal of Christian perfection in the business world. When John Wesley had been asked at the Conference in 1745, "But would not one who was thus sanctified be incapable of worldly business?" the answer had been an unequivocal "He would be far more capable of it than ever, as going through it without distraction."[107] As one Wesley scholar has remarked, "for Wesley, personal transformation is the key to moral problems. Because he believes these transformations are possible, he can set aside many of the institutional issues that arise when society tries to deal with intractable personal characteristics. Prisons, workhouses and slums were the scenes of his ministry, but they do not figure in the intellectual landscape of his ethics."[108]

Because the centre of that landscape was the soul of the individual, young Burwash had felt perfectly qualified to preach on business ethics, national prosperity, and world progress. And his faith in the moral growth of the individual meant that he could hold out the same ideal of Christian perfection to "young society men" in Belleville, students in Toronto, and businessmen in Hamilton, and then go home and chart his own spiritual struggle in his journal. Christian perfection, like conversion, was a means of bringing together people of different temperament, background, and way of life. Thus the experience of the pastorate was really not very different from the college revival at Victoria in his student days.

That much admired college revival had occurred without the assistance of a revivalist; its manifestations had been ethical rather than emotional. Now, in the like manner, Burwash's interpretation of Christian perfection de-emphasized the role of the professional revivalist. The same had been true in his view of Christian nurture. As the mother had been the pivotal figure in the nurture of the child, so the educator and the pastor were essential for guiding the individual on to perfection. Even the itinerant preacher was at a disadvantage, for Christian perfection required continuity. Not surprisingly, when Burwash came to Belleville in 1861, there had been at least two previous preachers stationed there with a marked interest in the doctrine, George F. Playter, and of course, John Carroll.[109] Moreover, laypeople like the Jacksons and Jane Clement Jones were at least as important as the minister in elevating the spiritual life of the membership. There was probably no new development here, for our knowledge of early Canadian Methodism has, of necessity, centred on the preacher and the revival, rather than the class meeting and popular piety. It may, however, be important that in Burwash's published writing laypeople were very visible and very prominent, whereas his ministerial colleagues had only a minor place in his reminiscences.[110]

Here the timing of his ministry deserves notice. Mention has been made of the fact that during these years Methodism in Canada began increasingly to draw on the financial resources of the members to satisfy the need to educate the young and erect larger and better places of worship. John Wesley had left the property of the Connexion in the hands of lay trustees, and as that property expanded, so did their influence within the denomination.[111] In 1874, only seven years after Burwash left the pastorate, the status of laymen was further enhanced when for the first time they were granted seats in the General Conference as an inducement to the New Connexion Methodists to unite with the Wesleyans to form the Methodist Church of Canada.[112] Clearly, therefore, in the relationship between the ministry and the laity, the 1860s were a period of change.

To cope with that change could be a threatening experience to those who stood to lose most. There are indications that some of Burwash's older ministerial colleagues were afraid that their style and status were in danger of being devalued in these new circumstances. At Burwash's ordination in 1864, Anson Green, who was venerated for his years of active service, felt compelled to make some rather pointed remarks, all faithfully recorded in the *Christian Guardian*:

He had discovered – he hoped he was mistaken – some little want of the aggressive spirit which characterized the fathers of this conference. He was afraid there was scarcely that degree of heroic self-denial which was the secret of the rapid advancement made by Methodism in the early days of this country and without which these young men would not have such a field before them as that upon the moral cultivation of which they were now entering.[113]

Two years earlier, Conference had voted to add George F. Playter's recently completed (and commissioned) work, *The History of Methodism in Canada* to the ministerial student reading list.[114] And three years later, in 1867, that other minister of the heroic period, John Carroll, published the first of his voluminous *Case and his Cotemporaries*. Somewhat pretentiously written, "after the manner of Herodotus," Carroll's five volumes were intended to evoke the excitement of the revival and the self-sacrifice of the early itinerant preachers, as well as record their personal idiosyncracies for posterity.

Thus, when *The Memorials of Edward and Lydia Jackson* appeared in 1876, a tradition of memorializing Canada's Methodist past had already been started. Slim in size but sublime in moral pretension, Burwash's book had none of the rambling, anecdotal style of John Carroll. Rather, it presented the reader with the edifying atmosphere of middle-class respectability and reverent piety. The environment of Methodism had obviously changed. But was this also the sign of a new period? As far as Burwash is concerned, the answer is simple. At his ordination he had made the customary pledge to preach faithfully the gospel of salvation. However, at that time he had promised not only to preach "Christ a free Saviour," but also to "preach a perfect Saviour."[115] To the doctrine of justification he had added that of Christian perfection. And when the time came a little later to pay tribute to "Methodist worthies," he added to the already published lives of the itinerant preachers his own version of the sanctified lives of two eminent laypeople. After the example of John Wesley and in the fashion of the Victorian age, he saw himself merely adding to and improving upon what already existed. After all, as he had reminded his audience in Belleville in 1862, "Progress is preeminently the watchword of the present age" – even for those whose business it was to save men's souls.

POSTSCRIPT

Progress in spirituality would remain a consistent note in Burwash's teaching, preaching, and writing for the rest of his life. With his frequent appeal to such concepts as "the higher Christian life" and "a more perfect consecration" he stood in the mainstream of late nineteenth-century evangelicalism with its emphasis on holiness. But though he was probably familiar with some of the non-Methodist expressions of holiness, such as the famous Keswick Movement (which originated in the English Lake District in 1875 and quickly spread to the United States), the authority to which he appealed in his exposition of the theme was invariably John Wesley.[116] In keeping with his own more mature understanding of Wesley's teaching on Christian perfection and under the influence of the thought of the American Methodist theologian, John Miley, he stressed the gradual nature of the sanctification without, however, ever ruling out the possibility of the experience as a crisis, a "baptism of the Spirit."[117]

Christian perfection figured as a prominent subject in his *Manual of Christian Theology*, as in *Wesley's Doctrinal Standards, Part I.*[118] The doctrine even provided the inspiration for the choice of a text from St John, "The truth shall make you free," which graced the front entrance of Victoria's academic building in Toronto.[119] And when the Methodist era began to draw to a close in 1906 and a doctrinal statement for a new United Church was drawn up, he was able, as chairman of the Committee on Doctrine, to make one final bequest that expressed his continuing commitment to Christian perfection. The wording of the last sentence of the twelfth doctrinal article, "sanctification" was due to his intervention (Burwash's contribution is italicized):

We believe that those who are regenerated and justified grow in sanctified character through fellowship with Christ, the indwelling of the Holy Spirit, and obedience to the truth; that a holy life is the fruit and evidence of saving faith; and that the believer's hope of continuance in such a life is in the preserving grace of God. *And we believe that in this growth in grace Christians may attain to a full assurance of faith, and to that maturity of faith working by love which the Scriptures call the love of God made perfect in us.*[120]

In 1911 in an effort to calm the fears of those critical of union, he explained that the wording of that article ensured that Christian perfection "in Mr. Wesley's favourite form of perfect love" had been safeguarded in the new Basis of Union. At that date Nathanael Burwash could look back on exactly half a century of exposition and application of Wesley's doctrine. Moreover, in 1911 as in 1861, he did not hesitate to admonish his less optimistic brethren to continue confidently to "follow the line by which God had led us up to the present and in which His providence and Spirit still seem to say "Go forward."[121] In matters spiritual, therefore, progress had remained "pre-eminently the watchword of the age," and it was this unquestioning confidence that would ultimately lead both Methodism and Burwash to accept church union. However, that decision would not be made until after two other significant developments – the formation of a college-educated ministry and university federation.

CHAPTER FOUR

Professor of Natural Science and Dean of Theology: Baconians, Methodists, and the Higher Criticism

The six years Burwash spent in the pastorate did more than formulate the contours of his piety and establish valuable links with Methodism's financial elite. Even in his first year as a probationer, fresh on the Newburgh circuit, he had been so presumptuous as to confide in the privacy of his journal an overriding, but at the time scarcely practicable ambition, "an honour which I covet above all others ... to build up the church or train those who may be the instruments of saving others."[1] Fifty years later that ambition had been more than realized, and on 23 September 1910 his contribution to Canadian Methodism was gratefully recognized in a special ceremony commemorating his fiftieth year in the ministry: "To you, perhaps more than to any other, the church owes the splendid position which Victoria University holds in the Higher Education of our land," were the words with which the Theological Alumni Association acknowledged the influence of one of its most illustrious members.[2]

Burwash had first become involved in higher education in 1867 as an underpaid and inadequately trained professor of natural science in a college facing bankruptcy. However, that year had marked the nadir of the college's financial troubles, and in large part thanks to the generosity of a few well-to-do Methodists, most notably Edward Jackson, William Gooderham, and Hart and Chester Massey, Victoria's fortunes underwent a remarkable recovery. Burwash's own career kept pace. The position of professor of natural science proved only to be a stepping stone to that of dean of theology in 1873, followed by his appointment as chancellor of Victoria University in 1887 after the sudden death of Samuel Nelles. As chancellor he presided over the federation of Victoria with the University of Toronto and its subsequent move from Cobourg to Toronto.

The extravagant praise bestowed on Burwash at his jubilee did have some basis, for during his years on the faculty of Victoria he played a pivotal role in the education of the Methodist ministry as it made the transition from training on the circuit to the college classroom. Whereas in 1872 only 25 theological students had been enrolled at the college, by 1910, the year of his jubilee, the number had increased to 212, and by that date four other colleges – Mount Allison, Wesleyan Theological College in Montreal, Wesley College in Winnipeg, and Columbian College in New Westminster – were sharing the task of Methodist theological training.[3] At any time well over half the candidates for the Methodist ministry could be found in these colleges, completing a full BA or the three-year post-graduate BD, or simply enrolled for three years as "conference students" after a two-year probation on a circuit.[4] During that time also, Victoria's faculty of theology had grown from one man to nine, of whom three, J.F. McLaughlin, R.P. Bowles, and George Blewett, were the college's own graduates. In 1900 Burwash had relinquished the administrative duties of dean to his colleague, F.H. Wallace, but in his capacity as chancellor he continued to preside over faculty meetings and to direct the nature of ministerial training at Victoria as well as in the larger setting of the church. Here he often warned that the denomination must remain alert to the demands of an increasingly sophisticated public and be fully convinced of the "imperative necessity of maintaining the standard of our ministry at a point corresponding to the growth of our country in intelligence."[5]

But not everyone agreed. Since 1890 when George C. Workman, Burwash's colleague and former student, had delivered a highly controversial lecture on Messianic prophecy at the annual meeting of the Victoria College Theological Union, rumours had been spreading that Victoria's dean and faculty were questioning the infallibility of the Scriptures and blindly following scholars who had forsaken time-hallowed biblical truths for the "negative theories of the 'Higher Criticism.' "[6] During the next twenty years it had become increasingly evident that at Victoria the authorship and interpretation of the various books of Scripture were being treated as matters of historical criticism. At the same time those persons who adhered to the familiar interpretation of the Bible were being condescendingly dismissed as "unawakened to the intellectual needs of the age."[7] In a denomination whose ministry had as model John Wesley, the "man of one book," such a divergence of views created great unrest and anxiety. It was not until 1910, the year of Burwash's jubilee, that the matter was finally resolved. At the eighth quandrennial Conference of the Methodist Church held in Victoria that year, an attempt to restrict theological professors to a literal understanding of Scripture was soundly defeated and the new critical teaching was allowed to continue, subject only to doctrinal guidelines, which would be safeguarded by a Committe of Trial composed of five ministers "of good repute for their knowledge of questions of doctrine."[8]

The debate over the teaching of the higher criticism in Methodist theological colleges between 1890 and 1910 has been one of the few issues in Canadian ecclesiastical history to attract the interest of modern scholarship, and has been seen as a significant stage in the modernization and secularization of Canadian culture. The decision by the Conference of 1910 to accept the higher criticism has been variously hailed as a great victory for academic freedom[9] and as the symbol of the decline of Methodist orthodoxy.[10] More recently the teaching of biblical criticism at Victoria has been treated as an example in the "taming of history," with Divine Providence becoming increasingly identified with the Whig idea of progress.[11] And on the premise that what ultimately mattered in the controversy over the higher criticism was piety, not classroom knowledge, the controversy has also been regarded as a classic case in the shift in modern thought away from abstract theory to concrete practice.[12]

Interpretations may differ, but all are in agreement that as in any significant turning point in history marked by controversy, there were two distinct sides, representing the old and the new. In the opinion of present-day scholarship, there were the "evangelicals" headed by Albert Carman, the elderly general superintendent of the Methodist Church, and the "liberals" headed by Victoria University's Chancellor Nathanael Burwash, equally advanced in years.[13] Contemporaries preferred to use the terms "conservative" and "modern," but they also had little difficulty in distinguishing between the combatants. Since February 1909, when the quarrel over the higher criticism was first publicly aired in the Toronto *Globe*, Albert Carman had presented himself as the champion of "competent and loyal ministers and members of the Methodist Church" who had become alarmed by a lecture on the first chapters of Genesis, delivered to the Toronto YMCA by Victoria's recently appointed professor of English Bible, the Rev. George Jackson.[14] And it was equally clear that although Nathanael Burwash had carefully avoided public involvement, he represented those parties who had jumped to Jackson's defence and who included such highly respected and affluent Methodist laymen as Chester D. Massey, H.H. Fudger, and Joseph Flavelle. It was also evident that this was a confrontation between the forces of progress and conservatism. Whereas Chester Massey accused Carman of displaying the intolerance of a medieval pope, the Rev. Solomon Cleaver accurately voiced the fears of many others when he argued at the 1910 Conference that "the very foundations of the faith" were under attack by false teaching.[15] Those who followed the proceedings of the Conference were at times struck by the apparently inconsistent behaviour of the "modern," or "liberal," side. It was to be expected that Burwash was one of the most ardent supporters of church union at the 1910 Conference. Yet his strong speech against a large-scale denominational revival and his proposal instead of "a more deeply spiritual method" was not quite what one would expect from a liberal attacking the foundations of the faith.[16] Moreover, as a leading member of the General Conference's Committee on Evangelism, he had helped write a forceful report recommending renewed emphasis on the traditional Wesleyan experiences of the witness of the Spirit and Christian perfection. In fact, that report had been praised by his former student and editor of the *Christian Guardian*, W.B. Creighton, as an unequivocal sign "that Methodism in British North America, no matter what pessimists may say, is very much alive to her great evangelistic mission and is not, as some aver, losing her passion and enthusiasm for the saving of men."[17] Such support for old-time revivalism did confuse the conservatives, and as Burwash confided in one of his many letters relaying home the dramatic stages of the controversy, "this was new light on our position to them."[18]

To know that Victoria's chancellor was at one and the same time championing the old Wesleyan doctrines and a new reading of the Bible may indeed shed new light on the introduction of the higher criticism into Canadian Methodist theological colleges. Was the great decision of the 1910 Conference a clear step in the history of modernization and secularization, or was something else at issue? To attempt to answer that question, it is necessary to return to the early 1860s, when young Nathanael Burwash first realized that not all the educated laity in his Belleville congregation had been swept away by the moral fervour of experiential religion. And it was from that period that he officially dated his own efforts to raise the standard of education for the Methodist ministry.

THE NEED FOR IMPROVED
MINISTERIAL EDUCATION

As a young minister in Belleville, Nathanael Burwash had not limited himself to earnestly proclaiming and practising the experiential Christianity of John Wesley. One of only a handful of men in the Methodist ministry in possession of a college degree, he had continued to study privately. In his aspiration to greater things to come, he had begun to emulate the well-known biblical exegete, Albert Barnes, who had started his career by devoting an hour each morning to biblical study with his Greek Testament and Hebrew grammar.[19] Because he had been forced to repeat a number of his college courses for the annual ministerial examination, Burwash had managed to complete the entire four years of the course of study in a record two – unfortunately, however, without the expected advance in his date of ordination.[20] Not to let knowledge go unused, he had been able in the pulpit to draw on his familiarity with his college texts in Christian apologetics and metaphysics to demonstrate to the younger members of his congregation, in particular, the complete harmony between religious experience and scientific knowledge. Forcefully he had reminded them that for ages the Scriptures had withstood "the test of the analysis of human reason and the cavillings of scepticism."[21]

Not everyone appeared to be convinced, and in the autumn of 1862 he became aware that two books, Bishop Colenso's recently published volume on the Pentateuch and Theodore Parker's *Ten Sermons on the Absolute Religion* were creating doubt in the minds of a group of students and young professionals in his congregation, the very group, in fact, that had previously threatened the moral welfare of Mrs Nathan Jones's class of young ladies. His crisis of faith resulting from the reading of these books has already received attention in an earlier chapter. However, more was at stake than his own peace of mind. For some time Burwash had been making the salvation of this group of potential religious libertines his special concern in his private prayer and in his preaching.[22] His personal crisis of faith now aroused in him a pastoral concern for the vulnerability of every educated young Methodist. As he mused fifty years after his bout of unbelief:

I was discovering that many of our most gifted and intelligent young men were drifting away from our evangelical faith under the influence of the modern scientific spirit and that if the church was to save such she must meet them not with anathemas but as a candid seeker for truth, with full faith in the harmony of truth; and so at twenty-four years of age I was squarely face to face with the problems of a lifetime and the labour which those problems involved.[23]

It should be pointed out that these words more accurately reflected the serene contemplation of an aging theologian intent on seeing the hand of Providence in his career than the reality of the time. The sermons of the Belleville period testify that for a while at least, Canadian Methodism's young "candid seeker of truth" fell back on the comfortable weapon of the weak and fulminated against "the quibblings of Colenso, the neology of Parker and the Germans, and the scoffings of Paine."[24]

This proved to be only a temporary expedient for coping. He had in fact learned one valuable lesson, namely, that his own college education and, even more certainly, that available to ministerial candidates in the course of study was no longer able to retain the more inquiring, better educated members for the Methodist Church. The incident in Belleville, therefore, gave a totally new direction to his pastoral concerns and to his own private study, and soon the usual self-chastisement in his journal began to shift from time wasted to too much time devoted to study.[25] For a time he contemplated the possibility of attending one of the Methodist theological institutes in the United States,[26] but eventually opted for a program of private study concentrating on metaphysics and, with a view to Colenso, on Old Testament Hebrew. In Hamilton he received strong encouragement from the Jacksons and his new district superintendent, Ephraim Harper, a biblical scholar reputed to be able "to make his way in thirteen languages." During this period he began to give weekly lessons to the half dozen men on his circuit preparing for the ministry, as well as serving on the district examination committee.[27]

For a Canadian Methodist minister who aspired to teach theology, the 1860s were a propitious time. Denominational self-awareness was on the upswing as new lay affluence found visible expression in a decade of church construction inaugurated by Hamilton Centenary in 1866. It was also becoming clear that increased work on the circuit was taking up too much time to permit adequate preparation for the ministerial course of study.[28] At the same time, when laymen like Edward Jackson were exposed to Burwash's unsatisfactory replacement in 1866, they were quick to note that more was required of a minister in an urban pulpit than conversion and zeal alone.[29]

In Great Britain and the United States the trend to a college-educated ministry had already begun in the 1830s and 1840s.[30] In Canada it was not until the American centenary in 1866 that the editor of the *Christian Guardian* began to issue a summons for a "School of the Prophets," arguing that "the times demand not only an educated ministry, but a ministry deeply schooled in Biblical lore and thoroughly trained in theological thought." But the Methodist Conference did little that was concrete, other than beginning a "centenary fund" for the purpose and establishing a committee two years later to look into possible sites for a theological institution. During the 1860s the *Christian Guardian* had to content itself with warning its readers of the "infidel propagandism" of such controversial writings as Charles Darwin's *Origin of Species* and *Essays and Reviews*.

Finally, in 1870, E.H. Dewart, its newly appointed editor, began to demand whether in the face of all such "modern skeptical philosophy ...

is it wise or right to thrust out as teachers of the people, young men, without any proper mental training, whose theological views are crude because their minds are not thoroughly instructed and grounded in truth?"[31] Laymen apparently thought not, and in 1872 a highly attractive offer of $50,000 was made to the Conference by Messrs Ferrier, Torrance, Glendenning, and others in Montreal to establish a theological institute in their city.[32] Meanwhile, Lachlin Taylor, then secretary of Missions and Nathanael Burwash's uncle, had not been idle either. Shortly before the death of Edward Jackson in the summer of 1872 Taylor had managed to persuade the Jacksons to endow a chair of theology at Victoria.[33] It was taken as self-evident that the appointment to that chair would be Nathanael Burwash.

PROFESSOR OF NATURAL SCIENCE: A THEOLOGIAN'S APPRENTICESHIP

For Samuel Nelles, Victoria's principal, the previous decade of the 1860s had not been easy. Increased denominational self-awareness and the possibility of a conservative backlash against scientific thought appeared to undermine the non-sectarian Christianity he had been promoting for the past twenty years at the college. To Nelles, unlike some of the *Guardian*'s readers, the answer to the new conflict between science and religion lay, not in denunciation, but in the affirmation of science and in the continuation of the "devout scholarship" which had been one of the hallmarks of the Victoria curriculum: "It may be well enough for theologians to call attention to the apparent antagonism of science to religion, but those in this case who ring the firebell are not the best to extinguish the flames. It is the man of science himself who is most competent to detect the errors of his co-worker in his special department.[34]

Fortunately, such a "man of science" had been teaching at Victoria since 1867. When the college's financial situation had been at a record low and Confederation threatened to end the annual government grant, Nelles had been forced to fill two vacancies in natural science with one inexpensive appointment. At that time he had gladly taken on his former graduate, Nathanael Burwash.[35] Clearly indicating that his real interest lay in theology, Burwash had accepted the appointment on the condition that he be allowed to help teach a number of the theology options in the arts program.

At Victoria, as in other evangelical colleges, the recent publication of Darwin's *Origin of Species* had suddenly made the chair of natural science a sensitive position. Students like W.R. Riddell (later a justice of the Supreme Court of Ontario) for example, were taking a strong stand for evolution, even though "at that time Darwin and his kind were taboo in orthodox circles," and respected an instructor who could remain neutral. Looking back on his college days many years later from the lofty heights of the Ontario Supreme Court, Riddell reflected on Burwash's attitude in the 1860s towards the hotly debated issue of evolution: "No one could detect the least theological bias in his teaching, Doctor Burwash stated what he understood to be the facts, but did not attempt to enforce any theories ... I do not remember any animadversions on the evolutionary theory at any time, although no one could doubt the Christianity of Doctor Burwash."[36] It was the proper attitude of the scientist faced with an unverified theory.

This also probably explained why Nelles abandoned his traditional hostility to establishing a faculty of theology at Victoria in 1872, even to the point of opposing Egerton Ryerson, who had curtly dismissed the college's science professor and aspiring theologian as a mere "stripling."[37] Therefore, when the faculty of theology was formally organized in 1873, the appointment of the new dean went without question to the man who for seven years had been serving his apprenticeship as a scientist. For his part, Burwash had not cast himself totally upon the mercy of Providence and two years earlier, had preveniently taken the examination for the degree of Bachelor of Divinity at the Garret Biblical Institute at Evanston, Illinois, to be followed in 1876 by the STD from the same institution.[38] And so, on 28 May 1873, under the leadership of a "fully qualified" professor in biblical and systematic theology, Victoria College formally began its experiment in the formation of a college-trained ministry.

THE SCIENTIST AS THEOLOGIAN

The introduction of a faculty of theology at Victoria did not proceed without internal strain. During the first ten years of the faculty's existence, the new dean fought a losing battle to prevent the Jackson endowment and the centenary fund from disappearing on general college expenses. Nelles, on the other hand, in addition to his financial worries, had to find ways to extend his already thinly manned staff in arts to help teach a constantly expanding theology curriculum.[39]

In the matter of educational aims, however, both shared an optimistic, progressive attitude. Burwash, who was secretary of the Education Society with the special task of publicizing the financial needs of theological education, began to spend almost every weekend away from home. During those trips he attempted, in sermons delivered in churches throughout central Canada, to make the denomination more sensitive to the need for a college-educated ministry as well as to the nature of that education. As with Nelles a decade earlier, the reception was not always favourable. Some ministers, for example, took offence on reading in the *Christian Guardian* in May 1876 that, at the closing exercises of the Wesleyan Theological Institute in Montreal, Victoria's dean of theology had made pointed references to "uncultured men" who from the pulpit "may hurl forth the red hot shot of denunciation against opinions such as Huxley's and Tyndall's." Such preaching, he had concluded, simply bred religious scepticism in young men who had been educated abroad and who "can weigh these opinions not founded on study or sound views. Those preachers may be popular, but they do more evil than good."[40]

Remarks of this nature were all the more infuriating because the dean refused to engage in public debate, preferring instead "the sincere and earnest presentation of truth for its own sake."[41] Displaying the single-mindedness of the academic and not a little intellectual arrogance, he made no effort to hide the fact that the new generation of college-educated ministers, through their study, had laid the foundations for "an intelligent Christian faith ... free from dogmatism, scientific skepticism and all juggling with Scripture such as is too fashionable in modern times."[42] There was clearly an aggressive, self-conscious attitude to theological education at Victoria, aptly summed up many years later by Dean Wallace, who had himself imbibed some of his predecessor's propagandizing spirit: "From the first, Dr. Burwash made the college course of study less dogmatic, less speculative and more biblical than was usual in those days, and his exegesis was of the modern, scientific, and historical type, not the confessional."[43]

As an undergraduate, Burwash had come to share the antipathy of his mentor Samuel Nelles for the twin enemies of true religion: dogmatism and sectarianism. Both these tendencies, he taught his students, had confused the true meaning of Scripture: "In every age the church has professed to derive its doctrine from the Word of God. But it has always mixed that teaching with human traditions and philosophy and often obscured it by misconceptions and errors of human understanding."[44] Opposed to the "dogmatic assumptions and metaphysical generalizations" of earlier theologians, including the once-revered William Paley and even of the Wesleyan commentator, Richard Watson, Burwash proposed to create "a scientific theology ... based on indisputable facts, observed by methods proper to itself." Far from being suspicious of science, he was confident that science could be turned into "the hand-maid of religion for our own age." In fact, the solution to the threatened rupture between science and religion in the 1860s was disarmingly simple. The scientific method of induction, first introduced by Francis

Bacon in the seventeenth century, would now be applied to the study of Scripture.

To nineteenth-century evangelicals, this confidence in the reconciliation between science and religion through the application of the inductive method was not particularly novel. Orthodox Protestants had long expressed the belief that the Baconian method, with its emphasis on facts rather than on "speculations and theories," would support Christian belief. Since the reincarnation of Francis Bacon and to a lesser extent Isaac Newton as the devout fathers of modern science in the writings of Thomas Reid and Dugald Stewart, a generation of American evangelicals schooled in the Common Sense tradition had eagerly and uncritically adopted the inductive method to ensure the continued union of faith and knowledge. And theologians such as Charles Hodge at Princeton had extended the scientific method to the study of Scripture, firmly convinced that it could serve as "the handmaid of the science of divinity" and that only in this way could science and religion be saved from infidel assault.[45]

Burwash had experienced this enthusiasm for Baconian science first-hand in 1866 in Yale when he briefly attended the chemistry lectures of Benjamin Silliman, a strong supporter of the inductive method and a leading exponent of science as spiritual enrichment.[46] Now drawing upon his own recent use of the Baconian method while functioning as professor of natural science, as well as on his familiarity with the Common Sense tradition, he began to construct a theology soundly rooted in empiricism. "Realism is the watchword of all the best educated of our day," he reminded his students, and therefore only "an inductive study of the facts" was acceptable:

We study not words nor formal definitions, not second-hand observations however perfect or excellent, but wherever possible, the things themselves. Hence we must get at, not volumes of theology constructed to hand, not creeds and dogmatic canons, but the original facts with which theology deals: – the living sin, the living Christ, the living God himself ... Where shall we find our facts as to these? In the Bible and in the heart of humanity.[47]

These would form the field of scientific investigation for the theologian, and in "carefully controlled research," conducted in a variety of courses, students began to examine the evidence in order to construct a theology firmly based on fact.

Grandiose in its conceptual framework, Baconianism was not for the faint-hearted. Those who could recall the dean's classes in natural science knew that "the conclusions slowly arrived at are the nearest to truth." Moreover, the same painstaking accuracy required in the analysis of matter was also necessary when it came to discovering the meaning of Scripture. Here, the first step, known as the analytical, or grammatico-historical method, was without doubt the most important, as well as the most difficult. When he was a young minister in Toronto in 1864 engaged in his private search for an answer to the "quibblings of Colenso," Burwash had already begun to make use of this method and had carefully laid out its basic principles: "We lay down as a first principle that every sentence of Scripture has a Definite meaning and is intended to express a certain sense or idea. This idea is that in the mind of the writer as inspired by the Spirit of God, the business of the Interpreter is to seek to ascertain this idea.[48]

The study of ancient history now received a renewed emphasis, and Greek and Hebrew, which had never been considered necessary in the training of the Methodist ministry, became indispensable. At Victoria there had usually been an arts option in the Greek New Testament, and in his second year as science professor, Burwash had begun to give lessons in Hebrew grammar. However, after 1874 linguistic study became mandatory with the addition of a new subject, Biblical exegesis, to the ministerial course of study. Second-year students examined the gospels of Matthew and John, and third-year students the Epistle to the Romans, aided in their efforts by a variety of grammars, lexicons, and concordances. After 1887 Burwash's own *Handbook of the Epistle of St. Paul to the Romans*, the result of many years of classroom work, became available as a model of the grammatico-historical method and three years later became the prescribed text for all ministerial candidates.[49]

Biblical exegesis, although arduous and time-consuming, was only the initial step to the scientific approach to theology. It was in their classes in biblical and systematic theology that students began to see the real fruits of the inductive method. A study of the book of Acts, for example, revealed the basic doctrines of the early church to have been human sinfulness and divine forgiveness through the atonement.[50] Since these two doctrines were also the cornerstones of evangelical revivalism, theological studies, far from undermining experiential Christianity, only served to vindicate it with the indisputable evidence of biblical scholarship.

The third step, systematic theology (the reduction to an orderly system of the various doctrines discovered in biblical theology) was the culmination of their studies. For anyone unable to attend the dean's lectures and to follow his careful reconstruction of a systematic theology, the methodology, as well as the finished product, was presented in his two-volume *Manual of Christian Theology on the Inductive Method*, published in 1900.

Whereas the first part examined the nature and authority of the Christian religion, the second explored its doctrines. Beginning with the doctrine of God and proceeding to man's relation to God, human responsibility and sin, redemption, personal salvation, and the role of the church, it concluded with Christian eschatology and divine judgment. As might be expected of any product of scientific study, this systematic study was considered irrefutable, and the hope was expressed that "the defined truth so won, will abide the test of the ages, and will build and perfect the spiritual life of the world."[51] Like biblical theology, however, systematic theology was studiously non-sectarian. Though the Wesleyan doctrines were dealt with, there was no mention of John Wesley or of Methodism, indeed, of any specific branch of the Christian faith. Nevertheless, the implications for Methodism were entirely reassuring, since the new systematic theology was presented simply as "the old truth in its evangelical fulness."[52]

This reassurance was more than a pious hope, because the various steps in the inductive method were unmistakably controlled and directed by a fourth area of study, a class in practical theology. In his *Manual of Christian Theology*, Burwash had insisted that "the primary requisite ... to a student of theology is strong, clear religious faith." Now using Wesley's Standard Sermons, he presented his students with Wesley's own account in practical form of the essential features of experimental Christianity.[53] His analytical studies of Wesley's Standard Sermons, published in 1881, soon became a college text, finding its way not only into the course of study for his own church, but also into that of the Methodist Episcopal Church South.[54] Wesley's sermons, supplemented by various other tracts, in particular the "Plain Account of Christian Perfection," had of course been listed on the ministerial course of study since its inception. But under Burwash experiential Christianity became a vital component of the scientific method applied to religion. Students were also enrolled in the traditional class meeting, and with Burwash as leader this now became "a laboratory in which the elements of the inner life were observed, recognized by name, and analyzed as they existed in the actual lives of men."[55] In his view there was nothing incongruous at all in this union between "the founder of modern science" and John Wesley's practical Christianity, for the two movements were progressive and mutually supportive. In the words of his eldest son (who had received his theological training at Victoria and faithfully echoed his father's theological views): "It was surely not accidental in an age when experimental science held the field intellectually, that an experimental or experiential form of religion should make its appearance. The Methodist's appeal to subjective experience as his ground of assurance in religion was a strict parallel and response to the scientist's appeal to objective experience as a sure foundation for his intellectual structure of laws and theories."[56] Through the application of the scientific method to Scripture, therefore, Burwash and his students merely saw themselves creating a systematic theology soundly rooted in Wesleyan spirituality.[57]

None of this insight, of course, had been acquired in a vacuum. To Burwash it was particularly gratifying to recognize that simultaneously with his own humble efforts, the English-speaking world in general had been forging ahead in scientific theological study. Beginning in the 1880s, through guest editorials in the *Christian Guardian* and articles and book reviews in the monthly *Canadian Methodist Magazine*, he began to inform the Methodist public of the noteworthy advances for evangelical Christianity resulting from these efforts. In 1880 for example, Bishop J.B. Lightfoot's "meticulous external historical testimony" on the authorship of the Fourth Gospel was a resounding victory over the German developmental school of F.C. Baur, as well as a golden opportunity to preach the benefits of Baconian science: "The truly scientific method always puts facts before theories; and it is encouraging to the faith of Christians to learn from conscientious and impartial labourers, such as the author of this little volume, that the *facts* were thoroughly in harmony with the old faith of the Christian Church."[58]

The publication of the revised version of the New Testament the following year brought Protestants another step closer to the faith of the early church, while at the same time striking a blow at sectarianism. As Burwash explained to the readers of the *Christian Guardian*, in this new translation it became clear that the Calvinist doctrine of a limited atonement had rested on a faulty rendition of the original text and that the New Testament now indisputably vindicated the Arminian teaching of the universal offer of salvation to the world. Again, such a significant clarification was a great advance "in the direction of progress and unity, and [would] provide a blessing especially to evangelical protestantism."[59]

A parallel, but even more important, development of this return from dogmatic speculation to Scriptural fact was the new emphasis by Albrecht Ritschl and others on Christ's ethical message. This, too, if properly understood, clearly worked to the advantage of evangelical Christianity:

The old form of evangelicalism, which had become almost a verbal and logical formalism, a learning to accept and repeat the cant phrases of the language of Canaan, is being abandoned by the thoughtful part of the Church for a broader and deeper spiritual conception. Faith in Christ can no longer be conceived as a mere saying, even sincerely, "He died for me," or "He paid my debt." It must mean the far deeper and broader act of taking him as the Lord and Master, the example and guide of my life.[60]

For one who as a young minister had chafed under the emotionalism of the old-fashioned revival meeting, such a change could only be welcomed and publicized.

SELECTIVE ACCEPTANCE OF THE HIGHER CRITICISM

Ironically, this new interest in the life and words of Christ also became for Burwash the key to a new interpretation of the inspiration of the Bible and to the selective acceptance of many of the findings of the higher criticism.[61] This discovery was not publicized, but to those who attended his lectures, followed his defence of George C. Workman in the 1890s and George Jackson in 1909–10, or read his *Manual of Christian Theology* the change was unmistakable. Its date can be traced to the academic session of 1885–6. It was at that time that Burwash first read the 1885 Bampton Lectures on the history of biblical interpretation delivered by Canon Frederic W. Farrar.[62] Farrar's devout scholarship, his use of Baconian language, and his fulminations against clerical opposition to science (with his help as canon, Charles Darwin had been buried in Westminster Abbey with Christian rites) had long made him a favourite with Burwash and Nelles, and in 1881 his *Witness of History to Christ* had been made a text in apologetics.

Now, in the Bampton Lectures, Farrar traced the history of biblical interpretation from the days of Jesus to the present, pointing out that since the rabbinical period the principal error in interpretation had been to over-emphasize dogma and external form at the expense of the Scripture's moral and spiritual message. Reading the lectures, Burwash began to see a new way of solving such thorny critical problems as Jesus' references to the Mosaic authorship of the Pentateuch and to David as the writer of the Psalms. Both of these had been laid open to question by his own study of the Old Testament following the grammatico-historical method. It now became clear that Jesus' aim had been to overturn false rabbinical interpretations of the Scripture, replacing them instead with moral and spiritual ones, consistently doing this, however, in "the language and modes of thought of his time with its human limitations and imperfections." If Jesus himself had accepted the restraints of the knowledge of his time and had shown that the supreme purpose of the Scriptures was "to arouse and enlighten the conscience and to turn the heart in faith to God," this hermeneutical principle could be applied without hesitation to all critical study of the Bible. It was evident, therefore, that the Bible contained a human as well as a divine side. It was "a heavenly treasure given to us in earthen vessels."[63] Matters of history, chronology, and science could now be examined by their appropriate methods. Finally, all obstacles to the reconciliation between science and the Bible had been removed: "This recognition then of the human setting of the Divine word with clear acknowledgement of the human limitations of this setting clears the way for the harmony and cooperation of all science with the Bible, and this includes even historical criticism."[64] Such a discovery he considered "a profound relief ... to the conscience and religious heart of all intellectual men."

The very first to benefit from his new insight were his own students in theology. One day in 1885 or 1886 while lecturing on Isaiah, Burwash had unexpectedly set his old notes to one side and confided to his students his changed view on the book's authorship. Until then he had contented himself with references to the considerable scholarship arguing that the Book of Isaiah was the product of two authors writing at totally different times.[65] He had taken no stand on the question himself, for the greatest stumbling block in accepting the dual authorship had been Jesus's reference to a single writer, Isaiah. To question this would be to undermine the omniscience and deity of Jesus. Farrar's *History of Interpretation* had, however, removed this obstacle and the way to accepting modern scholarship on the issue was now open.[66] To R.P. Bowles, one of the six students present and later his successor as chancellor, this revelation to the class was "the beginning of a new era in theological training in our Canadian divinity schools."[67] To Albert Carman, addressing the matter of biblical inspiration at the 1910 General Conference, such a reading simply "made the Saviour speak like a drivelling idiot."[68]

CONTROVERSY

Divisions within Canadian Methodism on the question of biblical inspiration did not, however, occur until the 1890s, and at that time it was not Burwash but his former students and colleagues who were openly criticized. Since his early years as dean of theology, Burwash had provided opportunities for students, as well as for ordained ministers, to express and share their theological insight. In 1877 Victoria College had formed a theological union whose highlight had been an annual lecture and sermon delivered by leading Canadian Methodist ministers. Twelve years later, in 1889, a highly ambitious theological journal, *The Canadian Methodist Quarterly*, began publication under the auspices of the Victoria and Mount Allison Unions.[69] Although its

editorial staff included older, more conservative figures like Albert Carman and William Shaw, principal of the Wesleyan Theological College
in Montreal, the *Quarterly*'s tone was aggressive and modern. Echoing
Burwash's own attitude, its foreword described Christian theology as
"the progressive science of God as revealed in Christ," and the Christian religion as "Divine life in the human, subject to all the laws of
vitality and growth."[70]

Unfortunately, the *Quarterly* became the subject of controversy the
following year, when it published a seventy-page essay on Messianic
prophecy by Victoria's professor of Old Testament theology, George
C. Workman. Starting boldly with the statement "Prophecy is a phenomenon peculiar to all primitive religions," Workman replaced the
traditional view that Messianic prophecy referred to the historical
Christ with an "ethical interpretation," which argued that the true purpose of prophecy was "to persuade men to faith in God."[71] Two years
later it was the turn of the journal's business manager, A.M. Phillips, to
be in difficulty. In this case it was for preaching in the Euclid Avenue
Methodist Church in Toronto an ethical interpretation of the atonement, intended to correct certain popular views which in Phillips' opinion "were neither Scriptural nor Methodistic."[72] Although he was
exonerated, suspicions lingered, and in 1895 the *Canadian Methodist
Quarterly* ended its short but dramatic existence.

George Workman, who had been excluded (against Burwash's wish)
from teaching biblical and theological subjects at Victoria, had resigned
in 1892. There followed a period of relative calm with only the occa-
sional rumbling as Workman fought indefatigably in print and at
annual Conferences to clear his name of alleged heresy.[73] In 1909, however, the college suddenly found itself again in the eye of the storm as
its newly appointed professor of English Bible, George Jackson, was
called to task for confessing that he accepted neither the Mosaic authorship of the Pentateuch nor the first chapter of Genesis as "an anticipa-
tion of the discoveries of modern science."[74]

During these decades no one defended the scholarship of Canadian
Methodism's alleged heretics more actively than Burwash. Although his
own acceptance of the progressive development of revelation was com-
paratively recent, he was quick to point out to Workman's critics that
"the historical method of interpretation which he follows is now recognized as the only legitimate method of universal scholarship."[75]

Moreover, although Burwash never accepted the principle of natural
selection, after 1885 he had come to subscribe whole-heartedly to the
theory of evolution, calling it "the most influential scientific doctine of
our time."[76] He now saw the early chapters of Genesis "as pure philosophy or religion realized for infant minds," neither a historical nor a

mythical account of man's beginnings; rather they laid the foundations for "the law of spiritual evolution, which seems to lie in the deepest nature of all intellectual, moral and religious life."[77] When he was a young professor of natural science, Burwash had refrained from taking a stand on evolution by rigidly adhering to the Baconian method of investigation. Now thirty-five years later, in his *Manual of Christian Theology*, which was based on that same inductive method, he was ready to champion evolution as a concept essential to religious insight: "The Christian theologian my thus with all boldness lay claim to this and all modern science as pillars in that great temple of truth, in which religion is the throne of glory from which God reigns supreme in His universe, and on which He is worshipped in spirit and truth."[78]

THE ROLE OF BACONIANISM

The question should now be asked whether the Baconian method really lay at the root of these changes in Burwash's thought. Most nineteenth-century intellectuals who tried to unite science and religion through the inductive method ended up rejecting both the higher criticism and evolution. In fact, historians are generally in agreement that by 1860, when Victoria College was about to embark on its experiment with Baconian science, the movement was already on the wane in major evangelical centres of learning in the United States.[79] Moreover, far from leading to an acceptance of the higher criticism, Baconianism has been considered one of the main intellectual forces behind the biblical fundamentalism of the late nineteenth century.[80] In 1873, at the time when Burwash was beginning to shape his own systematic theology on the inductive method, Charles Hodge at Princeton published his massive *Systematic Theology*. Based on that same method, Hodge's work was intended to provide a well-integrated theology of biblical authority and to be a bulwark in the defence of biblical infallibility.[81] In fact, to the Old School Presbyterians at Princeton in the decades after Darwin's *Origin of Species* and the *Essays and Reviews*, Baconianism had become a tool for protecting the faith from "visionary hypotheses" and "rash speculations."[82] An appeal to the "facts" could, therefore, be reactionary as well as progressive.

Nowhere was this more clear than in Canadian Methodist circles, where the two most vociferous critics of advanced biblical scholarship, E.H. Dewart and Albert Carman, both took their stand on Baconian principles. In his numerous diatribes against George Workman's teaching, Dewart sought to demonstrate that the higher critics were advancing "speculative theories which have not been tested by time" and were relying on "utterly unscientific" methods of proof.[83] Similarly, when

Albert Carman attacked Jackson in the *Globe* in February 1909, he presented himself as a man of science, ready to expose unverifiable hypotheses, claiming "we are not, like the higher critics after theories, but after facts, and facts in their logical and historic order."[84] Baconianism was a game both sides could play equally well.

THE ROLE OF METHODIST DOCTRINE

As Burwash soon made clear, doctrinal interpretation was a different matter. In the United States, as in Great Britain, despite controversies analogous to those in Canada between 1890 and 1910, Methodists did not join the ranks of Protestant fundamentalism.[85] And when it came to defending the higher criticism, Burwash, like Workman, Phillips, and Jackson, rested his case on the Methodist Standards of Doctrine and on the distinguishing characteristics of experiential Christianity.

In the first place, unlike those Baconians of the Calvinist tradition who have almost exclusively formed the subject of American scholarship, not all nineteenth-century Protestants saw the future of Christianity to be totally dependent on the infallibility of the Scriptures. Anglo-Catholics, for example, avoided the biblicist dilemma by an appeal to tradition.[86] Methodists on the other hand had the additional certainty of religious experience. Using the term "the Wesleyan Quadrilateral," American Methodist scholarship has drawn attention to the fact that in his formulation of doctrine John Wesley considered four sources to be necessary to a complete understanding of faith: Scripture, tradition, experience, and reason.[87] As he examined the thorny issue of the authority of Scripture in his *Manual of Christian Theology*, Nathanael Burwash also had detected in the history of the Christian religion four "collateral or co-ordinate authorities." Following the example of late nineteenth-century British biblical criticism, and in keeping with the evangelical emphasis on the Gospel, or the message of salvation, Burwash considered the "Apostolic Word" to be the essence and the culmination of the teaching of the Bible, but otherwise his authorities followed Wesley's. These were, first, "the written Apostolic Word"; second, "a continuous tradition of teaching, which expands and enlarges the truth to be gathered from the written word"; third, the church, which especially through its ministry carried on "the Apostolic authority and gift of declaring God's Word"; and finally, the gift of "the inner light which is given to every true Christian."[88]

It was this "inner light" that had come to the rescue of Nathanael Burwash in Belleville when Colenso's and Parker's arguments had shattered his intellectual defences. And as he explained in his *Manual of Christian Theology in the Inductive Method*, he considered an "inner assurance of faith" rather than "rational, scientific, or historical investigation" to be the basis of the faith of most of mankind. As a corollary, only those who possessed this inner assurance of faith could discover and preach the truth of the Scriptures, for "authority alone cannot command living faith. That implies the vital touch of truth itself with the living spirit."[89] This position was re-emphasized in a statement by Victoria's faculty of theology published in the *Christian Guardian* in March 1909 after the outbreak of the Jackson controversy: "No one, however he may excel in scholarship or whatever may be his intellectual endowments, is qualified to interpret the Word unless in his own heart there dwells the spirit of God testifying of the things of Christ."[90] Thus, to Burwash religious experience was the foundation of biblical study at Victoria, and by means of the course in practical theology it had been incorporated into the curriculum and made a vital component of the scientific method.

Secondly, in the Anglican, and by derivation the Methodist traditions, the attitude to biblical authority differed significantly from that of most Reformed Protestants. Not biblical authority but the doctrine of the Trinity came first in the Methodist and Anglican articles of faith, unlike those of most sixteenth-century continental confessions.[91] Moreover, when defining biblical authority, the articles spoke only of "the Sufficiency of the Holy Scriptures for Salvation," clarifying that the Holy Scriptures contain all things "necessary to salvation; so that whatsoever is not read therein, nor may be proved thereby, is not to be required of any man that it should be believed as an article of faith, or be thought requisite or necessary to salvation."[92]

Using this article, Burwash was able to turn the tables on his opponents. At the 1910 General Conference he argued successfully that it was not the teaching of biblical criticism at Victoria, but the desire of certain ministers to limit Methodists to a literal interpretation of Scripture that was unorthodox and an innovation: "We cannot settle anything here. This is a court of legislation. It is not a court of trial – not a judicial court. And it is not a court competent to establish any new standards of doctrine. The standards of our doctrine are beyond the reach of this general conference."[93] Therefore, as long as biblical interpretation continued to clarify the central doctrines of salvation, there was nothing to fear from "the modern view of the Bible." Indeed, by distinguishing the human from the divine and by following Christ's example of drawing out moral and spiritual truth, the modern view presented "more fully the spiritual power and the Divine truth of the Holy

Scriptures."[94] There was no question of piety becoming divorced from the teaching of the classrooms. Rather, piety could be reinforced by that teaching.

By asserting the sufficiency of the Scriptures for salvation, Wesley had allowed much room for the philosophical and scientific developments of his time.[95] Nineteenth-century Methodist Baconians could therefore maintain an orthodoxy far more accommodating to the results of scientific investigation than, for example, their Reformed colleagues. When Burwash defended George Workman's teaching on Messianic prophecy against the criticism of E.H. Dewart and other Methodists, he had based his case on the impeccable authority of John Wesley. Insisting that the right of private judgment was fundamental to Protestantism, he had asserted that "this same liberty, especially in the critical study of the word of God, was an essential element of early Arminianism, and was fully maintained by John Wesley ... in his own method of work in his *Notes on the New Testament*, a work in which he adopted the most advanced results of the critical scholarship of his age."[96]

He repeated this same point in his defence of George Jackson at the 1910 Conference. In fact, Burwash considered it to carry such weight that in his preparation for the defence he frantically telegraphed his secretary at Victoria College to send him the section in the minutes of the Wesleyan Conference of 1774 where Wesley himself had directed "a thorough and free discussion of all questions."[97] The opponents of the higher criticism, on the other hand, made no comparable attempt to base their case on Methodist doctrine. In the end, the Conference accepted the fact that it was impossible to create a new doctrine of Scriptural infallibility and limited itself to establishing machinery to deal with future allegations of departure from Methodist doctrine at church colleges. In fact, with the addition of a sentence "that this General Conference affirms ... its faithful adherance to the Word of God which liveth and abideth forever," the vote of acceptance became virtually unanimous.[98]

DIFFERENT MODELS OF METHODISM AND THEIR SIGNIFICANCE

There was no doubt that those who championed the old view of biblical interpretation at the 1910 Conference were motivated by the same commitment to experiential Christianity as Burwash and his group. Indeed, a statement by Victoria's theological faculty published in the *Globe* during the 1909 debate clearly recognized that both "the conservative view of the Bible," as well as "the modern view" were acceptable and that John Wesley's *Notes* and *Sermons* could, in fact, be quoted in support of either.[99] Simply put, both sides were Methodists and both were anxious that, to quote the *Christian Guardian*, "Methodism [should] remain alive to her great evangelistic mission." Moreover, each side realized that that mission had to be carried out within an existing culture. Albert Carman reminded the assembled delegates at the 1910 Conference in the opening sentences of his controversial address as general superintendent that Methodists could never retreat in "quiet and fruitful mysticism," for "the Church is the army of the living God, fighting His battles in an enemy's country."[100] Military metaphors were, of course, commonplace in evangelical Christianity, but in this case a closer examination of Carman's analogy may help to distinguish the two camps in the higher criticism controversy more clearly.

Since 1880 an offshoot of Methodism, the Salvation Army, had unashamedly adopted military terminology and organization. More than once Nathanael Burwash had expressed his admiration for that group's evangelistic zeal and, even during the Jackson controversy, had given his blessing to a pious but disgruntled Methodist who had threatened to join the followers of General Booth, should the 1910 Conference approve of the teaching of the higher criticism. In Burwash's estimation, such a decision was understandable for those who considered scientific study to be unimportant and who simply concentrated, like the Salvation Army, on practical and spiritual Christianity. Questions of the authorship of the books of the Bible or the science of the early chapters of Genesis were irrelevant to those preaching the message of salvation. "And," he had added, "in so doing we should be largely following the example of Wesley himself, or I might even say with reverence, of Christ and the Apostles." Such an attitude to scientific study was correct "wherever the church is being gathered anew from a world submerged in sin."

Methodists in the late nineteenth and early twentieth centuries, however, he considered to have a greater responsibility. Living in a Christian civilization, it was their duty to carry "the expansive and leavening power" of Christianity into science, philosophy, literature, political, and social life, into everything "which belongs to the God-given activity of the race." Unlike the Methodists of John Wesley's day the task of contemporary Methodists went beyond the salvation of the soul to the permeation of all culture with the moral and spiritual truths of Scripture. And it was for this reason that, committed to the Christianization of culture, they were to seek their own true scientific foundation, "which will we believe be one with our foundation in the grace of our Lord Jesus Christ." It would be the work of generations, "but the principles which should guide us in this long and arduous labour are quite clear, and will bring us at once into harmony with all true science and will set our religious faith at once clear from all imputation of being unscientific, or opposed to true science, or shifty or dishonest toward any form of truth."[101]

That optimistic attitude toward culture is what divided Burwash from some of his Baconian contemporaries. Historians have drawn attention to the ambivalence towards culture that was shared by many of the evangelicals schooled in the Common Sense tradition. When Baconianism no longer served as a bridge between science and religion after 1860, "they found themselves clinging to an increasingly out-moded concept of nature and science and drifting gradually from vital contact with the scientific learning of their times."[102]

Burwash, however, with his unquestioning belief in the ultimate unity of scientific and religious truth, had been alert to the results awaiting those who had first adopted a favourable attitude towards science and then became critical once science no longer appeared to support revealed religion. Not only would their science be outmoded, but in his opinion, those who had criticized science would capitulate in the end and accept its findings. In the meantime, however, the cause of the Christian faith would have been irreparably damaged.[103] In a private letter to Albert Carman during the controversy, he had warned that to crush the scientific spirit of the age which demanded that every-thing be thoroughly investigated would only be a confession of weakness:

We believe that the Bible will bear such investigation, and we propose to meet the demand of the age in the spirit of quick confidence and honest candour ready to admit truth wherever we see it and quite fearless that any truth will overturn the authority or Divine power of the Word of God. Such an attitude will we believe command the respect of all honest men and will itself do more than anything else to maintain their confidence in the Bible.[104]

But who were these "honest men?" In Belleville in the 1860s they had been a small group of professionals and students who had begun to question the intellectual validity of Methodism. Later, as dean of theology, Burwash's concern had expanded to the entire denomination, but again in particular to the more critical and better educated segment. And by the 1890s another group had been added, for Methodism's responsibility had gone beyond the Canadian borders to distant nations like Japan which, being highly civilized, "will accept our science and discard our religion": "To replace at once their ancestral religion and philosophy by our own, we must go to them as Paul did with the united strength of reason and revelation and shew that the God of Nature who giveth rain and fruitful seasons is the God whom we preach."[105]

Albert Carman, on the other hand, had also expressed the view that "we have a constituency in this world," but by the use of military terminology he had made it clear that he did not expect the world to fall so quickly to the sweet sounds of reason and religion. Like Burwash, Carman, as a young probationer in the ministry, had struggled to maintain his spirituality in a sinful world. Burwash, it may be recalled, had re-emphasized John Wesley's doctrine of Christian perfection and had illustrated its practice in the lives of eminent Methodist lay people. Carman, too, had been concerned with the corrupting power of wealth, and in 1858, after his own experience of perfection had drawn up a private "covenant." In it he had dispensed hypothetical amounts of money to "religious, benevolent, and charitable purposes," and on a sliding scale had promised increasing amounts, until the time when his income reached fifty thousand, and he would give it all away.[106]

Unfortunately, Albert Carman was never called upon to make that heroic gesture, for he continued in the ministry of the Methodist Episcopal Church and, as its bishop, had to bow to changing socio-economic conditions and lead that church into union with the larger, wealthier, and more urban Wesleyans.[107] There as general superintendent of the new Methodist Church, he was confronted for the first time with the phenomenon of lay representation in the church's highest courts. These laymen did not appear to bow easily to clerical authority, and Carman found himself repeatedly defending the itinerancy system against lay claims to the right to appoint ministers.[108] In 1906 he had even had to resist an attempt led by such influential Torontonians as Joseph Flavelle and Newton Wesley Rowell to unseat the general superintendent and other aging members of the church hierarchy.[109]

The invitation of the Sherbourne Street Methodist Church to a foreign minister, the Rev. George Jackson of Edinburgh, was only one more example of lay independence, and a careful reading of Carman's attacks on Jackson in the *Globe* in 1909 leaves little doubt that his first concern was "the unmethodistic and utterly unconnexional" appointment made by Sherbourne Street's wealthy laity.[110] In his capacity as chairman of the Board of Regents at Victoria, Carman could not have been totally uninformed of the nature of biblical teaching in the faculty of theology and, in any case, there had been complaints since 1890. There was nothing that George Jackson taught concerning the first chapters of Genesis that could not be found in Burwash's own lectures in systematic theology, available since 1900 in published form or, less explicitly, in his analytical studies of Genesis, printed for lay and clerical use in the *Canadian Methodist Quarterly* in 1894.[111] Moreover, at the 1910 Conference Carman, like Burwash, had had to manoeuvre within the guidelines set by John Wesley and had been forced to rule out of order an amendment to limit theological professors to a literal interpretation of Scripture.[112] At that Conference he had indeed quoted John Wesley, but his was a Wesley who took a stand against, not for, cultural change: "It seems at times necessary to recall the words of John Wesley, the originating spirit of our Methodism, that we are to beware lest we make rich men a necessity to us and in a way to our ecclesiastical movements. The money power is a tremendous power, and even in the hands of wellmeaning men it may be misdirected."[113]

To Burwash, on the other hand, these "rich men" were exemplary Methodists whose careers were a witness to the doctrine of Christian perfection that he had been extolling since his early ministry. They were actively involved in Sunday school and missions and frequently acknowledged the effectiveness of the new interpretation of the Bible in these areas.[114] Not only had they brought George Jackson from Great Britain to teach it to their young people, but Chester Massey had even gone so far as to point out in the *Globe* during the debate with Carman that "a crying need of the Methodist Church is more ripe scholarship in the pulpit, and more earnest study of the Bible."[115]

Such a sentiment would not sit well with ministers whose own academic careers lay in the dim past or whose knowledge had been acquired painfully in the midst of a heavy load of circuit work. As Owen Chadwick has reminded readers in his study of the Victorian Church, it was often not the layman in his pew, but the preacher in the pulpit who felt most threatened by the higher criticism.[116] In Canadian Methodism this fact was particularly relevant, for of the four hundred delegates at the 1910 Conference, one half were laymen. Moreover, the defence of the higher criticism had been shared by a minister and a leading layman, Newton Wesley Rowell, KC, recently elected with Burwash to represent the denomination at the Methodist Conference of Great Britain.[117] Although Rowell was well versed in biblical scholarship, he had taken his stand on Methodism's traditional mission of salvation, and in true ministerial style had concluded his remarks with the exhortation, "Brethren, let us go forth as men to preach that God is able and willing to save men from their sins, and let us cease this haggling about non-essentials."[118]

Thus, in the matter of ministerial training, biblical inspiration, and even lay evangelization, the spirit of John Wesley had become firmly entangled with new cultural forces. It was not that Methodists, by adopting the higher criticism, had unwittingly accepted the idea of progress. Progress had always been part of their piety. However, by conscientiously following in the footsteps of Francis Bacon and John Wesley, Burwash could claim in 1910 that the Bible he was teaching his students was still the old Gospel but that the new understanding of its form expressed Methodist spirituality more clearly. Piety had simply been updated.[119] As with Burwash's wealthy lay supporters, progress and piety had become indissolubly linked.

There is one final illustration of that union. In 1909 when the controversy over the teaching of the higher criticism was at its stormiest, a layman, H.H. Fudger, president of the Robert Simpson Company and a founding member of the Sherbourne Street Methodist Church, asked Burwash if he would "write something which may help our young people in the settlement of the difficulties which at present disturb their religious faith." Fudger's eye was to the future of Methodism. What he received was an account of Burwash's own past spiritual development, beginning with Anne Taylor's doctrinal instruction of her sons, including a description of his faith crisis in Belleville, and the final solution of his difficulties with the higher criticism through reading Farrar's Bampton Lectures. While political tact decided against publication, Fudger expressed himself more than satisfied.[120] So he should have been for, as the title of Burwash's account, "The Old Religion and the New Learning," already indicated, the new was simply an improved version of the old. And on the title page the author, without any apparent thought of incongruity, had presented two verses:

Tis the oldtime religion
And 'tis good enough for me. Torrey and Alexander

Let Knowledge grow from more to more
But more of evidence in us dwell
That mind and soul according well
May make one music as before. Tennyson[121]

To a Baconian and a Methodist there was no incongruity in linking evangelical revivalism with moral and intellectual progress. Indeed, the two were inseparable.

CHAPTER FIVE

Chancellor of Victoria University: The Federation of Learning, Culture, and True Religion

"You speak of 'moving' to Toronto. How do you move a University? What sort of fellows are you Canadians – are you more of Yankees than we are? It must grind an Englishman's bones to hear of such a movement." "Such a movement" – the removal of Victoria University from Cobourg to Toronto in order to enter federation with the publicly funded University of Toronto – was indeed under serious consideration in the spring of 1884 when Samuel Nelles received this astonished reaction from an old friend of Genesee Wesleyan days.[1] But it was not until October 1892 that Victoria's students were able to occupy their new academic bulding, located on a choice four-acre site in Queen's Park. When they did, it was only after one of the most divisive debates in Canadian Methodism, and under the leadership of a new chancellor, Nathanael Burwash.

As dean of theology and Nelles's right hand, Burwash had been one of the most ardent advocates and a principal architect of university federation. When Samuel Nelles, worn out by the strain of the attendant controversy, had suddenly succumbed to typhoid fever in October 1887, there had been little surprise at the appointment of Burwash to succeed him as president and chancellor. Hailed by Victoria's students as "among the foremost theologians and exegetes of the century," he was cast by the denominational press in the equally progressive (but safer) role of modern university administrator, "worthy to rank with those great college presidents, Patton, McCosh and Eliot."[2] There was a reason for this reference to such well-known modern institutions as Princeton and Harvard, for from the beginning of the federation movement Burwash had placed himself on the side of progress in education. As he argued, university federation was an opportunity to be seized and would give Canada in an instant "a grand national university scarcely inferior to any upon this continent," for which the country might otherwise "be required to wait for perhaps half a century."[3]

To some of his Methodist confrères, on the other hand, Burwash's vision entailed the inevitable demise of Victoria as a self-consciously Methodist college as well as the probably disappearance of Methodism's distinctive voice in Canadian higher education. "No man has done more to rob Methodism of her University than the successor of our late lamented chancellor," an anonymous Victoria alumnus wrote to the Cobourg *World*. And he sardonically concluded his criticism with the prophecy, "There is a grim gratifaction in knowing that the man who has done most to strip her will be the first to exhibit her nakedness."[4]

Burwash, who had studiously avoided controversy when he was dean of theology, did not for a moment hesitate to risk his reputation in defence of federation. He devoted his lengthy tenure as chancellor, from 1887 to 1913, to convincing his denomination by both precept and practice that the new university arrangement met "the highest interests of the Church and country."[5] He was convinced that the terms of federation would safeguard Victoria University's stress on moral formation and its commitment to the harmony between reason and religion. By the 1870s that harmony, once the cornerstone of the classical curriculum, had been severely undermined by the impact of evolutionary science and extensive university reform. Richard Hofstadter, Lawrence Veysey, and others have demonstrated that because of these changes religion came to be seen as obstructionist and at best irrelevant as it gradually receded from the university curriculum and campus in the United States.[6]

Though there are no comparable studies for higher education in Canada, A.B. McKillop has drawn a distinction between Ontario's colleges of the nineteenth century, which were founded to cultivate a pious disposition or "character," and the "research ideal" of the University of Toronto, which in the 1880s began to rival the earlier stress on cultural formation. Such a contrast, however, is only partially correct, because it fails to take into account the significance of the division of labour between the colleges and the university within the University of Toronto, embodied in the Federation Act of 1887.[7] As conceived by Nathanael Burwash, this division was intended both to preserve the traditional emphasis on religious values in higher education and to promote research and the expansion of the sciences. Moreover, under Burwash as chancellor of Victoria, religion on the campus acquired a new stature as the humanities, and literature especially were called upon to assist in the task of moral formation.

By accepting and promoting university federation, Burwash's response to change was characteristic. As had been the case in his support of theological education and the higher criticism, he attempted to affirm selectively both the old and the new. Again, where some of his colleagues preferred to erect a wall against new cultural developments, he tried creatively to adapt these to the exigencies of religion. In this way he hoped to advance the influence of evangelical Christianity in Canadian society.

BACKGROUND TO FEDERATION

To Samuel Nelles's surprised American friend, as to many Canadians, moving a university appeared unorthodox, but in North American university circles the 1880s were not orthodox times. In the words of Noah Porter, president of Yale University, "College and university education are not merely agitated by reforms, they are rather convulsed by a revolution – so unsettled are the minds of many who control public opinion, so sharp is the demand for sweeping and fundamental changes."[8] The pattern of that revolution in American university education was everywhere the same. The introduction of electives, the constantly increasing demand for professional and graduate training, and the availability of new surplus capital brought about such fundamental changes that by 1900 the complexity of the new universities made the old college of mental discipline of half a century earlier appear little more than a boys' school in contrast.[9]

Ontario's denominational colleges and publicly endowed University of Toronto had not been unaffected, and by the 1870s they were faced with increased pressure to expand their facilities and curriculum. To the Liberal government of Oliver Mowat, and especially to William Mulock, elected vice-chancellor of the University of Toronto in January 1881, the answer, as with most Canadian problems, lay in federation. Under Mulock's aggressive leadership a concerted effort was made to consolidate the province's system of higher education while at the same time meeting the University of Toronto's need for expansion and additional government grants. As a result, by 1885 St Michael's, Wycliffe, Knox, and the Toronto Baptist College (later McMaster) had entered into affiliation with the University of Toronto, thus adding weight to that institution's request for funding.[10]

Nathanael Burwash had been watching this development with keen interest. Many years earlier, in 1868, in response to the proposed termination of annual government grants to denominational colleges, he had expressed his fondness for statistics by compiling an analysis of the occupations of Victoria's graduates. His intention had been to show that the work of the college was not narrowly denominational or sectarian, as opponents argued in order to justify the cessation of the grant. Unfortunately, though presented as part of a memorial to the government by the Board of Regents, the study had not had the desired effect, and the denominational colleges were forced to fall back on the resources of their constituencies.[11]

When in January 1881, following Mulock's election, the possibility that the University of Toronto would be expanded was reported in the *Globe*, Burwash was quick to seize the opportunity to tie this proposal to a larger scheme of government support for all the province's institutions of higher learning. Outlining this view in a letter to the *Globe*, he made no mention of federation, but he did suggest that there were points of interest between the various colleges where "harmony or unity is desirable." These might include a uniform standard of matriculation, a common curriculum for the first year, and a board of university regents representing all the colleges to ensure such uniformity.[12] The letter was not sent but "pigeon-holed" on the advice of Samuel Nelles. The latter had been busy behind the scenes with his colleague, George Grant, principal of the Presbyterian Queen's College, Kingston, devising a plan of action now that the question of government funding had been reopened.[13] Later, when the contents of the letter had acquired historic value, Burwash would treasure it as the first in a series of personal papers documenting his role in university federation.

According to his later testimony, this letter was only part of a larger vision that had begun to take shape in his mind a little earlier when he was visiting Toronto on a preaching assignment to raise funds for the Educational Society of the Methodist Church. At that time he had taken the opportunity to attend a lecture by Sir Daniel Wilson, president of the University of Toronto. "Rambling up and down" Queen's Park, which at that time was still bordered to the north by cow pasture and forest, he had given rein to his imagination and began "to picture in fancy a series of colleges facing the ravine with a fine winding drive from College Street to Bloor."[14]

It would take only eleven years before Victoria as the first of those colleges took up its location on a site in the eastern section of the park, leased from the provincial government at a nominal annual rent of one dollar. The various steps towards federation, which have already received considerable scholarly attention, will not be given here in detail.[15] What should be noted, however, is Burwash's prominent part in the negotiations.[16] These began at the instigation of William Mulock in January 1884 and were attended by representatives of Toronto and its affiliated colleges, the Church of England's Trinity College, Queen's College, and by Nelles and Burwash for Victoria. In every instance Victoria's conditions for entering federation were presented by Burwash, although they had beforehand received a thorough critical review by Nelles.[17]

By mid-December a formula had been reached whereby the colleges would teach the humanities and the university the sciences. The initial suggestion put forth by Nelles and Grant had been that the denominational colleges receive a share in the university endowment and would not have required the colleges to move to Toronto.[18] The principle of basing federation on a division of labour was Burwash's idea, and though it did undergo a series of permutations in its details, its acceptance was a source of no little pride to him. As his private notes support, it was he who suggested at the negotiations that the university be "organized on the German principle for the promotion of higher learning," and the colleges be "organized on the English basis for a broad liberal culture." The model of the university had been suggested to him by a brief description of the Prussian universities in *Schools and Universities on the Continent* by Matthew Arnold, the well-known English school inspector and literary critic.[19] In practice, however, expediency had dictated some inconsistencies in this division, for at the insistence of Sir Daniel Wilson, history was made a university subject, as were metaphysics, Italian, and Spanish, while ethics remained in the hands of the colleges.[20] In later years, the logic of this division of the curriculum would not always be readily apparent to university administrators and would call forth repeated explanations from Burwash, whose proprietary pride in the arrangements had quickly turned expediency into principle.[21] Like Arnold, he had assumed the responsibility of instructing his fellow countrymen on the nature of higher education in a changing world.

The instruction to his own denomination began almost immediately after G.W. Ross, the minister of education acting on behalf of the government, accepted the proposed division of labour in late December 1884. Opinion among Victoria's Board of Regents on the desirability of federation was far from unanimous.[22] When it became clear that Queen's was dissociating itself from the proposal, the board decided to defer a final decision on Victoria's stand until the Quadrennial Conference of the Methodist Church, to be held in September 1886.

By that date the opposition had so escalated that Nelles, disappointed that Victoria appeared to be the only denominational college still actively considering federation, and mistrusting the intentions of the government and the University of Toronto, spoke against federation at the Conference.[23] In this he was supported by Burwash. It was the one occasion when the latter briefly found his enthusiasm on the issue waning.[24] Though he later attributed his stand to concern for Nelles's health and to his own pessimism concerning the denomination's unwillingness to make the necessary sacrifices for federation, his dark mood may also in part have been caused by the death that spring of his mother, Anne Taylor.[25]

When the Conference voted by a narrow margin (carried by the lay delegates) to proceed with federation, he quickly resumed his earlier position. Nelles, on the other hand, was disappointed, even though he loyally promoted federation as the policy of the Methodist Church for the remaining months of his life.[26] The brunt of the defence, however, was eagerly carried by Burwash, who together with E.H. Dewart, editor of the *Christian Guardian*, became the leading Methodist spokesmen on behalf of federation.[27]

In 1887 the details of this new arrangement for higher education in Ontario were spelled out in the Federation Act. By its terms any denominational colleges entering into federation agreed to hold their degree-conferring power in abeyance except in theology. Instruction in the sciences and in those courses specified in the 1884 negotiations, as well as all professional training would be surrendered to the state. The colleges, however, would continue to provide instruction in theology and in the humanities. Though they would be represented in the university Senate, they also retained their own internal organization, received the tuition fees of their students, and remained responsible for the life and conduct of the student body.[28]

The Act was not proclaimed until 1890, when Victoria as the only denominational college finally decided to accept its terms and move to Toronto. Notwithstanding the decision of the 1886 General Conference, in the intervening three years Methodism in Ontario was wracked by controversy, all of which received wide publicity in the secular press.[29] Those three years of bitter warfare included obstinate resistance by the Senate, not to mention an injunction served on the Board of Regents by the town council and several members of the Senate, including the vice-chancellor, William Kerr, prohibiting the removal of the college.[30]

Indeed, federation became a *fait accompli* only after a negative court decision was handed down on the injunction, and the denominational press was closed to the anti-federationists. Finally, in a desperate attempt to end their opposition, the latter were ousted from the Board of Regents by some high-handed manoeuvring on the part of the new chancellor.[31] That Burwash was forced to resort to such action underscores the fact that a strong case for independence had been made in Canadian Methodist circles.

THE CASE FOR INDEPENDENCE

The battle over university federation happened to coincide with a heightened denominational awareness that historians have detected in North American Protestantism in the latter decades of the nineteenth century.[32] During those years Canadian Methodism had witnessed a second effort at consolidation of a very different nature. In 1884 the various branches of Methodism in Canada had finally united to form one Methodist Church, thereby creating the largest denomination in the country. One of the tangible products of that union had been the federation of two colleges, Albert College, belonging to the former Methodist Episcopal Church, and Victoria. Together they would form Victoria University, with Albert College becoming a preparatory school. It was in May 1885 at the first annual convocation of this recent product of union that Nelles and Burwash had presented the plan for university federation. However, they had found the response to be far from favourable, for the new denominational self-consciousness had become a rallying point for all who were opposed to the move to Toronto.[33]

The case for independence was strong, and ably presented by Alexander Sutherland, secretary of missions, who briefly offered his candidature as Burwash's only rival for the vacant chancellorship in November 1887.[34] To Sutherland the time was right to create one strong national Methodist university, with its own affiliated colleges and schools, rather than accept federation with a "godless" university. The alternative to locating such a university "amid the temptations and dangers of a great city" was simple: it could either remain in Cobourg, but with improved facilities, or possibly be moved to Hamilton, that great centre of Methodist patronage, or even Ottawa, the nation's capital. A strong, independent Methodist university would provide "a bond of union to the Connexion, the strength and value of which can hardly be overstated." Moreover, Sutherland warned, in a time of intellectual unrest and religious scepticism, co-operation with a secular university was dangerous. By carrying out Methodism's traditional mission "to spread Scriptural holiness throughout the land," an independent Methodist university would be able to act as "an immovable breakwater against the floods of Agnosticism and Infidelity which threaten to overflow the land."

Burwash and the defendants of federation had extolled the opportunities that that would be provided for denominational co-operation as various church affiliated colleges gathered around the nucleus of a state university. Sutherland did concede that there were certain matters in which the different denominations might advantageously co-operate, such as the printing and circulation of the Bible, and the promotion of temperance and the public observance of the Lord's day. But he was not at all convinced that "there are as good reasons for co-operating in the work of higher education by uniting to sustain a common secular university." The real question in his mind was: could the different denominations provide better service in the cause of higher education by uniting in the support of a single state institution, or would they be more effective if they maintained several autonomous universities in various parts of the country and remained in charge of their own curriculum?[35]

Many of Victoria's alumni shared his fear that by entering federation the college would soon lose its distinctive nature as an arts college and become a theological faculty of the University of Toronto, as some of that institution's officials openly preferred.[36] The town council of Cobourg, on the other hand, saw the proposed departure of the college as one more step in the town's economic decline from its former promising position.[37] Both groups rallied to the support of independence. Finally, though less openly expressed, there had remained also a strong voluntarist sentiment among some of the members of the former Methodist Episcopal Church who had entered into the 1884 union. Historically they had had reservations about accepting public funds for a denominational institution like Victoria.[38]

In 1887 the decision was made to take no steps toward removing the college to Toronto until pledges had been secured for the full $450,000 estimated to be needed to cover the costs of relocation.[39] As the case for independence gathered momentum, opportunities to finance this rival scheme began to present themselves. In 1886 the Hamilton Board of Trade had already put out feelers exploring the conditions under which the college might consider establishing itself in that city. Two years later, not to be outbid, the town of Cobourg made an attractive offer of additional land and funding for the improvement and maintenance of college buildings.[40] In October 1888 an even more irresistible offer by Hart Massy of a quarter million for improved facilities in Cobourg made the case for independence practically uncontrovertible. In the end, however, William Gooderham's bequest of $230,000 in September 1889 on the condition that Victoria move to Toronto swung the financial pendulum in favour of federation. Nevertheless, though Gooderham had not stipulated moving as a condition, even he had favoured independence and had already picked a suitable site.[41]

Within Canadian Methodist circles, therefore, there had been strong support for an independent denominational university with improved resources to meet the new exigencies of university education. Indeed, at the time, for church colleges, federation with a secular university turned out to be the exception rather than the rule for dealing with the revolution in higher education. Principal George Grant of Queen's College had already rejected federation by April 1885, and in only three years managed to raise $375,000 within the Presbyterian denomination and the college community to meet the need for expansion.[42] The Toronto Baptist College and Trinity, the two other denominational arts colleges that had initially expressed a similar interest in federation, followed the same route.[43] Mount Allison University, Victoria's counterpart in the Maritimes, also briefly considered "consolidation" with Dalhousie University but soon opted to remain independent and began a successful fund-raising campaign to improve its science department.[44]

In short, the availability of surplus private wealth for the time being enabled denominational colleges to weather the revolution in university education. In 1906, when the Carnegie Foundation for the Advancement of Teaching prepared a list of totally non-denominational colleges as potential recipients of its philanthropy, it was able to come up with only fifty-one.[45] The decision by Nelles and Burwash to seek federation with a state university had therefore to be based on more than financial considerations.

THE CASE FOR FEDERATION

Federation in itself was not a new concept, for since the early 1840s the various administrators of Ontario's denominational colleges – Ryerson and Nelles for Victoria, Principals Liddell, Leitch, and Snodgrass for Queen's – had tried unsuccessfully to create a unified provincial university system giving all the colleges a share in public funding.[46] It was out of loyalty to this ideal that Samuel Nelles had lent his support to the university federation scheme of the 1880s, even though his own preference and that of his faculty (with the exception of Burwash) had been to remain in Cobourg.[47] As Nelles pointed out in his defence of federation at the 1885 Convocation, "My life's best energies have been put forth in her venerable halls, and I will bear no part in doing injury or dishonour to the institution. But I am a Canadian as well as a Methodist, and I am a lover of all sound learning; and finding, as I believe, all important interests likely to be promoted by this scheme of academic federation, I am inclined to give it my support."[48] However, when first Queen's, and then Trinity and McMaster, withdrew from the federation negotiations, Nelles's support for the project cooled considerably, and though he loyally accepted the decision of the 1886 General Conference to proceed with federation, he did so with great private reservations.[49]

Burwash, on the other hand, felt much less restrained by the realization that Victoria would be the only denominational arts college entering federation. Throughout the negotiations he had forged ahead, and at times Nelles had worried openly that his impetuous dean of theology seemed too willing to compromise the interests of the college.[50] For Burwash, federation was less a duty to be loyally but painfully followed than an opportunity to be grasped. Where Nelles looked to the past for motivation, his emphasis was optimistically on the future. Nelles's mind was that of the philosopher, subtle and always aware of the ambiguities inherent in every aspect of the human condition. Burwash's was that of the theologian and the Baconian, which once it had seized upon certain principles by means of the inductive method, never let them go or re-examined the process by which they had been reached. As a result, his defence of federation had a tenacity and dogmatism foreign to that of his older colleague. Those qualities probably account in part for the hostility he evoked among those of his Methodist colleagues committed to independence. However, taken in combination with the fortuitous death and legacy of an heir of the Gooderham and Worts distillery, they are also responsible for the eventual acceptance of federation and for its successful implementation during his long tenure as chancellor.

When William Mulock had first sounded out the denominational colleges concerning the possibilities of federation, Burwash's concept of the available possibilities had been hazy. However, as an educator who, thanks to the need for retraining, had first-hand knowledge of American universities, he was familiar with the recent changes that were revolutionizing university education. His mind quickly detected in these changes certain underlying principles to which he would adhere for the rest of his life.

During the negotiations, opportunities for implementing these principles began to present themselves and he seized them eagerly. Soon pragmatism and principle were indissolubly joined, and the result was a detailed blueprint of the nature and needs of the modern university, which in turn became his rationale for the proposed system of university federation in Ontario. The contours of the plan were clear to him by the summer of 1884, for by then he had hit upon the idea of dividing responsibilities between the colleges and the university, with "culture" or the humanities for the colleges and the "higher learning" or the sciences for the university. C.B. Sissons has argued in his examination of Ontario university federation that this device of dividing the labour between the colleges and the university on the basis of a rigid assignment of areas of instruction "distinguishes and has conserved federation at Toronto."[51] In practical terms, therefore, Burwash's contribution was no mean feat, even though the principles on which it was based would elude a later generation.[52]

He made the first formal presentation of his blueprint for the modern university before Victoria's Alumni in May 1885. Burwash's tone was optimistic, progressive, and clearly in agreement with the recent changes that were revolutionizing university education. As a former professor of natural science, he had watched with interest "the entrance into modern education of the vast circle of the physical natural and political sciences." On more than one occasion he had expressed his pride in the fact that under Eugene Haanel, his successor in the chair of natural science, Victoria had in 1877 opened the first building in Ontario to be entirely devoted to science, Faraday Hall. Now in his 1885 address, with a characteristic opportunistic reading of history to the advantage of Methodism, he placed Victoria College in the vanguard of progress. As he reminded his audience, "it was the impetus given by Faraday Hall that moved the entire university work of Ontario off the old lines forever." Calling on his familiarity with the educational scene in Europe as well as America, he proceeded to explain the effect of the explosion of the sciences on the university curriculum.

In the past, he pointed out, the goal of university instruction had simply been "the production of educated men, men of culture, intellectual, moral and social," a task that had been performed adequately by Ontario's various colleges with their classical curriculum and limited budgets. With the recent expansion of scientific knowledge, however, this tranquil state of affairs had come to an abrupt end. A second objective had now become part of university education, "the promotion of higher learning and the advancement and diffusion of science." This entailed specialization and expansion of the university curriculum, making the earlier system of competing colleges obsolete and inefficient. Unity, not diversity, was the proper approach to this new state of affairs.

Closely linked to this call for centralization was an appeal to national sentiment. Adversely comparing Canada's limited resources in higher education to those of the United States, he drew an optimistic picture of the stature and size of the institution that would be created through federation. Its benefits to the nation would be immeasurable. University education would now serve the interests of the common man in a totally unprecedented manner since its studies bore directly upon every aspect of commerce, industry, and domestic life. Elitism would finally place its services at the disposal of the nation: "The university henceforth will not merely send forth learned clergymen and lawyers, cultured and skilled in the beauties of Latin prose, but it will send among you men brimfull of knowledge which will help every worker in all the land, in every sphere of daily toil."[53] All these themes – utilitarianism, nationalism, the benefits of centralization, and an optimistic attitude towards change would recur often in his later defences of federation.

Whereas the opponents of federation were of the opinion that Methodism could best meet the needs of the nation by maintaining an independent university, Burwash urged co-operation with the state. By combining the resources of church and state, federation in his view would allow Methodists to provide higher education "more efficiently, more economically, and with a wider influence for good, both to our country and to ourselves, than any other scheme."[54] "If God has given the Methodist Church a million to spend as His steward, is an independent University the best that can be made of it?" he asked in November 1887 when support for independence was beginning to gain momentum. His answer had been "If with that million we can bless the whole country as well as ourselves, should we not do so? Is there not a nobler way than to use our means merely for denominational aggrandizement?"[55]

To those who objected that centralization limited the usefulness and influence of higher education, he scoffed that all that could be saved by the distribution of colleges was a little railway fare and a few hours of travel, while "both economy and efficiency may be promoted by centralization."[56] In 1889 a representative of the Victoria Alumni Association, James Allen, published the results of a private fact-finding tour to leading American universities. In it he concluded that the much vaunted revolution in university education was greatly exaggerated and that in times of change it was best to proceed with caution.[57] Burwash's scorn at such conservatism was unmistakable. To call a halt and not to take part in change would soon reduce Victoria to the sphere of a "country college," to cheap mediocrity in "a little town." Such a position, he was convinced, the Methodist Church would never consent to occupy.[58]

In this uncritical acceptance of change and his utilitarian emphasis, Burwash expressed the attitude of many late Victorians. In *The Transformation of Intellectual Life in Victorian England*, T.W. Heyck describes a very similar approach by British Whigs, Liberals, Utilitarians, and Dissenters as they attempted to make their country's ancient universities more responsive to the needs of a modern industrial nation and, in particular, to the middle class.[59] Some of the themes Heyck has detected weaving through the forces of change in intellectual life – specialization, professionalization, and the need for the division of labour – also figure prominently in Burwash's advocacy of university federation. However, under his hand they underwent a peculiar change, for he appeared determined to preserve most of the old while at the same time accepting the new.

He would achieve this goal through the division of labour between the subjects taught at the university and the colleges. Accordingly, the principles on which this division had been based formed Burwash's main defence of federation to the Methodist constituency. His exposition rested on a distinction between "learning" and "culture." Learning consisted of the dissemination of technical, industrial, and commercial expertise. Of direct benefit to the nation, it allowed the country to make the most of its natural resources and acquire a leading position in the world economy. This part of the university curriculum, comprising the sciences and professional training, was essentially secular, having a "bread and butter basis" and an intellectual rather than a moral aim. For these reasons learning belonged to the university and was to be financed by the public purse.[60] At the same time this designation of "learning" as secular also happened to meet the scruples of those members of the former Methodist Episcopal Church who had objected to public financing for a denominational institution.

Though this new funding arrangement neatly took care of the changes introduced by the revolution in higher education, Burwash also managed to retain what he considered best in the classical curriculum, namely, its goal of cultural formation. "Culture," which he defined basically in moral terms as including "high ideals of right, of honour, of beautiful sympathies and affections," was to be the special concern of the denominational college.[61] Since moral formation was the task of the church, the colleges would continue to be church-funded and would represent the various denominations of the Christian religion. It was true that in this scheme the existing arts college of the University of Toronto, University College (and until 1905 the only arts college besides Victoria in federation), was something of an anomaly. Hence Burwash did concede later that a state college might be of use "to provide for a large part of the population which cannot support church colleges, as well as set a common standard of excellence below which no college can afford to fall."[62] In theory, however, the college was under the fostering care of the church and its task was formidable: "To mould and perfect the man. To form his intellect, his entire fashion of thinking and expressing his thought, giving him not only the best material but also the best form. This implies fulness, strength and beauty of intellectual life.[63]

A college education could be summed up in three words: "breadth, depth and culture."[64] Burwash considered the ideal subjects in the curriculum for achieving these goals to be the humanities, specifically literature and languages. For this concept, like the rest of his educational philosophy, he was heavily indebted to the writings of Matthew Arnold. Arnold's distinction between the goals of the university and the college now became the means by which Burwash tried to assure recalcitrant Methodists that under federation the denomination would be able to continue its traditional involvement in higher education. At the same time, by linking itself to the publicly funded university and by its physical presence on the campus of the University of Toronto, Victoria College would ensure that the university was Christian in character and that the nation's leaders in a new age of technical and scientific progress were men of culture and high moral standards.

Ideally, Victoria would be one of several denominational colleges clustered around the nucleus of the university, each imparting to the university its special ethic and religious flavour.[65] When in 1890 only two theological colleges, the Presbyterian Knox College and Anglican Wycliffe College, entered federation along with Victoria, Burwash saw no need to alter his vision of the role of the arts college or of the national scope of the university. In his estimation, taking into account that the Roman Catholic St Michael's College had remained in affiliation, two-thirds of the province's population were still represented in the University of Toronto. Accordingly, with his central Canadian bias, he considered that the university might claim itself "to be national in spirit as well as constitution."[66] Ever optimistic, but with little charity concerning the decision of Queen's, Trinity, and McMaster to remain independent, he assured his fellow Methodists that general acceptance of federation was inevitable and that their fears that Victoria would lose her Christian character were totally unjustified.

This visionary optimism enabled him to continue in the face of overwhelming opposition. The years that preceded Victoria's move to Toronto were not an easy introduction to his new position as chancellor. They were marked not only by public controversy but also by private tragedy. In the space of one week in June 1889, he and his wife, Margaret Proctor, lost four children to black diphtheria: twin sons aged five, an eight-year-old son, and their only daughter, aged ten. The grief of the parents was immense, and the loss marked Mrs Burwash for the rest of her life.[67] However, Burwash's public response was characteristic: without comment, he submitted the last of a series of articles on John Wesley's doctrine of Christian perfection to the *Canadian Methodist Quarterly*, and he published yet another pamphlet defending university federation as more efficient, more economical, and "with a wider influence for good both to our country and to ourselves, than any other scheme."[68] This blending of Methodist spirituality with a confident acceptance of educational reform would also be his approach to implementing the scheme he had so ardently defended, once the college took up its new site on the University of Toronto campus in 1892.

PRINCIPLE BECOMES PRACTICE: THE NEW VICTORIA UNDER FEDERATION

Though Victoria's new academic building in Toronto was not yet completely finished and furnished, it was occupied in October 1892 and formally opened by the Lieutenant-Governor; with addresses by Albert Carman and Prof. Goldwin Smith, and the welcome presentation of a cheque for forty thousand dollars by Hart Massey.[69] The latter had made his peace with the new arrangement and, thanks to the generosity of the Massey family, first Hart, and later his children Lillian, Walter, and Chester, Victoria College in its new location was able to present itself before the nation as an example of sound Methodist financial responsibility.[70]

Completed at the cost of $212,000, the building had been designed by an old student of academy days, W.G. Storm, RCA, with suggestions from Burwash, especially on those aspects of symbolic significance.[71] These were readily evident. Above the main door and bearing the text "The Truth Shall Make You Free," the head of Plato was represented in stained glass, with a motto from the fifth book of Plato's *Laws*, "Truth is the beginning of every good to the gods and to mankind." The modern period was represented by a depiction of the man who had enabled truth to break through by his inductive method, Francis Bacon, captioned by his misquotation from Aristotle, "Nature shows herself best in her smallest works."[72]

On the second floor, in four windows in the apse of the chapel, it was even more apparent that the new Victoria did not represent a break with the past. In the first window John Milton with the line to "assert eternal providence and justify the ways of God to men" reminded students of the moral purpose of literature. Next to Milton John Wesley's final words, "The best of all is God is with us," testified to the experimental nature of religion. To the right of Wesley, Martin Luther with his famous line at the Diet of Worms pointed to the duty of conscience and the triumph of freedom in religious thought. And, in the final window, Isaac Newton, confident yet humble in his pursuit of truth, repeated the favourite line of a generation of Baconians, "The great ocean of truth lay all before me undiscovered."

However, though the thought of Plato, Bacon, and Newton had been acknowledged in stained glass in the new academic building, their study would take place elsewhere. The inductive method would continue to be used at Victoria but only in theology, for the sciences as well as philosophy were now taught in the university. By the arrangements of the 1887 Federation Act, half the traditional college curriculum had been handed over to the public university. This had been the cause of no little concern to the critics of federation, and the onus would be on Burwash to demonstrate that this loss would not in any way weaken the religious faith of Victoria's students.

Burwash's own attitude to the departure of the sciences and philosophy from the college curriculum reflected his appreciation of the impact of historical development. His defence of federation had not come to a stop once the college was moved to Toronto, for he believed that the denomination needed to be constantly reminded of its duties to higher education. Whereas in the past he had often explained why the sciences and philosophy properly belonged to the university, during a fund-raising address in 1900 he also clarified why they should not be taught in a church-supported college. It was the triumph of the Baconian method which had finally allowed the sciences to be taught (and funded) in their proper sphere, a state university. In Burwash's words, "it would be a misfortune if the Church undertook to teach universal science bound hand and foot in the claims of dogmatic preconceptions. An absolutely infallible church can logically make such a claim, Protestant Christianity cannot. She must permit each great truth to speak for itself, and to unfold itself freely to the mind of man. She must permit the inductive method everywhere to prevail." Thus in the university "philosophy, biology and cosmogony must yield to no theological bias, and its political economy to no political necessity."[73]

However, practice did not always follow principle. It was rumoured that one of the University of Toronto's most gifted chemistry professors, Lash Miller, of Unitarian persuasion, found his opportunity for advancement blocked by Victoria's chancellor, who objected to his "atheism."[74] The teaching of philosophy by the university also soon became a cause for concern to both Burwash and General Superintendent Albert Carman. The one issue on which the two were in prefect harmony during the famous 1910 Conference was that in the philosophy program of the University of Toronto there appeared to be "a distinct tendency to render the conception of personality less definite, thus weakening the foundations both of morals and religion."[75]

Though theory and practice might not always agree, as a Baconian, Burwash applauded the fact that the sciences and philosophy had been emancipated from the tutelage of the church. Nevertheless, the new division of labour between the university and the colleges was also a tacit recognition that along with the revolution in university education the old harmony between natural and revealed knowledge had been irrevocably lost.[76] To maintain that balance had been one of the aims of the college curriculum, once explained by Egerton Ryerson as "intended to maintain such a proportion between the different branches of literature and science as to form a proper symmetry and balance of character."[77] That same symmetry had been captured in architecture in the Greek revival style of Victoria's academic buildling, which now stood abandoned in Cobourg.

The new structure that had replaced it in Toronto, with its turrets and the impregnability of late-Victorian Romanesque was evocative more of a fortress or a church than a classical hall of learning. There may have been some truth to the remark by a student of one of the university's other colleges that to enter Victoria College made him feel he had walked into a church.[78] With half the university curriculum no longer available to form the student's "proper symmetry and balance of character," the moral task of the college had become awesome and not unlike that of the church.

By dividing the curriculum into "learning" and "culture" Burwash had openly recognized that the responsibility for moral formation had ceased to be shared between "the different branches of literature and the sciences" and had devolved entirely on the humanities, to be taught by the denominational college. Under this new dispensation the burden of the church in higher education had increased, not decreased, as the critics of federation had predicted. Baconianism precluded a devout and inquiring mind that trusted in the harmony and ultimate unity of all truth. The task of the church-supported college, therefore, was to ensure that the nation's intelligentsia were not simply experts in their field, but were above all men and women of culture and integrity who had, to use Burwash's phrase, "reached the true plane of higher spiritual life."[79]

Influenced by Matthew Arnold, Burwash had seized on the point that "spiritual development is promoted by literary rather than by scientific studies."[80] Accordingly, in an age of university options, there were two compulsory subjects: English literature and a foreign language.[81] Both, as Egerton Ryerson had pointed out in 1842, were of recent addition to the classical curriculum.[82] But with the fragmentation of that curriculum, their importance became formidable.

The personal element in literature held special value in the task of moral and spiritual formation. As Burwash explained, "the world's greatest and best men have stamped their personality on the literature which they left behind them. And the young secure the richest intellectual treasures and at the same time the most perfect intellectual form from converse with the world's best literature."[83] Whereas Samuel Nelles in the midst of a moral philosophy class had been able to transport his students with recitations of Wordsworth and Robert Burns, poetry and literature did not have any noticeable place in Burwash's own creative expression.[84] He did confess to a liking for Shakespeare,

Tennyson, and Gray (though they were only secondary to the Bible), but it was really the moral lessons of literature that captured his interest and on occasion led to sermonic addresses with such didactic titles as "The Use and Abuse of Books."[85]

Sharing a well-known Methodist prejudice that the reading of novels was liable to create "an utter moral and spiritual wreck," he was of the opinion that a book could only be evaluated by "the greatness of the Spirit which embodies it." As he said to one audience in 1907, "fifty years of a Tennyson spent in England in the glorious Victorian era may represent almost all that is best and highest in human life and so be a perfect mine of spiritual riches."[86] This happened also to be the sentiment of Alfred Reynar, Victoria's professor of English since 1868, though not of all the college's students.[87] By the first decade of the twentieth century, some of these, contrary to the wishes of the administration, began to avail themselves of an unintended benefit of federation by seeking a more contemporary interpretation of literature at the secular University College.[88]

Literature was not the only available avenue, however, for moral formation. Burwash never grew tired of insisting that the college was only one component of a much larger educational program that began with infancy and comprised both "culture" and "learning." Whereas the elementary and intermediate school and the university were primarily concerned with learning, or "working knowledge," the kindergarten and the college represented the first and crowning stages of the individual's cultural formation:[89] "If these [church-controlled] colleges are anything, they should be the homes, the nurseries of the highest Christian life, the inner sanctuary of religion, as well as of high intellectual life."[90] Building directly on the moral formation provided by the family and the church, the college would, therefore, act as a transition, a rite of passage from childhood to the responsibilities of adult life.

The model for this instrument of Christian nurture was not difficult to find and had already been in existence since the 1850s, when Samuel Nelles had begun to change the old school of mental discipline into the new Christian college.[91] However, under Burwash, the Yale model was not, as appeared to be the case in the United States, a transitional stage. Thanks to federation with its distinction between the college and the university, this model became a vital and permanent component of the new university. The familiar elements were easily visible: exhortative and inspirational annual convocation addresses, an even larger assortment of student activities than had been available in Cobourg, and the example provided by godly professors.

Burwash had set the tone with his first convocation address as chancellor in May 1888. Paying tribute to his predecessor, he had compared

Nelles's recent death to that of "the aged father whom children remember as all their life-long filling the old arm-chair and offering up the morning devotion."[92] It was a chair that for the next twenty-five years Burwash would fill with ease in a wide variety of ways: responding to students' letters with fatherly advice, on occasion even acting as matchmaker, delivering annual introductory lectures to first-year students on methods of studying, personally finding suitable student accommodation, and quietly but persistently eradicating all vestiges of "the smoking habit" from the college.[93]

Students appeared to respond to this moral earnestness in a fashion not unlike that of his Belleville congregation during his early ministry. A few chose to attend college elsewhere, but generally they tried to live up to his expectations of "moral manliness' and "true womanhood," at least in his presence, and then filled their time according to their own inclinations and the opportunities available for social interaction.[94] Of the latter, as might be expected in a college that prided itself as a community of Christian nurture, there was no lack. The student journal, *Acta Victoriana*, assuming the Chancellor's paternal tone, periodically admonished, "We have multiplied social functions and college organizations till our time is spent, a little here, a little there – anywhere except in the lecture room or study."[95]

If the pages of *Acta* are any indication, students generally had little difficulty in adopting the tone and ideals of their chancellor, and uncritically repeated many of his favourite themes. Thus, a student at Victoria benefited from "the society of good people – people of clear heads and pure hearts and high ideals" and was reminded that "the qualities of leadership that are the special gift of some men are often best developed in college life."[96] Another writer showed she had understood well the purpose of the college curriculum by concluding that the ideal of Victoria was not "the decorative, the marketable ... but the creative."[97]

The sense of community in a Christian college was also fostered in a more tangible way by the college residence. In Toronto, unlike Cobourg, lodgings in a morally safe environment were not always readily available. In 1888 Burwash had had the opportunity to visit the campuses of a number of American state universities. Through the *Christian Guardian* he had submitted an enthusiastic account of the influence of the college residence in refining "the boisterous rudeness which arises from the constant association together of boys whose physical strength is every day increasing."[98] It was not until 1913 that he was able to provide a residence for Victoria's male students.[99] The college's female students, however, who had been growing in numbers since they were first admitted in 1878, had been a matter of more immediate concern. In 1902 they had been provided with a women's residence, Annesley Hall, again funded by the Masseys and furnished and equipped by the Barbara Heck Association, presided over by Margaret Proctor Burwash.[100]

Of all the vital influences that together made up the Christian college, none was as important as the college faculty. Sheldon Rothblatt has drawn attention to the model that Thomas Arnold, the famous headmaster of Rugby, provided to a generation of early Victorian teachers who made loyalty to themselves rather than the imposition of impersonal rules the force behind college instruction.[101] By the time of university federation, this ideal of the professor as moral influence, had begun to yield, under pressure from Oxbridge dons, to the image of the professional academic researcher.[102] Under Burwash, however, at Victoria the role of the godly professor became indispensable.

Under the original classical curriculum, the college professor had been able to demonstrate the perfect harmony between natural and revealed knowledge and thus to lead the mind of the student into direct contact with the works of God. Under federation, however, the sciences were taught in the university, and the course in Christian Evidences, whose obsolescence Burwash had already recognized as a young minister, was quietly dropped and replaced by a college course in "ethics and theistic philosophy." Where the curriculum no longer served in its entirety to achieve the goal of Christian nurture, the godly professor now stepped in to fill the lacuna. In the intimacy of the college classroom he instructed both through moral influence and through intellectual discipline. Classes, therefore, were to be small: "A college professor who sits down with a class of twenty very soon knows each one intimately, understands fully his intellectual, moral and social peculiarities and brings upon him the power of his own personality. His high ideals of scholarship, his love of truth as coming from and revealing the great Father of our spirits, all this he imparts to the little circle around him."[103] To do his work properly, the professor was not merely to excel in scholarship, but even more, he had to represent "the very highest type of manhood."

Accordingly, when some of the members of Victoria's Board of Regents would contrast the faculty's light student load to that at University College or tried to impose the efficiency of business practices upon the college, Burwash was quick to remind them of the high moral responsibilities placed upon the Christian college professor.[104] University College's faculty, in contrast, was little more than a branch of the government "like other civil servants many of whom seem to be satisfied with rendering a minimum of service in a perfunctory way."[105] At University College, as well, the ominous spectre of specialization had in Burwash's opinion begun to supplant cultural formation as the goal of the college curriculum. To ensure that this goal continued to be met, Victoria's faculty had the additional burden of carefully guiding the student in the choice of electives. In practice, however, the work of both the student and the faculty adviser was considerably lightened by the fact that a wise administration had included the electives in the various course programs in an effort to counteract the harmful side-effects of the revolution in university education.[106]

Victoria's faculty appeared to have little difficulty in accepting the moral responsibilities of their profession. Eight of the ten who made the move to Toronto were the college's own graduates. Subsequent appointments continued to draw heavily on former students, although some of them, like George Blewett, appointed to the chair in ethics in 1906, had received considerably more graduate training than their older colleagues.[107] The latter were remarkable for their longevity, and by the first decades of the twentieth century investigations by Burwash (on the insistence of the Board of Regents) showed that the balance between saintliness and scholarship was not in all cases being maintained.[108] In the students' view the aging faculty came to form part of the Old Guard, a term applied also to the hierarchy of the Methodist Church, some of whom, like John Potts, secretary of the Educational Society, and Albert Carman, president of the Board of Regents, were actively involved in the college's administration. To E.J. Pratt, who described them in a lengthy twenty-five stanza poem, "The May Examinations," they seemed "a great array of doctors aged ... Reverend, hoary sages, Heaven-born to Educate."[109] And when in time they were eased into retirement or died, their colleagues memorialized them in terms that aptly summarized the ideal of the godly professor who "led rather than drove, perhaps suggested rather than taught, inspired more than educated."[110]

Nevertheless, as a result of the longevity of the faculty and by maintaining and intensifying Samuel Nelles's concept of the college as a Christian community, as well as by readjusting the curriculum, Burwash was able to maintain a continuity between the old Victoria of Cobourg days and the new college in Queen's Park. Not surprisingly, therefore, the earlier opposition to federation within Canadian Methodism disappeared. In 1906 in response to a royal commission investigation into the government and management of the University of Toronto, Victoria's Senate and its Alumni Association, which only sixteen years earlier had gone to such extreme lengths to halt a "visionary and erroneous" federation, were ready to acquiesce in the existing arrangement of university federation. In the words of the Senate, it "seems to us the best that has hitherto been devised for this country."[111]

There was an additional reason why the fears of the anti-federation-ists were in time allayed. For Burwash the practice and teaching of experimental Christianity remained a vital component of Victoria's program of Christian nurture.[112] This was promoted in a variety of ways: a Sunday afternoon Bible class, led by J.F. McLaughlin, profes-sor of New Testament, attendance at Toronto's various Methodist churches, and daily compulsory chapel services.[113] References by students to religious conversions in their correspondence with Burwash are frequent enough to suggest that this aspect of Methodist spirituality was maintained.[114]

It was especially the ideal of Christian perfection to which Burwash directed Victoria's students in his annual convocation addresses, and J.F. McLaughlin, writing in Burwash's *History of Victoria College*, has drawn attention to its prevalence in the religious life of the college in Toronto.[115] "You have by precept and practice inspired in our hearts the truths of the gospel, and have sanctified the truths by your godly example," a student address to Burwash had remarked when the college took up its new location in Toronto.[116] In 1910 an enthusiastic gradu-ate, describing in *Acta* the success of the recent three-day alumni con-ference where Burwash had spoken on Scriptural holiness, was even more explicit about the chancellor's role in directing the spiritual life of the college community: "Talk about Evangelism! Why for those three days the Chancellor himself was our 'Evangelist' and he could have had us all on our knees in penitence and consecration on the spot. We were in the grasp of the Spirit of Truth, and he could have led us whither-soever he would."[117]

The exposition of Christian perfection to Canadian Methodists had continued to concern Burwash, and from the three essays he had pub-lished in 1889 in the midst of family tragedy and the controversy over university federation, it can be seen that his interpretation was espe-cially applicable to higher education. In one of these essays he wrote that, though the experience of Christian perfection was never to be regarded as "a superseding of our intelligence by a religious python-ism," it did follow the "universal law, that the religious spirit is in *sym-pathetic harmony* with all truth, and especially with all moral and theo-logical truth." In his understanding, those scholars who had come to experience God's perfect love would "as a natural consequence more quickly, easily, perfectly and profoundly apprehend truth, and espe-cially all truth concerning God and duty than will the common man."[118] In one of his repeated efforts to describe the nature of the Christian col-lege, Burwash had defined it as "essentially a unity of individual men seeking a higher spiritual life."[119] This moral and spiritual elitism was also an attendant mark of Christian perfection, and thus the doctrine to him naturally found its home in the Christian college. In this emphasis he was not alone, for his colleague and friend, Alfred Reynar, professor of English, had also written a short study, "The Higher Life" in 1905.[120]

Like Burwash's revision of the college curriculum, the prominent place assigned to Christian perfection at Victoria indicates a continuity with the ideals and spirituality of the earlier period of revivalism known as the Second Great Awakening. Historians have noted the prevalence of perfectionism at Oberlin College in the 1830s under the presidency of Charles Finney, the prominent Congregationalist revivalist of the awakening.[121] Within American Methodism Timothy Smith has also detected a continuous strand of perfectionism from the 1830s to the end of the century.[122] Whereas Smith has seen a direct link between this doctrine and the social gospel movement, Burwash's understanding of Christian perfection was especially conducive to encouraging individual moral leadership, whether in private philanthropy or in intellectual life.

CHRISTIAN UNITY AND MORAL NATIONALISM

Though support for federation did increase, Burwash was at no time ever able to cease his defence of Victoria's decision to enter federation. First there had been those members of his own generation who had favoured independence; later he had to contend with certain members of a younger generation who considered the concept of church-supported colleges outmoded and favoured Christian instruction through university extension programs.[123] To one of these young critics he pointed out with pride in 1902 that not only was Victoria College reported to be "the centre of the strongest religious life in our Church today," but "men of other churches have said that it has lifted the whole tone and religious life of the University."[124] This reputed vitality of religious life at the University of Toronto was a cause of great satisfaction for Burwash and was never omitted in his annual reports to the Board of Regents and the Educational Society of the Methodist Church.[125] To him it was a vindication of a point he had repeatedly emphasized in the course of the federation debates, that Victoria's entry into federation would guarantee that "the Christian forces are planted to do their work within the University, and no longer stand as mere indirect forces from without."[126]

This prospect had been the main inspiration behind his vision of a national university, and it informed the moral nationalism that became a dominant note in his speeches and thought after federation. To understand that vision and place it in context, it is necessary to return briefly to his visit to Toronto in January 1881, when he first began to picture a national university in the provincial capital. Upon his return to Cobourg he had drafted, in addition to his letter to the *Globe*, a letter to the then minister of education, Adam Crooks.[127] Like his other letter, it had not been sent either, on Nelles's advice, although the latter subscribed unreservedly to its sentiments. In the drafted letter to Crooks, Burwash encouraged the creation of a national university comprising the province's denominational colleges, and argued forcefully that in the past these colleges had been excluded from government funding on the pretext of sectarianism. Such an accusation, he argued, was utterly unfounded: "The parties most deeply interested, the Methodist, Presbyterian and Evangelical Churchmen are all distinguished by a truly Catholic spirit and would be willing to make large concessions for the best welfare of the country and its educational interests."[128]

This ideal of an educational system based on a non-sectarian Christianity was not new. Egerton Ryerson's system of common schools for Upper Canada had similarly been rooted in a Christianity that stressed "the fundamental principles of Religion and Morality."[129] Nor was this ideal limited to Methodists. As Goldwin French has observed in a brief study, "The Evangelical Creed in Canada," Christians of evangelical background generally supported a public or national system of education based on Christian principles, with a limited provision for separate schools. This support included college as well as elementary education.[130] In the 1840s, for example, the Rev. Robert Alexander Fyfe, principal of the Canada Baptist College in Montreal (and, unlike Ryerson, a strict voluntarist) had subscribed to this view and had suggested "that a provincial university [would] be invaluable as a nation-building force."[131] Fyfe's fusion of national sentiment with the ideal of a Christian educational system had been shared by evangelicals of his generation. Their "incipient nationalism," French has noted, "expressed as a common feeling of identification with Canada ... arose naturally out of the experience of the churches in creating acceptable syntheses from imported and local materials."[132]

Efforts to create a system of higher education based on Christian principles had appeared to come to an end in 1867. By the terms of the British North America Act education was assigned to the provinces, and in 1868 the Ontario legislature had ceased its annual government grant to denominational colleges. As a result, in a period of growing denominational awareness, the colleges were totally thrown back on their own constituencies for funding. At the same time the revolution in university education and the evolutionary teaching of Charles Darwin had begun to undermine seriously the harmony between reason and religion that had characterized the standard college curriculum in the public as well as denominational colleges. It could no longer be taken for granted that the university curriculum would act as a unifying factor, ensuring that the country's system of higher education continued to teach "the fundamental principles of Religion and Morality."

Far-reaching changes, therefore, separated the aspirations of an earlier generation of evangelicals from Burwash's concept of a national university described in his 1881 letter to Crooks. The need to create a public university that would be neither secular nor sectarian had become urgent, and Burwash had drawn Crooks's attention especially to the ability of a university to ensure the Christian nature of the country. "A National University need not be godless," he had pointed out. "It will not become so unless the nation becomes godless first. The National University of a Christian people must be permeated by the living power of religion. To secure this it must combine the learning and piety of all the great religious communities of the land."[133] Like his colleagues who had opted for independence, Burwash had been determined that the nation would not be "godless." Unlike them, however, he had looked back to the educational ideals of an earlier generation and had seen that the battle would not be won by encouraging denominational distinctiveness, but by co-operating with the various Christian churches.

He had not been the only one to take this approach. Samuel Nelles, too, was convinced that "the purely secular type of higher education must not, and cannot prevail in this land," and had warned, quoting Gladstone, "Let us beware of a Christianity of isolation."[134] Other participants in the federation debate had expressed a similar concern. At the annual convocation in 1884 Chancellor Edward Blake of the University of Toronto angrily retorted to charges of "godlessness" that the university was not "a sect of secularists," but consisted of "a Christian people belonging to the various denominations into which the Christian Church is divided in this country, believing this is the best practical plan of carrying out the great object of higher education in which we are concerned."[135]

Once federation was completed, Burwash would be equally zealous in defending the Christian character of the University of Toronto against charges of godlessness from members of his own denomination. These, like Albert Carman, tried to guard the orthodoxy of biblical teaching in the university's Department of Religious Knowledge as jealously as they did that of Victoria's Faculty of Theology.

The creation of this Department of Religious Knowledge at the University of Toronto in 1906 became a source of considerable satisfaction for Burwash. Some of his colleagues, most notably Carman and S.H.

Blake, an Anglican and an influential member of the university's Board of Governors, expressed their concern about the advanced biblical criticism allegedly taught in the new department, and maintained that the teaching of religion by the university clearly contravened the terms of the 1887 Federation Act. Burwash, however, was not averse to laying aside his Baconian principles when an opportunity to further the cause of religion presented itself. Thus, he insisted that in their courses in religious knowledge, students received "a thoroughly intelligent grasp of religious truth including the Bible ... and the great basal truths of Christianity held by all Christian Churches in common, in their relation to history, science and philosophy." Seeing the department as a venture in ecumenism, he lauded the opportunity now available for the professors of the various denominational colleges to co-operate "without any indication of sectarian strife."[136]

For Victoria's students too, the opportunities for such co-operation had increased dramatically as a result of federation. Principal Sheraton of Wycliffe conducted a Bible class open to all students. At University College they were able to attend a special class for Bible study leaders, while the YMCA, which had a tradition of interfaith co-operation, also sponsored Bible study courses. The University Settlement House, a common *University Hymn Book* compiled in 1912, and the Canadian Intercollegiate Missionary Alliance were further visible signs of the strength of the Christian religion in the "national univesity." And as the university went, so went the nation, for to Burwash "the university becomes to the nation the very fountainhead of its whole spiritual life."[137]

It would be the special task of the university's graduates to give shape to the nation's spiritual life. Not only, therefore, were Victoria's students exposed to the high ideals of Christian perfection and to a curriculum that promoted spiritual development, but through the pages of *Acta* the faculty also reminded them of the duties of Canadian citizenship. Succinctly summarized, these consisted of "clean life, devotion to duty, sound judgment, unselfish work."[138] As evidence that Victoria's graduates did take their responsibilities seriously and were a credit to their alma mater, *Acta* regularly published a review of the careers of the more noteworthy. In 1904 it was able to list four graduates in "Legislative Halls." The best known of these was Clifford Sifton, minister of the interior, whose aggressive immigration policy among eastern Europeans of non-Anglo-Saxon background was already making the burden of natural cultural and spiritual formation more difficult.[139]

Federation and the move to Toronto had opened up a number of new channels for Methodists to involve themselves in matters of national and provincial concern. The importance of Victoria's entry into federa-

tion in government eyes had already been underscored by the presence
of Prime Minister John A. Macdonald, the provincial Premier, the minister of education, and the chancellor and vice-chancellor of the University of Toronto at the 1886 General Conference debates.[140] Though in
principle Burwash was as opposed to "sectarianism" in politics as he
was in religion, this had not prevented him from making clear from the
beginning of the federation movement his own sympathies towards the
province's Liberal government, as well as his uncritical adulation of
Vice-Chancellor William Mulock. The latter's "broad patriotic appeal"
to establish a national university had struck a highly responsive chord
in Burwash.[141] Equally firm was his respect for Sir Wilfrid Laurier, the
Liberal Prime Minister after 1896. On occasion he could be counted on
to use his influence with "Sir Wilfrid" to further the careers of Methodists, including William Kerr, KC, Victoria's litigious vice-chancellor during the federation controversy.[142] In addition, as chancellor of one of
the University of Toronto's colleges, he was often called upon to lend
his support to public causes of a moral nature, such as the temperance
movement, the Canadian Peace and Arbitration Society, the Lord's
Day Alliance, the fight against juvenile delinquency, and women's
suffrage.[143]

His own favourite area of moral reform however, was national
education. In keeping with many of his contemporaries, Burwash held
the view that national character could be classified according to type.[144]
This type he considered to be determined by education. Thus whereas
the Scottish educational system emphasized the importance of the common people, the English was "elitist," and the American "patriotic."
Canadians, he suggested, ought to make their type of education "spiritual." In an address to the Dominion Educational Society in Winnipeg
in 1904, he drew attention to the great part to be played by education in
national unification. Regretting that education was "still" not national,
but in the hands of the provinces, he believed that the way to unity lay
in making this spiritual type the distinguishing feature of Canadian
education. Success depended entirely on the moral character of the
teacher: "I care not whether he be Catholic or Protestant, Episcopal or
Independent or Baptist, Methodist or Presbyterian, provided he is a
high minded, reverent Christian – one who by his example, his government and his teaching keeps before his pupils the fundamental principles of piety and righteousness."[145] Though a Faculty of Education
was only formally established at the University of Toronto (and at
Queen's) three years later in 1907, the presence of Victoria College in
the "national university" since 1892 was already a visible promise for
Burwash that the country's educational system would indeed be of the
"spiritual" type.

Equally important in shaping national character was the influence of literature. In 1864, E.H. Dewart, Burwash's partner in the federation debates, had published a collection of Canadian verse and deplored the country's "universal absence of interest and faith in all indigenous literary productions."[146] By 1907 this state of affairs had apparently been sufficiently rectified for Burwash as a member of the Royal Society of Canada to read a paper on the question "Our Canadian Literature. Has it reached such a position that it can be introduced into our Schools and Colleges as a subject of study?" Using the moral and aesthetic criteria that he had applied to the study of literature at Victoria, he replied in the affirmative. Never one to pass by an educational opportunity, he concluded his survey with an admonition to the young writer "so to weave the very form of his best thought, the very words in which it has been embodied, into the higher spiritual life and culture of a nation that they will go on repeating it from generation to generation in the self-same words in which it was born from his own soul. It is like the force of gravitation, it works forever." Thus Canadian literature was brought into the mainstream of education and allowed to assume its "prophetic mantle of weighty responsibility."[147]

Alexander Sutherland had therefore been proved wrong when he predicted in 1885 that within ten years Methodism would disappear "as a distinct factor in the work of higher education." What had separated him from Burwash at that time had been more than his desire that Victoria College remain an independent institution. Where the two had differed was in their understanding of the nature of Methodism. For Sutherland Methodists had been raised up to do a special work, "to spread Scriptural holiness throughout the land," and this task could best be done "as a separate ecclesiastical organization."[148] For Burwash – educator, empiricist scientist, and Methodist theologian – Methodism was not the church, nor was it meant to be only "a distinct factor in higher education." Rather, by its experimental nature, Methodism was itself an educational force. For this reason he had seized upon higher education as an essential instrument in evangelization.

And so, when the opportunity suddenly presented itself for Methodists to enter into a more intimate relationship with the provincial university, Burwash did not hesitate. As a Baconian, his mind cut through the complexities of federation and simplified them to a few principles. These principles had admirably linked the optimism and uncritical acceptance of change of the late-Victorian period to the earlier ideal of evangelicals in order to establish a provincial system of higher education on a Christian basis. Thus, in an age of growing Canadian nationalism he welcomed the opportunity of federation as a means whereby Methodism might transmit its moral values to the future leaders of the country. In fact, as a result of university federation, "Methodist" had become linked to "Canadian" in Burwash's mind. On one occasion in 1896 when the possibilities provided by university federation appeared unlimited, he let slip, "We certainly have the elements from which the several college types might be evolved, an English type from Trinity or Wycliffe, a Scottish type from Knox or Queen's, a puritanical type from McMaster, a Canadian type which we shall not attempt to explain from Victoria."[149] Such identification was a prize he would not easily relinquish but would attempt to seal with church union in Canada.

CHAPTER SIX

Evangelical Statesman: Doctrine, History, and the Postmillennialism of Church Union

"A crisis is upon us which seems to us to demand that we should unite our forces for the one object of promoting the Kingdom of Christ in this land which God has given us: and in this effort we desire nothing more earnestly than the sympathy, prayers, and help of our brethren, both Methodist, Presbyterian and Congregational, in the Old Land." With these words, Nathanael Burwash broached to the Methodist Ecumenical Conference assembled in Toronto in 1911 the admittedly delicate subject of a proposed organic union of the Canadian Methodist, Presbyterian, and Congregational churches.[1] Only seventy-two years earlier, John Wesley's followers in primitive chapels scattered through the frontier settlements of central and eastern Canada had joined with fellow societies in Great Britain, Ireland, and the United States to celebrate the first centenary of Methodism. Now in 1911, after a period of steady and at times spectacular growth as one great Methodist Church of Canada with a membership of 340,091 and far-flung missions in West China and Japan, Canadian Methodists were expressing the wish to end their historic identity as a denomination.

To the assembled delegates, Canadian Methodism, far from appearing to be in a crisis, gave every appearance of having fallen upon good times. From the moment of their arrival in Toronto every effort had been made to impress them: a lavish brochure extolling the cultural attractions of their host city, a specially staged autumn convocation of Victoria College federated with the University of Toronto, "the largest university of the British Empire," and finally, a statistical survey of the collective institutional wealth of Toronto Methodism, presented in the evocative surroundings of Metropolitan Methodist Church by William Briggs, steward of the Methodist Book Room and Publishing House.[2]

But as they soon came to know, all this was in danger of disappearing. "A crisis is upon us," Nathanael Burwash, the seventy-two year old chancellor of Victoria College, solemnly informed them. During the past ten years Canada's population had jumped from five to eight million, as waves of immigrants entered the country from Europe, Asia, and the United States. These had presented the Canadian churches with a new phenomenon, for unlike earlier immigrants, "two thirds or three fourths of the population pouring in upon us are Christless, and if our country is to remain vitally Christian, we must bring upon them the saving power of the gospel." Nor could Canadians dare retrench their work in the foreign field in order to meet their commitments at home. Already Chinese, Japanese, and Indian immigrants were entering Canada, and a brisk international trade with their home countries was only a matter of time. The question was "Shall we meet them as Christian brothers or as despised heathen?"[3]

Fuel was added to the fire by Burwash's lay colleague, Newton Wesley Rowell. Recently returned from the World Missionary Conference in Edinburgh, Rowell chose to speak on the topic "interdenominational co-operation." Though the past ten years had shown remarkable advances in the foreign mission field, the home situation had deteriorated and church membership had, in fact, recently begun to decline. "Why is it," the assembled delegates were asked, "that leadership in great movements of social and moral reform, which of right belongs to the church, has in many cases passed into other hands?" Could it not be because the church was simply not using its ministry effectively and expending far too much time keeping the machinery of its organizations running, rather than concentrating on the true task of preaching "the living Christ?"[4]

Both Rowell and Burwash argued, that the issue at stake was the continuation of Canada as a Christian nation, and in these new times denominational competition could simply no longer be afforded. However, far from despairing over the difficulties presented by modern life, Canadian Methodists offered a new solution, church union. The underlying tone, therefore, was one of confident optimism, eloquently captured by the co-superintendent of the Methodist Church in Canada, S.D. Chown, in a stirring address, "Adaptation of the Church to the Needs of Modern Life."[5]

Did such adaptation in the form of church union mean the abandonment of John Wesley's teachings in Canada? Rowell had prefaced his address with Wesley's own call to Christian brotherhood, quoting the words "I desire to form a league, offensive and defensive with every soldier of Jesus Christ" and "If thy heart be as my heart, give me thy hand." Burwash expressed his church's desire to retain "our old filial relations" with Methodism after union and also assured the delegates that the doctrinal statement of proposed union conformed to all the essentials of John Wesley's experiential Christianity. Even more explicit on this point was another Canadian minister, J.S. Ross of Guelph, who only a year before had been locked in mortal combat with Victoria's chancellor over the teaching of the higher criticism. As Ross reminded delegates at the Ecumenical Conference, the nineteen articles drawn up to summarize the belief of the three negotiating churches were awaiting perusal in one of the lecture rooms of Metropolitan Methodist Church. He would be greatly surprised if anyone examining them could find that one vital Methodist belief had been omitted, for "it is all there in black and white in the basis of union."[6]

Whereas some of the delegates, primarily from colonial countries, were indeed sympathetic to Canadian Methodism's plight and solution, those from the older seats of Methodism, Great Britain and the United States, expressed grave reservations. Rather than act precipitately and "cut the connection with Methodism's glorious activity and become a sort of nondescript religious community," as one British Wesleyan termed it, Canadian Methodists were reminded of their traditional mission to spread Scriptural holiness through the nation and not be overly obsessed with "the problems of the day." The true Methodist response to the difficulties caused by immigration and urbanization lay not in the "adaptation of the church to the needs of modern life," but in prohibition, a "great Methodist revival," and a more concerted effort to draw the poor into the church.[7]

By 1911 there was little the members of the Ecumenical Methodist Conference could do to prevent the departure of their Canadian brethren. The previous year the 1910 Quadrennial Conference at Victoria had voted 220 to 35 to proceed with union.[8] A Basis of Union, drawn up by a joint committee of the Congregational, Presbyterian, and Methodist Churches had been approved at that time by the General Conference and submitted in 1911 to the eleven annual conferences, where all but the Newfoundland Conference had endorsed it.[9] By the time of the Ecumenical Methodist Conference in October 1911 there remained only the vote of the general Methodist membership, in the summer of 1912.

Though the membership, too, voted overwhelmingly in favour of union, debates in the *Christian Guardian* in 1911 and the spring of 1912 did register voices of dissent as had been the case at the Ecumenical Methodist Conference.[10] Again Burwash was the official spokesman for union. Reiterating his arguments on the imperative need for union in order to facilitate evangelization at home and on the foreign mission field, he again insisted that all the essentials of Methodist belief were safeguarded in the new doctrinal statement of the Basis of Union. This time, however, unlike earlier suggestions in 1911 that Canadian

Methodists were abandoning their traditional doctrines, the criticism was more explicit. Two elderly colleagues, both senior to Burwash, Stephen Bond and W.S. Griffin, subjected the new doctrinal statement and Burwash's defence to a scathing review. Neither had had the benefit of a formal theological training at college, but both had acquired a thorough familiarity with the writings of Wesley, and comparing the new statement with their familiar doctrines, they found the former sadly wanting.[11] Griffin could not "resist the conviction that our own men who were a party to this legislation have ceased to be Methodists after the old orthodox style."[12] A third dissenting colleague, W. Jackson, remarked pointedly in a letter to the *Christian Guardian* that "if Methodists had a grip on their doctrines as intelligent and firm as was formerly the case, union on this Basis would not be dreamed of."[13]

While these critics were in a distinct minority, they received unexpected support from pro-unionists, as well as later from historians of church union. For example, the editor of the *Christian Guardian*, who strongly favoured union, reminded readers just before the membership vote on the Basis of Union that whereas in the past the church had emphasized doctrine, "today we emphasize *life*. The spirit of this age is intensely practical, and while it does not discredit dogma, it insists that applied ethics are of greater importance."[14]

Historians of church union agree that doctrine was without a doubt of little concern to those who negotiated the Basis of Union. C.E. Silcox, whose *Church Union in Canada*, published in 1933, is still the most detailed analysis of the movement, regretted that the new doctrinal statement revealed little sensitivity to the issues of the day.[15] Drawing on the conclusions of a 1923 study by a Presbyterian opponent to union, E. Lloyd Morrow, he agreed that the members of the subcommittee on doctrine did not appear to have overworked, for their work was completed speedily and aroused little controversy. Morrow's own research had already revealed that the Methodist contribution to the doctrinal statement was minor. As he demonstrated, the sources for the nineteen (later twenty) articles of the statement were exclusively Presbyterian, consisting of a brief statement of the Reformed faith prepared by the Assembly of the American Presbyterian Church North, and to a lesser extent a similar document, the Articles of the Faith, published by the English Presbyterian Church. At the same time, the articles contained "interjected parallelisms of Methodist doctrine which do not fuse." Morrow could only conclude that the church union movement was a "non-theological, non-doctrinal affair."[16]

Fifty years later, C.G. Lucas, examining the Methodist contribution to union, saw no reason to revise this evaluation. He pointed out that whereas Wesley had been greatly concerned about catholicity and the continuity of the apostolic church, his successors in early-twentieth-century Canada were parochial in outlook and chose to emphasize the Canadian nature of the three uniting churches. Worried by a decline in numbers, Methodists considered union primarily as a practical business arrangement.[17] In a more recent analysis of the doctrinal statement of the Basis of Union, N. Keith Clifford has again drawn attention to its indebtedness to the Reformed tradition, and in an earlier historiographical study of church union he summarized environment and a pattern of growing national consensus as the two factors essential for understanding the origins of the United Church.[18] Doctrine, one can only conclude, was of secondary importance to those who championed church union.

Against such an array of evidence, Burwash's own writings and actions appear strangely contradictory. A strong supporter of church union from the moment it was first proposed informally by the Presbyterians in 1902, he acted as the chairman of the Joint Committee's subcommittee on doctrine. After it had completed its deliberations in 1906, he tirelessly defended the new doctrinal statement before his Methodist colleagues as chairman of the Church Union Committee at the 1910 General Conference, as well as before the Methodist Ecumenical Conference and the readers of the *Christian Guardian*.[19] At the same time, he continued to guard jealously such traditional Methodist doctrines as the witness of the Spirit and Christian perfection. Both of these were reaffirmed by the 1910 General conference, and in the 1906 revision of the Methodist ritual the doctrine of infant depravity had been unequivocally retained. Even after the membership had endorsed church union and the realization of the new United Church only awaited Presbyterian approval, Burwash continued to preach, teach, and promote Methodist doctrine and to extoll the virtues of Canadian Methodism in historical studies and commemorative addresses.[20] He rarely made explicit reference to church union in his teaching and in these speaking engagements. Nevertheless, it is here that one finds the key to his repeated assertions that precisely by entering into union the Methodist Church in Canada was remaining true to its doctrinal heritage and dealing responsibly and effectively with the problems confronting Canadian Christians in the early twentieth century. In fact, unlike later critics, Nathanael Burwash saw doctrine to be the very basis of church union.

PLOTTING THE ROAD TO CHURCH UNIONS: THE LESSONS OF HISTORY

Unlike university federation, church union had required little of Burwash's time and energy. Nor after its acceptance by the general membership in 1912 did it lead to any change or emphasis in his theology and teaching. The reason was not that church union was unimportant – but simply that in Burwash's opinion the groundwork had already long been laid. In his public pronouncements advocating church union, Burwash might have cited the example of his own religious upbringing: his mother's instruction in the basic doctrines of the Christian faith through the use of the Westminster Assembly's Shorter Catechism, supplemented by his father's emphasis on the experiential nature of Methodism.[21] Moreover, in the 1840s there had been no denominational Sunday school at Baltimore, and young Burwash had attended a Union Sunday school, where a Presbyterian lay preacher had rounded out the boy's rudimentary knowledge of theology, again using the Shorter Catechism but carefully refraining from emphasizing the controversial Five Points of Calvinism.[22] Though Burwash refrained from drawing on his own personal experience for illustration, it does serve as a reminder that thanks to the religious revivalism and inadequate denominational facilities of the first half of the nineteenth century, the Methodist identity of a number who voted in 1912 to enter church union was still of relatively recent origin.

To Burwash, however, the roots of church union lay in the period after 1850, in that general transition in Canadian Methodism which he had begun to experience during his college days away from emotional revivalism to a quieter, more spiritual piety which could stand the test of reason. Students at Victoria, exposed to a non-sectarian curriculum based on broad Christian principles, had been instructed by Samuel Nelles in the ideals of "essential Christianity," defined once as "the minimum of ritual and sacerdotalism with the maximum of loyalty to Christ."[23] Catholicity" had been a frequent theme in Nelles's informal addresses, and in one such address in 1857 he had directed his students to cultivate "a Catholic spirit," that is, "a spirit of wide charity, of generous sympathy with all truth and beauty." Seventeen years old at the time, and devout and idealistic, young Burwash would not have been unaffected by Nelles's closing rhetorical question, "Identity of opinion or of form seems as far off as ever, if not farther, and may not be palatable: but what is to hinder universal love?"[24] John Wesley, however, despite his own similar call to Christian tolerance, had in practice been forced to devote considerable time to pointing out the errors of antinomianism and Calvinism. And while Samuel Nelles and his Presbyterian friend and colleague, Principal George Grant of Queen's College, shared a frustration with what Grant once termed "the weakness, the unbelief of mere traditionalism" which hid "the great truths of Revelation," neither lived to see the union of their churches.[25]

Burwash, however, was a generation younger. In his mind there existed one great difference between his own time and the days when Nelles and Grant had had to battle against overzealous "sectarian interference," or, even earlier, when John Wesley had taken on the Calvinists in theological debate.[26] As an ardent Baconian, Burwash was convinced that "the triumph of the scientific spirit" would finally make the union of the churches possible. In Canada this new attitude had already led to university federation, but federation was only a sign of things to come. Thus his colleague F.H. Wallace recalled how one day in 1884, after the first session of federation negotiations with the government, he had been summoned to pray at the sickbed of a totally exhausted Burwash. It was then that the latter confided to him his hope that one day the union of the universities would lead to that of the churches.[27]

Ten years later, in 1894, Burwash was able to elaborate publicly on this sentiment at one of the interdenominational gatherings made possible by university federation, the jubilee of the Presbyterian divinity school, Knox College. Characteristically he began with a tribute to the University of Toronto, which in his opinion had become a centre of religious unity through education. He then expressed his dream that "in these divinity schools, the seedplots of the higher life of all the churches for the future, I see a possibility of cooperation which from the schools may spread as a Divine leaven of unity until *all* our Churches are one." Here he thought his own insight and experience might be of some value, and pointed out that as a theologian he had long since ceased to "lecture on polemical Theology." Instead he had adopted "the historical method of comparative Theology striving from the centre of unity of all our doctrines to work out into a more perfect grasp of truth than could ever be possible from within the Chinese wall of my own 'ism.' " The outcome of his field of study had been "an amazing revelation of the extent of territory which we occupy in common and the narrowness of the field in which we diverge." "How clearly even in that field a truly scientific spirit brings us within sight of each other," he had concluded.[28]

Now though the reference to "polemical Theology" can be attributed to hyperbole suitable for the occasion, Burwash's emphasis on the "scientific spirit" as the distinguishing feature of theological instruction at Victoria requires closer scrutiny. What Samuel Nelles and George Grant had seen as the road to Christian unity, the instruction of the mind, or in Grant's words, "cleaving away from the fair face of truth, the dust and grime of centuries," Burwash as dean of theology had tried to implement with all the rigour of the scientist and fervour of the Baconian. In practical, systematic, and biblical theology the inductive method had been employed as the means for arriving at a clearer understanding of "the facts of religion," stripped of dogmatic of speculative accretions. This scientific method, as demonstrated in an earlier chapter, also happened to lead to an unqualified vindication of Burwash's own "ism," the religion taught and practised by John Wesley, and its systematized form, Arminian theology.

Therefore, commendable though Burwash's comments at the Knox College jubilee might be, it should be remembered that in the search for truth and Christian unity, the Methodist theologian, supported by scientific proof, had a distinct advantage over his colleagues in other denominations. More accurately reflective of the ecumenical insight gained by the scientific spirit are the words of the introductory statement of the *Canadian Methodist Quarterly*. Launched in 1889, it promised to propagate Methodism "as the best form of Christianity, and Wesleyan Arminianism as the best expression of Christian theology."[29]

Baconian science, however, involved more than a method; it also provided the devotee with a concept of history.[30] In the first place, Baconianism was iconoclastic. To Burwash, the inductive method had finally freed contemporary scholarship from the distorting influence of such "idols of the theatre" as rabbinical and medieval scholasticism and the generalizations of modern philosophic or scientific skepticism.[31] To be a Baconian really meant that one took on a giant house cleaning, George Grant's, "cleaving away ... the dust and grime of centuries," in order to arrive at truth in all its pristine purity. However, once that work was completed, the windows were thrown open to let in the new light of science. What had begun as a conservative process now became the basis for unlimited growth and progress. At this point the thought of another scientist, Charles Darwin, became relevant. Darwin's concept of natural law and evolution had been welcomed and transferred to the spiritual world, in highly edited form, by such progressive evangelicals as Henry Drummond of Scotland and James McCosh of Princeton.[32] To Burwash, who was committed to the harmony between science and a religion, and to the recovery of New Testament spirituality and the progressive work of the Holy Spirit, the combination of Bacon and Darwin was irresistible.

Nowhere was this commitment more ably executed than in the study of comparative theology, following the historical method, sometimes also referred to simply as "the history of doctrine." And, Burwash had suggested at the Knox College jubilee, it was precisely in that field that the hope for the future union of the churches lay. Burwash's lecture notes in the history of doctrine after 1897 are of special interest, for at that time the monumental *History of Dogma* by the German church historian, Adolf von Harnack, began to be made available to English readers.[33] Burwash had applauded Harnack's efforts to provide a synthesis of the religious and intellectual forces that had shaped the dogma of the early church, and F.H. Wallace, his successor as dean of theology, spent a few months attending Harnack's lectures in Berlin in 1910. However, while both appreciated Harnack's emphasis on the importance of personal Christian experience rather than the intellectual formulation of doctrine, they also had reservations about Harnack's neglect of the work of the Holy Spirit in the church after the apostolic age.[34] Burwash's own lectures on the history of doctrine, therefore, were a correction of Harnack's interpretation and revealed his own scientific and evangelical concerns.

The history of doctrine was a dynamic process, he argued, for it was the continuing presence of the Holy Spirit that enabled the words of Scripture to enter "the Christian Consciousness, the religious life," before receiving intellectual formulation. Accordingly, the biological analogy of evolution and natural law was a favourite, and students were always reminded in the first lecture that "history is the science of life. All life implies growth. History traces the living processes and forces by which that growth is accomplished."[35]

When applied to Christian doctrine, however, evolution did not mean unending change. Here the Baconian and the theologian stepped in to set matters straight. Doctrine, like the Christian faith of which it was the expression, was dependent on divine relevation, of either new facts or new inspiration to interpret these facts. Since the "objective revelation" had ended with Pentecost and the "subjective" with the apostolic age, the task of the church had been to give intellectual formulation to these spiritual facts and to guard them against error. But because each age had to contend with new influences that threatened to obscure the religious truths of Christianity, doctrinal expression was an ongoing process, continuing into the students' own days.[36]

As he examined the thought of individual theologians in the history of Christian doctrine, Burwash extolled the theology of the early church up to the fifth century. The entire medieval period with a few notable exceptions, such as the eleventh-century theologian, Anselm, however, he cast in a negative light. Not only in science apparently, but also in theology, truth had become obscured by the philosophical speculation and scholasticism of the Middle Ages. Progress, rightly understood, began only in the sixteenth century when Martin Luther took the first great step in recovering the spiritual life of the New Testament by insisting on the centrality of justification by faith and the authority of the Scriptures.

Unlike Harnack, Burwash did not stop his history of doctrine at this point nor, following the example of his favourite church historian, George Parker Fisher of Yale, did he concentrate primarily on continental Europe.[37] Though the Protestant Reformation was unquestionably significant, it did not constitute the full recovery of New Testament spirituality, he argued, for Protestantism quickly became divided by sectarian quarrelling and linked itself with the state. Soon new creeds and institutional forms were imposed that retained many of the errors of the medieval church as well as the peculiar circumstances of their origin.

At this point Burwash transferred the focus in the history of doctrine definitively to Great Britain. Dogmatism, he argued, had reached its limit by the time of John Wesley, and "the Methodist revival was a baptism of new life, and the new life cast out much old leaven, returning once more to the foundations of living truth." Quoting at times from his 1881 introduction to Wesley's Sermons, Burwash reminded his students that Wesley had made no attempt to create a new church or to impose a new dogma, but instead had pruned down an existing creed, the thirty-nine articles of the Church of England, leaving twenty-five that more closely reflected Scriptural truth. And the Sermons and Notes on the New Testament, which were left behind as doctrinal standards, were simply an explanation of the Scriptural plan of salvation, unlike earlier Protestant confessions of faith. Introduced into every trust deed of a chapel or church in the Methodist Connexion, they were only intended to ensure the continuation of "an Arminian evangelical preaching and exposition of God's Word for all time."[38] Because of his training in the Church of England, Wesley was able in these simple doctrinal standards to bring together the essential doctrines taught by the Church since the apostolic period. On this point, Burwash's enthusiasm shone forth unabashed: "It was not the glory of Wesley or of Methodism that he discovered or preached a new gospel. But all the elements of gospel truth were in him combined in a burning focus of spiritual light and heat, as, perhaps they had not been since the Apostolic age."[39]

This glorification of Wesley's role in history did not wane when church union negotiations began in 1902. Nor did it have to, for as Burwash saw it, Wesley had not instituted a new creed or denomination but had only recovered New Testament spirituality. In the New Testament and apostolic age, the new birth had been marked by the overwhelming power of the Holy Spirit. Now, thanks to Methodism's recovery of this experience, the Spirit could again continue its work of conversion untrammelled. "It was thus in the providence of God reserved for the age of Methodism, not first to experience this form of religious life, but for the first time since the days of the Apostles to make it the central idea of a worldwide gospel preaching."[40]

Seen in this light, Methodism rightly ranked first in the progressive march to truth. Not only had Wesley reinstated the importance of conversion, but this renewal of apostolic spirituality had become the basis for further progress in religion and theology, exactly in fact, as Bacon's inductive method had led to the great expansion of scientific knowledge in the nineteenth century. Equally important, because of the resulting interaction of reason and religious experience, a clear definition was finally possible of the "essential" Christian doctrines – the doctrine of the Word, responsibility and holiness, and the future judgment and life. This had been a liberating development, and theology could now accept without fear the discoveries of science, including the historical criticism of the Bible. Methodism, therefore, was linked with progress, scientific advance, and a distrust of traditionalism. Revivalism and science appeared natural partners. This partnership, Burwash argued, had been especially fruitful in the clarification and simplification of doctrine. Theologically, Wesley had placed his evangelical religion within the Arminian tradition. As a more biblical and less dogmatic theology, Arminianism had modified Calvinism, an older system of thought, forcing it to shed many of its theories and peculiarities created by the period of controversy in which its creeds had first been formulated.

This "purification" of the creeds had not yet been completed, and the lectures on the history of doctrine always terminated with a brief section on "modern movements in Christian theology." Here students came to realize that many of the controversies that in the past had divided the church and given form to its doctrine were now "obsolete." So, too, was the historic claim of the church and at times the state to control religious thought through creeds and confessions of faith rather than by "the convincing power of truth itself." Following the example of Wesley, there was a tendency in the modern period to relax formal subscription to church standards. Greater allowance was made for individual interpretations and convictions, and certain groups like the Salvation Army avoided religious standards completely and made the Bible their one statement of faith.[41]

By adopting a historical approach to theology and placing Methodism's doctrinal standards within the dynamic framework of the simplification of doctrine and the return to the "essentials" of Christianity, Burwash made church union appear not only distinctly probable, but inevitable. As early as 1889, when there had been a brief flurry about overtures concerning union by the Church of England, the student editor of Victoria's *Acta* had ventured the opinion that before long some of the Protestant Churches would be united. "A man can be a Methodist today and believe far differently from what Methodists believed half a century ago," he had concluded.[42] In the process of simplification, which was the true task of the scientific spirit, a student apparently might outstrip even the lessons of his mentor. However, while the statement oversimplified Burwash's lectures in the history of doctrine, it did capture their mood. While Burwash did insist that its essential beliefs remain fixed, Methodism was undeniably progressive.

This progressive nature of Methodism became even more apparent in Burwash's lectures in church history. Here, too, the approach was intended to be irenic. Called upon to exercise his "historical imagination," the historian was to be "in sympathetic touch with the living movement," while taking special care to avoid "misleading sympathies and prejudices and party spirit."[43] Burwash's own sympathies, of course, led him directly to view church history within the framework of revivalism, using the Protestant Reformation as his point of departure. In later years the focus was sharpened even further by a course dealing exclusively with church history among the Anglo-Saxon people.[44] In each case, he depicted the Methodist revival (whose forerunners could already be faintly distinguished in the fourteenth-century Lollards) as the first stage of a much greater movement, the evangelical Christianity of the nineteenth century.

In the final year of the nineteenth century, in an essay entitled "1799–1899 – the Contrast and Outlook," Burwash offered the readers of the *Canadian Methodist Magazine* a brief summary of church history after the Methodist revival. Whether the reader gazed backward into the past, or forward into the future, the scene was one of unbounded optimism, thanks to the efforts of John Wesley and the "little band of evangelical Christians" he had left behind. Insisting that the power of Wesley's evangelical preaching had broken through denominational confines, Burwash was able to list without difficulty fifteen examples of its overwhelming impact on the Christian world. These began with the Sunday school movement and proceeded to the evangelization of the British colonial empire and the United States, the "awakening of the Greek Church in Russia," the Oxford Movement, and a host of interdenominational organizations from the YMCA to the King's Daughters. The list had climaxed with the "vast collateral work of social reform reaching out into the fields of politics and legislation, including temperance, social purity, prison reform, care of the poor, and all such lines of work." Especially proud of this last example of the all-pervasive influence of the Methodist revival, Burwash had concluded, "An age of dogmatics and ecclesiastics seems to be giving place to an age of strenuous pragmatics." Every type of evil was now coming under attack, and under the influence of this pragmatic spirit, a deeper spiritual power had begun to touch the hearts of humanity. Thus, there was every reason to be confident that the end of the next century would see "the liquor traffic curse, the social impurity curse, the political corruption curse, turned out of human life as great institutions."[44]

Another prominent sign of progress was the extent to which the missionary spirit had taken hold of the Christian church, and here too, there was reason to hope that the next century would see the evangelization of the entire world. In an earlier address that year, printed in the same journal, Burwash had traced in detail the relationship between the Methodist missionary movement and developments in modern theology. At that time he had called attention to the providential fact that Methodism's missionary efforts among the Japanese and Chinese, "the oldest and most subtly intellectual civilizations of the world," had taken place precisely at the end of the nineteenth century, when the conflict between science and religion had finally been resolved. The resolution of that conflict had been beneficial in more ways than one. Because of the intimate connection between science and religion, the missionary movement could no longer be seen as an "outcome of fanatical zeal," but rather as "the onward movement of light and truth, bringing higher civilization and better life."[46] Therefore, owing to the work begun by John Wesley, it would appear that in the year 1899 evangelical Christianity was at home in the world. Moreover, it was there to stay, and its light and truth would continue to transform the decaying institutions and the prejudices of earlier times and different civilizations.

When it came to this transformation, Burwash was convinced that Canada, a new, growing, and British nation, had a decided advantage. His two main works in Canadian history, the *Life of Egerton Ryerson* and the *History of Victoria College* had not yet been published, but in 1899 the contours of that history were already firmly in his mind, and just as at an earlier date he had used the argument from history to justify university federation, he also read into the story of Canada's religious development the inevitable triumph of evangelical Christianity. "In our own country what was the outlook one hundred years ago?" he had asked in his essay, "1799–1899": "Fourteen preachers, and about two thousand members represent the Methodism of Canada in the year 1800. The evangelical forces of the country were very little indeed beyond this. Even down to the middle of the century the writer can remember the sneers of members of other Protestant Churches at the evangelistic work of Methodism."[47]

In later years, in his *History of Victoria College*, he would commit to writing the means by which this unpromising outlook for evangelical Christianity in Canada had changed: the interdenominational week of prayer held in 1860 after the great Indian Mutiny, the influence of the missionary spirit, the YMCA, whose revivalism had penetrated and strengthened "all the Churches," the evangelism of such international and interdenominational figures as Dwight Moody and John R. Mott, chairman of the Student Volunteer Movement for Foreign Missions, and of course university federation, with the many opportunities it had opened up for contact with students and faculty of different denominations.

Again, as with the history of doctrine, the focus was on Methodism. However, it was not the enthusiastic revivalism of the Methodism of the earlier period that he believed had brought about the shift to evangelical Christianity, but the quieter more sober evangelism of his own college days in the 1850s, when the alliance between reason and religion had begun to take effect. Education had been the great leveller of sectarian differences in the years after 1850 and had led to a quieter type of evangelism and a "life less impulsive and emotional than that of the early days of our century." This had already been apparent at the 1860 interdenominational week of prayer, which had brought "the earnestly religious people of all the Churches together, Anglican and Presbyterian, Baptist and Methodist and Congregational ... Their sectarian peculiarities were dropped. The great essentials filled their thoughts. Each absorbed something of the special quality of the other, the Presbyterian Methodist fervour without its eccentricities and the Methodist Presbyterian sobriety without its coldness. A new form of spiritual life was developing, a form at once congenial to and caught up by College halls and youthful intellectuals."[48]

IMPLEMENTING THE LESSONS OF HISTORY: THE DOCTRINAL STATEMENT OF UNION

Burwash did not confine his optimistic reading of history to Methodist circles. Just as in 1894 he had shared with his Presbyterian colleagues at Knox College some of his insight acquired through the study of comparative theology, so in 1898 as a fraternal delegate to the General Assembly of the Presbyterian Church, he described at length his reading of church history. Again, the approach was selective. Largely a preview of his essay the following year for the *Canadian Methodist Magazine*, the address to his Presbyterian brethren did not focus on the pivotal role of Methodism but on the buoyancy of evangelical Christianity. In glowing terms he described the latter as "a mighty army moved forward to positions of wonderful vantage for the immediate conquest of the world for Christ."[49] In his recorded remarks there was no mention of church union. However, in his speech at Knox College five years earlier, union had already been in his mind as a theoretical, if not yet a practical goal.

Four years later, in 1902, that goal suddenly appeared to come within reach when Principal William Patrick of Manitoba College, as a fraternal delegate from the Presbyterian Church in Canada, made a strong plea for church union at the Methodist Quadrennial Conference in Winnipeg. Less circumspect than Burwash had been in similar circumstances in 1898, Patrick's entreaties were unofficial, but the Conference responded favourably.[50]

Seven days later Conference accepted a report by a church union committee that negotiations to formulate a possible basis of doctrinal, practical, and administrative union be undertaken with the Presbyterian and Congregational Churches. Chaired by William Shaw, Principal of the Wesleyan College, Montreal, the committee declared itself "in favour of a measure of organic unity, wide enough to embrace all the evangelical denominations in Canada." This, however, appeared to be practicable at the time only with the two mentioned denominations, "since their relations are already marked by a great degree of spiritual unity, and they have already become closely assimilated in standards and ideals of Church life, forms of worship and ecclesiastical polity."[51]

Burwash was not a member of the committee at that time, but the report's expression of the unity that had already been reached through time, and its stress on evangelical Christianity would have met with his unqualified approval. When a committee to draft a Joint Basis of Union was formed in 1904, he was appointed chairman of the subcommittee on doctrine. That December, in an address, "Is a Positive Doctrinal Basis for the United Churches Possible?" he expressed cautious optimism. His reasons were a succinct summary of his course in the history of doctrine. On the basis of practical religion, not dogmatic theory, he saw every possibility for success. Indeed, if the Presbyterian Shorter Catechism was placed next to the Methodist Catechism, or Wesley's introduction to the *Standard Sermons* next to the brief statement "The Sum of Saving Knowledge" of the Westminster Assembly's Confession of Faith, agreement could well be expected. Both of these two short statements rightly put the emphasis on Scriptural truth rather than on dogmatic definition. A quick perusal of Wesley's sermons showed how easily the essential doctrines of Methodism could be summarized in a form as succinct as the brief Calvinist statement of faith.

The point of departure for a basis of union he proposed, therefore, was the shortest statement available. Such a statement of faith would merely summarize the essential beliefs of experimental and practical Christianity, not their dogmatic explanation and defence as found in the confessions of the Reformation or, for that matter, in Calvinist and

Arminian theology. "The question thus assumes this form," Burwash concluded, "can this unity be so expressed apart from Calvinistic theory on the one side and Arminian theory on the other as perfectly to guard the essential truths of Christianity and of the Gospel salvation?" It was a serious question, but he did feel that he could reply in the affirmative. The solution would require "a gracious freedom from prejudice, a clear grasp of fundamentals, a lofty purity of motive, a simple fidelity to truth, and a candid humility in the tenure of mere opinions or theories such as the grace of God and the influence of his truth and Spirit alone can give."[52]

None of these appeared to be wanting when the subcommittee on doctrine met, and it had already completed its work by December 1906. Information on the committee's actual negotiations is, unfortunately, sparse, and what is available has already been laid out in the principal studies of church union.[53] Burwash's private papers yield little additional information. Unlike university federation, where he had carefully guarded every scrap of evidence for later documentation and justification of his role, church union, at least in Methodist circles, did not arouse much controversy. From his private correspondence, however, we do know that he considered the formation of a doctrinal statement to be the most important step in bringing about union.[54] From his letters to concerned individuals and from his public defence in the *Christian Guardian* in 1912, it is clear that he felt this task had been successfully accomplished, even though, like the Congregationalists, he would have preferred an even simpler statement.[55] It can also be concluded from his lectures on the development of doctrine that he sympathized with the objections of the Congregationalists against ministerial subscription to a doctrinal statement, and saw this as an expression of the general trend in theology to a more personal understanding of faith.[56]

The most detailed analysis of the work of the subcommittee on doctrine, based primarily on interviews with surviving members was published in 1923. It was written by E. Lloyd Morrow, a Presbyterian who was highly critical of the doctrinal statement of the Basis of Union. While Burwash made no public comments to this effect, it is clear from Morrow's account that he did argue for a more explicit statement of the Methodist doctrine of the witness of the Spirit and that the second part of the article on sanctification followed his formulation exactly.[57] In this way he sought to maintain the distinct doctrines of experimental religion in the doctrinal statement. However, his strongest (and most criticized) contribution was his attempt to formulate the Christian faith in terms that used neither Arminian nor Calvinist "theory."

To many of his older colleagues in the Methodist ministry who had not been subjected to the irenic lessons of the history of doctrine, and whose opposition to Calvinism was still expressed in the succint "Five Points," such a task was by its nature impossible. John Potts, for example, in a lengthy opening address at the first conference on doctrine had categorically asserted that "there never could be any reconciliation between Calvinism and Arminianism." Potts had been refuted by F.B. Duval of Knox Church, Winnipeg, one of the western Presbyterians on the union committee, and had been directed to Scripture with the reminder "to get back to the foundation which is Jesus Christ."[58] However, the historical development of Calvinism as well would prove Potts's assertion to be wrong.

Historians are generally in agreement that during the nineteenth century the Calvinist tradition in the United States had been transformed under the impact of revivalism and Scottish Common Sense Realism, facilitating a rapprochement with Arminian theology impossible in John Wesley's day. Burwash's analysis of the changing nature of Calvinism in his lectures on the development of doctrine had, therefore, in substance been correct. As Lefferts A. Loetscher has observed, "in nineteenth century America even strict Calvinists like Dr Charles Hodge were inclined toward mollifying rather than accentuating aspects of their heritage."[59] In 1902, for example, the American General Assembly had adopted a number of moderate revisions of the Westminster Confession along with a "Brief Statement of the Reformed Faith."[60] Consisting of sixteen articles described as "religious rather than speculative in tone," this approach was very much in keeping with Burwash's own criteria for a statement of faith.

This "Brief Statement" was quickly accepted as a working document by the Toronto section of the subcommittee on doctrine, which at its first meeting had divided into four regional sections. According to one Presbyterian participant the discussions had reached an impasse, when someone presented the "Brief Statement." Church union suddenly became a "practical possibility" as it became apparent that both Burwash and William McLaren, the new principal of Knox College, expressed a willingness to accept this summary of faith.[61] The breakthrough was all the more significant since in the past Burwash had gone to some lengths in his lectures on the history of doctrine to refute his Presbyterian colleague's assertion that Arminianism was "merely a negation of some elements of Calvinism."[62] McLaren had little enthusiasm for union, unlike his predecessor, William Caven. The latter, as Chairman of the Canadian Society of Christian Union, had already memorialized the Presbyterian General Assembly in 1902, presenting suggestions for a doctrinal statement that tallied closely to those offered by Burwash two years later.[63]

The "Brief Statement" was in turn placed next to a statement written by the Montreal subsection, which had drawn on a similar statement of faith formulated by the English Presbyterian Church.[64] From these two documents emerged a simple statement of faith consisting of nineteen (later twenty) articles. When the subcommittee on doctrine had completed most of its work by December 1906, the speed of this accomplishment was a clear sign to W.B. Creighton, editor of the *Christian Guardian*, "that the matter of doctrine offers fewer difficulties to union than any other."[65]

To critics of the doctrinal statement, however, the ease with which the committee completed its work was evidence that the committee had not overworked or, in its eagerness to bring about union, compromised the essential features of Arminian and Calvinist theology. Part of the ease with which the committee completed its task can be attributed to a mutual acceptance of the changes that had taken place in Calvinist theology. Another factor contributing to the swift success of the committee's deliberations went largely unnoticed, and that was the influence of Burwash's own theological formation at the hand of a Presbyterian mother, Anne Taylor. Only F.H. Wallace, Dean of Theology, at Victoria, appears to have made note of the fact that the new Methodist Catechism published in 1897 had used the Shorter Catechism of the Westminster Confession of Faith as a model for a number of its statements.[66] Burwash had had a considerable hand in its writing. Though the section on the "conditional benefits of the atonement" was unmistakable proof of his own teaching on the atonement, other articles, such as those on the purpose of man, the nature of God, and the sinful state of the human condition, were very similar to those in the Shorter Catechism. Since its publication the new catechism had been one of the assigned texts for first-year students in the Methodist ministry.[67]

Burwash later reflected in his autobiography that by the time he was eleven the doctrines of the Shorter Catechism had become as sharply defined in his mind "as were the theorems of geometry or the definitions of Grammar, as a result of his mother's and his Presbyterian Sunday school teacher's thorough instruction."[68] With the help of Anne Taylor's training, the catechism's stress on human sinfulness and God's righteousness had been incorporated into his mature understanding of the atonement. As has been noted previously, in 1906 he had also succeeded in ensuring that the doctrine of infant depravity was clearly stated in the official forms of his denomination. This no doubt made doctrinal agreement with the Presbyterians easier. While the Montreal subsection of the committee had submitted a more ambiguous statement on depravity under the title "Of Man," the article which was adopted followed verbatim the American Presbyterian statement "Of the Sin of Man." In keeping with Burwash's own views on the matter, this article stated that "all men are born with a sinful nature ... and ... no man can be saved but by His grace."[69]

Finally, as a minister and a theologian, Burwash had frequently drawn upon the resources of Calvinist thinkers. In Belleville the writings of Jonathan Edwards and Timothy Dwight had formed part of his small library, and later in his teaching and writing he made it a practice to consult the *Systematic Theology* of Charles Hodge.[70] With Hodge he was a proponent of the inductive method in theology. While his views on evolution and the higher criticism were very different, Burwash shared Hodge's opposition to the progressive displacement of divine grace by the human will in contemporary Calvinist as well as Methodist theology.[71] Thus on the one hand, his upbringing by a Presbyterian mother had served as a retarding agent against the liberalizing tendencies of nineteenth-century American Methodist theology. At the same time it had facilitated a doctrinal rapprochement with those Presbyterians at church union who had a high regard for the teachings of Charles Hodge and the Princeton faculty.[72]

This dual allegiance was not always understood by his Methodist critics. Whereas they considered the articles on the sovereignty of God in the doctrinal statement of the Basis of Union to be a triumph for Calvinist theology, Burwash pointed out that the statement also confessed "the individual responsibility of man for the use of God's grace."[73] The juxtaposition of John Wesley's Arminianism and George Whitefield's Calvinism, which Burwash's critics said was impossible, had already existed in his own theology and in the catechism their church had adopted in 1897.

His childhood training may also account for Burwash's tacit acceptance of a reversal of two of the articles in the Presbyterian "Brief Statement" as finally adopted in the Basis of Union. In the face of criticism by Canadian Presbyterians that "logically the action of God precedes the act of faith on man's part," the American articles had been reversed so that "Of Regeneration" preceded "Of Faith and Repentance."[74] In the eyes of Methodist critics, however, such an order was "absurd," "unphilosophical," and "unscriptural." They argued that, following the new order "a minister would have to teach that a man is "born again" before he repents and believes.[75] Though Burwash did not answer their criticism, it should be noted that in his own teaching and in keeping with his personal experience he took pains to emphasize the importance of prevenient grace. Because of divine grace, even before conversion, the Holy Spirit was already "in the heart convicting, enlightening ... man."[76] For these reasons – his own peculiar religious upbringing and the changes he had observed taking place within Calvinism – Burwash was unable to understand the criticism of those who insisted that the

Basis of Union's statement of doctrine contained "all the objectionable elements of Calvinism."

However, rather than citing his own theological insight or repeating a lesson on the development of doctrine (which, given the pivotal role he had assigned to Methodism, might well have been offensive to Presbyterians), he preferred to direct critics to the words of Scripture. In his defence of union in the *Christian Guardian* in 1912, he maintained that whereas in the past "theory" had divided Calvinist and Arminian, the words of Scripture had finally reunited the two: "The Scriptural elements of faith we held to be essential, the theories human and at best imperfect, and changing with the progress of human science and philosophy. We strove to include all the prominent elements of religious faith, and to eliminate all speculative theory, especially where its harmony with Scripture might be questioned."[77] The result might not be perfect, he argued, but any "candid and intelligent man" who took the nineteen doctrinal articles and placed them next to "the plain words of Scripture" would have to admit that this was "a reasonable statement of Scriptural saving truth."

From these words it may be inferred that in his mind the doctrinal statement of the Basis of Union in essence conformed to the ideal of John Wesley. In the preface to his *Standard Sermons*, Wesley too had professed a desire to "abstain from all nice and philosophical speculations" and to set down only what was "found in the Bible concerning the way to heaven."[78] Thus to Burwash the new was only the old – but it was the old improved. What had been impossible in John Wesley's day, a union between Methodists and Presbyterians, was now possible thanks to the scientific progress in biblical studies.

When viewed in this light, the doctrinal articles for the proposed united church constituted an advance for both Methodists and Presbyterians. Had not the former gained in "fulness of Scriptural doctrine?" he queried. And had not the Presbyterians, who in the past had placed such great emphasis on God's sovereignty as to obscure human responsibility, "now gained something in the statement more clearly and emphatically of God's universal love or the provisions of the atonement for the whole world, and in the emphasis of man's individual and the Church's collective responsibility?"[79]

Such a conclusion arose logically from his revivalist reading of history, which meshed well with the Baconian emphasis on the recovery of "facts" from the theories and speculations of a less enlightened age. Burwash's enthusiastic acceptance of the doctrinal statement can be explained by his conviction that in the new creed the spirituality of the early church had finally been recovered in simple, unadorned expression. Thus union had been made possible by time or, more accurately, by the Spirit working through time, not by compromise or ignorance of doctrine as critics insisted.

Pursuing this argument, it was not difficult to interpret the past development of the uniting churches as a prelude to church union. Concentrating almost exclusively on the Presbyterians and Methodists (between whom the differences in doctrine and religious behaviour had in the past been most contentious), he pointed out that denominational differences had originated outside Canadian soil and during an earlier period. As he had done in his historical analysis of doctrine, he linked religious revivalism, with its emphasis on essential doctrines and on the effacement of all denominational differences, to the forces of spiritual progress.

In this reading of history Methodists and Presbyterians had each undergone a series of internal unions followed by periods of revival that had brought them closer to each other "in revival spirit, in methods of work, and in the great message of evangelistic truth which is proclaimed alike from all pulpits." Thus the old denominational distinctions had given way to a new modern evangelical Christianity. Indications of this were that the Methodists had shed much of their emotionalism at revivals and had begun like the Presbyterians to devote greater attention to the nurture of their children, and in theological training their ministers had become the equal of Presbyterians. In this last area university federation had made a major contribution, for ministers of both denominations were now trained at the same university. In this common environment they had come to realize that they shared "the great evangelical doctrines of the atoning work of Christ and the regenerating work of the Holy Spirit." Finally, as an affirmation and seal of this interpretation of history there had been "the inner oneness of the Spirit," which he believed had united all the members of the union committee. It was this unity that had so greatly facilitated the task of formulating a common doctrinal basis: "We had been learning and absorbing each from each other, all that was truest and best in our neighbour's ways and thoughts until we found that in every essential we were one, and that there was little or no difficulty in finding a common expression for that unity ... Surely such a history could only point to one conclusion, that God was making ready His people for the day of His power."[80]

Seen in this perspective, church union was not simply an option but a duty. On this matter the title of the first article in the *Christian Guardian*, "Is it Right?" had left no doubt. This, he argued, was to be the first and fundamental question for every Methodist, and it had long before been answered by the founder of Christianity in his prayer for the unity of his followers so that the world might believe. Accordingly, church union was the ultimate expression of religious revivalism, a return to Christ's own ideal for the salvation of the world. There was only one hindrance to recapturing this ideal, Burwash told his readers, and that was the desire to retain traditional ties. While such a desire was natural, even beautiful, "it is only sentiment, not duty and if it stands in the way of duty it may be sin."[81]

THE CRITICS OF UNION

Not all the members of his denomination were inclined to see church union in this moral light or to subscribe to Burwash's reading of history. Throughout the year 1911–12 the *Christian Guardian* had opened its columns to opinions for and against church union, although the editor made no effort to hide his own strong pro-union bias. In January and February 1912, just before the Methodist membership voted on union, one minister, Stephen Bond (who had also served on the subcommittee on doctrine but whom Burwash privately considered too old for his objections to be taken seriously), was given the opportunity to represent officially the case against union. His articles ran parallel to Burwash's plea for the unionist cause.[82] Bond was ably supported by letters from a number of ministers, but most strongly by two, William Jackson and W.S. Griffin.[83] As secretary of the superannuation fund, the latter was especially anxious to safeguard the financial interests of Methodist ministers in the proposed union in light of the apparently weaker funds of the two other denominations. All three critics, it should be noted, had behind them a lengthy ministry in the Methodist Church, Bond having entered the ministry in 1856, Griffin in 1849, and Jackson in 1862. Though the last two had attended Victoria College, their attendance had predated the establishment of a faculty of theology.

Their stand was antithetical to that presented by Burwash. Whereas he had rested his case for union on a developmental understanding of revivalism, they countered with a defence of denominationalism based on a logical but scathing review of the doctrinal articles and showed that not everyone had abandoned the "theories" of doctrine in favour of the bare essentials. Stephen Bond found it important to make a distinction between union in the "academic and abstract sense," which all might be able to endorse, and union on the terms of the Basis. In the case of the latter, he found it impossible to see how anyone entering the ministry who held "clear cut views of what are Methodist Arminian doctrines" could ever accept the doctrinal articles without reservation. While he conceded that the Basis did contain Wesley's essential experimental doctrines, he also argued that they lacked the clarity, fullness, and logic of Wesley's teaching.[84] Following Burwash's lead, supporters of church union proclaimed that Methodists had come to share these doctrines with other denominations.[85] However, to Bond and the other critics of the Basis, these experimental doctrines, rather than being shared (and in the process watered down), represented for Methodists "the peculiar characteristics of our teaching specially committed to our keeping."[86] In opposition to Burwash's optimistic view of spiritual progress they offered a different reading of history that stressed the antithesis between unbelief and faith, with faith forever fighting a rearguard action.

Griffin, who in the distant past had often directed his wit at denominational fanaticism with his friend Samuel Nelles, had nothing favourable to say about what he considered to be its latest expression in favour of a passing fad.[87] In his opinion the Methodist people were not simply being urged into union, but were being stampeded into it without really understanding its implications. His rejection of an optimistic reading of history also left him free to assign a less lofty motive to church union. A preoccupation with size and status was, in his opinion, leading Methodists to replace the "sect" by "a large ecclesiastical combine, and become a real church authorized by Act of Parliament." To Griffin, Burwash's interpretation that earlier internal unions had been the prelude to a wider union was at best naive, and a reading of revivalism that was "altogether wide of the mark." In the past, he pointed out, the great revivals of Christianity had not been the result of a combining of forces but rather the breaking away from "mighty church organizations." Where Burwash had excelled in vision, Griffin surpassed him in imagery and concluded one of his letters with a funeral oration on "the passing of the sect": "It went stark mad and committed suicide. In its insanity it tore off the well known garments which, as a 'sect', it had always worn, left them on the beach behind it, and threw itself in the wild swollen current of organic union, never to be seen or heard of again."[88] Thus in the eyes of critics, church union, far from marking a major step in the triumphant march of the Spirit, was an act of suicide ending a glorious history of revivalism.

The arguments advanced by the critics against union have a familiar ring and have been repeated by later historians. At the time, however, keen as their insight may have been, Griffin, Bond, and Jackson represented an aging minority who as spokesmen for the losing side have passed into oblivion. It was the Presbyterians, not the Methodists, who subjected the doctrinal articles of the Basis of Union to the most probing review and who put forth the strongest case against union.[89] However, as Allan Farris has pointed out, many of the Presbyterians who chose not to enter union in 1925 were motivated not so much by opposition to union *per se* as by the desire to preserve a historic church and its creeds. Nevertheless, these non-concurring Presbyterians did favour some form of federation.[90] More recently this same group and their case for denominationalism as opposed to ecumenism has been the subject of a detailed analysis by N. Keith Clifford, who has rightly argued that the fundamental problem with a trans-confessional statement such as the doctrinal articles of the Basis of Union is that "churches cannot unite [in this way] unless they are willing to die."[91]

The Methodist critics had also recognized this. Both Bond and Griffin had taken pains to point out that, while they were willing to consider a federal union, their misgivings were directed against the organic union proposed by the Basis. Like the arguments of many of the Presbyterian dissidents, their arguments against the doctrinal articles were also a plea for the continuation of the denomination as a distinct tradition. At the 1911 Methodist Ecumenical Conference in Toronto, American and British representatives had cautioned against union on similar grounds.[92]

Within Canadian Methodism, however, opposition was confined to the expression of individual misgivings and did not lead to organized collective resistance, as it did in the Presbyterian Church. Methodists voted overwhelmingly for union, with 234,449 members and adherents in favour, and only 38,075 against.[93] Simply requested to vote for or against union as outlined in the Basis, the members were not given the opportunity to register specific misgivings. Thus, the only conclusion which can be safely drawn from the vote is that, whatever criticism might exist concerning the actual terms of union, Methodists en masse, unlike Presbyterians, were willing to end their historic existence as a separate denomination. This decision in 1912 would later act as a strong moral reason for some Presbyterians like George Pidgeon to continue with union in the face of escalating internal opposition.[94]

The question, therefore, is not why so many Methodists favoured union, but why they were willing to cut their historic ties. Given the influence which that decision had on the later stages of the union movement, the question is of more than academic significance. Here Burwash's contribution to Canadian Methodist self-awareness is crucial and deserves to be examined briefly within the religious and social context of the church union movement.

REVIVALISM AND THE POSTMILLENNIALISM OF CHURCH UNION

Critics have argued that church union took place at a time "when old credal affirmations were not only being called into question, but ... were increasingly considered to be irrelevant."[95] Others have suggested that by the time of union Canadian Methodism had long lost its earlier evangelical fervour. Therefore there was little to prevent the denomination from exchanging its "authentic Wesleyan tradition" for a new identity as the United Church of Canada.[96] Both these analyses, however, fail to take into account that church union also affirmed a great deal that was old, though not in the same terms as the creeds and standards of the uniting churches.

In the first place, the members of the Joint Committee on Union who, as C.E. Silcox has noted, represented the real leadership of the churches at the time, were decidedly elderly. They were men, it has also been remarked, "from whom no radical departure would probably be expected." Thus critics of the doctrinal statement have commented (and the present study has agreed) that "the old school of theology very largely predominated." The average age of the Methodist group was the highest of the three, sixty years, and of the twenty-eight ministers present at the first union committee meeting, twenty-one, including Burwash, did not live to see the consummation of union in 1925.[97] Secondly, it should be remembered that the same General Conference of 1910 which voted to proceed with the two very modern ventures of church union and the teaching of the higher criticism also, through its Committee on Evangelism, reaffirmed the need to preach the old Wesleyan doctrines.

There is a further evidence that old ideals had not been abandoned in the face of the new venture of church union. The leading spokesmen for union, such as Burwash, Rowell, and Chown, consistently rested their case on the need to continue Methodism's traditional evangelical mission, and they did so with a good deal of revivalist fervour. When union was finally achieved and celebrated in an inaugural service in the Toronto Arena on 10 June 1925, revivalist language set the tone.[98] The service was described the next day as "rivalling in intensity of religious fervour and attendance any Protestant revival which the world has ever witnessed." It had included a communion address, "The Cross at the Heart of Life," delivered by S.P. Rose, a Methodist minister and Victoria graduate who would continue to mine the Wesleyan tradition after union.[99] At that service representatives from the three uniting congregations had reaffirmed that each group was contributing its own particular tradition to union. In the case of the Methodists this was "to make disciples of all nations, more especially in the manifestation of the Spirit in evangelical zeal and human redemption."[100] It would appear, therefore, that while Methodists had retained their sense of mission, they did not see this to be tied necessarily to their historic identity as a separate denomination.

Here it is fruitful to examine first, not the manner of "the passing of the sect," but the manner of its rising. By comparing the Methodism of the first decades of the twentieth century to the revivalism and awakening of the mid-nineteenth, points of contact can be discerned between the earlier period and the church union movement. The way that the ideals of the old college curriculum made the leaders of Canadian Methodism receptive to church union has already been noted in an earlier chapter.[101] However, outside the college classroom as well there were values conducive to interdenominational co-operation. Richard Hofstadter, in his examination of the views of mid-nineteenth-century American evangelicals has stated that the bond which held most denominations together was not "traditional, inherited, confessional bonds – that is, not a historical system of doctrinal belief – but goals or motives more or less newly constituted and freshly conceived." As a result of this de-emphasis of confessional unity, rational discussion of theological issues which in the past had been a great source of discipline in the churches, now came to be seen as a distraction and a source of division.[102]

This simplification and pragmatic approach was also adopted by Burwash in his teaching of theology, and it characterized the official attitude to doctrine, as formulated by decisions of the General Conference.[103] Even at the period of his life when he was most denominationally self-conscious, Burwash emphasized in the introduction to Wesley's *Sermons* in 1881 that the Methodist standards were not to be interpreted or applied "after the manner of Articles of Religion, or Creeds, or Confessions of Faith which categorically define the doctrines to be professed or believed." Rather, he insisted, they were simply to be seen as a model for preaching experimental Christianity.[104] Similarly, his systematic theology, when stripped of the elaborate reasoning of the inductive method, was only a restatement of the basic teachings of Methodism.

The emphasis on experience rather than creed also allowed him to argue at the time of union that there was no danger that Methodism would lose its distinctive doctrines, as critics of the Basis of Union warned. "Was not this the characteristic quality of Methodism from the beginning, its emphasis upon a definite religious experience of salvation by faith?" he asked in one of his 1912 articles in the *Christian Guardian*. Methodism's origins, he reminded his readers, lay in just such a religious experience, when John Wesley's heart had been strangely warmed, and so it had continued. This experience, he urged, was "the fundamental thing today, with a Congregational Moody, with a Presbyterian Drummond, as well as with a Methodist Sankey or Hugh Price Hughes."[105]

This reductionism, or what Hofstadter has called anti-intellectualism, did provide a common meeting ground for church union. George Pidgeon, first moderator of the United Church, noted with approval in

1928, "these [doctrinal articles] are accepted by all evangelical Christians. There is nothing here to alienate believers from one another or to perpetuate divisions."[106] Thomas Kilpatrick, one of the Presbyterian participants on the subcommittee on doctrine, repeated this assertion in a detailed commentary on the articles, adding "we are not offering a theory. We are describing an experience, and bearing a witness."[107]

Secondly, as Donald Mathews has pointed out, one of the distinctive features of the Second Great Awakening in the United States was that revivalist sects like the Methodists "were not restructuring church life so much as extending it." As a missionary movement, revivalism was therefore not confined to an ecclesiastical institution but extended itself beyond the church to a large number of voluntary institutions whose purpose was to implement and maintain Christian values and morals.[108] In Canada such institutions included the Union Sunday Schools, the YMCA, the Evangelical Alliance, and a variety of temperance movements. C.E. Silcox has stressed their importance to church union in promoting a spirit of co-operation among Protestants. Other historians have emphasized as well their effectiveness as agents of acculturation.[109]

Both these goals had motivated Burwash in his strong support of university federation. In his analysis of the background to church union in 1912 he had argued that federation was a direct precursor to union, for its shared milieu for theological training had fostered spiritual unity among Methodist and Presbyterian ministers. The facts, however, do not support his argument. Analysing the formative influences of non-concurring Presyterians, N. Keith Clifford has concluded that "the typical Presbyterian minister who stayed out of the union was born in rural Ontario [and] educated at the University of Toronto and Knox College before 1908."[110]

Nevertheless, in the case of Methodism, one aspect of university federation can be linked to church union. During the increased denominational consciousness that followed the 1884 union, Canadian Methodists had made the decision, be it unwillingly, to abandon their traditionally independent role in higher education in central Canada for an untried co-operative venture. This meant that the tradition of united Protestant effort that had been one of the distinguishing features of the earlier period of revivalism was extended to university education. Secondly, by participating in the "national university," Methodists were now in the front ranks of the ongoing effort to Christianize the nation, at least in the eyes of those who took the addresses by Victoria's chancellor seriously. Thus, by de-emphasizing confession and creed in favour of religious experience and by co-operating with other Protestant groups, Methodists had maintained continuity with the earlier period of revivalism. At the same time, this approach helped prevent the formation of a strong sense of denominational distinctiveness and facilitated contact with other traditions.

Finally, there was a third feature of the revivalism of the mid-century which favoured co-operation. This was the continuation of a post-millennialism in which evangelism, social reform, economic progress, and democracy were all interpreted as heralds of Christ's rule on earth. In the United States this postmillennial optimism transcended denominational lines, forming a common bond among evangelical Christians in their efforts to reform the nation.[111]

While there exists less comparable research for Canada on this topic, postmillennial expectation was consistently expressed in the annual addresses and reports of the Methodist conferences in the 1830s and continued throughout the pre-union period.[112] This view of history, of course, also underlay Burwash's optimistic prognosis for the advance of Christianity in his own time. To him, John Wesley's conception of the coming of Christ meant "the extension of Christ's spiritual kingdom in the hearts of men by individual conversion such as *was taking place in* his own day. This he expected to go on in still greater power till the world should be regenerated by the saving power of the Gospel which was doing its work in his own time" (emphasis his).[113]

In the nineteenth century this postmillennial hope had found a natural ally in an evolutionary reading of history which assumed that Christianity and culture were marching together "onward and upward" toward "the grand consummation of prophecy in a civilized, and enlightened, and a sanctified world."[114] Otherwise known as religious progress, this concept found expression in Canadian Methodist circles in a large number of ways, from the annual statistical stock-taking to such writings as *Religious Progress in the Nineteenth Century* by W.H. Withrow. Like his old college friend Nathanael Burwash, Withrow considered "the humanitarian character of the century" to be one of the period's "noblest notes."[115]

While this postmillennial optimism was without doubt the predominant note in Canadian Methodism, it was not the only religious understanding of history. George Marsden and others have pointed to the continued existence of a second view that tended to think in terms of antitheses or simple dichotomies and saw truth to be basically "fixed aspects of reality from which could be derived rather different laws, so that there was little concept of development."[116] Historians have drawn a direct link between this view of history and the fundamentalist movement with its adherance to biblical inerrancy, opposition to evolution, and belief in the premillennial return of Christ.[117] Though they were certainly not premillennialists, the critics of the doctrinal statement of the Basis of Union had countered Burwash's optimism with a reading of history which did have strong overtones of this more static, antithetical approach. Thus their views were very much in contradiction to the prevailing mood within Canadian Methodism.

Historians have observed that by the 1890s the world had begun to alter and close in on many North Americans, and for some evangelicals, postmillennial sanguinity began to waver under the impact of urbanization and foreign immigration. While their response would differ, Canadian Methodists did not escape these changes. With alarm it was noted in 1898 that the annual increase in membership had begun to decline.[118] For the quadrennium ending in 1902, when union negotiations seriously began, the increase stood at less than a third of what it had been only twelve years earlier.[119] There were other causes for concern: in 1906 Conference was informed of an alarming decline in the number of class leaders since 1894. Attention was drawn to the fact that the old "evangelistic tone" appeared to be absent from too many pulpits, while a scarcity of suitable candidates for the ministry was greatly lamented.[120] At the 1910 Conference there were encouraging signs that a change for the better had set in, but the spiritual stocktaking continued to show weaknesses, and local preachers were now added to the already existing decline in class leaders.[121]

Resources appeared to be diminishing at the time when they were most needed. Clifford Sifton, Victoria's gold medallist of 1880 and since 1896 minister of the interior, reputedly considered a good-quality Canadian immigrant to be "a stalwart peasant in a sheep-skin coat born on the soil." By 1900 six thousand representatives of such hardy stock – Poles, Russians and Ukrainians – had entered Canada. These were only a small segment compared to the British and American settlers who flocked into the country as a result of Sifton's aggressive immigration policy. Though a few had to be deported, most became moral citizens. But unlike earlier immigrants, the majority (including those of the Roman Catholic and Orthodox faiths) were considered to be in need of the Gospel.[122] In addition there were the heavy demands of foreign missions, a point underscored in 1910 by the Methodist Laymen's Missionary Movement as it reminded General Conference of the "clear duty of the Churches of Canada to evangelize all those in the Dominion and who come to our shores who have not been led into the Christian life, and also to provide for the adequate preaching of the gospel to forty million of souls in the non-Christian world."[123]

It was an awesome prospect, and Nathanael Burwash considered it to be a crisis. His response had been characteristic: a calling for a "baptism of the Holy Spirit" in an address at the 1910 General Conference, the reaffirmation of the old Wesleyan experimental doctrines in his report from the Committee on Evangelism, and finally, the presentation to Conference of the Basis of Union.

Historians of church union have concluded that the movement in large part represented an attempt by Canadian Protestants to maintain a national consensus of values which they saw threatened by immigration and increased industrialization, and Burwash does not prove to be an exception. John W. Grant, for example, has noted that as long as the various denominations were primarily concerned with church extension through their auxiliary organizations, they took an optimistic view of their resources. By the late 1890s, however, this was no longer possible, and accordingly, "when it became apparent that certain churches could only perform the role in national life to which they believed themselves called by merging their identities, union became a serious issue almost overnight."[124]

For Methodists, some of the structures for such a union were already in place from the earlier period of revivalism: a tradition of inter-denominational co-operation in education, social reform, and missions and an understanding of religion which valued experience over creed. What remained, however, was their sense of identity as a distinct denomination.

The loss of that identity would not take place through the formulation of any systematic statement of ecumenism. As N. Keith Clifford has observed, it was not the Methodists, or for that matter the Presbyterians or the Congregationalists, but the Anglicans, who dominated ecumenical thinking in the nineteenth century.[125] In fact, the one Canadian Methodist who did make a contribution to ecumenical thought, James Roy, in *Catholicity and Methodism; or, The Relation of John Wesley to Modern Thought*, published in 1877, was severely condemned for propagating heretical views.[126]

Methodists would not terminate their historic existence in this way because such a route to church union, besides being contrary to the prevailing anti-intellectualism and potentially divisive, was also in contradiction to their own laws. By the 1883 Basis of Union, established as law by Act of Parliament, the General Conference was forbidden (in keeping with earlier practice) to "revoke, alter or change any Article of Religion, nor establish any new standards or rules of doctrine." Thus C.E. Silcox has quite rightly stated that in accordance with its own laws, in order to enter union, the Methodist Church faced a twofold task. It had to reaffirm its doctrinal standards and also prove that the new statement of faith was not "contrary to existing and established standards of doctrine."[127]

It is not surprising therefore, that in a tradition which continued to see itself as a missionary movement, and where a series of church unions had forestalled any strong denominational awareness, the intellectual road to church union did not proceed through ecumenical thought but through a reading of history. Here Burwash's developmental approach to doctrine and church history, outlined in the first part of this chapter, played a critical role. A generation of Methodist ministers, whatever they might have forgotten of their studies, did remember that in an age of change they were not called to serve a backward-looking, static denomination, wedded to a historic creed and tradition. On the contrary, theirs was an aggressive, evangelical movement in tune with the time. Moreover, they had also been led to view all contemporary developments in religion in the best possible light for Methodism, whether it be the Ritschlian emphasis on the ethical message of Christ or the findings of the higher criticism.[128] As a corollary, anything not in agreement with this favourable reading of religious progress, be it Hegelian thought or denominational differences, was simply dismissed by Burwash as a passing fad or a remnant of a less enlightened past, both destined to burn on the rubbish pile of history.[129]

A similar optimistic understanding of the pre-eminence of Methodism existed at the more popular level. In 1891, the centenary of Wesley's death, the *Canadian Methodist Magazine* devoted five issues to Wesleyana. In these the founder of Methodism was linked without exception to every conceivable expression of nineteenth-century progress.[130] By 1903, with the bicentennial of Wesley's birth, tributes to an ecumenical Wesley were added, with Alfred Reynar examining "Wesley and the Reunion of the Churches."[131] In a similar vein, Alexander Sutherland, writing the first official history of Canadian Methodism, published in 1904, took pains to emphasize that his account was not that of "a denomination cast in a narrow groove, intent upon its own sectarian theology ... but the history of a great evangelistic movement."[132] For Sutherland, denominationalism had simply been limited to opposition to university federation, not to church union.

When the time came to place the Basis of Union before the membership in 1912, Burwash's defence in the *Christian Guardian* followed a similar path. The historical argument for union could not help but strike a responsive chord in a denomination which already had a tradition of interdenominational co-operation, where postmillennialism had always promised a glorious future, where the old revivalist fervour was not dead, and which now saw its values threatened by immigration. What Burwash did was to simplify the complexities of the present and unify the disparate elements of the past into one account of the ongoing triumphal march of revivalism. "Surely this is a call to unite our forces with a work which shall hasten the millennium," he argued, insisting that if John Wesley had been alive, he would have joined hands "with all evangelical men in such a work as this."[133]

This postmillennialism and appeal to history to promote ecumenism was in no way new or unique to Methodism in Canada. It is a consistent theme throughout the second half of the nineteenth century, in the writings of Philip Schaff, the founder of the American Society for Church History, in those of Schaff's pupil George Parker Fisher, whose works were on the ministerial reading course, as well as in the writings of Walter Rauschenbusch, whose *Christianity and the Social Crisis* in 1914 had become compulsory reading.[134] Moreover, the year of the membership vote on union, 1912, saw the publication of *The Way to Union* by A.S. Morton, a former student of Adolf von Harnack's and lecturer in church history at the Presbyterian College in Halifax. What Burwash had done for doctrine, Morton did for polity, using an environmentalist approach and arguing that in this area too, the three churches had already reached a remarkable similarity by the time of union.[135]

CONCLUSION: AN AMBIVALENT LEGACY

The road to church union via the study of history was therefore well travelled, and would continue to be after union, for a developmental approach lent itself to an environmentalist as well as to a nationalist reading of the past.[136] However, by its nature, this kind of historical awareness was also problematic. As Michael Polanyi has perceptively observed, such a view really treats "scientific progress" as a function of human experience rather than of impersonal information.[137] Church union was effected by an aging leadership, who whatever their concerns for the future, had a great deal at stake in preserving the past. It may be noted that in summarizing some of the significant signs of the past that pointed to union, Burwash had in fact recounted his own experience: the increased emphasis on child nurture, a less emotional revivalism, improved theological training, and university federation. There was nothing to prevent others, in turn, from imposing their reading upon church union. Indeed, one of the strongest arguments the Methodist critics had advanced against the doctrinal statement of the Basis of Union was that its ambiguous wording would lead to confusion and uncertainty, as some ministers imposed an Arminian reading of the articles, and others a Calvinist, depending on their tradition before union.[138]

Secondly, Burwash's postmillennial reading of history with its positive attitude to change bore a close resemblance to the Whig view of history that dominated Canadian historical writing at the time of union.[139] Whereas to Burwash progress meant the recovery of truth, to others progress could just as easily mean continuing change. S.D. Chown, for example, who expressed great respect for Burwash and echoed much of his teaching, persistently went a little further in his optimism and in the process distorted the lessons of his former mentor. Thus, in his post-union study *Church Union in Canada*, Chown insisted "in all candour" that "the theology of Methodism had developed far beyond the initial tests of orthodoxy which John Wesley had provided in the Articles of Religion, his own sermons, and his sketchy notes upon the New Testament." Such a view flatly contradicted the laws of the former Methodist Church. However, the point Chown had wanted to make was that Methodist theological scholarship had advanced to the same high level as that of the Presbyterians by the time of union, thereby making the work of the doctrinal subcommittee a negotiation between equals.[140]

Moreover, in keeping with the Whig view of history, to others, doctrinal reformulation could continue and in time render obsolete what the framers of the statement of faith stated to be "the essentials of Scriptural saving faith." Not surprisingly, the Presbyterian critic E. Lloyd Morrow was able to find a Methodist clergyman who considered the doctrinal articles to have been only a matter of expediency to accelerate church union, but open to revision after union.[141] He found another, also unnamed, but one of the members of the subcommittee on doctrine, who in 1923 argued that the statement of the faith was "not at all a vital organic expression of the real living church of today. It is 20 years old, and is no more vital than the Westminster Confession nor the Twenty-five Articles of Methodism." It would appear that Burwash may have read more "inner oneness of the Spirit" into the deliberations of the subcommittee on doctrine than had actually existed.[142]

Burwash's inability to recognize a pluralism of viewpoints was characteristic of his progressive understanding of history. As a result he failed to recognize the variety of expectations which lay behind the union movement. The critic who had found the doctrinal statement dated, for example, had especially regretted the fact that it made no mention of the social gospel. While an analysis of the origins of the social gospel lies beyond the limits of this study, both Richard Allen and William Magney have pointed to its evangelical background.[143] At the time the doctrinal statement was framed, there were still many points of contact between the individualistic and perfectionistic approach to social reform of an older generation like Burwash, and the more radical critique of society advanced by Methodists like Salem Bland.[144] Thus Burwash's celebration of "practical religion" in his 1899 article "The Contrast and the Outlook" and his Baconian iconoclasm of the "speculations and theories of the past" coincided with the views of the social gospel. This movement, as Allen has noted, "in its orientation to the future, and its emphasis on life rather than form ... looked upon creeds and institutions as temporary habitations."[145]

Similarly, while as an empiricist Burwash was critical of British idealism, there were elements in idealist thought which facilitated co-operation. In his analysis of the relationship between British idealism and liberal Protestantism in Canada, A.B. McKillop has suggested that one of idealism's attractions for Methodists as well as Presbyterians interested in union was that "it made doctrinal or denominational differences seem essentially unimportant, if not simply irrelevant or even harmful, especially in an age of rapid social and industrial change."[146] It can be argued that this cavalier attitude to doctrine and creed was as characteristic of the older generation as it was of those schooled in idealist thought. But the fact remains that by placing church union within the framework of evolutionary history, Burwash and his colleagues left a confused legacy to the United Church. By assuming the obsolescence of all opposing views, this approach ignored the pluralism of opinions and expectations that lay behind union.[147]

A pluralism of opinions was not a new phenomenon in Methodism. It had been there at the time of Burwash's ordination in 1864 when Anson Green had cautioned against losing the old aggressive spirit of revivalism, and it had manifested itself in the controversy over the higher criticism, the moral status of children, university federation, and finally church union. In each case, Burwash's approach had been to affirm both the experimental doctrines of John Wesley and the new developments in thought and society. To defend tradition with the tools of innovation, it may be recalled, was the method of his old college curriculum. In church union the irony of that method caught up with him. In the name of religious progress he had urged his denomination to abandon Wesley's doctrinal standards, the very tool with which he himself had always been able to accommodate the new and the old.

Church union would not be effected until 1925, seven years after Burwash's death. Had it taken place during his lifetime, there is no doubt that he would have continued to apply his Methodist biases to it, as on an earlier occasion he had interpreted the terms of university federation in such a way as to promote his own understanding of the relation between reason and religion. However, university federation had been completed in 1890, when Burwash was still in his prime. By 1912 he was an old man, who regardless of his optimism on paper, was finding it increasingly difficult to maintain the balance between the old and the new. In October of that year he submitted his resignation as chancellor. To a contemporary observer like Charles Sissons, the issue that led to the resignation appeared petty: a disagreement over minor infractions of the curfew by the women of Annesley Hall, with Chancellor and Mrs Burwash siding against the more progressive position of the dean of women, Margaret Addison.[148] As Sissons commented, "thus ended a great presidency." And he mused, "The manner of its ending invites the reflection as to how much better it would have been had the resignation attended his victory for freedom of thought in 1910 rather than his defeat on the lesser issue of freedom of manners two years later."[149] What Sissons failed to appreciate was that while superficially the two issues represented opposite poles, to Burwash they were linked. Both were a reflection of his understanding of Methodism.

And so, the man who had ardently urged his denomination in the name of progress and John Wesley to give up its Methodist tradition would spend the remaining six years of his life chronicling and defending that heritage as a guide for future generations.[150] Not surprisingly perhaps, after 1912 he made little reference to church union, and there is no evidence that he ever used the doctrinal articles of the Basis of Union in his teaching. From this it can be concluded that what Nathanael Burwash had been defending all along in church union was not so much the new as the old.[151]

Conclusion

To the Japanese reporter who interviewed Nathanael Burwash on board the *Siberia* of the Pacific Steam Ship Company on 27 January 1913 the chancellor of Victoria University appeared a very old man "whose forehead furrowed with a thousand wrinkles, the eyes with warm glimmers and kind and gentle entertainment all make one at once to feel that he was in the presence of a loving grandfather instead of a stranger."[1] Accompanied by his wife, Margaret Proctor, who, the reporter noted approvingly for the benefit of Japanese women, appeared to be "faithfully obeying the words of her husband," Burwash was about to begin a four-month tour of Methodist missions in Japan. A solicitous but misinformed Japanese minister and Victoria graduate had added five years to the chancellor's age, making him seventy-eight. Unfortunately, this had not deterred church officials and Victoria's graduates in missions from arranging a gruelling schedule that would have taxed a man of forty.

Frequent bouts of exhaustion soon led to a pruning of activities, but the list still remained formidable. In the space of four months, Burwash attended two Methodist Conferences, visited his former students and lay workers at specially arranged gatherings, and delivered lectures at the Imperial University in Tokyo and the Kwansei Gakuin, a mission school just outside the city of Kobe, where since 1910 Canadian Methodists had been co-operating with the Methodist Episcopal Church South in providing academic, commercial, and theological training to a total of over twelve hundred Japanese students.[2]

Burwash's reports home, published in the *Christian Guardian* and the *Missionary Outlook* were enthusiastic. What he detected taking place in Japan appeared to him to be a vindication of his own teaching on the nature and methods of revivalism. His accounts of the Japanese tour and his lectures can therefore also be read as a summary of the themes of his own long career as a Methodist preacher, theologian, and educator.

Again, as in his recent defence of church union, he defined the Christian faith, not as a matter of doctrine, but as the "essentials" of New Testament spirituality. In his first article in the *Missionary Outlook*, under the title "Japan's Need for Christ," he pointed out the importance of getting "into sympathetic touch" with the Japanese people to learn how far they felt their need of Christ. He quickly concluded, "If we do that, we shall soon discover that what Japan needs is not the theological systems we have built through eighteen centuries upon Christianity, but the inward spiritual life which Christ brought and still brings to the world."[3]

He proceeded then to demonstrate how the Christian faith had begun to penetrate the Japanese way of life in the last fifty years. Quietly and almost imperceptibly the work had proceeded. First there had been only the efforts of a few individuals, "earnest, deep-hearted, receptive souls, touched by the Holy Spirit"; this had been followed by the work of the church, but also by the penetration of "Christian ideas," which were now beginning to show themselves in the Japanese press, the schools, and politics. Rather than forcing Christianity upon the Japanese, as earlier attempts at evangelization had done, this quiet, slow method was allowing the Japanese to adapt Christian ideas to their own needs. In all of this, higher education was playing a leading role, and Burwash applauded the efforts of Charles Eby, a Canadian Methodist missionary and Victoria graduate who twenty-five years earlier had located the Methodist Central Tabernacle near the gates of the Imperial University in Japan.[4] During his own visit there he had been able to witness a revival meeting conducted by John R. Mott, travelling secretary and evangelist for the Student Volunteer Movement, where hundreds of students had been converted or had expressed an interest in the Christian faith.[5]

When asked to address members of the Imperial University himself, Burwash gladly accepted. In his report in the *Missionary Outlook* he drew attention to the encouraging sign that the Japanese Imperial Government, recognizing the intimate relationship between religion and morality, had met with representatives of the Christian, Buddhist, and Shinto faiths in order to discuss the best method for providing moral education to the country's youth.[6] It was a subject Nathanael Burwash was more than eager to examine, and therefore his lecture topics for the Imperial University were chosen advisedly.[7] Recognizing the criticism with which the Japanese press was meeting Canada's recent backlash against Chinese and Japanese immigration, he spoke first on "Some Problems in the Development of Canada." Here he outlined the country's relatively recent economic expansion as a result of the National Policy, but also dwelt at some length on the loss of spiritual values that had accompanied the growing material prosperity. To countervail this increased materialism, he pointed out that hope lay in the country's moral resources: "pure homes, and a motherhood, intelligent, moral and religious," a strong educational system, in religion, and in its "old population ... descended from the best stock of the British Isles, and of France, Germany and Holland," as well as more recent immigrants "of the best moral type."[8]

In the second lecture, "Christian Ethics," he explored the relationship between religion and morality. Many years earlier, interested in helping some of his Japanese students "who approached the study of Christian truth from a point of view quite different from that of their European brethren," he had revised one of his drafts for the *Manual of Christian Theology* in order to present experimental Christianity in terms which he hoped would be intelligible to the Japanese mind.[9] Now in his lecture at the Imperial University he proceeded to demonstrate how religion and morality were inextricably connected. He first examined the salient features of Buddhism and then proceeded to compare it to Christianity. The latter, he epitomized for his audience as a "religion felt in the heart as well as influential in the life." This became clear when an individual repented of sin, accepted Christ as Saviour, and thereby experienced "the supreme Christian enlightenment," or "illumination of the spirit," which expressed itself in a new relationship to God and a new moral life. This life was characterized by "the fruits of the Spirit, love, joy, peace, long suffering, gentleness, goodness, fidelity, meekness, temperance."[10]

Thus what Nathanael Burwash was preaching in Japan under the title "Christian Ethics" was simply a rephrasing of John Wesley's description of the new birth. Though the medium might vary according to time and circumstances (for the same description was referred to as "Practical Christianity" in his lectures at home), the message of sin, salvation, and sanctification remained largely the same. And in his opinion the results were no different from what they had been in Wesley's day. As he enthusiastically commented to the General Board of Missions upon his return to Canada, the experience of the last thirty to fifty years of mission work had definitely proved that "the Japanese can become converted in the old-fashioned Methodist sense, and that when so converted they make most excellent, spiritual and exemplary Christians."[11]

However, was this model of Christian evangelization which he was presenting to Canadian Methodists, and which tallied closely with his own experience really conversion in the old-fashioned Methodist sense? Scholars like Patricia Hill and Jane Hunter who have examined the work of women overseas missionaries have drawn attention to the confusion of motives that often directed the work of those in missions and led to a misreading of the results. What Burwash interpreted as a quiet expression of revivalism with Christian ideas slowly infiltrating the Japanese way of life through education and contact with the West has also been seen as Christian acculturation, a "gospel of gentility," from a female perspective.[12]

While he too was aware of some of the cultural ramifications of missions, Burwash saw these as flowing naturally out of the acceptance of evangelical Christianity. For this purpose he had rephrased the Wesleyan doctrines in an effort to make them intelligible to the non-Christian mind. These doctrines he had continued to teach at the Methodist National Training School after his retirement, and through the required reading of the *Standard Sermons* they were also conveyed to those training as medical missionaries, as well as to anyone entering the ministry of the Methodist Church.[13]

In his view, Wesley's teaching of experimental Christianity and the Christianization of society through education and other forms of moral reform were both part of revivalism. The second merely followed from the first. As he had pointed out three years earlier in the controversy over the teaching of the higher criticism, for Canadian Methodists living in the early twentieth century the field of revivalism had expanded from the days when John Wesley called sinners to flee from the wrath to come. Living in a Christian civilization, their task was not only to call sinners to repentance but also to urge them "to go on to perfection" and, through "sanctified lives," to permeate all the culture with "the moral and spiritual truths of Scripture."[14]

In his own teaching and preaching, with the exception of a few zealous efforts when he was a young minister in Belleville, he had appeared to devote more attention to the last two of these tasks than to the first. This was largely due to the nature of late Victorian Methodist society and the university environment in which he lived. However, in his teaching of experimental Christianity in his classes in practical theology he had stressed repentance as much as sanctification. Moreover, in the face of a prevailing tendency to accept the innocence of the child he had insisted that the church unequivocally recognize in its formal documents in 1906 the doctrine of human depravity and the need for children as well as adults to be converted.

While Burwash had been consistent in his teaching of the evangelical doctrines, the medium he had used to convey these requires some attention. Because of his view of the ultimate harmony of reason and religion, he had tried to use reason in the defence of religion and had sought to express what he considered to be unchanging moral and spiritual truth in the language of his listeners and thus in the modes of contemporary cultural expression. At a time when scientific and critical thought had appeared to be undermining these truths, he had worked for thirty years to perfect a systematic theology following the inductive or scientific method. As he had concluded in the resulting *Manual of Christian Theology*, it was his hope that through this new expression of the old evangelical truth he might be able to turn some of his readers away "from the obscuring mists of modern controversies to this pure light of truth which shines within."[15]

Convinced through his childhood training, his reading of Scripture, and his own experience that the basis of all religion was an "inner assurance of faith," he had simply and unquestioningly proceeded from this premise and had tried to update the form but not the beliefs of Wesley's teaching. Theological instruction at Victoria, following the inductive method, had intended to provide for students in the Methodist ministry what he personally had found wanting during his brief bout of religious doubt in Belleville in 1862. What he had needed at that time was an apologetic of the Christian faith that recognized its experimental nature and at the same time showed it to be "neither irrational nor unreasonable." In his efforts to supply this need he had considered himself to be faithfully following in the footsteps of two impeccable authorities: the apostle Paul, who had gone to the Greeks "with the united strength of reason and revelation," and John Wesley, who had insisted that religion and reason went hand in hand and that "all irrational religion is false religion."

However, he had also been following the model of his college curriculum of that period of thought referred to as the "didactic Enlightenment" of Protestant Scholasticism when moral philosophers like Francis Wayland and James McCosh had marshalled the arsenals of reason in defence of religion in order to ensure that in a rapidly changing progressive society Christian values would be retained. To maintain this desired stability they had placed a heavy emphasis on education, hoping that through the proper exercise of reason the student would recognize the teachings of the Christian religion as absolute and implement and practise them in his daily life.

While Burwash had attempted to rectify the epistemology of the moral philosophers and had balanced reason with "the inner assurance of faith," he had not questioned the basic suppositions. He had merely corrected the "facts" on which they had based their system of Christian ethics. Thus he had retained both their uncritical attitude to culture and their supposition that, given the ultimate harmony between reason and religion, all new knowledge, if rightly understood, would prove supportive of revealed religion.

Following their example he had accepted social change but at the same time had tried to control it by harnessing it to religious truth. To Methodist businessmen he had preached the doctrine of Christian perfection; to meet the needs of an increasingly sophisticated laity he had urged that the ministry receive a college training which recognized both the new critical thought and the old Wesleyan experimental teachings. The answer to university reform and expansion had been found in a system where Christian colleges teaching moral and religious truth were federated with a secular university dedicated to the study of the sciences and to professional training. Finally, to meet the changing ethnic and demographic condition of early-twentieth-century Canada there had been the answer of church union. Here, it had been his conviction that evangelical Christianity would continue to find expression in the simple, biblical statements of the articles of faith in the Basis of Union. The result had been that religion and culture had become closely tied together not only in Burwash's mind, but also, through a variety of institutions, in actual fact.

However, while his approach had been intended to ensure that culture would continue to be influenced by religion, the reverse was equally possible. Some observers have noted a shift in the social composition of late-nineteenth-century Canadian Methodists and have wondered whether this was not indicative of the fact that culture had indeed affected religion and weakened its message. At the 1911 Methodist Ecumenical Conference in Toronto, one of the British Wesleyan delegates who had been impressed neither by William Briggs's growing statistical survey of Canadian Methodism nor by the solid splendour of his setting, Metropolitan Methodist Church, had pointedly asked how many "working men such as John Wesley had had in his day" had worshipped in Toronto's Methodist churches that past Sunday? In other words, in the view of this delegate, Canadian Methodism, at least in Toronto, had become too closely identified with upper-middle-class respectability. Rather than transforming society as it had done in John Wesley's time, Methodism was now seen to be in danger of being radically changed by its cultural environment.[16]

J.S. Woodsworth, who had received his BD from Victoria College in 1900, made a similar observation in somewhat different terms in a 1913 article in the *Missionary Outlook* entitled "How to Help Our European Immigrants." Sent by the church to North Winnipeg to "convert the foreigner," Woodsworth, who was already troubled by religious doubt, also found himself at odds with the apparent callousness of many Methodists to the West's growing immigrant population. Rather than converting the foreigner, he had become impressed with "the need of converting the Canadians who through their selfishness and indifference are degrading him." Woodsworth had darkly concluded his article with the ominous and prophetic warning that he was nearing "a parting of the ways," and that "either the Church must adopt an altogether different attitude and policy or some other organization must be raised up to do the work that must somehow be done for immigrants."[17]

Burwash did realize that Canadian society in 1913 was not what it had been in the 1860s when as a young minister in Belleville he had been impressed by the moral and spiritual leadership provided by the laity and by their commitment to Wesleys' doctrine of Christian perfection. As he had pointed out to his audience in the Imperial University in Tokyo, Canadian wealth unfortunately was becoming increasingly concentrated in the country's major centres and in the hands of capitalists and captains of industry, while the number of "utterly helpless and hopeless and even depraved" was increasing. At the same time he had expressed the hope that these evils would be rectified in time as the country began to rely again on its "moral resources."[18]

At home on the other hand, he became increasingly critical, and as he longingly looked back to a simpler era, a nativist tone began to enter into his addresses. Speaking at the jubilee of the Centenary Methodist Church in Hamilton in 1918 shortly before his death, he emphasized that Methodism in Canada had been "planted in material of high moral quality." The first British immigrants who had settled the Hamilton area, he pointedly remarked, had been "men with ambition and looking for a better life," not like the current "pauper immigrants ... shipped out by paid passage because they were not wanted at home."[19]

Not only did he speak out in an increasingly critical voice against Canadian society in his final years, but he also found the spiritual resources with which to rectify the apparent evils to be wanting. And so he called frequently for a religious revival, urging the formation of small holiness bands such as he had known in his short stay in the pastorate in the 1860s. "Better a lonely messenger of God without a church but baptized with the Holy Spirit than a worldly half dead church with great numbers and all worldly attractions," he exhorted members of the Nova Scotia Conference in 1915.[20] At that time there was none of the triumphalism of his church union addresses, for Burwash began to see himself more and more as "a lonely messenger of God," not unlike the apostle Paul or the New Testament Church, both of which he admired and often held up as models. Like them he was now not in agreement with, but critical of, society.

This was one of the ironic results of his implementation of the teachings of the moral philosophers, for society, unlike "moral and religious truth," continued to change. As a college student he had been taught to see a correlation between society as it functioned and a divinely

ordained moral law. His friendship later with such Methodist philan-
thropists as the Jacksons and Chester Massey had only served to affirm
him in this belief. However, in the final years of his life he became increasingly aware that practice and precept were diverging widely. The
law which appeared to direct society in the final years of his life and
which he saw reflected in the terrible war that was killing Victoria's
students overseas was more akin to the law of the jungle than the moral
law of God.[21] Once the apparent close fit between culture and Methodist piety began to break down and the wealthy no longer went on to
perfection, and the poor were not converted, and even Victoria's
women in Annesley Hall refused to follow the model of "true womanhood," the only option left was to take what appeared to be a reactionary stance and again to call people to repentance.

The second irony of his college training was that the principle that
had guided its curriculum, the harmony between reason and religion,
was itself conditioned by time and circumstance. As Owen Chadwick
has noted in his study of the Victorian church in Britain, by 1900 the
conflict between faith and reason, between science and religion, appeared to be over. Few intellectuals spoke of the problem, while to the
man in the pew it had only barely if ever existed.[22] However, Burwash's
defence of the Christian religion had rested on the premise that reason if
rightly exercised would be supportive of religion, and that premise was
the guiding principle of his great opus, *The Manual of Christian Theology on the Inductive Method*. As a result he had been successful (to
repeat the assessment of his work made by Thomas Langford) in enun-
ciating a theology that was receptive "to the rising scientific ethos" but
that also conserved "the central ligaments of the Wesleyan tradition."
However, as Langford and others have also demonstrated, by 1900
Methodist theology in England and the United States was moving away
from the empiricist base to which Burwash and contemporaries like the
American theologian John Miley had anchored it.[23] Though Burwash
did incorporate into his *Manual* some of the insights of later theologians such as the Methodist Borden Parker Bowne of Boston University, his systematic theology, as well as his selective use of philosophy,
expressed the intellectual concerns of an earlier period.

His colleague at the Wesleyan Theological College in Montreal until
1911, William I. Shaw, was a Victoria graduate of 1861 and avowedly
conservative. Those teaching theology in Canadian Methodism's other
theological institutions were either of Burwash's generation and had
little formal training, or were his former students.[24] Of the three who
might have been able to lead Canadian Methodist thought in new direc-
tions, two – George Jackson and George C. Workman – ran into difficulties with the church's hierarchy over their advanced views on bib-

lical criticism, while the third and most likely candidate, George Blewett, whose work in ethics was highly acclaimed, died prematurely in 1912.[25] Thus, when Canadian Methodists voted to enter into church union in 1912, they did so with a great deal of sincere revivalist fervour, but also with a systematic formulation of Wesleyan doctrine which was more a reflection of the conflict between science and religion than of the problems faced by religion in the new social and intellectual conditions of the early twentieth century.

Thirdly, and this was the final irony of Burwash's commitment to the harmony between reason and religion, in seeking to express Methodism in terms meaningful to a changing environment, he was at the same time quite unintentionally undermining the very religion he was trying to preserve. Baconian science had been for him a means of accepting selectively the findings of modern critical and scientific thought and at the same time reaffirming Wesley's evangelical Christianity. Some of his students like S.D. Chown and A.M. Phillips eagerly accepted the inductive method and saw it as a means to be at the vanguard of scientific knowledge.[26] However, they were less concerned than Burwash about also preserving the old verities. A.M. Phillips had to face accusations of preaching a heretical understanding of the atonement, while S.D. Chown's replacement of Pauline theology with a sociological interpretation of the Kingdom of Heaven has been termed "unadulterated theological liberalism" by Ramsay Cook in a recent analysis of the decline of orthodox religious belief in Canada.[27] Another scholar examining Chown's thought has noted that his confidence in the inductive method led Chown to conclude that theology had become a process, "ever open to further development and adjustment," for to him Protestantism's endorsement of the scientific method meant that everything, including dogma, was now open to investigation.[28]

However, a note of caution against too hasty a verdict of religious heterodoxy is in order. Though both critics have taken Chown's rhetoric at face value, they have overlooked the fact that his evangelical roots remained unshaken. The library of Salem Bland, another Methodist whom some historians have identified with the decline of revivalism, contained a short but revealing manuscript written by Chown after church union, entitled *The Influence of Wesley Upon Canada*. In it Chown cited Wesley as the authority not only for Canadian Methodism's decision to enter church union, but also for the call made by the 1918 Methodist General Conference for complete social reconstruction by Canada after the war.[29] Described by Richard Allen as "the most radical statement of social objectives ever delivered by a national church body in Canada," to Chown it was "supremely Christian ... and essentially Wesleyan."[30] At the same time, while socially radical, his reading of Wesley remained spiritually conservative, and he regretted in later years the loss of "such evangelical truths as repentance, saving faith, the witness of the spirit and such other beliefs as formerly developed a clear and understanding type of evangelical Christian."[31] In his old age, Chown too, once known for his progressive spirit, would, like Burwash, begin to look nostalgically to the past.[32]

In his later writings, Burwash was equally aware that the accommodation of both the old and the new was becoming problematic, but his protests were private or expressed in veiled form. Thus addressing himself to those who, like the novelist George Eliot, placed their confidence in a religion of humanity, in a universal brotherhood, he agreed that the New Testament demonstrated the interrelatedness of human lives. However, he cautioned, "it teaches us at the same time that there is a supreme Lord who governs the Universe and guides the history of all human life."[33]

More direct but probably known to very few was his encounter with George C. Workman in 1910 at the very time of the controversy over the teaching of the higher criticism at Victoria. Workman had found in Burwash a staunch defender of his teachings on Messianic prophecy, a defence which had not wavered in the face of private criticism of Workman's unsettling effect on the faith of the students of Wesleyan Theological College in Montreal, where he had gone after resigning from Victoria.[34] In reply to this criticism, Burwash had reminded the writer that Workman was "one of my boys and almost if not the very first who was converted at College after I commenced my work there."[35] To Burwash, conversion resulting in an "inner assurance" was a guarantee that religious faith would be maintained in the face of any challenge by modern scientific thought. Nevertheless, in January 1910, he regretfully refused to endorse a manuscript on the life of Christ sent to him by Workman. "You make Christ almost human," he had pointed out and suggested a thorough revision using the inductive method in the reading of the New Testament evidence.[36] Workman, it appeared, had embraced change, but not the method by which change was to be tested.

Woodsworth, Chown, and Workman have been considered by a number of historians to have been directly though unwittingly responsible for a profound shift in religious thought in early-twentieth-century Canada. In the opinion of Ramsay Cook this shift was so radical as to deserve the name "secularization," for it resulted in "the substitution of theology, the science of religion, with sociology, the science of society."[37] In such an interpretation the position of Nathanael Burwash in his final years seems doubly ironic. On the one hand, in his frequent calls to the Methodist denomination to repentance, he may be seen as the last bastion of a crumbling Christian faith against the onslaught of secularization. On the other hand, as a teacher and a theologian he bore a direct responsibility for the thought of those who have been accused of contributing to the decline in the influence of religious values in Canadian society. Strangely enough, while he frequently expressed his disenchantment with the lukewarm state of Methodist spirituality in the final years of his life, Burwash remained supportive of his former students, even though theologically they might be branching out into new territory.[38] This would lead to the conclusion that there is another way to interpret his calls to the denomination to return to the old faith and the old ways. The key to this interpretation lies in the nature of religious revivalism and its accompanying cultural expression of "awakening."

That revivalism, it may be recalled, had begun in central Canada as part of the cultural disorientation experienced by new immigrants, who like the Burwash clan and the Taylors had arrived from the American colonies and Great Britain and who, under the preaching of itinerant evangelists, had undergone religious conversion. Drawing on that recent religious experience, they in turn had tried to direct and shape the values and beliefs of their children both through Christian nurture in the home and through educational institutions like Victoria College. Thus, what had begun as a religious revival, a re-orientation of beliefs, by the time of Burwash's childhood had turned into an "awakening," a period of cultural revitalization. Burwash and his colleagues who formed the hierarchy within Canadian Methodism in the late nineteenth and early twentieth centuries, had played a critical role in implementing and thereby prolonging the consensus of values which had resulted from the earlier period of revivalism. Drawing upon contemporary scholarship in an age of growing religious doubt, Burwash had made it his special task to interpret John Wesley's experimental Christianity to a new generation of increasingly sophisticated and educated Methodists. Thus, by insisting on the continued need for childhood repentance and conversion, by his emphasis on the importance of the witness of the Spirit and Christian perfection, through the use of the inductive method in theology, and institutionally through university federation and church union, he had tried to give a permanent expression to the religious experience of the revival.

At the same time, this "old religion" with its emphasis on repentance, forgiveness through the atonement, the witness of the Spirit, and a life of holiness, and acceptance of postmillennialism also appeared to him to represent a satisfactory understanding of all of human experience. Individual responsibility, moral perfectibility, the reliability of the senses, and a confidence in the inevitability of progress were, as Walter E. Houghton has outlined in *The Victorian Frame of Mind*, part of the

Victorian consensus of values.[39] In his analysis of the relationship between revivals, awakening, and reform, William McLoughlin has seen these values to be central as well to the Second Great Awakening in the United States.[40]

In the case of Nathanael Burwash they had become so woven into the fabric of his life that he simply could not view reality in any other terms. Quite naturally he had assumed that the means and institutions which were intended to give concrete expressions to these values would be permanent. In the conclusion of his *Manual of Christian Theology on the Inductive Method*, the work of a lifetime, he had expressed the hope that "the truth so won will abide the test of the ages and will build and perfect the spiritual life of the world." This aspiration also held for university federation and church union and was reinforced by his post-millennial interpretation of history. As William McLoughlin has noted, such an expectation is part of all human experience, for "human institutions generally assume that there is a fixed or normative relationship of one man or group to another, of one generation to another. They prepare men for continuity, not change; they are the means by which men try to ensure stability, order, regularity, and predictability in their lives." While such is the expectation, in reality, however, as Burwash painfully had come to realize in the final decades of his life, "times change, the world changes, people change, and therefore institutions, world views, and cultural systems must change."[41]

In the United States, McLoughlin has discerned such a time of change occurring between 1890 and 1920, a period he has designated as the "Third Great Awakening."[42] Attendant to this were signs similar to those which had accompanied the earlier awakening that had so profoundly affected Burwash's parents and his generation: a period of individual stress and cultural disorientation, followed by the appearance of leaders able to create a new consensus or "new mazeways" and to convert the aspirations of the group into "beliefs which can be validated by experience."[43]

The socio-economic changes which in McLoughlin's analysis were responsible for this new awakening were also experienced in central Canada. Large-scale non-Anglo-Saxon immigration, increased urbanization, religious scepticism, a changing lifestyle among Methodists that had penetrated even the walls of Victoria College's women's residence, not to mention the shatteringly disillusioning effect of the Great War – all of these were threatening to overturn the world to which Burwash had become accustomed. As a theologian and chancellor he had been able to exert some influence over that world, but by 1913 had resigned as chancellor, unable to stop the encroachment of the world upon the habits of Victoria's women students.[44] By that date most of the Old

Guard of Methodism had lost their positions of influence, whether through death, retirement, or as was the case with Albert Carman, by being teamed as general superintendent with a younger, energetic man like S.D. Chown, who was considered more "in tune with the time."[45]

For Burwash, all these changes had led to disorientation and to repeated attempts to call society back to the old faith and the old values. However, his correspondence during the final decades of his life reveals that members of the younger generation as well were experiencing disorientation and were groping for their own expression of self-identity. Such is apparent, for example, in the letters sent home by his eldest son, Edward, who had graduated with a BD from Victoria in 1903. Theologically a faithful reflection of his father, Edward was nevertheless in a state of constant unrest and found himself enticed by a dizzying array of professional possibilities, all of which he briefly tried out: artist, secretary to his father, Methodist itinerant, missionary in Mexico, settlement house worker in London, England, instructor of science at Methodism's Columbian College in New Westminster, British Columbia, geologist, official biographer for his father after the latter's death, and finally, teacher at Upper Canada College in Toronto. Moreover, the perplexity of the future was aggravated by periodic doubts about his call to ministry. These were shared by his youngest brother, Proctor, who finally settled for homesteading in Ponoka, Alberta, thereby reversing the career opportunities which had presented themselves to his father, who as a young boy had chosen the ordained ministry rather than farming.[46]

Self-identity as a Methodist itinerant similarly failed to exert its old charm for Edward's friend and Burwash's former student, young Charles Currelly. A probationer in the Methodist ministry, Currelly had been appointed curator of the projected Royal Ontario Museum in 1907. Only a few years later, however, he made the decision that he would not seek to combine an academic career with that of an ordained minister, though he would remain a local preacher. Burwash, who had a lively interest in archeology and had been the recipient of various "trinkets" which Currelly sent home from his various expeditions, had remained in touch, and when consulted he acquiesced. As he noted at that time, Currelly's decision appeared to be part of a general trend he had perceived in academic circles.[47]

The disorientation experienced by his sons and former students was in part a result of the bewildering number of career opportunities which had opened up for young Methodists by the turn of the century and which had been unavailable in Burwash's own day. However, there are indications that some of the unease experienced by young college-educated Methodists arose from an awareness that they were no longer able to find a legitimation of their understanding of themselves and of society in the faith of their elders. Examples of this can be found at both sides of the ideological spectrum. On the one side were those who wished to turn back to an earlier era of biblical understanding and who protested against the teaching of the higher criticism at Victoria. One angry theological student, for example, dropped out of the probationer's course in 1908 because, as he informed Burwash, his recent baptism with the Holy Spirit had finally revealed to him the pernicious threat to his faith contained in his college texts.[48] On the other side were those like George Workman who chafed very visibly against the efforts by the Old Guard to keep Methodism on its familiar tracks. In addition to his efforts to reinterpret Biblical prophecy and the work of Christ, Workman had also been at odds with the denomination's teaching of infant depravity. At the 1906 General Conference his had been one of the voices of protest raised against Burwash's insistence on maintaining this doctrine and the need for childhood conversion as part of the essential teachings of Methodism.[49] While these teachings had been retained in the form for infant baptism and in the *Discipline*, this time Workman ultimately proved to be on the winning side.

By 1918 only twelve years later, far-reaching changes in childhood religious preparation were to take place within the official practices of Canadian Methodism. In large part these arose out of the preparation for church union, which required a greater emphasis on the religious instruction of the young in order to synchronize with Presbyterian efforts in this area.[50] Nevertheless, while doctrine and the form for infant baptism would continue to remain unchanged, in practice a Bushnellian view of Christian nurture was accepted in 1918. Following the model of progressive American educators like George A. Coe, the church now placed baptized children in a streamlined program and enrolled them in a "cradle roll" in Sunday school up to age five. Thereafter until they were eighteen, they were entered as catechumens in the circuit register until the time when they publicly undertook on their own behalf the obligations set forth in the ritual for reception into adult membership. Though Burwash did protest in print, as well as in the more veiled form of frequently recounting his own childhood religious upbringing as a model, nurture and decision had finally triumphed over repentance and conversion.[51] That such a reversal took place within such a short time seems to suggest that a sufficiently large number of Methodists wished to reinterpret religious practice in the light of significant changes in society.

A more personal and poignant expression of this same need can be found in young J.S. Woodsworth, whose religious doubts have been noted with interest in a number of studies examining the process of secularization.[52] When he was a student at Victoria, Woodsworth had, according to his own testimony, accepted without question the answers of his instructors to the challenges they believed were being levelled at the Christian faith. But after his ordination and "in the quiet of the pastorate," these answers failed to satisfy him. Plagued by growing religious uncertainty, he finally appealed to Burwash for help in 1902, trusting that the latter's "liberal spirit" would allow him to understand.[53]

As Woodsworth confessed to his former instructor, while his faith in God and in God's personal guidance remained unshaken, he was no longer able to believe or preach many of the doctrines found in the Methodist doctrinal standards, to which as a minister he was obliged to assent formally. As a young college-educated Methodist searching for "ultimate truth," he found himself especially to be struggling with the problem of biblical authority. In the light of modern criticism, the Bible had become for him a book whose interpretation varied according to time and circumstances.[54] Unlike young Burwash, who had experienced a similar predicament at an earlier date, Woodsworth found himself unable to fall back on the certainty of conversion and assurance. Raised in a devout Methodist home, he had never experienced conversion, and thus his dilemma was specially perplexing. As he pointed out in print on a later occasion, because he had not been converted, his own religious faith did not match the definition of Methodist spirituality that Burwash had outlined in his edition of Wesley's *Sermons*, a definition that Woodsworth considered normative.[55] And so, since he was unable to turn to the certainty of the witness of the Spirit, the only final authority to which he could appeal was his "religious consciousness," which he considered to be synonymous with "reason, conscience, intuition, or commonsense."[56]

Burwash's reply has not been saved, but from later correspondence it appears that he advised Woodsworth to remain in the ministry.[57] There, until he finally departed in 1918, Woodsworth continued to experience a troubling disjunction between his own experience and that officially required of a Methodist minister. For example, in a caustic analysis, "Heterodoxy or Hypocrisy – A Minister's Dilemma," published in *Acta Victoriana* in 1913, he drew attention to the casuistry to which he felt many Methodist ministerial candidates were forced to resort at the annual district meetings. Expected to assent to doctrines in which they no longer believed, they found themselves in a predicament which, he was convinced, was shared in even stronger form by Presbyterians. His solution was simple: "Sweep away an impossible solution! Is not sincerity of greater importance than orthodoxy? The Master's denunciations were not against erroneous doctrines or independent action, but against all forms of insincerity."[58]

Statements such as these have been interpreted by Ramsay Cook as evidence of the triumph of "a secularized theological liberalism" whereby religion had adapted itself to secular culture.[59] To do so, however, is to overlook the nature of evangelical revivalism, whose essence was experience, not "dogma." To Woodsworth, doctrine no longer accurately reflected experience, and thus he appealed to the founder of Christianity as his authority and called for reform. However, in his recognition that religion was in the first place a matter of experience, not doctrine, he was also simply expressing a view shared by Methodists and nineteenth-century evangelicals generally. As Burwash had demonstrated by both precept and practice during his long career, religion could not separate itself from society but constantly had to address itself to the needs of individual men and women.

However, because Burwash had drawn so deeply on the experiential nature of religion as a force of direct relevance to the way people raised and educated their children, spent their money, and associated with one another, he had also helped ensure that Canadian Methodism could never remain static and isolated from developments in society. Thus, in time, under the impact of significant socio-economic, demographic, and intellectual changes, all of which began to put a considerable strain on the earlier consensus of beliefs and values, there followed a period of unrest and a call for change within Canadian Methodist thought and practice.

The contours of those changes were already becoming evident during Burwash's final years. A recent study of Methodist piety in Canada between 1884 and 1925 has drawn attention to signs of the beginning of an "eclipse" of the piety represented by Burwash and his generation, and a shift in emphasis from a definite crisis experience to nurture and education. Though the social gospel movement in Canada would not find full expression until after the First World War, Methodism was also beginning to lay a greater stress on social service, although in its official pronouncements it continued to balance the regeneration of society with that of the individual as part of the church's mission.[60] The social gospel, complex in its origins and goals, has been summarized by Richard Allen as "a call for men to find the meaning of their lives in seeking to realize the Kingdom of God in the very fabric of society," and Methodists would play an important role in providing leadership and giving official church support.[61]

However, while changes were indeed discernible, these did not, it should be emphasized, represent an abrupt change with the past. As Allen and others have pointed out, the social gospel movement had already been prepared by the evangelicalism of the nineteenth-century English-speaking world.[62] Whereas Burwash would continue to see the essence of the Christian faith in the evangelical doctrines of individual repentance, forgiveness through the atonement, assurance, and Christian perfection, members of a younger generation would place a greater emphasis on the incarnation and on social regeneration.[63] At the same time through his interpretation of Christian perfection, as through his support of university federation and church union, Burwash had taught young Methodists that their responsibility extended beyond the practice of personal piety to the moral reform of the nation. In his old age, therefore, he had applauded the ethical concerns that in his view motivated many of the young. Thus he had helped provide an important measure of continuity between evangelicalism and the social gospel, even though the two might differ in theological emphases. Following the example of Burwash and his generation, those who espoused the social gospel would continue to recognize the mandate of Christianity to respond to concrete human needs. For them as well, religion was not a matter of custom or tradition, but a force of revitalization.[64] Despite his religious doubts, young J.S. Woodsworth had understood this, and it was for this reason that he had been so critical in this 1913 article in *Acta*. He had concluded that article, not merely with a cry to sweep away orthodoxy, but with the hopeful affirmation of the revivalist: "That Church surely cannot go to ruin that places the emphasis where the Master placed it!"[65]

This understanding of the intimate relationship between evangelical revivalism and its cultural expression makes it clear that what Burwash and Woodsworth and their respective generations were struggling with was not secularization (an elusive term whose origins can be traced to almost any point in the history of Christianity). Rather, they were facing a dilemma which has been part of the Christian experience since its beginning, and which has been compellingly analysed by Richard Niebuhr as "the enduring problem" between Christ and culture. As Niebuhr and others have demonstrated, because Christianity exists in a give and take with a cultural whole, its history has been marked by constant re-evaluation and readjustment. This has been especially true in Protestantism, where readjustment has become a continuing tradition. In order to remain prophetic, religion has had to be both responsive to and yet distinct from the changing culture.[66] Thus, nineteenth-century Canadian Methodists had to face not only the challenge to transform culture through religion but also the apprehension that culture itself might transform religion and make it ineffective. That apprehension had constantly resurfaced: in Anson Green's criticism of the quieter style of revivalism represented by young Burwash, in Alexander Sutherland's opposition to university federation, in Albert Carman's battle with Methodism's wealthy laity over biblical instruction at Victoria, and in the protests against church union in the *Christian Guardian*. More recently it had found expression in Woodsworth's accusation in Winnipeg in 1913 that a claim to conversion on the part of a Methodist entrepreneur was no guarantee that he would deal justly with foreign immigrants. Finally, it found expression in Burwash's laments about the spiritual state of Methodism in his final years. However, normally his approach had been positive. As a scholar and a theologian forced to come to grips with the intellectual currents that unsettled religious belief in the late nineteenth century, he was able to reappropriate the resources of the faith in order to ensure its continued vitality. In this way he demonstrated that biblical fundamentalism and religious scepticism were not the only two responses to modernity available to Victorians. This was no mean feat and should not be overlooked by historians.

A number of scholars examining the origins of unbelief in the western world have emphasized that one of the reasons for the decline of orthodox Christianity was that well-meaning Christians tried to save religion from obsolescence by translating it into terms relevant for the times, thereby "bringing God into line with modernity."[67] As one such critic, James Turner has written, "Reconciling belief with the standards of science, attending more to the immediate moral relevance of religion than to its incomprehensible mysteries, were ways of keeping belief meaningful in a radically different environment."[68] There is a measure of truth to such a conclusion, but it should not be overlooked that, in the case of earnest evangelicals like Burwash, their response flowed naturally out of their understanding of the nature and claims of their religion. Unable to ignore the changes of their own time, they were at the same time fully confident of the power of evangelical Christianity to make effective use of new thought and thereby further its mission to transform the individual and society. Thus, at the heart of Methodism, as of evangelical Christianity, there existed a tension between God's transcendence and human reason, between divine purpose and individual responsibility that gave the movement a dynamism, or in its own phraseology, "a moral momentum." Many years earlier another Methodist preacher and historian, George Playter, had used an evocative analogy to describe this relationship. Recounting the activities of the early Methodist itinerants in Upper Canada, he compared their task to that of a mill grinding wheat. Like the stream that ran the mill, the work of spreading the Gospel was in the first place God's, whereas the task of the ministry, like that of the mill, was secondary. But there was one significant difference: "a mill is an instrument, while man is an agent having thought and will – God's agent, not an instrument as is mistakenly said."[69]

It was precisely because Burwash placed himself within that tradition, as a preacher and as God's moral agent "having thought and will," that he was able to speak throughout his long life with such magisterial confidence on the complex issues that his denomination faced in the late nineteenth century. At his death on 31 March 1918, it was noted in the *Globe*, "No man in Canadian Methodism has influenced and guided the thinking of the ministry of the church to so great an extent."[70] That influence did not stop at his death. By taking the experiential Christianity of John Wesley as seriously as he did, he ensured that the history of evangelical revivalism cannot be confined to the study of mid-nineteenth-century religious behaviour and that its bounds would extend beyond the Methodist tradition in which he had been born. Revivalism would put its mark on a young country's system of higher education, its developing literature, and the statement of faith of a new United Church, as well as on the schedule of Victoria's students for almost a century, as they travelled across the University of Toronto campus to study history, because it was a science and therefore neutral, and then rushed back for a class in literature, which belonged to the moral field of culture.[71] By effectively mining the resources of Methodist faith and practice, Nathanael Burwash helped ensure that through a variety of institutions and practices religion would continue to remain a vital component of Canadian society well into the twentieth century. As one recent historian, Michael Zuckerman, has cogently remarked, arguing for the importance of ideas in bringing about changes in society, "The world we bequeath our great-grandchildren may as nearly be the one we envision most compellingly as the one we build most bulkily."[72] Nathanael Burwash and his fellow Methodists would have been in complete agreement with such a sentiment. As evangelicals the world they envisaged was a world transformed in their own image. Ultimately that was not the world they bequeathed, but having examined their vision and its cultural expression, we may also question whether it was indeed, as some have suggested, the secular city.

Notes

ABBREVIATIONS

CMM   *Canadian Methodist Magazine*, 1875–88
      Methodist Magazine, 1888–95
      Methodist Magazine and Review, 1895–1906
      (Format and editorship remained constant from
      1875–1906.)
CMQ   *Canadian Methodist Quarterly*, 1889–94
CMR   *Canadian Methodist Review*, 1894–5
NBP   Nathanael Burwash Papers
UCA   United Church Archives

INTRODUCTION

1 Massey, *What's Past is Prologue*, 41–4.
2 See for example [Margaret Proctor Burwash], Address on the Education of Methodist Women [1901], NBP 14:385. As president of the Barbara Heck Memorial Association, she led the financial campaign after 1897 to raise money for the building of a women's residence. When a residence, Annesley Hall, was constructed in 1902 she played an active role, along with other Toronto Methodist women, in choosing its furnishings. See Mrs Burwash, "The Victoria Women's Residence and Educational Association," *Acta Victoriana* 32, no. 6 (1908–9): 343–6. For a biographical sketch, written by her eldest son, Edward Moore J. Burwash, see Typed Drafts of Biography, n.d. chap. 13, "Margaret Proctor," NBP 28:634. Victoria's women students paid tribute to her efforts on their behalf in 1912. Mrs F.H. Wallace, "Mrs. Burwash – An Appreciation," *Acta Victoriana* 35, no. 6 (1911–12): 384–8.

3 For E.M.J. Burwash see H.J. Morgan Papers, vol. 4, 1401–2, microfilm, Univ. of Western Ontario, Weldon Library. Lachlin Burwash received notice in the *Star Weekly*, 31 Mar. 1934, as did E.M. Burwash, in the *Star Weekly*, 18 May 1935. For an obituary and comments on Lachlin Burwash see the *New York Times*, 22 Dec. 1940, p. 30.

4 Lachlin Taylor Burwash, *Coronation Gulf Copper deposits: report of an inspection of the known mineralized areas in Coronation Gulf and Bathurst Inlet districts, 1928–9* (Ottawa: Acland, 1930). Edward Moore Jackson Burwash, *The Geology of Vancouver and Vicinity* (Chicago: Univ. of Chicago Press, 1918). Edward published one short study in theology, which faithfully echoed his father's views. E.M.J. Burwash, *The New Theology*.

5 Taylor, "The Darwinian Revolution."

6 Boyle, "Higher Criticism and the Struggle for Academic Freedom in Canadian Methodism"; Gauvreau, "The Taming of History"; Sinclair-Faulkner, "Theory Divided from Practice."

7 Berger, *The Sense of Power*, 86, 230, 237.

8 McKillop, *A Disciplined Intelligence*, 6–7, 88–9, 224–5.

9 Reid, *Mount Allison University*, 1:370–3. In response to the request by Queen's University for government funding to establish a School of Forestry as part of its School of Mining, Burwash and President James Loudon of the University of Toronto issued a very negative report. Queen's, Burwash asserted, had turned down state aid when she refused to enter university federation in the 1880s, and the province could not afford two publicly supported universities. President Loudon and Chancellor Burwash, *Queen's University and the University Question* (pamphlet, n.p., n.d.).

10 Sissons, *History of Victoria University*, 160–204; Falconer, *University Federation in Toronto*; Loudon, *Sir William Mulock*, 76–8; Langton, *Sir Daniel Wilson*, 118–19.

11 As reported by Burwash's cousin, Bertie St Denis. Bertie St Denis to Nathanael Burwash, n.d., NBP 10:146. Mrs St Denis was requesting that Burwash intervene on behalf of her brother-in-law, John W. Thompson, for "some substantial appointment."

12 Obituary Tribute to Burwash, 4 Apr. 1918, NBP 26:581.

13 "In Memoriam: Rev. Nathanael Burwash, MA, STD, LLD, FRSC," *Victoria College Bulletin*, Burwash Memorial Number (1918–19): 63.

14 R.P. Bowles, "The Spirit of Victoria," in Victoria University, *On the Old Ontario Strand*, 171.

15 Langford, *Practical Divinity*, 283.

16 McKillop, *A Disciplined Intelligence*, 205–28; Cook, *The Regenerators*. Cook, in turn, cites as an authority two analyses of secularization which have also been of use in this study: Chadwick, *The Secularization of the European Mind in the Nineteenth Century*, and Hutchison, *The Modernist*

Impulse in American Protestantism.

17 Cook, *The Regenerators*, 4.

18 See for example Armour and Trott, *The Faces of Reason*; Berger, *Science, God, and Nature in Victorian Canada*; Shortt, *The Search for an Ideal*; Westfall, "The Sacred and the Secular."

19 Airhart, "The Eclipse of Revivalist Spirituality"; Semple, "The Decline of Revival"; and "The Impact of Urbanization on the Methodist Church in Central Canada, 1854–1884"; Manning, "Changes in Evangelism"; W.W. Patterson, "The Doctrine of the Ministry in the Methodist Church 1884–1925"; Kleinstuber, *More Than a Memory*, 70–5.

20 Clark, *Church and Sect in Canada*, 399, 431.

21 I am grateful to Prof. Fred Dreyer, Department of History, University of Western Ontario, for first alerting me to this point. For the Model Deed, see Wesley, *The Works of John Wesley* 8: 330–2. In Canada after 1883 the Basis of Union and the Model Deed, with appropriate changes, were printed in the manual *The Doctrine and Discipline*. The Model Deed was incorporated in the Dominion Statute 47 Vict. cap. 106, assented to 19 Apr. 1884. The clearest and most concise analysis of the authority of the Methodist standards is W.I. Shaw, "Doctrinal Standards of the Methodist Church of Canada," *CMM* 13 (1882): 444–50.

22 Ibid., 448. See also W.I. Shaw, *Digest*.

23 Rawlyk, *Ravished by the Spirit*, 110.

24 Sweet, ed., *The Evangelical Tradition in America*, 1–86; Sweet is quoting W.G. McLoughlin.

25 French, "The Evangelical Creed in Canada". For other studies acknowledging the impact of evangelicalism on Canadian society, see Rawlyk, *Ravished by the Spirit*, and James, "The Historical Imagination."

26 French, "The Evangelical Creed in Canada," 33.

27 For a thoughtful examination of contemporary evangelicalism see Marsden, ed., *Evangelicalism and Modern America*. For definitions of eighteenth- and nineteenth-century evangelicalism see Kincheloe, "European Roots of Evangelical Revivalism"; Ballard, "Evangelical Experience: Notes on the History of a Tradition," Helmstadter, "The Nonconformist Conscience," 140–4; Hudson, *Religion in America*, 135–6; Marsden, ed., *Evangelicalism and Modern America*, ix–x.

28 The most concrete international expression of this was the Evangelical Alliance, founded in 1846. See Silcox, *Church Union in Canada*, 85–8.

29 Sweet, ed., *The Evangelical Tradition in America*, 2–7; the Reformation roots are briefly explored in Ballard, "Evangelical Experience: Notes on the History of a Tradition." The mutations which occurred in the normative pattern of conversion between the seventeenth and nineteenth centuries are traced in Brauer, "Conversion: From Puritanism to Revivalism."

30 Wesley, *Works* 5:333.

31 Kincheloe, "European Roots of Evangelical Revivalism," 262. Kincheloe's survey deals with the German Pietist and Dutch Reformed, as well as the Methodist roots of evangelical revivalism.

32 The best summary of these and their social impact in the United States is T.L. Smith, *Revivalism and Social Reform*. Unfortunately, Smith offers no definition of the term "revivalism."

33 Miller, *The Life of the Mind in America*. See also for example Mathews, "The Second Great Awakening as an Organizing Process."

34 McLoughlin, *Revivals, Awakenings, and Reform*, xiii.

35 Both remarks are in Grant, "Asking Questions of the Canadian Past."

36 Moir, "American Influences on Canadian Churches Before Confederation." See also Kewley, "Mass Evangelism in Upper Canada before 1830"; McNairn, "The American contribution to early Methodism in Canada, 1790–1840"; Airhart, "The Eclipse of Revivalist Spirituality"; Bush, "James Caughey, Phoebe and Walter Palmer and the Methodist Revival Experience."

CHAPTER ONE

1 Autobiographical Essay, "Sixty years of Canadian Methodism," NBP 19:498; Essay, "The Old Religion and the New Learning," 1906–9, NBP, box C. This material was added to an unfinished autobiography by E.M. Burwash after his father's death. References to the autobiography will be to the typed draft, which faithfully follows Burwash's handwritten manuscript. NBP 28:613–28.

2 N. Burwash, *Memorials of the Life of Edward and Lydia Jackson*, vii.

3 Cockshut, *Truth to Life*, 21.

4 For example, for the period 1829–1900, fifty-four apparently biographical items are listed as publications under the auspices of the book stewards of the Methodist Church. Pierce, ed., *The House of Ryerson*, 9–45. The importance of "ministerial lives" in carrying on the Wesleyan tradition was recognized at an early date in Great Britain. "Under the editorship of Thomas Jackson, the *Lives of the Early Methodist Preachers* (1837–8) provided a link with Wesley's helpers who first began to make the Methodists a reading people with their saddlebags filled with Mr Wesley's books." Davies, *A History of the Methodist Church in Great Britain* 2:104.

5 Carroll, *Case*, 5 vols.

6 Carroll, *Case* 1:3.

7 Essay, "The Old Religion and the New Learning." 1906–9, NBP, box C.

8 Troeltsch, *The Social Teaching of the Christian Churches* 2:723; Niebuhr, *The Social Sources of Denominationalism*, 20–1; Clark, *Church and Sect*, 329.

9 Niebuhr, *The Social Sources of Denominationalism*, 20.

10 Semple, " 'The Nurture and Admonition of the Lord,' " 158.

11 For an analysis of the unsuitability of the sect-church model for Methodism as organized during Wesley's lifetime, see Dreyer, "A 'Religious Society Under Heaven.' "

12 Davies, *Methodism*, 111–12.

13 For a brief treatment of the importance of the atonement in evangelical theology and piety, see Helmstadter, "The Nonconformist Conscience." For Methodism see Chiles, *Theological Transition in American Methodism*, 144–84.

14 Autobiographical essay, "Sixty Years of Canadian Methodism," NBP 19:498.

15 F.H. Wallace, "In Memoriam: Rev. Nathanael Burwash, MA, STD, LLD, FRSC," *Victoria College Bulletin* (1918–19): 59–65.

16 In 1915 Edward, the oldest, volunteered as chaplain to the Canadian forces; the second, Lachlin, was with the First Canadian Pioneers, first in England and then in France; the third, Albert, was wounded while serving in France and in 1917 was sent home. Proctor, the youngest, who had already once volunteered unsuccessfully for the Boer War, was turned down for medical reasons. For Burwash's pride in five generatioans of military service see Nathanael Burwash to Major General, the Hon. Sir Samuel Hughes, 22 Dec. 1915, NBP, box A.

17 See for example Greven, *The Protestant Temperament*, 335–65; Bailyn, *The Ideological Origins of the American Revolution*, 257–71; McLoughlin, *Revivals, Awakenings, and Reform*, 80–97.

18 "It was a day of revivals and the little country circuit which [the Rev. George] Farr found with forty members rose that year to ninety, the next to a hundred and fifteen under Richard Jones, in two years more under Cyrus Allison to two hundred and eighty-three, and finally after the great revival under Hurlburt and Brownell in 1836, to six hundred and sixty-seven. In ten years the membership multiplied by sixteen and two-thirds." Autobiography, chap. 1, "Family History and Religious Training," NBP 28:622. Burwash's figures for the 1836 revival agree generally with those in Carroll, *Case* 4:50–4.

19 Within three years, 1830–33, the population of Upper Canada increased by nearly 50 per cent. A large number of the newcomers were considerably more well-to-do than the immigrants of an earlier period. Politically and socially, they were considered conservative. Craig, *Upper Canada*, 129–30, 228–30.

20 *Christian Guardian*, 31 Aug. 1881; Lachlin Taylor Papers and Personal File, UCA; Carroll, *Case* 4: 262, 5:76 on Taylor's conversion.

21 Metcalf, a Methodist Episcopal preacher had "located" in 1836 and had strongly opposed union with the Wesleyans. French, *Parsons and Politics*, 139.

22 Wesleyan Methodist Church in Canada, *Minutes* (1824–5): 219.

23 Carroll, *Case* 3: 136, 249.

24 For the history of Methodist unions before 1850 see French, *Parsons and Politics*, 138ff.; after 1850, Caldwell, "the Unification of Methodism in Canada 1865–1884."

25 George Ryerson to Egerton Ryerson, 6 Aug. 1831, quoted in full in Burwash, *Egerton Ryerson*, 317.

26 On the conservativism of British Wesleyan Methodism under Jabez Bunting see Davies, *A History of the Methodist Church in Great Britain* 2: 102–240.

27 Wesleyan Methodist Church in Canada, *Minutes* (1824–45): 132.

28 [Wesley] *Minutes*, 1:43, 67–9, 686–9. Wesley's advice was reprinted in Canada in *The Doctrine and Discipline* from 1833 to 1905.

29 References to the importance of the Sabbath school were frequent in Burwash's sermons, for example, "And wisdom and knowledge shall be the stability of thy times." n.d., NBP 13:336. On the transition from Union to Methodist Sunday schools in central Canada during the 1850s see Semple, "The Impact of Urbanization," 282ff.

30 For a well-documented discussion of the importance of family prayers in the evangelical household see Bradley, *The Call to Seriousness*, 178–93.

31 Autobiography, chap. 1, NBP 28:622.

32 For a description of John Burwash see "Rev. John Burwash – An Appreciation," *Acta Victoriana* 34, no. 1 (Nov. 1910): 56–8.

33 Notebook, "Sermons and Sketches," vol. 10, Nov. 1861.

34 *Christian Guardian*, 24 May 1886. See also "Reminiscences" by Emma G.J. Graham in the *Christian Guardian*, 6 Nov. 1918.

35 Autobiography, chap. 1, NBP 28:622, "Sixty Years of Canadian Methodism," NBP 19:498.

36 Ibid.

37 Greven, *The Protestant Temperament*, 64–5.

38 N. Burwash, "The Rev. Donald G. Sutherland: A Tribute," *CMM* 41 (May 1895): 372. Also Sermon, "What Owe I to Christ?" 24 Feb. 1883, NBP 12:187.

39 Lectures, "Religion and Ethics," 1913, Kwansei Gakuin and Elsewhere in Japan, IV, "Moral Education," NBP 18:464. The sentiment may well be derived from the *Works* of Timothy Dwight, a favourite source for moral education for Burwash as a young minister in the early 1860s. Compare to the discussion of Dwight's pedagogy in Slater, *Children in the New England Mind*, 100–4.

40 Sermons, NBP 12:184, 13:255. For the ideals of "true womanhood" (the feminine counterpart of "moral manliness"), see Welter, "The Cult of True Womanhood"; Bloch, "American Feminine Ideals in Transition"; Hunter, *The Gospel of Gentility*; Kathryn Kish Sklar, "The Last Fifteen Years," in H.F. Thomas and R.S. Keller, eds., *Women in New Worlds* 1:48–65.

41 Greven, *Child-Rearing Concepts*, 46–7.

42 For example "Susanna Wesley" in Withrow, *Makers of Methodism*, 23–41.

43 John Potts, "John Wesley and his Mother," *CMM* 33 (1891): 255.

44 Hart Massey to Nathanael Burwash, 6 Dec. 1892, NBP 10:140.

45 Joseph Flavelle to Nathanael Burwash, 29 May 1905, NBP 2:22. See also, for example, Egerton Ryerson's tribute, "But that to which I am principally indebted for any studious habits, mental capacity or decision of character, is religious instruction, poured into my mind in my childhood by a Mother's counsels, and infused into my heart by a Mother's prayers and tears." Ryerson, *The Story of My Life*, 25.

46 N. Burwash, "Lydia Jackson," *CMM* 3 (Feb. 1876): 97–104; "Jane Clement Jones," *CMM* 42 (July 1895): 37–44; "Anna Vincent Massey," *CMM* 63 (Mar. 1906): 209–14; "Margaret Hopkins Cox," *CMM* 63 (May 1906): 401–7.

47 "Anna Vincent Massey," 213.

48 Slater, *Children in the New England Mind*, 50–1; McLoughlin, *Revivals, Awakenings, and Reform*, 46–58; Greven, *The Protestant Temperament*, 22–4.

49 McLoughlin, *Revivals, Awakenings, and Reform*, 115–17; Douglas, *The Feminization of American Culture*, 143–273.

50 Slater, *Children in the New England Mind*, 104.

51 Douglas, *The Feminization of American Culture*, 96–159; McLoughlin, *Revivals, Awakenings, and Reform*, 119.

52 McLoughlin, *Revivals, Awakenings, and Reform*, 115–17; Aries, *Centuries of Childhood*, 38ff.

53 Douglas, *The Feminization of American Culture*, 55.

54 Semple, " 'The Nurture and Admonition of the Lord,' " 158.

55 Douglas, *The Feminization of American Culture*, 161.

56 Chiles, *Theological Transition in American Methodism*, 58–166 passim; T. Otto Nall, "Methodist Publishing in Historical Perspective 1865–1939," in Bucke, ed., *The History of American Methodism*, 3:155–6; Langford, *Practical Divinity*, 20–49.

57 Langford, *Practical Divinity*, 45–6.

58 On the influence of the Oxford Movement on Wesleyan Methodism see Bowmer, *Pastor and People*, 232–43. Canadian Methodists were very anxious to eradicate from Wesley's thought any hint of baptismal regeneration; see for example the *Christian Guardian*, 17 June 1874; or for a view similar to Burwash's, "Baptismal regeneration is a strange conceit, calculated to do much harm ... Baptism does not change our nature, but merely our relation to the visible church." Green, *The Life and Times*, 414.

59 Hugh Johnston to Edward Moore Burwash, n.d., NBP 6:86. Johnston was Nathanael Burwash's successor at Berkeley Street Methodist Church in Toronto in 1865.

60 Notebook, "Sermons," Sept. 1862, Belleville, NBP 11A:169.

61 Bushnell, *Christian Nurture*, 3–8.

62 Notebook, "Anniversary Addresses," Nov. 1860, "To the Belleville Sabbath School on the Death of Clara Meacham," NBP 14:357.

63 Diary, 4 Nov. 1861, NBP 11:152.

64 *Christian Guardian*, 7 Dec. 1864; NBP 23:565.

65 Hibbard, *A Treatise on Infant Baptism*, 5–6.

66 *Christian Guardian*, 11 May, 29 June, 24 Aug., 7 Sept., 6 Nov., 7 Dec. 1864.

67 *Christian Guardian*, 29 June 1864.

68 In 1870 John Carroll, then one of the most prominent Canadian Methodist ministers, wrote a short treatise defending the Methodist practice of infant baptism against the teachings of the Baptists, in which he echoed the view earlier stated by Hibbard that "infants are born in a state of initial justification by view of the atonement of Christ, in which state, they continue till it is forfeited by personal transgression." Carroll, *Reasons for Methodist Belief*, 34.

69 H.F. Bland, *Student; Preacher; Pastor*, 86; Sermons, Henry Flesher Bland Papers, UCA, 3:132; H.F. Bland, *Universal Childhood*; the original sermon was inserted in the *Sunday School Banner* (1876): 226–8, 257–9.

70 H.F. Bland, *Universal Childhood*, p. 13. The issue had been strongly debated in the *Christian Guardian*, 14 Jan. 1874, 6 Jan., 13 Jan., 10 Mar., 1875. One of the other best-publicized stands came from Alexander Sutherland, secretary of the Missionary Society. In a series of lectures given to the Toronto, London, and Montreal Conferences in 1876, Sutherland argued that, though born in sin, every child had been placed within the kingdom of Christ because of the Atonement. Conversion was unnecessary, provided the child was kept in this position through proper Christian nurture. Sutherland, *The Moral Status of Children*.

71 N. Burwash, *The Relation of Children*. The essay was published as "The Moral Condition of Childhood" in the *Christian Guardian*, 25 May 1881.

72 For the debate see the *Christian Guardian*, 14 Dec. 1881, 2 Mar., 5 Oct., 16 Nov. 1882; for Bland's private reaction Diary 1882, 153–4. Henry Flesher Bland Papers, box 2, UCA.

73 N. Burwash, ed., *Wesley's Doctrinal Standards*, 118, 127, 190.

74 Langford, *Practical Divinity*, 78–86, 113–15. Ahlstrom, *A Religious History of the American People*, 1:532. Chiles, *Theological Transition in American Methodism*, 58–61, 129–34.

75 For a more detailed analysis see N. Burwash, *Inductive Studies in Theology*.

76 N. Burwash, *The Relation of Children*, 14–15.

77 Ibid., 26.

78 Ibid., 27.

79 Ibid., 7.

80 *Christian Guardian*, 1 June, 21 June, 5 July 1882.

81 *Christian Guardian*, 5 July 1882.

82 "Appendix," H.F. Bland, *Universal Childhood*, 21.

83 Shaw, *Digest*, 79.

84 Quoted in Bucke, ed., *History of American Methodism* 3:155.

85 The controversy had begun with the "dropping" from society membership of Ryerson's friend, J. George Hodgins, for failing to attend class meetings. The fullest treatment of this is in Sissons, ed., *Egerton Ryerson* 2:285–95. See also N. Burwash, *Egerton Ryerson*, 282–5.

86 "Sixty Years of Canadian Methodism," NBP 19:498.

87 The names of the children were to be enrolled in the list of probationers, "and if they shall continue to give evidence of a principle and habit of piety, they shall be admitted into full membership in the Church, on the recommendation of a leader with whom they have met at least three months in class, and publicly assenting before the Church to the baptismal covenant, and also to the usual questions on doctrines and discipline." Wesleyan Methodist Church in Canada, *Doctrine and Discipline* (1864), 79.

88 Methodist Church (Canada, Nfld., Bermuda), *Methodist Catechisms*, 3.

89 Methodist Church (Canada, Nfld., Bermuda), *Catechism*, 8. See also NBP 8:104, containing correspondence concerning the catechism between N. Burwash, W.H. Withrow, and A. Carman.

90 Methodist Church (Canada, Nfld., Bermuda), *Journal* (1883): 41. Methodist Church (Canada, Nfld., Bermuda), *Journal* (1902): 80.

91 N. Burwash. "The Revision of our Ritual," CMM 59 (Jan. 1904): 759.

92 Methodist Church (Canada, Nfld., Bermuda), "Agenda," *Journal* (1906): 184; "At least once in each year all the young people who give evidence of such attainment [repentance, decision for Christ, and the exercise of saving faith] shall, after examination by the pastor, be publicly received into the membership of the Church, furnished with our rules, and enrolled in a class." Methodist Church (Canada, Nfld., Bermuda), *Journal* (1906): 144.

93 Burwash, *The Relation of Children*, 31. See also Methodist Church (Canada, Nfld., Bermuda), *Doctrine and Discipline* (1906), 37.

94 *Christian Guardian*, 26 Sept. 1906.

95 Niebuhr, *The Social Sources of Denominationalism*, 21.

96 Semple, "The Decline of Revival," 18.

97 Bradley, *Call to Seriousness*, 22.

98 McLoughlin, *Revivals, Awakenings and Reform*, xiii.

99 Autobiography, n.d., chap. 1, "Family History and Religious Training," NBP 28:622.

100 Geertz, *The Interpretation of Cultures*, 89–90.

101 Semple, " 'The Nurture and Admonition of the Lord,' " 164. Semple's essay on the changing Methodist attitude to childhood conversion appears to

contain one major contradiction. On page 164 he states, "The preeminent belief was that children were the fragile and preferred subjects of Christ. With supervision, discipline and a sound environment, conversion would not be necessary and the safety of childhood could be extended for all children at least into adolescence." However, on page 171, the contrary is asserted: "In general, by the second half of the century, the Methodist Church was prepared to accept not only that children should be prepared for future conversion and, thus, church membership, but that their immediate conversion was both possible and real." Here two models of "modernization" appear to be in conflict: the acceptance of childhood innocence, and the institutionalization of rites of passage.

102 See especially Helmstadter, "The Nonconformist Conscience," 142. For an example of the use of the atonement as a pedagogical device, note the following advice to young children: "As we think of Heaven, we should remember that only the good are there. Within those gates of pearl there shall in no wise enter anything that is impure or unholy or that loveth or maketh a lie. The inhabitants all have washed their robes and made them white in the blood of the Lamb." Editorial, "A Talk With Children About Heaven, CMM 5, (1877): 269–72.

103 N. Burwash, ed., Wesley's Doctrinal Standards, 118; Lectures on Comparative Theology 1890–1891, Victoria College, NBP 17:454.

104 N. Burwash, Inductive Studies in Theology, 7.

105 Ibid., p. 58.

106 "It [the atonement of Christ] is the example to man, and to the universe of moral beings, of Divine righteousness in all its fundamental elements – 1. As right. 2. As how. 3. As obedience. 4. As self-sacrifice. 5. As love. Lastly, by the power of its moral value as a work of right, of law, of obedience, of self-sacrifice, of love, it gives infinite strength to that moral power in which the government of God stands eternally secure." N. Burwash, Manual of Christian Theology 2:189.

CHAPTER TWO

1 For examples of "honest doubt" see Willey, More Nineteenth Century Studies; Turner, Without God, Without Creed; McKillop, A Disciplined Intelligence; Cook, The Regenerators.

2 See for example sermon, "Train up a child in the way he should go," n.d., NBP 13:330; Address Given at Farewell Luncheon for Dr Burwash in Praise of Work Done by his Predecessor Dr Nelles, 17 Oct. 1913, NBP 15:406.

3 Chadwick, The Secularization of the European Mind, 161.

4 For a strongly expressed opinion in support of this view see Thompson, The Making of the English Working Class, 385–440; Buckle, History of the Civilization of the English 1:303. For an analysis of the relationship

between revivalism and critical thought, see Hofstadter, *Anti-Intellectualism in American Life*, 67–121.

5 Quoted in French, *Parsons and Politics*, 121.

6 McKillop, *A Disciplined Intelligence*, 20.

7 Kewley, "Mass Evangelism in Upper Canada" 2:355.

8 Semple, "The Decline of Revival," 17–18.

9 Chiles, *Theological Transition in American Methodism*, 37–61. On the influence of Common Sense Realism on theology in America see Ahlstrom, "The Scottish Philosophy and American Theology," 257–72, and Scott, "Methodist Theology in American in the Nineteenth Century," 87–99.

10 Wesleyan Methodst Church in Canada, *Minutes* (1830), 38. '

11 Quoted in Victoria University, *On the Old Ontario Strand*, 60.

12 McKillop, *A Disciplined Intelligence*, 13–21.

13 For a description of the "Yale Report on the Classics" see for example Schmidt, *The Liberal Arts College*, 45–56. For its adoption at Victoria see Victoria University, *On the Old Ontario Strand*, 115; and draft, "The Founding and Development of Victoria College," July 1914, NBP 29:650.

14 *Christian Guardian*, 6 Dec. 1830.

15 Schmidt, *The Liberal Arts College*, 31–2; T.L. Smith, *The History of Education in the Middle West*, 278; Winthrop Hudson, "The Methodist Age in America."

16 May, *The Enlightenment in America*, 307–57; Meyer, *The Democratic Enlightenment*.

17 On Scottish Realism in America see Ahlstrom, "The Scottish Philosophy and American Theology"; Noll, "Christian thinking and the Rise of the American University"; Sloan, *The Scottish Enlightenment and the American College Ideal*.

18 Persons, *American Minds*, 189.

19 May, *The Enlightenment in America*, 341–7.

20 For the only study of Samuel Nelles see *Dictionary of Canadian Biography*, vol. 11, *1881–1890*, "Nelles, Samuel Sobieski (1823–1887), by G.S. French, 640–2.

21 *Christian Guardian*, 24 May 1843; Address at the First Annual Exhibition of Victoria College, "Spirit of Inquiry," 20 Apr. 1843, Nelles Papers 2:20, UCA.

22 Journal, "Random Thoughts and Mental Records," Toronto, 24 Oct. 1848 – 3 Feb. 1849, p. 96, Nelles Papers 3:31, UCA.

23 Burwash frequently acknowledged Nelles's influence. See for example, Address Given at Farewell Luncheon for Dr Burwash in Praise of Work Done by his Predecessor Dr Nelles, 17 Oct. 1913, NBP 15:406.

24 See for example Address to Victoria College Students re: Love of Learning and Love of Goodness, Winter Session, 1854–5, Nelles Papers 8:174, UCA.

25 Journal, 5 Feb. 1849–19 July 1849, Nelles Papers 3:32; S. Nelles to J.G.

Hodgins, 9 Apr. 1877. Correspondence between J.G. Hodgins and S.S. Nelles (1876–80), Nelles Papers 1:12.

26 Typed Drafts of Autobiography, n.d., chap. 3, "Entering College," 19, NBP 28:624.

27 N. Burwash, *The History of Victoria College*, 462.

28 Meyer, *The Instructed Conscience*. Meyer's excellent study of moral philosophy as taught in American colleges in the pre–Civil War period has provided much of the insight needed to reconstruct Burwash's college education.

29 Journal, "Random Thoughts and Mental Records," vol. 2, 5 Feb. 1849–19 July 1849, Nelles Papers 3:32.

30 Upham, *Mental Philosophy*, vi.

31 For the most comprehensive treatment of Common Sense see Grave, *The Scottish Philosophy of Common Sense*. See also works cited in notes 16 and 17.

32 Lectures on Stewart, 1873, Nelles Papers 10:238, UCA.

33 Meyer, *The Instructed Conscience*, 39; Grave, *The Scottish Philosophy of Common Sense*, 224–57. As Upham concluded, "We feel authorized, therefore, in asserting, that originally, supreme love to God was an essential element of human nature, and that, at the present moment, it is, or ought to be in every human bosom, a distinct and operative principle." Upham, *Mental Philosophy*, 398.

34 Quoted in typed Drafts of Biography, n.d., chap. 5, "Devotions and Opinions," p. 39, NBP 28:626.

35 Ibid., 44–6; Notebook of Essays, "An Essay on Beauty," 1859, read before the Literary Association of the University of Victoria College in Cobourg, NBP 19:487.

36 N. Burwash, *History of Victoria College*, 183–4. Burwash was typical of his generation in this interest in natural science. See Berger, *Science, God and Nature in Victorian Canada*, 5–18.

37 Notebook, "An Essay on the Coincidence of the Geological with the Mosaic Account of Creation," Jan. 1858, NBP 19:486; Biography, 39–44, NBP 28:626.

38 Bozeman, *Protestants in an Age of Science*, 55–6.

39 For the influence of the thought of William Paley on North American educators see May, *The Enlightenment in America*, 342, and Meyer, *The Instructed Conscience*, 8–9.

40 Journal, "Book of Random Thoughts," Wesleyan Univ., Mount Pleasant, Newburgh, Port Hope, Toronto, 1846, Nelles Papers 3:29, UCA.

41 Essay, "The Old Religion and the New Learning," 1906–9, NBP, box C.

42 Notebook, "Sermons," Sept. 1862, Belleville [no. 33], NBP 11A:169.

43 May, *The Enlightenment in America*, 348.

44 College Speech re: Religion and Learning, Nov. 1857, Nelles Papers 8:180, UCA.

45 Wesley, "Romans 14:17," *Notes on the New Testament*, 395.

46 Wesley, "The Case of Reason Impartially Considered," *Works* 6:340.

47 Journal, "Random Thoughts and Mental Records," Toronto, 24 Oct. 1848–3 Feb. 1849, Nelles Papers 3:31, UCA.

48 N. Burwash, *History of Victoria College*, 460–1.

49 Typed Drafts of Autobiography, n.d., chap. 1, "Family History and Religious Training," 9, NBP 28:622.

50 Ibid.

51 "Sermon V: Justification by Faith," *Wesley's Doctrinal Standards*, N. Burwash ed., 49.

52 Joseph Butler, Bishop of Bristol, reproved Wesley with "Sir, the pretending to extraordinary revelations and gifts of the Holy Spirit is a horrid thing; yes sir, it is a very horrid thing." Quoted in Davies, *Methodism*, 65.

53 Quoted in French, *Parsons and Politics*, 53.

54 See for example "Sermon XLIII, The Scripture Way of Salvation," *Wesley's Doctrinal Standards*, N. Burwash ed., 426–36.

55 "Sermon X & XI, The Witness of the Spirit," *Wesley's Doctrinal Standards*, N. Burwash ed., 95.

56 Ibid., 102.

57 Ibid., 108.

58 Autobiography. Chap. 1, 10. NBP 28:622.

59 N. Burwash, *History of Victoria College*, 179. On the work of James Caughey in Canada see Bush, "James Caughey, Phoebe and Walter Palmer and the Methodist Revival Experience in Canada West, 1850–1858."

60 C.C. James, "Upper Canada Academy, 1836–1841," *Acta Victoriana* 28, no. 4 (Jan. 1905): 331–6; E.B. Ryckman to the editor, *Acta Victoriana* 23, no. 3 (Dec. 1899): 290–1.

61 "Reminiscences of Old College Professors and Old Times," *Acta Victoriana* 28, no. 2 (Nov. 1904): 152–6. The lack of discipline at Victoria appears to have been common in North American colleges of the period. See Schmidt, *The Liberal Arts College*, 82–3, and Reid, *Mount Allison University* 1:46–7.

62 Sissons, *A History of Victoria University*, 80.

63 N. Burwash, *History of Victoria College*, 178; "Reply to the Address of the British Conference," Wesleyan Methodist Church in Canada, *Minutes* (1853), 247.

64 N. Burwash, *History of Victoria College*, 180–1. For the most complete account of the 1854 college revival see Notebook, Tribute to Rev. Edward Baird Ryckman DD in the Sixtieth Year of his Ministry, n.d., NBP 15:409. Reference to the revival also occurs in Wesleyan Methodist Church in Canada, *Minutes* (1854), 277. At the Wesleyan Academy (Mount Allison) a similar revival took place in 1845 but was followed by controversy after non-Methodist parents complained about the aggressiveness of the evangelism. Reid, *Mount Allison University* 1:38–42.

65 Autobiographical essay, "Sixty Years of Canadian Methodism," 1910, NBP 19:498.

66 N. Burwash, *History of Victoria College*, 181; Autobiography, chap. 3, 22–3, NBP 28:64.

67 N. Burwash, *History of Victoria College*, 181.

68 See for example the description of the effects of fermented cider on the unsuspecting and studious element of the student body in *Acta Victoriana* (Dec. 1900): 182.

69 W.A. Warden to Nathanael Burwash, 5 July 1904, and Cornell Lane to Nathanael Burwash, 18 July 1904, General Correspondence (1905), NBP 2:20.

70 Cremin, *American Education*, 34; Schmidt, *The Liberal Arts College*, 90.

71 Louise L. Stevenson, "New Means to the Millennium: Noah Porter's College Reforms." I am indebted to Ms Stevenson's analysis of the Yale experience for the information in the preceding paragraph, as well as for the insight concerning the transition taking place at Victoria in the 1850s.

72 N. Burwash, *History of Victoria College*, 178–9. For examples of Nelles's lasting influence on two other students, J.H. Rogers and A. Burns, see *Acta Victoriana* 11, no. 2 (Nov. 1887): 4, 7.

73 College speech re: Religion and Learning, Nov. 1857, Nelles Papers 8:180.

74 N. Burwash, ed., *Wesley's Doctrinal Standards*, 181.

75 N. Burwash, "The Perfect Christian Character," *CMQ* 1, no. 2 (Apr. 1889): 118.

76 N. Burwash, *History of Victoria College*, 465.

77 Meyer, *The Instructed Conscience*, 56.

78 Chiles, *Theological Transition in American Methodism*, 27–61; Langford, *Practical Divinity*, 101–15.

79 For a short description of Miner Raymond's "governmental" theory of the atonement see Langford, *Practical Divinity*, 109. Burwash's criticism of this theory is given briefly in his introduction to Wesley's Sermon XX, "The Lord Our Righteousness," *Wesley's Doctrinal Standards*, N. Burwash ed., 190. Burwash is listed in the 1876 *Circular* of the Garrett Biblical Institute, p. 9, as "Nathan Burwash ... BD V[ictoria]. C[ollege]. Can. Wesleyan (Prof. in V. College). That year he was awarded an STD (Pro merito in sacris Literis). A second Canadian graduate in 1871 was Joseph Sparling, later principal of Wesley College, Winnipeg. Upon receiving the BD in 1871, Burwash presented a "theme" at convocation on the atonement, "The Self Sacrifice of the Son of Man," NBP 12:173. For a brief description of his studies at Garrett see Typed Drafts of Biography, n.d., chap. 13, "The Faculty of Theology," NBP 28:635.

80 Typed Drafts of Biography, n.d., Chap. 13, "The Faculty of Theology," NBP 28:635.

81 See for example sermon, "The Atonement," July 1881, NBP 12:180. For the

most complete exposition of his understanding of the atonement see N. Burwash, *Inductive Studies in Theology*.

82 N. Burwash, *History of Victoria College*, 468.

83 See for example manuscript "The Holy Spirit in the Work of Human Salvation," [1915-16], NBP 22:539-45; essay, "The Spiritual Life: Its Birth: A Definite Religious Experience," 1910, NBP 19:499; Address to the Ministerial Association and Theological Conference, "The Holy Spirit in the Work of the Church," 18 Nov. 1901, NBP 14:384.

84 Notes, n.d., "The Work and Baptism of the Spirit," NBP 22:551; N. Burwash, *History of Victoria College*, 466-9. For a more detailed analysis of the Canadian Methodist attitude to the Plymouth Brethren, see P. Airhart, "The Eclipse of Revivalist Spirituality," 102-14.

85 "Editor's Preface," *Wesley's Doctrinal Standards*, N. Burwash ed., iii-iv.

86 N. Burwash, ed., *Wesley's Doctrinal Standards* 1:92.

87 Methodist Church (Canada, Nfld., Bermuda), *Journal* (1910): 376.

88 Lecture Outlines for Methodist National Training School, part 2, 1916-17, NBP 18:469.

89 See for example typed Drafts of Autobiography/Biography, n.d., chap. 7, "Belleville," 52, NBP 28:628.

90 The best studies of the influence of critical scientific thought on Burwash's generation schooled in Common Sense Realism are Bozeman, *Protestants in an Age of Science*; Hovenkamp, *Science and Religion in America 1800-60*; Noll, ed., *The Princeton Theology 1812-1921*. For Canada see McKillop, *A Disciplined Intelligence* and Berger, *Science, God, and Nature*.

91 N. Burwash, *History of Victoria College*, 362-3. For a detailed examination of Burwash's own response to evolution see Robert John Taylor, "The Darwinian Revolution: the Responses of Four Canadian Scholars" (Ph D dissertation, McMaster Univ., 1976). The present study does not repeat the ground covered by Taylor but amplifies his analysis by demonstrating the relation between Darwin's theory of evolution and Burwash's articulation of Methodist doctrine. In 1896 Burwash considered Paley and Butler as "still useful," but needing to be supplemented by modern apologetics. See N. Burwash, "Modern Apologetics," *CMM* 44 (Oct. 1896): 372. In 1867 S. Nelles was less positive. Recording in his journal his difficulty in finding a suitable text in ethics, he noted, "Butler but a fragment of great principles. Paley unsound & c." Journal, 14 Dec. 1867, Nelles Papers 2:10, UCA.

92 McKillop, *A Disciplined Intelligence*, 217.

93 See for example Methodist Church (Canada, Nfld., Bermuda), *Address of the General Superintendent* (1910), 11-12. Carman used the terms "Rationalism" and "Pantheism." The present study disagrees with McKillop's conclusion that idealism influenced Presbyterians and Methodists in equal measure: "The pervasiveness of idealist assumptions in Canadian university circles is suggested by even the most cursory of examinations of stu-

dent newspapers such as *Queen's Journal* or Victoria College's *Acta Victoriana.*" McKillop, *A Disciplined Intelligence,* 207. My own detailed examination of *Acta Victoriana* (1887–1918) leads to the conclusion that what may appear to be idealism can just as easily be an expression of late-nineteenth-century postmillennialism and a modified form of Christian perfectionism (see chaps. 3, 5, and 6 of this study). J.G. Hume, professor of philosophy and ethics, University of Toronto, submitted a detailed review to *Acta* of John Watson's *The Philosophical Basis of Religion* (1907). While Hume highly recommended the book, he took issue with Watson's assertion that "evil is a necessary element in the development of a finite self-conscious being, who only becomes good by the exercise of his freedom." To Hume, such a view "seems to be diametrically opposed to the view that evil is a stage in a descent not an ascent, not a preparation for good, but a perversion of it." *Acta Victoriana* 31, no. 6 (Mar. 1908): 390–2.

94 Notebook of Lectures on Ethics (Kant), Fall 1878, Nelles Papers 11:241; "Sunday, May 27, 1866," Diary, Cobourg, 1 Jan. 1866–13 Jan. 1867. Nelles Papers 3:35, UCA. For Burwash on Kant see Lectures on Theological Themes, n.d., NBP 18:482; Lecture Series, n.d., NBP 19:483; and on Caird, his review of George Blewett's *The Study of Nature and the Vision of God,* NBP 19:496.

95 NBP 19:496.

96 N. Burwash, *The Genesis, Nature and Results of Sin,* 27–8.

97 N. Burwash, *Manual of Christian Theology* l:vi.

98 Ibid., 236–7.

99 Complementary accounts of his religious crisis are given in detail in typed Drafts of Autobiography/Biography, n.d., chap. 7, "Belleville," NBP 28:628; and in essay, "The Old Religion and the New Learning," NBP box C.

100 Typed Drafts of Biography, n.d., chap. 10, "The Fenian Invasion," NDP 28:630.

101 Typed Drafts of Biography, n.d., chap. 5, "Devotions and Opinions," 45, NBP 28:626. For a brief summary of the approach taken at Victoria College during Burwash's tenure as a professor and administrator see N. Burwash, *History of Victoria College,* 470.

102 N. Burwash, *Manual of Christian Theology* 1:11.

103 Essay, "Intuitive Certainty in Religion," Jan. 1900, NBP 19:492. For another draft of this address see Notebook, Address to the Students of Michigan University, "Intuitive Certainty in Religion," Jan. 1900, NBP 14:383.

104 "Sermon XII, The Witness of Our Own Spirit," *Wesley's Doctrinal Standards,* ed. N. Burwash, 110. For an examination of Wesley's debt to empiricism in forming his understanding of faith see J. Clifford Hindley, "The Philosophy of Enthusiasm," and Dreyer, "Reason and Faith in the Thought of John Wesley."

105 Samuel Nelles, 1 Sept. 1866, Diary, Cobourg; 1 Jan. 1866–13 Jan. 1867,

Nelles Papers 3:35, UCA. For the thought of James McCosh see Hoeveler, *James McCosh and the Scottish Intellectual Tradition*. McCosh retained the dualism of the Scottish realists. In the *Method of Divine Government, Physical and Moral* (1850), in language as much religious as philosophical, and dwelling emphatically on the role of Scripture and the Holy Spirit in changing human character, he demonstrated that conscience, or the moral faculty, had to be linked with the other faculties, the emotions, the intellect, and the will, if the individual was to be fully transformed, or in evangelical terms, converted. In this way it was possible to keep both religion and morality together without adding a religious faculty (pp. 504–10). Burwash, however, did add such a faculty.

106 Burwash acknowledged his debt to McCosh in *The History of Victoria College*, 470. His reference here to the need for the "full assurance and life-giving power of the Holy Spirit" contradicts McKillop's assertion that Burwash's "view that one might know God 'from that which we find within ourselves' could be seen as one similar to [John] Watson's idea of self-consciousness to those disposed towards idealism." McKillop, *A Disciplined Intelligence*, 210.

107 For a brief summary of the thought of Borden Parker Bowne see Langford, *Practical Divinity*, 119–24. A defence of Bowne's teaching, written by E.I. Badgley, professor of ethics and philosophy at Victoria College from 1884 to 1905, can be found in *CMQ* 5, no. 2 (1894): 267–70, and 5, no. 4 (1894): 430–2. Burwash's reference to Theism is taken from Lecture Series, n.d., NBP 19:484. See also Lectures on Theological Themes, n.d., NBP 18:482; and Lecture Series, n.d., NBP 19:483.

108 Mathews, "The Second Great Awakening as an Organizing Process," 29–31.

109 Paley's *Evidences* and Wayland's *Elements of Moral Science* are still listed on the course of study for 1870 but disappear after the 1874 formation of the Methodist Church of Canada. Burwash expressed his chagrin at having to repeat his college work in these areas when he entered the ministry in 1860. Typed Drafts of Autobiography/Biography, n.d., chap. 7, "Belleville," 56–7, NBP 28:628.

110 For a brief study of William H. Withrow's thought as expressed in the *Canadian Methodist Magazine*, see Steven Chambers, "*The Canadian Methodist Magazine*," For Albert Carman's formation and thought see Manning, "Changes in Evangelism within the Methodist Church of Canada during the time of Carman and Chown, 1884–1925." The present study, based on Burwash's role in directing ministerial education during the period 1871 to 1918, questions the pervasiveness of the changes noted by Manning and argues that the piety of the 1850s continued to direct the evangelism of the pre-1925 period. (See also chap. 4).

111 McLoughlin, *Revivals, Awakenings, and Reforms*, 17–18.

112 Dewart, Introduction," *The Canadian Methodist Pulpit: A Collection of Original Sermons*, ed. S.G. Phillips, xvii.

113 William H. Withrow, "Our Educational Work," *CMM* 2 (Dec. 1875): 556.

114 N. Burwash, *History of Victoria College*, 464–5; ibid., 235–68 for changes in the Victoria College curriculum and chaps 4 and 5 of this study. The influence of education upon the leading figures in Canadian church union has received attention in Burkold Kiesekamp, "Community and Faith."

115 Carwardine, *Trans-atlantic Revivalism*, 23–40.

116 Especially valuable for suggesting a relationship between the teachings of the moral philosophers and Victorian business ethics in North America is Meyer, *The Instructed Conscience*, 74–144. See also chap. 3 of this study.

117 Lovin, "The Physics of True Virtue," 14.

118 Address to Victoria College students re: Love of Learning and Love of Goodness, Winter Session, 1854–55, Nelles Papers 8:174, UCA.

CHAPTER THREE

1 After one year travelling on a circuit under supervision, the candidate was examined and "received on trial" or "on probation" for four years. Thereupon, after annual examinations, he was "received into full connexion" and ordained. In Burwash's case, the preliminary year was waived, and his year on the Newburgh circuit was allowed as the first probationary year. He had hoped to have his college education count for two of the years on trial, but since he had attended college before deciding to enter the ministry, the Conference of 1862 refused to allow his request – a severe disappointment. Diary "Sunset Thoughts," 25 June 1862, NBP 11:153; Autobiography/Biography, chap. 7, "Belleville," 62, NBP 28:628.

2 Diaries, NBP 11:150, 150A, 151, 152, 153, 153A; Sermons, NBP 11A: 160–169, 12:170–172; Autobiography, chap. 6, "Tutor and Probationer," NBP 28:627; Autobiography/Biography, chap. 7, "Belleville," NBP 28:628; Biography, chap. 8, "Toronto," NBP 28:629; Biography, chap 9, Hamilton, NBP 28:630.

3 The prominence of Wesley's doctrine of Christian perfection in nineteenth-century Canadian Methodism is the subject of current doctoral research by Alden Aikens, McGill University. For a brief treatment see French, "The Evangelical Creed in Canada," 20. For a detailed study of Christian perfection or the holiness movement in central Canada, as influenced by the preaching of James Caughey and Phoebe Palmer, see Bush, "James Caughey, Phoebe and Walter Palmer and the Methodist Revival Experience in Canada West, 1850–1858." The importance of Christian perfection in Albert Carman's faith is briefly examined in Kleinstuber, *More than a Memory*, 52–6.

4 Hudson, *Religion in America*, 202–5; Ahlstrom, *A Religious History*, 1:557–8, 2:287–91; T.L. Smith, "Righteousness and Hope" and "Holiness and Radicalism in Nineteenth Century America"; Peters, *Christian Perfection*, and the works listed in note 5 below.

5 T.L. Smith, *Revivalism and Social Reform*; Cross, *The Burned-over District*; Dieter, *The Holiness Revival of the Nineteenth Century*; Jones, *Perfectionist Persuasion*.

6 Wesleyan Methodist Church in Canada, *Minutes* (1859): 88.

7 The Toronto School of Medicine had been founded by Dr John Rolph in 1843 and was being conducted in Toronto by a staff of five. In 1854, after the discontinuance of medical teaching at the University of Toronto, Rolph's school turned to Victoria for its degrees and was known as the Medical Department of Faculty of Victoria College, although no instruction was given at Cobourg. This arrangement continued until 1875, when after a period of turmoil, students went over in a body to the Toronto School of Medicine. Sissons, *History of Victoria University*, 98, 102, 142.

8 "Schools and School boys," 25 June 1862, NBP 16:487; Notebook, Address to Juvenile Missionary Meeting (1864), NBP 16:420; Notebook of Addresses on Mission Work (1866), NBP 14:358.

9 Diary, "Sunset Thoughts," Fri. morning, 4 Oct. 1861, NBP 11:152.

10 Notebook, Address before the York Pioneer Club on Toronto in the 1860s, 7 Dec. 1915, NBP 15:409.

11 Pocket Diary, 1866, Hamilton, NBP 11:153A.

12 Biography, "Toronto," NBP 28:629.

13 Ibid.

14 N. Burwash, "Jane Clement Jones," *CMM* 42 (July 1895): 37–44.

15 Biography, "Hamilton," NBP 28:630; and Mika, *Historic Belleville*, passim.

16 Champion, *The Methodist Churches of Toronto*, 169–71.

17 *Dictionary of Canadian Biography*, vol. 11, "Gooderham, William (1790–1881)," by Diane Newell, and "Gooderham, William (1824–1889)," by Leo A. Johnson.

18 Biography, "Hamilton," NBP 28:630.

19 Annual District Meeting Minutes, 1866, Hamilton District, Wesleyan Methodist Church in Canada, UCA.

20 Biography, chap. 12, "Professor of Natural Science," NBP 28:631.

21 N. Burwash, *Memorials of the Life of Edward and Lydia Jackson*. Also in *CMM* 3 (Jan., Feb. 1876): 1–10, 97–104.

22 *Dictionary of Hamilton Biography*, "Jackson, Edward," "Moore, Dennis," "Sanford, William E."; *Dictionary of Canadian Biography*, vol. 10, "Jackson, Edward"; vol. 11, "Moore, Dennis."

23 Biography, chap. 9, "Hamilton," NBP 28:630, *Christian Guardian* 5 July 1865.

24 Note by E.M. Burwash in Biographical Data on the Life of Rev. N. Burwash, vol. 1, NBP 27:599.

25 Lachlin Taylor to S.S. Nelles, 29 July 1872, Nelles Papers 1:2, UCA.

26 Biography, chap. 13, "The Faculty of Theology," NBP 28:635. At the Conference held in Hamilton in June 1874, Lydia Jackson was able to add $10,000 to the fund. In her will she contributed an extra $10,000, plus personal legacies of $2,000 each to Lachlin Taylor, then secretary of missions, and to Burwash. The latter was thereby enabled to purchase a house in 1876 and leave his residence in the college building.

27 "My Eighty Years on Earth," vol. 1, William Hincks Papers, UCA.

28 Biography, chap. 10, "Close of the Pastorate," NBP 28:631.

29 Notebook, "Sermons," Sept. 1862, Belleville, "Soul thou hast much goods laid up for many years," NBP 12:169.

30 [Wesley], *Minutes of the Methodist Conferences*, 1:88.

31 Diary, "Sunset Thoughts," Sat. 4 Jan. 1862, NBP 11:153.

32 Diary, "Sunset Thoughts," 18 May 1861, NBP 11:151.

33 Diary, "Sunset Thoughts," 7 Oct. 1861, NBP 11:152.

34 Green, *Life and Times*, 402.

35 Diary, "Sunset Thoughts," 10 Aug. 1861.

36 Diary, "Sunset Thoughts," Wed. evening, 27 Nov. 1861, NBP 11:153.

37 Diary, "Sunset Thoughts," 10 Aug. 1861, NBP 11:150A.

38 Diary, "Sunset Thoughts," 18 Sept. 1861, NBP 11:152. For a totally different and very positive appreciation of that same revival, see Burwash's reminiscences, Autobiography/Biography, chap. 7, "Belleville," NBP 28:628.

39 Autobiography, chap. 6, "Tutor and Probationer," NBP 28:627.

40 Ibid.

41 Ibid.

42 Autobiography/Biography, chap. 7, "Belleville," NBP 28:628.

43 L.E. Smith, "Nineteenth Century Canadian Preaching," (DTH thesis, Emmanuel College, Toronto, 1953), See also for example, sermon notes in Personal Papers, W.S. Blackstock, William Shannon, UCA, and references in reminiscences in the personal papers of John Craig, Joseph Hill, William English (diary), UCA.

44 Green, *Life and Times*, 373. Also 34, 341.

45 Diary, "Sunset Thoughts," 7 Oct. 1861; NBP 11:152.

46 "Belleville," NBP 28:628.

47 Diary, Sun. 13 Jan. 1867, Nelles Papers 3:35, UCA.

48 Autobiographical Essay, "Sixty Years of Canadian Methodism," 1910, NBP 19:498.

49 Ibid.

50 Notebook, "Sermons," 3 July 1863, Toronto, NBP 12:171.

51 "Belleville," NBP 28:628; "Sixty Years," NBP 19:498.

52 Notebook, "Sermons," Sept. 1862, Belleville, NBP 12:169.

53 Notebook, "Sketches of Sermons" (1865), NBP 12:172.

54 Notebook, "Sermons and Sketches," vol. 10, Nov. 1861, Belleville, NBP 11A:167.

55 Sermon, "For the love of money is the root of all evil," n.d., NBP 13:321.

56 Notebook, "Sermons," Sept. 1862, Belleville, NBP 11A:169.

57 Notebook, "Sermons," 3 July 1863, Toronto, NBP 12:171.

58 "Schools and Schoolboys," 24 June 1862, Belleville, NBP 19:487.

59 Samuel Smiles' Self-Help is listed in Burwash's library of 1862, the date of the first recorded inventory of his books. Index to Library, 1862, NBP 23:569.

60 Meyer, The Instructed Conscience, 99-109.

61 Bliss, A Living Profit, 15-33.

62 McKillop, A Disciplined Intelligence.

63 For the clearest example of such an interpretation see Clark, Church and Sect. For a similar approach, but one which sees culture affecting religion in a positive manner, see Semple, "The Impact of Urbanization on the Methodist Church in Central Canada, 1854-1884."

64 For an illustration see T.B. Brown, Autobiography, 17.

65 Diary, "Sunset Thoughts," Mon. 7 Oct. 1861 and Sat. 12 Oct. 1861, NBP 11:152.

66 Diary, "Sunset Thoughts," Tues. 20 Aug. 1861, NBP 11:151.

67 Autobiography, chap. 6, "Tutor and Probationer," NBP 28:627. For a similar expression of Burwash's appreciation see Address to the Students of Alberta College, "Dealing with Souls," 1912, NBP 15:405.

68 N. Burwash, "Jane Clement Jones," CMM 42 (July 1895): 40.

69 "Sixty Years of Canadian Methodism," NBP 19:498.

70 Sermon 45, "The New Birth," in Wesley's Doctrinal Standards, N. Burwash ed., 454.

71 Wesley, "Plain Account of Christian Perfection," Works 11:368.

72 Ibid., 369.

73 Ibid., 380.

74 T.L. Smith, Revivalism and Social Reform; Peters, Christian Perfection; Langford, Practical Divinity, 92-99.

75 Peters, Christian Perfection, 116-17; Carwardine, Trans-atlantic Revivalism, 159-98; Davies, A History of the Methodist Church 2:234-8; Bush, "James Caughey, Phoebe and Walter Palmer," 81-141. A good account of Caughey's 1853 Hamilton revival is found on pp. 97-102.

76 T.L. Smith, "Righteousness and Hope," 43.

77 Bucke, ed., The History of American Methodism 2:611.

78 T.L. Smith, "Righteousness and Hope," 43.

79 There is already a brief reference to Christian perfection in the annual address in 1834, but in 1853 the doctrine is clearly described and urged upon the membership. However, sporadic references in Carroll, Case show

that entire sanctification never entirely disappeared from Canadian Methodist piety after Wesley's death. The first reference to a Canadian professing to the experience is Calvin Wooster, "sanctified, February 6th, 1792," Carroll, *Case* 1:46. For references to entire sanctification in the 1830s see Carroll, *Case* 4:24-25, 32-35.

80 Wesleyan Methodist Church in Canada, *Minutes* (1860), 84.

81 Wesleyan Methodist Church in Canada, *Doctrine and Discipline* (1859), 59.

82 Wesleyan Methodist Church in Canada, *The Course of Study* (1844). This new course was officially adopted by the 1856 Conference.

83 Autobiography/Biography, chap. 7, "Belleville," NBP 28:628.

84 Meyer, *The Instructed Conscience*, 79.

85 For example NBP 11:150A, and Diary, 10, 13, 17 Aug. 1861, NBP 11:151.

86 Diary, "Sunset Thoughts," Sabbath morning, 22 Sept. 1861, NBP 11:152.

87 Diary Wed., 25 Sept. 1861; NBP 11:152.

88 Diary, "Sunset Thoughts," Mon. 2 Dec. 1861, NBP 11:153.

89 N. Burwash, "Jane Clement Jones," *CMM* 42 (July 1895): 40.

90 Ibid.

91 "Sixty Years of Canadian Methodism," NBP 19:498. For another possible reference to an experience of "entire sanctification" in 1862, see 14 Nov. 1862, NBP 11:153.

92 "A great & glorious idea burst in upon my mind this morning ... It is this to organise in our society a little band who shall unitedly and daily devote themselves to the salvation of sinners. Could not such a band be formed in Belleville. Could not one be formed in every town, city, village, & hamlet in the world? Would not God own their labours & O what results might follow. But am I worthy to see such a scheme in motion. How holy how humble how self sacrificing I must first become." Diary, "Sunset Thoughts," Sabbath morning, 22 June 1862, NBP 11:153. In 1884 a similar band re-emerged in Belleville, again consisting of consecrated laypeople professing to the experience of entire sanctification. Clark, *Church and Sect*, 410.

93 "A Covenant," n.d., NBP 13:263; Handbook, "Growth in Grace or the Progress of the Christian from Penitence to Glory being a Selection of Scripture Illustrating the Attainment of Pardon and Perfect Love," n.d. NBP 23:568; Notebook, "Promise of the Gospel," 30 July 1862, Belleville, NBP 23:559.

94 According to the testimony of his son, E.M. Burwash, this chapter was written during the final days of Burwash's life. In the handwritten manuscript the narrative ends in mid-sentence. E.M. Burwash completed the chapter by adding to it the final portion of the 1910 essay, "Sixty Years of Canadian Methodism."

95 "Sixty Years of Canadian Methodism," NBP 19:498.

96 Hincks, "My Eighty Years on Earth," vol. 1.

97 Biography, chap. 9, "Hamilton," NBP 28:630.

98 Peters, *Christian Perfection*, 130.

99 Pocket Diary, 1866, Hamilton, NBP 153A.

100 For information on Ralph C. Horner and the holiness movement of the 1880s, see Clark, *Church and Sect* 417–18, and Ross, "Ralph Cecil Horner."

101 N. Burwash, "Jane Clement Jones," *CMM* 42 (July 1895): 41.

102 N. Burwash, *Memorials of Edward and Lydia Jackson*, vii.

103 Ibid.

104 Ibid., 21.

105 Ibid., 23.

106 Bliss, *A Canadian Millionaire*. 10–13. For an example of the discrepancy between Flavelle's motives and the effect of his actions see chap. 14, describing the "bacon scandal" during the First World War.

107 [Wesley], *Minutes* (1745), 1:10.

108 Lovin, "The Physics of True Virtue," 15.

109 According to Burwash's recollections in the Autobiographhny, George F. Playter gave "an excellent exposition of Mr. Wesley's great doctrine of Christian Perfection" at the 1861 camp meeting. In his diary this is not mentioned. Autobiography/Biography, chap. 7, "Belleville," NBP 28:628.

110 Exceptions are his classmate at Victoria, Donald G. Sutherland, and A.M. Phillips, a former student, and co-editor of the *CMQ*. N. Burwash, "A Living Epistle," *CMM* 41 (May 1895): 371–9; "The Rev. A.M. Phillips, BD," *CMM* 45 (Feb. 1897): 186–8.

111 On the role of laymen in British Methodism see Bowmer, *Pastor and People*, 163–226. For insight into the role of influential lay men and women in Hamilton Centenary Methodist church, see Smyth, "Centenary Methodist Church."

112 Caldwell, "The Unification of Methodism in Canada," 18–29.

113 *Christian Guardian*, 8 June 1864.

114 Wesleyan Methodist Church in Canada, *Minutes* (1862), 217.

115 *Christian Guardian*, 8 June 1864.

116 For Miley's interpretation of Christian perfection see Miley, *Systematic Theology*, 2:362–71, and Chiles, *Theological Transition*, 165–75. Miley's *Systematic Theology* was used until 1900 as a text on the course of study for Canadian Methodist ministerial students attending college. It was then replaced by Burwash's *Manual of Christian Theology*.

117 For a detailed analysis of the holiness movement in the United States see Marsden, *Fundamentalism and American Culture* 72–108. There is no evidence that Burwash attended a Keswick Conference during his visits to England, nor did his library appear to contain books by writers associated with Keswick. Catalogue of the Books of Dr Burwash in Victoria College Library, n.d., NBP 23:571.

118 N. Burwash, ed., *Wesley's Doctrinal Standards*, 181–8, 389–409, 426–35; *Manual of Christian Theology*, 2:311–36.

119 In an 1888 lecture on Christian perfection, Burwash quoted as evidence from the New Testament John 16:13, "When He, the Spirit of Truth, is come, He shall guide you into all truth." In the same way John 17:17: "Sanctify them through the truth" appeared frequently in his convocation addresses, for example, Address to the Graduates of 1889, "Scientific Morality or Conscientious Search for Truth," 1889, NBP 14:367. The words "the truth shall make you free," are from John 8:32.

120 The text of the entire article, in Burwash's handwriting, is preserved in Church Union Collection, 1:19, UCA. According to "Memorandum re Doctrinal Statement in the Basis of Union," Article 12 "is from the Congregational Statement down to 'Grace of God.' The last sentence was suggested by Dr. Burwash, Chairman of the Doctrinal Committee." Church Union Collection 1:4, UCA.

121 "To the Members of the Methodist Ecumenical Conference" (1911), NBP 8:107.

CHAPTER FOUR

1 Diary, 17 Aug. 1861, NBP 11:151.

2 Theological Alumni Association to N. Burwash, 23 Sept. 1910, NBP 5, 60.

3 Methodist Church (Canada, Nfld., Bermuda), *Journal* (1910): 208–11.

4 See Manuscript of Biography, n.d., chap. 20, NBP 28:620. In 1899, of 328 probationers in the ministry, 162 were at college, 20 on reserve or without a station, and 146 on circuit or missionary work. Address on the Development of Methodist Theology and Mission, 1899, NBP 14:382. In 1910, 1,054 probationers were reported to be attending college. Methodist Church (Canada, Nfld., Bermuda), *Journal* (1910), 189.

5 Methodist Church (Canada, Nfld., Bermuda), *Journal* (1910), 210.

6 For a detailed description of the controversy see Sinclair-Faulkner, "Theory Divided from Practice."

7 F.H. Wallace, "The Probationer's Course of Study," *Acta Victoriana* 32, no. 8 (May 1909): 495–9.

8 Methodist Church (Canada, Nfld., Bermuda), *Journal* (1910): 107–9.

9 Boyle, "Higher Criticism and the Struggle for Academic Freedom in Canadian Methodism."

10 Burkholder, "Canadian Methodism and Higher Criticism, 1860–1910."

11 Gauvreau, "The Taming of History."

12 Sinclair-Faulkner, "Theory Divided from Practice," 321–7. This view is repeated by Moir, *A History of Biblical Studies in Canada*, 38.

13 Sinclair-Faulkner, "Theory Divided from Practice," 319.

14 *Globe*, 26 Feb. 1909.

15 Methodist Church (Canada, Nfld., Bermuda), *Journal* (1910), 107; *Christian Guardian*, 14 Sept. 1910.

16 Nathanael Burwash to Margaret Proctor Burwash, 18 Aug. 1910, NBP 10:144.

17 *Christian Guardian*, 21 Sept. 1910.

18 18 Aug. 1910, NBP 10:144.

19 Autobiography, chap. 7, "Belleville," NBP 28:627.

20 Mention of his completion of four years of reading in two can be found in "Minutes, Belleville District, 1862," UCA.

21 Notebook, "Sermons and Sketches," vol. 10, Nov. 1861, Belleville, NBP 11A:167.

22 Essay, "The Old Religion and the New Learning," 1906–9, NBP, box C.

23 "Sixty Years of Canadian Methodism," 1910, NBP 19:498.

24 Notebook, "Sermons," Sept. 1862, Belleville, NBP 11A:169. See also a review by N. Burwash, "Dr. Freshman on the Pentateuch," *Christian Guardian*, 16 Mar. 1864.

25 Diary, "Sunset Thoughts," 11 Nov. 1861–25 July, 1866, NBP 11:153.

26 There is a resolution in the 1863 Belleville District Meeting Minutes that Nathanael Burwash "be permitted to attend some Theological Institution during the Coming Year." Why he did not do so is not clear, except possibly what at that time he was also considering missionary work in British Columbia. Notebook of Clippings, "Missions 1863," NBP 23:560.

27 Typed Drafts of Biography, n.d., chap. 9, "Hamilton," NBP 28:630.

28 See for example "The Centenary in Canada," *Christian Guardian*, 31 Jan. 1866.

29 Typed Draft of Biography, chap. 12, "Professor of Natural Science," NBP 28:631.

30 For a summary of Methodist theological education in the United States and Britain before 1850, see McCulloh, *Ministerial Education in the American Methodist Movement*, 1–34.

31 For a reaction to *Essays and Reviews*, see the *Christian Guardian*, 17 July 1861; on Colenso, *Christian Guardian*, 30 Jan. 1867; on the need for better theological education, *Christian Guardian*, 21 Oct. 1868; 15 June 1870; 21 Dec. 1870.

32 Wesleyan Methodist Church in Canada, "Minutes of Annual Conference 1872" (microfilm, Weldon Library, Univ. of Western Ontario); *Christian Guardian* 12 June 1872.

33 Typed Drafts of Biography, n.d., chap. 13, "The Faculty of Theology," NBP 28:635. Lachlin Taylor to Samuel Nelles, 29 July 1872, Nelles Papers 1:2; "Opinion on the Wills of Edward and Lydia Ann Jackson re Victoria College by Rose, Macdonald and Merritt, 17 July 1876," Nelles Papers 2:25. Edward Jackson left $10,000 "to aid in establishing a Theological Chair, or to aid such other funds of Victoria College as said Trustees might think

best." At the same time Lydia Ann Jackson gave a $10,000 cheque with a letter "in which she understands that a chair of Theology has been established and that it is the intention of the Trustee to apply the legacy given by her husband to the endowment of said chair, and she directs that the sum of $10,000 then given by her should be applied to the endowment of the said chair." At her death in 1875 she left an additional $10,000.

34 Published after his death. Samuel Nelles, "The Place of Theology Among the Sciences," *CMM* 27 (Feb. 1888): 180.

35 Confederation resulted in the termination of the annual provincial grant of $5,000. For a detailed description of the college's financial concerns see N. Burwash, *Victoria College*, 192–237; Sissons, *Victoria University*, 132–7. For Burwash's appointment see Minutes of the Board of Regents, Victoria College, 28 Sept. 1866, UCA. Burwash's mother and his uncle, Lachlin Taylor, urged him to accept the appointment for reasons of his poor health. Burwash himself appeared initially to be torn, but in the words of his eldest son, decided in the end "that a wider influence could ultimately be exerted through a professorship than through the pastorate." Chap. 12, "Professor of Natural Science," NBP 28:631.

36 Typed Drafts of Biography, n.d., chap. 12, "Professor of Natural Science," NBP 28:631.

37 Quoted in chap. 13, "The Faculty of Theology," 28:635. Ryerson may have preferred the appointment to go to the Rev. Morley Punshon, past president of the British Wesleyan Methodist Conference, who spent 1868–73 in Canada, and whose name was generally linked to a proposed chair in theology. See for example *Christian Guardian*, 17 May 1871, 21 June 1871.

38 In the 1876 Calendar of Garrett Biblical Institute, p. 9, there is an entry under "Class of 1871" for "Nathan Burwash BD and STD [Doctor of Sacred Theology] Prof. Theol. Vic. Col." His professor in Christian Apologetics in 1871 was the college's president, E.O. Haven, "a professor of the blessing of perfect love." The two continued to correspond after Burwash graduated.

39 For a while, at least up to 1882, there was sufficient friction between Nelles and Burwash over the spending of the Jackson Endowment that Burwash considered his dismissal to be impending and felt he would have to return to the pastorate. Manuscript of Biography, n.d., chap. 8, "Personal Relations to his Work," NBP 28:620. Part of the friction may have been due to the fact that Nelles initially had been opposed to the establishment of a faculty of theology at Victoria. A.L. Langford, "Our College: A Retrospect and Prospect, Victoria 1829–92," *Acta Victoriana* 31, no. 3 (Dec. 1907): 153. The establishment of the faculty only became possible with the cessation of the provincial grants in 1867 when it was no longer necessary for the college to maintain its "non-sectarian" status.

40 *Christian Guardian*, 3 May 1876.

41 Sermon, "And wisdom and knowledge shall be the stability of thy times," n.d., NBP 13:336.

42 Notes for Lectures on the English Bible Study, n.d., NBP 18:477.

43 F.H. Wallace, "The Faculty of Theology of Victoria College," *Acta Victoriana* 46, no. 6 (Mar. 1922): 248.

44 Lecture Series, n.d., NBP 19:484.

45 For the fullest treatment of the nature of Baconian thought see Bozeman, *Protestants in an Age of Science*. Except for brief references in McKillop, *A Disciplined Intelligence*, 94–5, and Gauvreau, "The Taming of History," 328–9, the importance of Baconianism in Canada has not received attention. For examples of Canadian Methodists other than Burwash who appealed to Baconian principles, see W.S. Blackstock, "The Higher Criticism," *CMM* 43 (Feb. 1896): 176–7, and Thomas Hurlburt, "Geology and the Bible," *Christian Guardian*, 1 Jan. 1862. In both cases the writers took an open-minded stance on the new scientific developments under examination.

46 Burwash refers without comment to attending Silliman's lectures. Pocket Diary, 1866, Hamilton, NBP 11:153A. On Silliman as a Baconian, see Bozeman, *Protestants in an Age of Science*, 61, 79.

47 Notes for "A System of Inductive Theology," no. 1, 1893, NBP 20:520. Partial but complementary descriptions of the inductive method in teaching can be found in N. Burwash, *Victoria College*, 470, and E.M. Burwash's Manuscript of Biography, n.d., chapter on inductive theology, NBP 28:621.

48 Notebook, "Theological Studies," 1864, Toronto, NBP 23:561.

49 Methodist Church (Canada, Nfld., Bermuda), *Journal* (1890), 180.

50 Lectures, "The Acts of the Apostles," 1885, NBP 17:452.

51 N. Burwash, *Manual of Christian Theology* 1:40.

52 Note one reference to Wesley: "From Peter, Paul, James, and John, to Rutherford, Wesley, Fletcher, Keble, Haverega, or Booth, its [Christianity's] examples of religious life stand unsurpassed in perfection of religious character" (1:85). These examples support the term "evangelical." The Wesleyan emphasis on assurance is dealt with in vol. 1, "Criteria of truth in theology," 10–21, and "The Holy spirit in Redemption," 2:200–12. Christian perfection is examined in 2:311–26.

53 N. Burwash, *Manual of Christian Theology* 1:8; Biography, "Inductive Theology," NBP 28:636.

54 As stated by E.M. Burwash, Manuscript of Biography, n.d. chap. XX, NBP 28:621. At approximately the same time, 1883, Burwash turned down an invitation to teach at a Southern Methodist university, which his son assumed was probably Vanderbilt.

55 "Inductive Theology," NBP 28:636.

56 Ibid.

57 As an example of student appreciation and use of the inductive method, see

A.M. Phillips, "Outline Study of the Life of Christ," *CMR* 7, no. 1 (Jan. 1895): 61–76.

58 N. Burwash, "The Authorship of the Fourth Gospel," *CMM* 12 (Nov. 1880): 470.

59 "The New Version and our Theology," *Christian Guardian*, 29 June 1881.

60 N. Burwash, "Current Tendencies in Religious Thought," *CMM* 43 (Jan. 1896): 83.

61 Burwash's selective acceptance of the higher criticism has been examined by M. Gauvreau in "The Taming of History." However, Gauvreau has not dealt with the importance of the 1885 Bampton Lectures as the turning point in Burwash's attitude. Secondly, Gavreau's study deals only tangentially with the nature of Methodism and as a result makes a stronger case for "a new spirit" at Victoria with respect to biblical studies than does the present analysis.

62 Essay, "The Old Religion and the New Learning" 1906–9, NBP, box C. This essay deals extensively with Burwash's attitude toward the final acceptance of the higher criticism, and is a key document for understanding his thought. For the 1885 Bampton Lectures see Farrar, *The History of Interpretation*. The section which so strongly influenced Burwash covered only a few pages, and it would appear that Burwash used Farrar's analysis of biblical interpretation primarily as a means to justify what his own critical study of Isaiah had already ascertained.

63 "The Old Religion and the New Learning," NBP, box C.

64 Ibid.

65 Lecture Notes on Isaiah, 1877, Victoria College, NBP 16:447. The approach taken was simply to give a historical survey of opinions on the authorship of Isaiah, beginning with Koppe in 1780, and concluding with Dean A.P. Stanley, and William Smith's *Dictionary of the Bible*.

66 In 1897 in his introduction to Workman, *The Old Testament Vindicated*, Burwash showered high praise on the following biblical scholars and theologians: George Adam Smith, S.R. Driver, Marcus Dods, and A.M. Fairbairn. His comment on these scholars was "In using the means thus provided, they hold as loyally to the inner faith of our moral and religious nature as they accept candidly the results of historical evidence and scientific investigation, believing that all truth is of God." Owen Chadwick comments on the slowness of English scholarship to accept the higher criticism and considers the years 1888–92 to be the turning point. See Chadwick, *The Victorian Church* 2:57–111 for a survey of the nature and acceptance of the higher criticism in Britain.

67 E.M. Burwash gives the year as 1885 in "Inductive Theology," NBP 28, 621, in keeping with his father's account. R.P. Bowles recalls 1883 as the date of Burwash's report to his class. Victoria University, *On the Old Ontario Strand*, 161.

68 Nathanael Burwash to Margaret Proctor Burwash, 18 Aug. 1910, NBP 10:144.

69 The journal was originally sent to every minister in the Methodist Church, Canada, and they, in turn, were requested to acquire new subscribers by drawing attention to the publication from the pulpit. In 1894 it changed to a bimonthly journal, and its name became the *Canadian Methodist Review*. *CMR* 6, no. 1 (1894). The following year, after staff and financial difficulties, it amalgamated with the *Canadian Methodist Magazine*.

70 "Salutatory," *CMQ* 1, no. 1 (1889): 94.

71 G.C. Workman, "Messianic Prophecy," *CMQ* 2 (Apr. 1890): 407; "Messianic Prophecy – A Sequel," *CMQ* 3, no. 4 (Oct. 1891): 407–55. Workman stated his approach to be "evangelical," p. 455.

72 A.M. Phillips, "The Eternal and Universal Fatherhood of God" *CMQ* 1, no. 1 (1889).

73 See for example G.C. Workman, "Religious Certainties; or, things which are not shaken," *CMR* 6, no. 4 (July–Aug. 1894): 287–301, and *Messianic Prophecy Vindicated*. Documentation of Workman's defence is in Correspondence re George Workman (1887–1904), NBP 8:113, and Victoria College, Minutes of the Board of Regents, 5 May 1891, 6 May 1891, 15 June 1891, 2 July 1891, 6 Jan. 1892. On the final date a resolution was passed (against Burwash's wishes) "that arrangements should be made as will not involve the teaching of Dr. Workman in the future, of Biblical and Theological subjects in Victoria University." This was followed by Workman's resignation. The controversy now wended its way through the church courts. On 31 May 1899 Burwash made an appeal to the Bay of Quinte Conference against a judgment by General Superintendent Albert Carman, who had overturned that Conference's earlier decision that Workman's teaching was not heretical.

74 Albert Carman, "The Records of Genesis: Not a Myth, a Fancy or a Legend." *Globe*, 26 Feb. 1909.

75 The defence included a very favourable assessment in 1899 of Workman's *Messianic Prophecy Vindicated*. With Principal George M. Grant, the American Methodist theologian Milton Terry and others, Burwash's defence was published as part of the book. In February 1912 Burwash was still concerned with Workman, this time in seeking hundred-dollar subscriptions for a fund to support Workman. In October 1907 the latter had been dismissed from the faculty of Wesleyan Theological College, again upon complaints of heretical teaching. See Sinclair-Faulkner, "Theory Divided from Practice," 330–1, and Correspondence re George Workman (1907–1912), NBP 8:114.

76 Lectures on the Pentateuch, n.d., NBP 18:478. Burwash's acceptance of evolution has been exhaustively examined by Taylor, "The Darwinian revolution: the responses of four Canadian scholars." Taylor's conclusion

is that the theory of evolution, stripped of natural selection, held no threat for Burwash, who "drew upon the intuitive certainty of his faith to explain the place of the Darwinian hypothesis within his concept of truth," p. 276. This interpretation is in agreement with the analysis offered in the present chapter concerning Burwash's acceptance of the higher criticism.

77 Lectures on the Pentateuch, n.d., NBP 18:478.

78 N. Burwash, *Manual of Christian Theology* 1:442.

79 Hovenkamp, *Science and Religion in America*, 209–10.

80 Bozeman, *Protestants in an Age of Science*, 167–73; Marsden, *Fundamentalism and American Culture*, 55–62. F. Sandeen, *The Roots of Fundamentalism* focuses more on the doctrinal roots of fundamentalism, and sees its two main sources to lie in premillennialism and the Princeton theology.

81 Bozeman, *Protestants in an Age of Science*, 150–7. Bozeman sees Baconianism to be in part a Presbyterian defence against the anti-intellectualism of denominations like the Methodists and Baptists, 132.

82 Ibid., xi–xv.

83 See for example, Dewart, "A Brief Examination of Professor Workman's Teaching and Methods," *CMQ* 3, no. 1 (Jan. 1891): 74–87, and Dewart, *Jesus the Messiah in Prophecy and Fulfilment.*

84 *Globe*, 29 Feb. 1909.

85 For a comprehensive but brief treatment of the encounter of British and American Methodism with the higher criticism see Langford, *Practical Divinity*, 119–30, 147–58. There were two major controversies in American Methodism: in 1904 Borden Parker Bowne was tried for heresy, but acquitted, and in 1895, 1900, and 1905 Hinckley G. Mitchell of Boston University became a centre of controversy for refusing to accept the Mosaic authorship of the Pentateuch. See also Bucke, ed., *History of American Methodism* 2:598. For a view which stresses the ease with which Methodism became liberal see Hutchison, *The Modernist Impulse*, 114.

86 Sandeen, *The Roots of Fundamentalism*, 106.

87 For a detailed analysis see Abraham, "The Wesleyan Quadrilateral." Abraham makes note of "little if any interest in the quadrilateral within British Methodism," 2.

88 N. Burwash, *Manual of Christian Theology* 1:236–7.

89 Lecture Series, n.d., NBP 19:483.

90 Statement to Board of Regents from Faculty of Theology re: Higher Criticism, 22 Mar. 1909, MBP, box D; *Christian Guardian*, 31 Mar. 1909.

91 For the significance of the order of the Anglican and Methodist articles of faith see Bassett, "North American Methodist Biblical Scholarship and the Authority of Scripture."

92 This same defence had been presented in the statement signed by the faculty on 22 March 1909.

93 Methodist Church (Canada, Nfld., Bermuda), *Journal* (1910): 109. For Bur-

wash's defence see Address to General Conference in Defence of George Jackson, Victoria, BC (27 Aug. 1910), NBP, box C.

94 Statement to Board of Regents, 22 Mar. 1909, NBP, box D.

95 Bassett, "North American Biblical Scholarship," 18.

96 N. Burwash in Workman, *Messianic Prophecy Vindicated*, 75. Burwash's position follows that taken by the Methodist Episcopal theologian Milton S. Terry (1846–1914) of Garrett Biblical Institute. See Langford, *Practical Divinity* 125–6. Terry also contributed a defence to Workman's *Messianic Prophecy Vindicated*, and like Burwash and George M. Grant pleaded for freedom of thought and emphasized the agreement between Workman's views and the Methodist doctrinal standards.

97 Nathanael Burwash to Bertha M. Toye, 12 Aug. 1910, NBP, box AS.

98 *Christian Guardian*, 14 Sept. 1910.

99 *Christian Guardian*, 31 Mar. 1909, 7. For a much earlier argument on the compatibility between the new biblical criticism and John Wesley's *Notes on the New Testament*, see "Watchman," "Wesley's Notes on the New Testament and the New Revision," *CMM* 14 (1881): 85. An editorial in the *Globe*, 29 Feb. 1909 also based its case for freedom of interpretation on Wesley: "He recognized the fundamental distinction between soundness of faith – a Christian temper and attitude to Christ – and soundness in doctrine – an acceptance of a formulated construction of faith." The *London Quarterly and Holborn Review* 189 n.s., 9 (Jan. 1901): 171 in a review of George Jackson's *A Young Man's Religion* also favourably compared Jackson to Wesley, proclaiming "these are such sermons as Wesley would now preach in Edinburgh."

100 Methodist Church (Canada, Nfld., Bermuda), *Address of the General Superintendent* (1910), 1–2.

101 Nathanael Burwash to the Revs. George Washington, MA, Joseph R. Gundy, DD, Joseph Philp, BA, BD, Richard Hobbs, Herman Moore, Thomas W. Blatchford, BA, George W. Dewey and W.E. Millson, 23 May 1910, NBP 8:116.

102 Bozeman, *Protestants in an Age of Science*, 167. See also Hovenkamp, *Science and Religion in America*, 173; Marsden, *Fundamentalism and American Culture*, 6–7, 55–7.

103 Nathanael Burwash to Albert Carman, 9 Oct. 1909 (unsigned), Carman papers 26:156, UCA.

104 Ibid.

105 Address on the Development of Methodist Theology and Mission, 1899, NBP 14:382.

106 Covenant, Belleville Seminary, 7 Oct. 1858, Carman Papers 26:151, UCA. In 1910 the annual salary for the general superintendent was three thousand dollars, and seven hundred for rent. Methodist Church (Canada, Nfld., Bermuda), *Journal* (1910), 404.

107 Semple, "The Impact of Urbanization"; Caldwell, "the Unification of Methodism in Canada, 1865–1884."

108 Albert Carman, "The Methodist Itinerancy, and the Stationing Committee," *CMM* 29 (Apr., May, June 1889): 310–21, 421–31, 517–25; *CMM* 30 (July, Aug., Sept. 1889): 27–39, 129–38, 224–34.

109 See Bliss, *A Canadian Millionaire*, 199–202. Bliss likewise focuses on the strength of lay opposition to Carman during the controversy. His conclusion, however, is different, for in his opinion "it was not laymen's money that finally triumphed when an anti-Jackson resolution was defeated at the 1910 General Conference, but rather the realization that the attacks on Jackson were a direct threat to freedom at Victoria and within the denomination generally" (p. 202).

110 *Christian Guardian*, 26 Sept. 1909.

111 N. Burwash, "Analytical Study of Genesis," *CMQ* (Jan.–Feb., Mar.–Apr. 1894): 64–83, 162–71.

112 Methodist Church (Canada, Nfld., Bermuda), *Journal* (1910), 107–9.

113 Methodist Church (Canada, Nfld., Bermuda), *Address of the General Superintendent* (1910), 9.

114 In 1902, for example, Timothy Eaton had offered to donate funds to Victoria to have A.M. Phillips give a two-year course in the analytical study of the English Bible. For reasons of political tact, Burwash did not accept. T. Eaton to N. Burwash, 7 May 1892, NPB 1:4.

115 *Globe*, 1 Mar. 1909, 1.

116 Chadwick, *The Victorian Church* 2:97.

117 Methodist Church (Canada, Nfld., Bermuda), *Journal* (1910): 85.

118 *Christian Guardian*, 14 Sept. 1910. For Rowell's stance on the higher criticism see Prang, *N.W. Rowell: Ontario Nationalist*, 70–90.

119 This concept is dealt with in R. Allen, "Providence to Progress".

120 H.H. Fudger to N. Burwash, 27 Dec. 1909, NBP, box A.

121 Essay, "The Old Religion and the New Learning," 1906–9, NBP, box C. While Burwash mentions no names and simply asserts that he is writing at the request of "one whose judgment and authority I respect," I have assumed from the letter of 27 December 1909 that this person was H.H. Fudger.

CHAPTER FIVE

1 R.C. Pitman to Samuel Nelles, 28 Feb. 1884, Nelles Papers 1:8, UCA.

2 *Acta Victoriana* 11, no. 3 (Dec. 1887): 5; *Christian Guardian*, 23 Nov. 1887.

3 N. Burwash, *History of Victoria College*, 533.

4 Clipping, Scrapbook on S.S. Nelles compiled by J.G. Hodgins, n.d., Nelles Papers 14:301, UCA.

5 N. Burwash, *Federation Vindicated: A Tract for the Times*, 5.

6 See for example Veysey, *The Emergence of the American University*; Hofstadter and Metzger, *The Development of Academic Freedom in the United States*, 346–63; Schmidt, *The Liberal Arts College*, 41; H.C. Johnston, Jr., "Down from the Mountain: Secularization and the American Public University."

7 McKillop, *Contours of Canadian Thought*, 78–95.

8 Quoted in Veysey, *The Emergence of the American University*, 2.

9 Ibid., 2–11; Schmidt, *The Liberal Arts College*, 160–8. For Canada see Harris, *A History of Higher Education in Canada 1663–1960*, 53–4; Masters, "Patterns of Thought in Anglican Colleges in the Nineteenth Century."

10 Sissons, *A History of Victoria University*, 161–2.

11 *Christian Guardian*, 15 Jan. 1868. See also 29 Jan. 1868.

12 "These letters were written in 1880–81 but by advice of Dr. Nelles not sent. This was the first beginning in my own mind of the federation scheme." These words are written on an envelope in the Burwash Papers which contained a "Letter to the Editor of the *Globe*, January 28, 1881," NBP, box B. Sissons makes a reference to the letter in *History of Victoria University*, 160–1.

13 On 23 December 1879 Nelles wrote a long letter to George Grant in which he expressed his refusal to consider any plan of "confederation" which entailed university centralization. His requirements for considering any proposal for confederation were "1. State aid to denom. Colls. 2. Perfect autonomy in all matters of religious teaching and moral discipline." For the present he advised (unlike Burwash) that the denominational colleges take a role of "masterful inactivity." S.S. Nelles to G.M. Grant, 23 Dec. 1879, G.M. Grant Papers 1071–1077, National Archives of Canada.

14 References to this incident are in N. Burwash, *History of Victoria College*, 281, and Notebook, "My Memories of Victoria College," no. 1, 1910, NBP, box E.

15 For a recent analysis see Ayre, "Universities and the Legislature: Political Aspects of the Ontario University Question, 1868–1906." Earlier accounts are Harris, "The Establishment of a Provincial University in Ontario"; Wallace, ed., *A History of the University of Toronto 1827–1927*. None of these examines the role of religious ideals in motivating Nelles and Burwash to support federation, nor Burwash's rationale behind the division of labour as outlined in the 1887 Federation Act. Burwash's own published accounts of university federation are in *History of Victoria College*, 271–409 and Wallace, ed., *The University of Toronto and its Colleges, 1827–1906*, 9–77. A short, clear summary of federation as it affected Victoria College is in Sissons, *History of Victoria University*, 158–204.

16 This is acknowledged in Sissons, *History of Victoria University*, 164–7, and in Neatby, *Queen's University* 1: 162 and Falconer, *University Federation in Toronto*, 44. See also Loudon, *Sir William Mulock*, 76–8.

17 N. Burwash, *History of Victoria College*, 305.

18 S.S. Nelles to G.M. Grant, 9 Jan. 1880, G.M. Grant Correspondence 1114–
1121, National Archives of Canada; N. Burwash, *History of Victoria College*, 280–3.

19 Notes, "The Colleges," n.d., NBP 22:553. Burwash simply refers to "Mat.
Arnold, p. 146." However the reference clearly alludes to Arnold's description of the Prussian universities. See Arnold, *Higher Schools and Universities in Germany*. Burwash appears to have hit upon the division in the late spring of 1884, possibly in response to a convocation address at Victoria by the Hon. G.W. Ross, where the latter suggested that denominational colleges look after "religious literary culture." *Christian Guardian*, 14 May 1884.

20 For the reason for the division of the curriculum see Sissons, *History of Victoria University*, 166. This agrees with Burwash's account in Address to the Royal Society of Canada, Section II. "A Review of the Founding and Development of the University of Toronto as a Provincial Institution," 25 May 1905, NBP 15:395. However, by that date Burwash appeared to have forgotten the original reason for the assignment of history to the university curriculum.

21 Memorandum for Senate re: University Commission, 1 Feb. 1906, NBP, box D.

22 Before this date Nelles had compiled a list of the positon on university federation by the members of the board. Of 39 members polled, only 14 were in favour. Of these, only 6 (including Burwash, but not Nelles), attached no qualification to their support. List of Members of Board of Regents of Victoria University Noting Their Attitude Toward Federation, n.d., [before 1883], Nelles Papers 15:322, UCA. See also Sissons, *History of Victoria University*, 168.

23 For Nelles's concerns, voiced on a number of occasions, see correspondence between J.G. Hodgins and S.S. Nelles (1885–7), Nelles Papers 1:15, UCA. In the summer of 1886 Nelles was in England and expressed the fear that in his absence Burwash might be prevailed upon to compromise Victoria's interests. See S.S. Nelles to J.J. Maclaren, 10 July 1886, Nelles Papers 1:17, UCA.

24 By 24 August 1886 Burwash, following Nelles, had opted for independence. On 30 August 1886 the *Globe* and the *Mail* published a letter by Burwash. In it he withdrew his support from federation and argued that for the present independence was the best policy. *Globe*, 31 Aug. 1886. See also Journal, "Notes by the Way," 24 Aug. 1886, Nelles Papers 3:39, UCA. Sissons remarked on this about-face, "It is doubtful whether in his long and honourable career Burwash on any other occasion erred so greatly in diplomacy." Sissons, *History of Victoria University*, 177.

25 Burwash explained later that he had not ceased to wish for federation but considered the danger of denominational disunity, as well as the apparent

lack of Methodist financial support to be insurmountable obstacles. N. Burwash, *History of Victoria College*, 339. These, along with Nelles's poor health are also the reasons he gave for his brief withdrawal of support in a very bitter exchange of letters with Alexander Sutherland in the *Mail*, 22 Dec. 1887, Notebook, Clippings and Addresses on the University Question, 1885-8, NBP, box F.

26 Notebook. Drafts of Address on Federation, July 1886, Nelles Papers 14:289, UCA. See also *Christian Guardian*, 8 Sept. 1886, and 22 Sept. 1886. Federation was carried by a vote of 138 to 113, with both Nelles and Burwash voting against. Names and votes were published in Methodist Church (Canada, Nfld., Bermuda), *Journal* (1886): 60-1.

27 See correspondence from Burwash to E.H. Dewart 1881-4, n.d., NBP, box A, and Dewart, *University Federation Considered in its Relation to the Educational Interests of the Methodist Church.*

28 First Draft of the Federation Act (An Act Respecting the University of Toronto and University College) with Burwash's Notes and Queries, 1887, NBP, box D; Minutes of Committee on Legislation, 29 Mar., 6 Apr. 1887, NBP, box D. A discerning evaluation of the Federation Act can be found in Sissons, *History of Victoria University*, 181-4.

29 Clippings from the *Globe* and the *Mail* dealing with the controversy are in Notebook, Letters and Clippings re: Federation 1888-1889, NBP, box F. Detailed accounts are in Sissons, *History of Victoria University*, 184-90, and N. Burwash, *History of Victoria College*, 258-409. Besides using the columns of the *Mail*, the *Globe*, the *Cobourg World*, the *Christian Guardian*, and the *Canadian Methodist Magazine*, both sides also issued a number of pamphlets.

30 N. Burwash, *History of Victoria College*, 374.

31 Against objections, Burwash succeeded in forcing the Board of Regents to accept a list of proposed candidates, all of whom strongly supported federation. His reason was that under the circumstances it was essential for the Board to speak with one voice. Victoria College, Minutes of the Board of Regents, 16 Oct. 1890. For a very critical reaction to this "gerrymandering" see H. Hough to N. Burwash, 22 Oct. 1890, General Correspondence (1890-1), NBP 1:3.

32 T. Smith, *The History of Education in the Middle West*, 40-49; Semple, "The Impact of Urbanization," 31-4.

33 In the 1883 Basis of Union it was explicitly stated that, in accordance with the traditional policy of the uniting bodies, "Colleges and Universities should be under the fostering care of the Church." Methodist Church (Canada, Nfld., Bermuda), *Journal* (1883): 309. This point was often emphasized by opponents of federation, for example, J.J. Maclaren to S.S. Nelles, 5 Oct. 1883, Nelles Papers 1:17, UCA.

34 Alexander Sutherland withdrew his candidature before a vote was taken on

the appointment to the presidency, and seconded the motion, "that the Rev. N. Burwash, STD be appointed to fill the vacancy occasioned by the death of the president of Victoria University." The motion was carried unanimously. Victoria College, Minutes of the Board of Regents, vol. 1, Toronto, 18 Nov. 1887.

35 Sutherland, *The Proposed Plan of College Confederation*.

36 See for example "Chancellor Edward Blake's address at the annual commencement exercises, Toronto University," the *Globe*, 11 June 1884.

37 Hodgetts, "Where Victoria Evermore Shall Stand."

38 See for example S.S. Nelles to J.H. Hodgins, 9 Jan. 1884, Nelles Papers 1:14, UCA. "Rice has been talking with Carman ... and those M.E. men are sensitive on this matter of state aid ... Our body is now heterogeneous and we cannot count fully on the M.E. men as to state aid." See also Moir, "Methodism and Higher Education, 1843-1849," and N. Burwash, *History of Victoria College*, 261.

39 C.B. Sissons, *History of Victoria University*, 184-5.

40 Supported by much statistical evidence, these two offers were unfavourably contrasted to university federation in "A catechism on college federation," by J.S. Ross in "The Present Aspect of University Federation," a pamphlet reprinted from *CMM* 26 (Nov. 1887). Inquiries from representatives of the Hamilton Board of Trade to Burwash during August 1886 are printed in Methodist Church (Canada, Nfld., Bermuda), *Journal* (1886): 200-2. Ibid., 202, for a letter of Cobourg's offer of twenty acres to the Board of Victoria University.

41 Sissons, *History of Victoria University*, 189. Gooderham left $200,000 in addition to an earlier $30,000. The site he had in mind consisted of eleven acres just to the west of the present Casa Loma. Burwash, in his defence of federation emphasized the financial disadvantages of independence in Toronto. N. Burwash, *Some Further Facts Concerning Federation*, 8-9.

42 Neatby, *Queen's University*, 1:162-167. Burwash was not averse to using Grant's successful fundraising as a means to emulate the Presbyterians in financial zeal. Addresses, "Methodist Education in Ontario," June 1886, NBP 14:363.

43 C.M. Johnson, *McMaster University* 1:47-52, 81-84; Wallace, ed., *The University of Toronto 1827-1906*, 146-7.

44 J. Reid, *Mount Allison University* 1:166-182; Harris, *A History of Higher Education in Canada*, 105.

45 Hofstadter and Metzger, *The Development of Academic Freedom in the United States*, 361.

46 Ayre, "Universities and the Legislature"; N. Burwash, *History of Victoria College*, 90-103, 168-76, 192-216. Burwash's account contains much documentary support from the *Documentary History of Education* edited by J. George Hodgins.

47 See Scrapbook on S.S. Nelles, compiled by J.G. Hodgins, n.d., Nelles Papers 14:301, UCA; S.S. Nelles to J.J. Maclaren, 17 May 1886, Nelles Papers 1:17, UCA.

48 N. Burwash, *History of Victoria College*, 528.

49 Notebook, Memoranda on College Matters, n.d., Nelles Papers 14:289, UCA.

50 Nelles was especially concerned that Burwash as dean of theology might give in to the desire of University of Toronto officials to change Victoria's status from an arts to a theological college. S.S. Nelles to J.J. Maclaren, 22 July 1886, Nelles Papers 1:17, UCA.

51 Sissons, *History of Victoria University*, 158

52 See for example Falconer, *University Federation in Toronto*, 47–9; correspondence between B.E. Walker and N. Burwash re University Finances (1897–8), NBP 8:118.

53 N. Burwash, "Appendix V, Dr. Burwash's Address to the Alumni on University Confederation in 1885," *History of Victoria College*, 529–33.

54 N. Burwash, *Some Further Facts Concerning Federation*, 13.

55 N. Burwash, *The Present Aspects of University Federation*, 11.

56 Ibid., 8.

57 J. Allen, *Facts Concerning Federation*.

58 N. Burwash, *Some Further Facts Concerning Federation*, 13.

59 Heyck, *The Transformation of Intellectual Life in Victorian England*.

60 N. Burwash, *The Present Aspects of University Federation*, 7.

61 Ibid., 4.

62 "The Future of the University," *University of Toronto Monthly* (June 1900), 33–4.

63 N. Burwash, "The College and the University," *CMM* 44 (Dec. 1896): 512.

64 Address, "The Broadest Facilities for Higher Education, the Duty of the Church," n.d., NBP 16:431.

65 N. Burwash, "The College and the University," *CMM* 44 (Dec. 1896): 514.

66 N. Burwash, *The Present Aspects of University Federation*, 11.

67 At the request of Chancellor and Mrs Burwash an investigation of the Victoria buildings was carried out, as the four children had died in the same building where two years earlier Nelles had died of typhoid fever. Carman Papers 26:156, UCA. For the permanent effect of the loss on Mrs Burwash see Typed Drafts of Biography, n.d., chap. 3, "Margaret Proctor," NBP 28:634.

68 N. Burwash, *Some Further Facts Concerning Federation*, 13.

69 N. Burwash, *History of Victoria College*, 405; *Christian Guardian*, 2. Nov. 1892.

70 "Mr. Massey's Will," the *Globe*, 27 Feb. 1896. For comments on Hart Massey's bequest to Victoria College see N. Burwash, "Our educational Work and Mr. Massey's Will," *CMM* 43 (May 1896), 472, and "Mr.

Massey's Bequests," 479. An itemization of subsequent bequests from the Massey family can be found in Sissons, *History of Victoria University*, 224, 247, 269–70. Hart Massey continued to favour independence, and Burwash repeated his defence of the amount of money to be saved by federation to the executors of Massey's estate. "Memorandum re Victoria University," Correspondence with Massey Family (1892–1907), NBP 10:140.

71 William George Storm to N. Burwash, 8 Mar. 1889. General Correspondence (1880–9), NBP 1:2.

72 For a successor's description of the meaning of Victoria's stained glass windows see Frye, *By Liberal Things*, 20.

73 Address, "the Broadest Facilities for Higher Education, the Duty of the Church," n.d., NBP 16:431.

74 I am indebted for this information to Prof. W.A.E. McBryde, Department of Chemistry, Faculty of Science, Univ. of Waterloo.

75 Carman expressed his agreement with Burwash on this point in Methodist Church (Canada, Nfld., Bermuda), *Address of the General Superintendent* (1910), 12.

76 See his comments on the influence of scientific thought on the college student in the period after 1859 in N. Burwash, *History of Victoria College*, 469–70. S.S. Nelles in 1879 expressed his concern that the Evidences of Christianity were "no longer taught or required at University College and the University of Toronto," S.S. Nelles to J.G. Hodgins, 23 Dec. 1879, Nelles Papers 1:2, UCA.

77 N. Burwash, *History of Victoria College*, 505–6.

78 Victoria University, *On the Old Ontario Strand*, 157–8.

79 Address, "The Broadest Facilities for Higher Education, the Duty of the Church," n.d., NBP 16:431.

80 N. Burwash, "The College and the University." *CMM* 44 (Dec. 1896): 512.

81 See for example "Courses of Study Possible," *Victoria College Bulletin* 1908–9, 13–15.

82 N. Burwash, *History of Victoria College*, 496–501.

83 N. Burwash, "The College and the University," *CMM* 44 (Dec. 1896): 512.

84 The moral and religious purpose of poetry was explained at length in Address, "Symbols," n.d., NBP 16:426, and Lecture, The Use and Abuse of Books, Oct. 1897, NBP 17:455a.

85 Ibid.

86 Ibid. In this connection see also Bliss, "Pure Books on Avoided Subjects," 89–108.

87 Criticism of Reynar's "morbid" enthusiasm for Tennyson's "In Memoriam" was shared by William Hincks and his son, two successive generations of Victoria undergraduates. William Hincks, "My Eighty Years on Earth," vol. 1, William Hincks papers, UCA.

88 N. Burwash to J.W. Flavelle, 22 Feb. 1902, NBP 1:17. Burwash was writing

in response to student criticism of the teaching of certain members of the faculty. See also Victoria College, Minutes of the Faculty, 29 Dec. 1910.

89 Address, "The Broadest Facilities for Higher Education, the Duty of the Church," n.d., NBP 16:431.

90 Ibid.

91 For the Yale model see Stevenson, "Between the Old-time College and the Modern University: Noah Porter and the New Haven Scholars." Burwash was not the only evangelical educator anxious to maintain traditional values in a changing academic environment. See for example Hoeveler, *James McCosh and the Scottish Intellectual Tradition*, 215–71, where the author examines the manner in which evangelical Christianity and Scottish Common Sense Realism shaped the educational reforms instituted at Princeton by McCosh. In the spring of 1888 Burwash visited both Yale and Princeton to gain firsthand experience of "college movements in the U.S." *Christian Guardian*, 12 Sept. 1988, 24 Oct. 1888.

92 *Christian Guardian*, 16 May 1888.

93 For an example of parental gratitude for Burwash's help with a "wayward" son, see Julien E. Dunne to N. Burwash, 26 Nov. 1901, Margaret Proctor Burwash Papers 1:8, UCA; of Burwash as matchmaker, F. Allan Patterson to Nathanael Burwash, 18 Oct. 1897, NBP 1:8; of Burwash's efforts to eradicate student smoking, Address to Conference on Higher Education, 1902, NBP 16:433; of methods of study, Notebook of Addresses [1894], NBP 14:374.

94 In the 1902 report of the Board of Regents of Victoria University, it was pointed out that "The very few who still avoid our College are mostly lovers of sport or persons to whom the high moral tone of the College is not an attraction." Methodist Church (Canada, Nfld., Bermuda), *Journal* (1902): 236.

95 *Acta Victoriana* 32, no. 5 (Feb. 1909): 415–16.

96 *Acta Victoriana* 37, no. 2.

97 *Acta Victoriana* 37, no. 5 (Feb. 1913): 258–60.

98 *Christian Guardian*, 24 Oct. 1888.

99 For Vincent Massey's appointment see N. Burwash to Vincent Massey, 13 Dec. 1912, NBP 10:141.

100 Address of the Education of Methodist Women [by Margaret Proctor Burwash, 1901], NBP 14:385, and *Acta Victoriana* 32, no. 4 (Jan. 1909): 343–6.

101 Rothblatt, *The Revolution of the Dons*, 180–9, 246.

102 Heyck, *TheTransformation of Intellectual Life*, 221–3.

103 N. Burwash, "The College and the University," *CMM* 44 (Dec. 1896): 513.

104 N. Burwash to J.W. Flavelle, 22 Feb. 1902, NBP 1:17.

105 N. Burwash to H. Hough, General Correspondence (1898), NBP 1:9. See also the petition made by the Victoria faculty to the Board of Regents for a salary increase, 4 Oct. 1901, NBP 1:13.

106 For an example of Burwash's criticism of specialization see Address to the University of Toronto Alumni Association, "The University," Jan. 25, 1910. Guelph, NBP 15:400.

107 Blewett underscored his respect for this former professors in a letter in 1906 responding to Burwash's request that he apply for a vacancy in ethics. G.J. Blewett to N. Burwash, 15 Jan. 1906, General Correspondence (Jan.-Mar. 1906), NBP 2:21.

108 Victoria College, Faculty Board Minutes, 29 Dec. 1910.

109 Acta Victoriana 32, no. 7 (Apr. 1909): 561.

110 Acta Victoriana 34, no. 2 (Nov. 1910): 55. The writer was referring specifically (and appreciatively) to A.H. Reynar.

111 Acta Victoriana 29, no. 4 (Jan. 1906): 289.

112 See for example "Special Aspects of the Religious Life of the College Since Federation, 1892–1917," in N. Burwash, History of Victoria College, 471–81, and Addresses, "Methodist Education in Ontario," June 1886, NBP 14:364.

113 Chapel attendance was listed as compulsory in the Victoria University Calendar until 1908–9.

114 See for example W.F. Adams to N. Burwash, 7 July 1904. General Correspondence (1904 Jan.-June), NBP 12:18; Margaret Proctor Burwash to Ned Burwash, 1 June 1909, Margaret Proctor Burwash Papers 2:20, UCA; N. Burwash, History of Victoria College, 473.

115 N. Burwash, History of Victoria College, 473.

116 A copy is in Notebook, Biographical Data on Life of Rev. N. Burwash, NBP 27:612.

117 Acta Victoriana 34, no. 1 (Oct. 1910): 19.

118 N. Burwash, "Perfect Love," CMQ 1, no. 1 (Jan. 1889): 10.

119 Article re Relationship between college and University, n.d., NBP, box C.

120 A.H. Reynar, "The Higher Life," CMM 62 (Sept. 1905), 279.

121 McLoughlin, Revivals, Awakenings and Reform, 129–30; Finney, Memoirs of Rev. Charles G. Finney, 339–51; T. Smith, Revivalism and Social Reform, 103–14.

122 T. Smith, Revivalism and Social Reform, 225–37.

123 Letter from Alfred Lavell re Methodist Educational Policy (1902), NBP 8:105.

124 N. Burwash to Alfred Lavelle [sic], 27 Mar. 1902, General Correspondence 1901–4; NBP; box A.

125 See for example "Educational," 1904, Committee Reports, NBP 8:102.

126 Methodist Church (Canada, Nfld., Bermuda), Journal (1910): 209.

127 Letter to Adam Crooks, Minister of Education, re National University, n.d. [January 1881], NBP 8:117.

128 Ibid.

129 Fiorino, "The Moral Foundation of Egerton Ryerson's Idea of Education"; Prentice, *The School Promoters*.
130 Goldwin French, "The Evangelical Creed in Canada," 31.
131 C.M. Johnston, *McMaster University* 1:10–11.
132 G. French, "The Evangelical Creed in Canada," 29.
133 Nathanael Burwash to Adam Crooks, n.d., NBP 8:117.
134 Address at 1885 Convocation, Nelles Papers 8:199, UCA.
135 *Globe*, 11 June 1884.
136 Correspondence between S.H. Blake and N. Burwash re Religious Teaching at the University of Toronto (1908–9), NBP 8:106. Along with Albert Carman, Blake objected strongly to the nature of biblical teaching in the department as being "absolutely opposed to the orthodox position connected with the Bible." For a brief summary of the controversy see Greenlee, *Sir Robert Falconer*, 127–34.
137 N. Burwash, "The University and the Nation," CMM 51 (Jan. 1900): 52–6.
138 *Acta Victoriana* 35, no. 7 (Apr. 1912): 349.
139 *Acta Victoriana* 28, no. 6 (May 1905): 464–7.
140 Methodist Church (Canada, Nfld., Bermuda), *Journal* (1886): 54, 59; *Christian Guardian*, 8 Sept. 1886.
141 Burwash credited Mulock and Senator John Macdonald, a Toronto Methodist, with having instigated the federation movement. N. Burwash, *History of Victoria College*, 445. In an early communication to the provincial government Burwash styled himself "a friend and supported of the present Ontario Government." N. Burwash to G.W. Ross, Minister of Education, 26 July 1884, Miscellaneous Documents, NBP: box F.
142 N. Burwash to Sir Wilfrid Laurier, 11 Oct. 1909, Laurier Papers 160786–7, National Archives of Canada. Earlier that year he had written on behalf of E.W. Thompson, who sought an appointment to the new department of foreign affairs. N. Burwash to Sir Wilfrid Laurier, 25 Mar. 1909, Laurier Papers 154026–8, National Archives of Canada.
143 On juvenile delinquency see N. Burwash to S.D. Chown, 11 Sept. 1909, NBP 4:50; on women's suffrage, Augusta Stowe-Gullen to N. Burwash, 20 Mar. 1909, NBP 3:45. The former had requested that he give a three-minute speech on behalf of the Canadian Suffrage Association Meeting at the Parliament Buildings.
144 See for example Berger, *The Sense of Power*, 128–52.
145 Address to the Dominion Educational Association, "National Education," 26 July 1904, Winnipeg, NBP 15:390.
146 Quoted in French, "The Evangelical Creed in Canada," 30.
147 N. Burwash, *Inaugural Introduction to Section II* 13.
148 Sutherland, *The Proposed Plan of College Confederation*, 19.
149 N. Burwash, "The College and the University," CMM 44 (Dec. 1896): 514.

CHAPTER SIX

1 N. Burwash, "To the Members of the Methodist Ecumenical Conference: A Plea for Canadian Church Union by a Canadian Methodist" [1911], NBP 8:107.
2 Methodist Church (Canada, Nfld., Bermuda), *Proceedings of the Fourth Ecumenical Methodist Conference*, 296.
3 N. Burwash, "A Plea for Canadian Church Union," NBP 8:107.
4 Methodist Church (Canada, Nfld., Bermuda), *Proceedings of the Fourth Ecumenical Methodist Conference*, 295–300.
5 Ibid., 290–5.
6 Ibid., 309–10.
7 Ibid., 311.
8 Methodist Church (Canada, Nfld., Bermuda), *Journal* (1910): 329; Silcox, *Church Union in Canada*, 167.
9 Silcox, *Church Union in Canada*, 168.
10 Ibid., 169–70. For the dissent in the *Christian Guardian* see especially the issues of 24 Jan., 14 and 21 Feb., 13 Mar. 1912.
11 Rev. Stephen Bond, "The Basis of Union," *Christian Guardian*, 24 Jan. 1912.
12 W.S. Griffin, "Why I Am Against the Basis of Union," *Christian Guardian*, 13 Mar. 1912.
13 W. Jackson, "The Doctrinal Basis," *Christian Guardian*, 21 Feb. 1912.
14 "Our Change of Emphasis," *Christian Guardian*, 5 June 1912.
15 Silcox, *Church Union in Canada*, 138.
16 Morrow, *Church Union in Canada*, 114–232.
17 Lucas, "Wesley Heritage in the United Church of Canada," 148–9.
18 Clifford, "The United Church of Canada and Doctrinal Confession"; "The Interpreters of the United Church of Canada."
19 Burwash's defence of union in the *Christian Guardian* took the form of four articles: "Church Union – Questions for the Methodist People. I. Is it Right?" 24 Jan. 1912; "Church Union – Questions for the Methodist People. II. When?" 31 Jan. 1912; "Church Union – Objections to the Basis," 7 Feb. 1912; "Church Union – Objections to Details of Organization, and also to the Principle of Organic Union," 14 Feb. 1912.
20 See for example Historical Address at Jubilee of the Centenary Methodist Church, 1918, Hamilton, NBP 15:412.
21 E. Lloyd Morrow noted, "It is interesting to learn that Dr. Burwash was brought up in a Presbyterian atmosphere, yet was Arminian by conviction. This circumstance no doubt enabled him to make very valuable suggestions and contributions of a conciliatory nature." Morrow, *Church Union in Canada*, 118.
22 Typed Drafts of Autobiography, n.d., chap. 3, "Entering College," p. 25, NBP 28:624.

23 Essay, "Shall We Hinder the Gospel of Christ?" (Distinction Between Actual Christianity and the Christianity of the New Testament), n.d., Nelles Papers 4:57, UCA.

24 College Speech re Religion and Learning, Nov. 1857, Nelles Papers 8:180, UCA.

25 George Grant to Samuel Nelles, 23 Sept. 1881, Nelles Papers 1:4, UCA. See also W. Grant and F. Hamilton, *Principal Grant*, 493; George M. Grant, "Organic Union of Churches," *CMM* 60, no. 9 (Aug. 1904): 123–8.

26 Burwash alluded to Wesley's debates with the Calvinists in his introduction to *Wesley's Doctrinal Standards*, xvii.

27 "Memories of the Manse, the Parsonage, and the College," Francis H. Wallace Papers 4, vol. 1, 324, UCA.

28 Notebook of Addresses [1894], "Divinity Schools," Knox Jubilee, NBP 14:374.

29 "Salutatory," *CMQ* 1, no. 2 (Jan. 1889): 94.

30 Brief references to the influence of the scientific method on the historical understanding of such a prominent American church historian as Philip Schaff can be found in Bowden, *Church History on the Age of Science*, 42–58.

31 Quoted by his eldest son, Edward M. Burwash, in Typed Drafts of Biography, n.d., chapter on inductive theology, NBP 28:635.

32 Drummond, *Natural Law in the Spiritual World*; Hoeveler, *James McCosh*, 180–211. On the effects of such an approach in undermining evangelical Christianity see Turner, *Without God, Without Creed*, 150–67, 179–87.

33 Notebook, Lectures on the History of Christian Doctrine, Oct. 1897, Victoria College, NBP 17:456.

34 See for example Burwash's comments in Notebook, Lecture, "Comparative Theology," Jan. 1899, NBP 17:456, and his review of Harnack's *History of Dogma*, "History of Dogma," *CMM* 43 (Apr. 1896): 371–2. F.H. Wallace voiced his concern from Berlin in F.H. Wallace to Nathanael Burwash, 21 Dec. 1910, NBP 5:62.

35 See for example Lecture Notes on the History of Christian Doctrine and Dogma, n.d., NBP 18:481.

36 Binder, "Church History Among the Anglosaxon Peoples" with Additional Notes on the European Reformation," n.d., NBP 23:558.

37 For George Parker Fisher's historical scholarship see Bowden, *Church History in the Age of Science*, 66. After 1898 Fisher's *History of the Christian Church* and *History of the Reformation* were assigned reading for all candidates for the ministry with a BA Methodist Church (Canada, Nfld., Bermuda), *Journal* (1898): 198.

38 Notes on "Comparative Theology," 1904, NBP: box E.

39 N. Burwash, ed., *Wesley's Doctrinal Standards*, xiii–xiv.

40 Notes on "History of Christian Doctrine," Oct. 1909, NBP: box E.

41 Notes on "Comparative Theology," 1904, and notes on "Comparative Theology," Feb. 1910, NBP: box E.

42 *Acta Victoriana* 12, no. 5 (Feb. 1889): 5–7; for the 1889 church union discussions see Millman, "The Conference on Christian Unity."

43 Lecture Series, "Church History from A.D. 1500," Oct. 1913, NBP 18:465.

44 Binder, "Church History Among the Anglosaxon Peoples," n.d., NBP 23:557.

45 N. Burwash, "1799–1899. The Contrast and Outlook," *CMM* 50 (Nov. 1899): 402–7.

46 N. Burwash, "The Ministry of Canadian Methodism and the College," *CMM* 50 (July 1899): 24–30.

47 N. Burwash, "1799–1899. The Contrast and Outlook," *CMM* 50 (Nov. 1899): 402.

48 N. Burwash, *History of Victoria College*, 464; see also Funeral Address for Reverend David Scott Houck. n.d. [1912], NBP 16:428.

49 Address given to the General Assembly of the Presbyterian Church in Canada, 1898, NBP 14:379. That same year Knox College's Principal William Caven and Dr Torrance, Moderator of the Presbyterian Church, were introduced as fraternal delegates by Burwash to the Methodist General Conference which met in Toronto. In reply to their overtures for a union of the two churches, the Conference moved, "We recognize that ... the Presbyterian and Methodist churches of Canada are being rapidly assimilated in thought, spirit and method, and we are convinced that in such approximation of the two leading Protestant churches of our Dominion there is an encouraging guarantee of an active evangelical influence which must result in the highest development of Christian intelligence and Morality." The Conference, in response to a plea for union in the general superintendent's address, also set up a committee on Church Union, "to confer with and consider any proposals from the representatives of other Christian denominations, and report to the next General Conference." Methodist Church (Canada, Nfld., Bermuda), *Journal* (1898): 38–9, 336. Surprisingly the 1898 church union references are completely overlooked in the most recent study of church union, which begins with Principal William Patrick's plea for union at the 1902 General Conference. Clifford, *The Resistance to Church Union*, 13–25. For Caven's fraternal address see *Christian Guardian*, 14 Sept. 1898.

50 Methodist Church (Canada, Nfld., Bermuda), *Journal* (1902): 71, 172–3.

51 Ibid., 172.

52 Address, "Is a positive doctrinal basis for the United Church possible?" Dec. 1, 1904, NBP 15:392.

53 The most comprehensive of these is Schroeder, "The Role of Theology in Church Union." See also Morrow, *Church Union in Canada*, 13–48, 114–213, and Silcox, *Church Union in Canada*, 133–8.

54 N. Burwash to the Rev. F. Louis Barber, 8 Feb. 1912, NBP 8:107.

55 N. Burwash to the Rev. Professor Patton, Wesleyan Theological College, Montreal, 28 Feb. 1910, NBP: box A.

56 "The Modern Revision of Creeds and the Position of Christian Doctrine Today," Notes on "Comparative Theology," Feb. 1910, NBP: box E.

57 Morrow, Church Union in Canada, 170; a copy of the twelfth artice, "Sanctification," written in Burwash's hand is in Church Union Collection 1925, 1:19, UCA; see also "Memorandum re Doctrinal Statement in the Basis of Union," Church Union Collection 1925, 1:4, UCA.

58 Morrow, Church Union in Canada, 114; for another example of Duval's irenic spirit see Clifford, The Resistance to Church Union, 32.

59 Hodge at Princeton had departed from the older Calvinism in his positive expectation that all dying in infancy, as well as a good proportion of the human race, would be saved. The more progressive wing of American Presbyterianism, the New School Presbyterians, had gone much further, denying both original sin and repudiating the determinism of predestination for an Arminian emphasis on human ability and free will. Expelled in 1837, the New School had reunited with the Old School Presbyterians in 1869 and had contributed significantly to a revision of the Westminster Confession which was taking place within both American and British Presbyterianism. Loetscher, The Broadening Church, 39-47, 83-9.

60 Ibid., 83-9.

61 Clifford, Resistance to Church Union, 40.

62 "What is Arminianism?" Lecture Notes on the History of Christian Doctrine and Dogma, n.d., NBP 18:481.

63 Silcox, Church Union in Canada, 118-20; Kiesekamp, "Community and Faith," 152.

64 Morrow, Church Union in Canada, 116.

65 Christian Guardian, 5 Dec. 1906.

66 F.H. Wallace, "Memories," F.H. Wallace Papers 4, vol. 1, 323, UCA.

67 Methodist Church (Canada, Nfld., Bermuda), Journal (1898): 195.

68 Typed Drafts of Autobiography, n.d., chapt. 3, "Entering College," p. 21, NBP 28:624.

69 "A Brief Statement of the Reformed Faith (U.S.A. 1905)," "The Articles of the Faith of the Presbyterian Church of England," the "Doctrinal Basis of Union" proposed by the Montreal Local Committee, and the doctrinal statement of the Basis of Union are in Morrow, Church Union in Canada, apps 1-4, 305-27.

70 Index to Library, 1862, NBP 23:569. For a reference to Hodge in his lectures see for example Lecture Notes on the History of Christian Dogma, n.d., NBP 18:481. A short, useful analysis of Hodge's theology and method can be found in Noll, ed., The Princeton Theology, 27-38, 145-52, 132-41, 177-84.

71 Hodge's opposition is described briefly in Meyer, *The Instructed Conscience*, 20.

72 A reference to the "Princeton sympathies" of especially William MacLaren, principal of Knox College, can be found in Clifford, *Resistance to Church Union*, 39–40. Unfortunately a more detailed analysis of the theological training and outlook of the Presbyterian members of the subcommittee on doctrine is still lacking.

73 *Christian Guardian*, 7 Feb. 1912.

74 Morrow, *Church Union in Canada*, 118–19.

75 W. Jackson, "The Doctrinal Basis," *Christian Guardian*, 21 Feb. 1912.

76 "Entering College," NBP 28:624.

77 *Christian Guardian*, 7 Feb. 1912.

78 N. Burwash, ed., *Wesley's Doctrinal Standards* preface.

79 *Christian Guardian*, 7 Feb. 1912.

80 Ibid.

81 *Christian Guardian*, 24 Jan. 1912.

82 Stephen Bond was eight years older than Burwash. For his criticism of the Basis of Union see "The Basis of Union," *Christian Guardian*, 24 Jan. 1912, 31 Jan. 1912, 21 Feb. 1912.

83 W. Jackson, "The Doctrinal Basis," *Christian Guardian*, 21 Feb. 1912; W.S. Griffin, "The Passing of the Sect," *Christian Guardian*, 24 Jan. 1912; "Why I am against the Basis of Union," *Christian Guardian*, 13 Mar. 1912.

84 *Christian Guardian*, 24 Jan. 1912.

85 Editorial, *Christian Guardian*, 15 May 1912.

86 S. Bond, "The Pessimistic Bishops; or do we emphasize our distinctive doctrines," *Christian Guardian*, 29 May 1912.

87 *Christian Guardian*, 13 Mar. 1912.

88 *Christian Guardian*, 24 Jan. 1912.

89 See for example Morrow, *Church Union in Canada*, 113–232; E. Scott, *"Church Union" and the Presbyterian Church in Canada*, 12–14; Clifford, *Resistance to Church Union*, 40–9 passim.

90 Farris, "The Fathers of 1925."

91 Clifford, *Resistance to Church Union*, 2.

92 As one delegate, the Rev. A.B. Leonard of the Methodist Episcopal Church warned, "Denominationalism is one thing; unity in Jesus Christ is another thing. I should deprecate that in the future all denominations should become one single organization. That happened once, and the dark ages followed," Methodist Church (Canada, Nfld., Bermuda), *Proceedings of the Fourth Ecumenical Methodist Conference*, 308.

93 See also Silcox, *Church Union in Canada*, 168–9, and 478 for an analysis of the vote by the individual conferences.

94 J.W. Grant, *George Pidgeon*, 70.

95 Chalmers, *See the Christ Stand!*, 135.

96 Lucas, "Wesley Heritage in the United Church of Canada," 142–6.

97 Silcox, *Church Union in Canada,* 127.

98 For the inaugural service on 25 June 1925 see Chown, *The Story of Church Union in Canada,* 118–30.

99 For S.P. Rose's continued interest in Methodism, see especially Rose, *The Genius of Methodism.* By 1930 this was one of the eight studies in the series, the "Ryerson Essays," edited by Lorne Pierce, specifically devoted to the teachings of John Wesley on subjects of current interest.

100 Chown, *The Story of Church Union in Canada,* 124. The Presbyterian contribution was described as "the manifestation of the Spirit in vigilance for Christ's Kirk and Covenant, in care for the spread of education and devotion to sacred learning," the Congregationalist as "the manifestation of the Spirit in the liberty of prophesying, the love of spiritual freedom and the enforcement of civic justice," p. 123.

101 See chap. 2 of this study.

102 Hofstadter, *Anti-Intellectualism in American Life,* 83.

103 See for example such statements as "While erroneous doctrine is not to be thought of as being as bad as immorality, yet the procedure for trial provided by Discipline is the same for both." Methodist Church (Canada, Nfld., Bermuda), *Journal* (1910): 169–70; and "Some sort of creed is essential to every religious or ecclesiastical organization … Harmony with principles held in common is essential to all organization. There is, therefore, no need of apologizing for creeds. They are a simple and palpable necessity." Shaw, *Digest,* ix. Shaw stressed that this attitude to doctrine followed Wesley's teaching.

104 N. Burwash, ed., *Wesley's Doctrinal Standards,* xviii.

105 *Christian Guardian,* 31 Jan. 1912.

106 Kilpatrick, *Our Common Faith,* vi. See also *The United Church of Canada,* 29.

107 Kilpatrick, *Our Common Faith,* 63.

108 Mathews, "The Second Great Awakening as an Organizing Process," 29.

107 J.W. Grant, " 'At least you knew where you stood with them' "; Silcox, *Church Union in Canada,* 73–102. Silcox makes detailed references to the importance of the Evangelical Alliance, whose first branch in Canada, as in the United States, was organized in 1867. Burwash, along with Principals Caven of Knox and Sheraton of Wycliffe, was active in the Alliance, which attracted, as Wilcox notes, "the best minds in the evangelical churches." Silcox also suggests that by 1902 the work of the Alliance for Christian unity had stalled and "was transformed to a different plane," p. 87.

110 Clifford, "The Interpreters of the United Church of Canada," 212.

111 T.L. Smith, *Revivalism and Social Reform,* 236.

112 See for example the exhortation in 1835 "We must never lay down our arms until the last enemy is conquered – and we must never quit the field or relax

our labours until our work is done; and that will not be until the world is converted." Wesleyan Methodist Church in Canada, *Minutes* (1835): 103; in 1847, calling for increased conversions, "May we be filled with the Spirit ... and may our whole bodies and souls be preserved blameless unto the coming of our Lord Jesus Christ." *Minutes* (1847): 47; compare to 1910, "Each age of the Church would seem to have its specific task. That of our own age the Christian Church is coming to recognize as the establishment of the Kingdom of God on the earth. The new conception of the Missionary enterprise as not only the salvation of individuals, but the uplifting and redemption of nations and races ... all these indicate ... that a new chapter in Christian history has been begun." Methodist Church (Canada, Nfld., Bermuda), *Journal* (1910): 416. Elsewhere, however, this latter report stressed continuity with the past: "Those who insist on individual regeneration and those who call for social reforms are coming together," p. 415. The same stress on conversion and on moral and social reform as signs of the coming of the Kingdom can be found in the 1836 and 1847 addresses. For a succinct summary of the millennial views of the Methodist Church of Canada as interpreted by S.D. Chown, see Schwarz, "Samuel Dwight Chown," 200-1.

113 These comments were made in one of the last recorded pieces of writing, just before his death, N. Burwash to G.C. Workman, 3 May 1917, NBP: box A. See also Sermon, "The Privileges and Responsibilities of God's Elect," n.d., NBP 13:248.

114 T.L. Smith, *Revivalism and Social Reform*, 225-37; Turner, *Without God, Without Creed*, 150-7. Turner examines the acceptance of an evolutionary reading of history by late-nineteenth-century American Christians but does not explore the points of contact between historicism and millennialism.

115 Withrow, *Religious Progress*, vii.

116 Marsden, "Fundamentalism as an American Phenomenon," 228; McLoughlin, *Revivals, Awakenings, and Reform*, 150-7.

117 Ibid.; Marsden, *Fundamentalism and American Culture*, 30-1.

118 Methodist Church (Canada, Nfld., Bermuda), *Journal* (1898): 260. In 1897 the annual increase was 5,733; in 1898 it was 2,412.

119 In 1902 the total increase for the preceding quadrennium was 11,358. Methodist Church (Canada, Nfld., Bermuda), *Journal* (1902): 137. For the period 1886-90 the increase had been 36,399. *Journal* (1890): 319.

120 For a shortage of ministers in 1902 see the letter by the Bay of Quinte Conference President, A.H. Reynar to N. Burwash, 8 July 1902, NBP 1:14. The decline in the number of class leaders was noted in Methodist Church (Canada, Nfld., Bermuda), *Journal* (1906): 222, as was the lack of suitable candidates for the ministry, p. 269, and the absence of the tone of evangelism from the pulpit, p. 268.

121 Methodist Church (Canada, Nfld., Bermuda), *Journal* (1910): 318. It was regretfully noted, "We are obliged year after year to send to the Mother Country for large numbers of young men who have been trained under the old system." Burwash also underscored the need for Canadian Methodists to seek lay ministerial supply in Great Britain in his Address to the Conference of Methodism is England on Urban Problems and Solutions. July 1911, NBP 15:402.

122 See for example R.C. Brown and R. Cook, *Canada 1896-1921*, 54-68, and Emery, "Methodism on the Canadian Prairies, 1896-1914."

123 Methodist Church (Canada, Nfld., Bermuda), *Journal* (1910): 285.

124 J.W. Grand, *The Canadian Experience of Church Union*, 94.

125 Clifford, *Resistance to Church Union*, 10.

126 Roy, *Catholicity and Methodism*. For a rebuttal, see *Spurious Catholicity or, Socinianism Unmasked*, by a Methodist Minister [W.H. Withrow], and W.H. Withrow, "Catholicity and Methodism," *CMM* 5 (June 1877): 25. Roy argued that Wesley had been indifferent to doctrine, and suggested an ecumenicalism which would subsume credal formulations. W.H. Withrow argued, however, "Mr. Wesley was truly catholic in his liberality towards those who differed from him; but not in the sense of placing a low estimate on the value of the orthodox doctrines." *Spurious Catholicity*, 50.

127 Silcox, *Church Union in Canada*, 135.

128 See for example N. Burwash, "The New History of Christian Doctrine" [review of A. Harnack, *History of Christian Dogma*], *CMM* 44 (Aug. 1896): 178-80.

129 In 1897, reviewing E.J. Gerhart, *Institutes of the Christian Religion*, he noted "Such a theology may well accord with the present popular Neo-Hegelian philosophy, but with the passing away of that philosophy and the return to a more strongly ethical concept of humanity we think the theology will also lose its hold." N. Burwash, "Systematic Theology," *CMM* 45 (Jan. 1897): 93-4.

130 Examples of Wesley's progressive outlook can be found in "Methodism, a power purifying and elevating society," *CMM* 33 (Jan. 1891); "John Wesley and his Mother" and "Wesley and his Literature," *CMM* 33 (Mar. 1891), and "The Moral Momentum of Methodism," *CMM* 33 (Apr. 1891). A similar reading of the evolutionary nature of Methodism, stressing continuity as well as change can be found in "The Old Methodism and the New," [review of George Jackson's recent publication]. *Acta Victoriana* 30, no. 4 (Jan. 1907): 259-60.

131 The 1903 commemorative issue contained thirty items of Wesleyana by such contributors as H.H. Fudger, Sir Oliver Mowat, N. Burwash, W.H. Withrow, and Albert Carman. *CMM* 57 (June 1903).

132 A. Sutherland, *Methodism in Canada*, 6.

133 *Christian Guardian*, 31 Jan. 1912.

134 For a brief evaluation of the historiography of Schaff, Fischer, and Rauschenbusch see Bowden, *Church History in the Age of Science*, 42–58, 66, 171–9.

135 Morton, *The Way to Union*, 242–44 especially. See also the chapter "Canadian Christianity: the Welding of the Canadian Provinces and Canadian Churches," 223–54.

136 The best summary of this approach is Clifford, "The Interpreters of the United Church of Canada," 203–14. Not cited by Clifford, but also environmentalist in their understanding of union are Chown, *The Story of Church Union in Canada*, 50–60; Pidgeon, *The United Church of Canada*, 24–6; and E. Thomas, "Church Union in Canada."

137 Polanyi, *Personal Knowledge*, 18–19.

138 W.S. Griffin also made the observation that "the originators and managers of this organic union were not the men who are engaged in the pastoral and evangelical work of this church, but principally were university professors and connexional officers, most of whom have passed away. *Christian Guardian*, 13 Mar. 1912.

139 For the influence of the Whig view in Canadian historiography see Windsor, "Historical Writing in Canada (to 1920)"; Berger, *The Writing of Canadian History*, 1–53. Berger does not use the term "Whig," but describes the evolutionary reading of Canadian history (with the progress of liberty becoming the central myth) in the work of such historians as George Wrong and Chester Martin.

140 Chown, *The Story of Church Union in Canada*, 77.

141 Morrow, *Church Union in Canada*, 177. Morrow also noted that he had not encountered one Methodist "anti-unionist" in all his investigations, p. 171.

142 Ibid., 173. Burwash did mention privately that two delegates of some authority on the subcommittee on doctrine had dissented. N. Burwash to Rev. Professor Patton, 28 Feb. 1910, NBP, box A.

143 R. Allen, *The Social Passion*, 3–17; Magney, "The Methodist Church and the National Gospel." The importance of religious revivalism among Presbyterian social gospelers is pointed out in Fraser, " 'The Christianization of Our Civilization,' " 35–44.

144 For Bland's own evangelical Christianity in the early part of his career see Bland, *The New Christianity*, xv–xvi. In this book, which first appeared in 1920, Bland was highly critical of the "type of Christianity which fixes its eye on heaven and abandons earth," and quoted one of Wesley's hymns as an illustration, pp. 20–2. He accepted as inevitable that the old order of capitalism and Protestantism had come to an end.

145 R. Allen, *The Social Passion*, 253.

146 McKillop, *A Disciplined Intelligence*, 222.

147 A good study of the background to union which makes this same point in different form, but in greater detail, is Kiesekamp, "Presbyterian and Methodist Divines." Kiesekamp emphasizes common threats, such as the challenge of French ultramontanism, and concludes that these were sufficiently great to have Methodists and Presbyterians lay aside their differences, pp. 222–34.

148 For detailed documentation of the controversy see Victoria University, Notes re Investigation, 1911, Annesley Hall, Margaret Addison Papers, UCA.

149 Sissons, *History of Victoria University*, 244.

150 Examples are many. In 1910, for example, he headed a fundraising drive to restore and reclaim the historic Hay Bay Church. Correspondence re Hay Bay Church (1910–11), NBP 8:109. Since 1899 he had also been collecting personal papers documenting the history of Methodism in central Canada. Thomas Webster to N. Burwash, 17 Jan. 1899, NBP 1:10.

151 A revealing indication of his allegiance to the continuation of Methodism in Canada is the remark he made in a letter in 1912, at the very time when he was urging the denomination to abandon its traditional identity. At that same date he counselled, "The foreign population and the American population coming into the West will require time before many of them can be won to Methodism, even though they may depend upon us for the means of grace." N. Burwash to C.E. Manning, Methodist Mission Room, 26 Jan. 1912, NBP 6:75.

CONCLUSION

1 Translation of article in the "Yorodzu Choho," 28 Jan. 1913, NBP 8:111. As early as 1902 there had been a request for Burwash to come for a visit. It was noted, "If the Japanese get the idea of a man that he is a highly educated high class man or that he holds some official post, then they are very eager to hear him." R. Emberson, Shiznoka, Japan, to N. Burwash, 29 Apr. 1902, NBP 1:14.

2 Methodist Church (Canada, Nfld., Bermuda), *Annual Report of the Missionary Society* (1914): xxv–xxvii.

3 Chancellor Burwash, "Japan's Need of Christ," *Missionary Outlook*, July 1913, 154.

4 Ibid. For Eby's efforts to make Christianity appeal to educated Japanese see Eby, *Christianity and Humanity*.

5 N. Burwash, "Japan's Need of Christ" *Missionary Outlook*, 154. Burwash and Mott kept in touch, and Mott made it a point to keep Victoria's chancellor informed of his evangelistic activities. See N. Burwash to J.A. Mott, 27 Jan. 1908, NBP 3:33, and 10 Feb. 1908, NBP 3:34.

6 "The Visit of Chancellor Burwash to Japan," *Missionary Outlook,* Nov. 1913, 247.

7 Lectures Before the Imperial University at Tokyo, 1913, NBP 16:463; Addresses Before the Imperial University at Tokyo, 1913, "Christian Perfection," "Christian Ethics – their Religious Basis," NBP 15:407.

8 "Some Problems in the Development of Canada," NBP 18:463. For Canadian reactions to Oriental immigration see Brown and Cook, *A National Transformed,* 68–72. Burwash professed ignorance of political matters when questioned by Japanese reporters on anti-Japanese feeling in British Columbia. "Translation," NBP 8:111.

9 N. Burwash, *Manual of Christian Theology,* 1:ii.

10 "Christian Ethics," NBP 18:463.

11 "The Visit of Chancellor Burwash to Japan," *Missionary Outlook,* Nov. 1913, 247.

12 Hunter, *The Gospel of Gentility,* 27–51; Hill, *The World Their Household,* 23–60.

13 For Christian doctrine, deaconesses were assigned Wesley's *Sermons* and the 1897 *Catechism* in the first year, and Wesley's *Plain Account of Christian Perfection* in the second. NBP 10:149. See also Methodist Church (Canada, Nfld., Bermuda), *Journal* (1914): 228, and Lecture Outline for Methodist National Training School, Part I and Part II, 1916–17, NBP 18:468–9.

14 N. Burwash to A. Carman, 9 Oct. 1909, Carman Papers 26:256, UCA.

15 N. Burwash, *Manual of Christian Theology,* 2:385.

16 Methodist Church (Canada, Nfld., Bermuda), *Proceedings of the Fourth Ecumenical Methodist Conference,* 307.

17 J.S. Woodsworth, "How to Help Our European Immigrants," *Missionary Outlook,* July 1913, 151.

18 "Some Problems in the Development of Canada," NBP 18:463.

19 Historical Address at Jubilee of the Centenary Methodist Church, 1918, Hamilton, NBP 15:412. In voicing this criticism of recent immigrants Burwash apparently appealed to the current mood among Canadians as described in Avery, *"Dangerous Foreigners,"* 16–38.

20 Addresses to the Nova Scotia Conference, June 1915, NBP 15:408.

21 One of his most bitter denunciations of contemporary society, directed against Canadian war profiteering, was a sermon written in 1915 and based on Amos 3:6, "Is there evil in a City and is not the Lord doing somewhat?" NBP 13:235. Here he did not appear to be in tune with the general Methodist interpretation of the war as described in Bliss, "The Methodist Church and World War I."

22 Chadwick, *The Victorian Church* 2:35.

23 Robert Chiles notes that by 1900 in the United States references to Wesley among Methodist theologians were rare and often served to correct, rather

than to find corroboration. Chiles, *Theological Transition in American Methodism*, 185. Langford stresses the influence of German philosophy upon such early twentieth-century Methodists as Borden Parker Bowne, in the United States, and John Scott Lidgett in Great Britain. Langford, *Practical Divinity*, 119, 150.

24 W.I. Shaw of Wesleyan Theological College died in 1911, and his place was filled by the Rev. James Smyth, BD, LLD who came from Belfast. Burwash at Victoria was succeeded in 1913 by his former student R.P. Bowles, MA, DD, LLD, formerly minister of Sherbourne Street Methodist Church. According to the 1914 quadrennial report of the Educational Society of the Methodist Church, the heads of Wesleyan Theological College, Victoria College, Wesley College Winnipeg, Mount Allison, Columbian College, Regina College, and Albert College had all either died or resigned in the previous four years. Methodist Church (Canada, Nfld., Bermuda), *Journal* (1914): 145–51. At Mount Allison systematic theology was taught by Howard Sprague, one of the college's first graduates and a Methodist minister in Sackville from 1899 to 1901. At his death in 1916 Sprague was replaced by John Line, who had taken his theological training at Victoria. J. Reid, *Mount Allison University* 1:271-3, 2:18.

25 For an analysis of Blewett's thought see M. Patterson, "The Mind of a Methodist," and Armour and Trott, *The Faces of Reason*, 321–53.

26 For Phillips' enthusiastic espousal of the inductive method, see A.M. Phillips, "Bible Study," *CMR* 7, no. 1 (1895): 62-3. For S.D. Chown, see Manning, "The Changing Mind-Set of Canadian Methodism."

27 Cook, *The Regenerators*, 229.

28 Manning, "The Changing Mind-Set of Canadian Methodism," 13.

29 S.D. Chown, "The Influence of Wesley Upon Canada." Mss, "taken from the Library of the late Rev. Salem G. Bland, D.D.," UCA.

30 Ibid.; R. Allen, *The Social Passion*, 71. For a good analysis of the 1918 statement see pp. 71-9.

31 Chown, *Some Causes of the Decline of the Earlier Type of Evangelism*, 5.

32 See Manuscript, My Life, S.D. Chown Papers 16:455 UCA. While he often disparaged doctrine as divisive, Chown agreed with Burwash that the doctrinal articles of the Basis of Union contained all the "essential truths" of Methodism. Schwarz, "Samuel Dwight Chown," 178.

33 Sermon, "The Aim of Life," Nov. 1897, NBP 12:178. The sermon was a response to a recent article by Goldwin Smith predicting the demise of Christianity and a moral interregnum.

34 For complaints concerning Workman's teaching at the Wesleyan Theological College see C.T. Scott to N. Burwash, 4 June and 11 June 1908, NBP 8:113.

35 N. Burwash to C.T. Scott, n.d. [after 4 June 1908], NBP 8:113. A little earlier that year Burwash had written Workman of his complete satisfac-

tion with the latter's recent public statement concerning his doctrinal views. At the same time he cautioned at length on the need to distinguish "between the great doctrinal facts which are clearly revealed in Scripture and the theories which have been advanced on the basis of those facts."

36 N. Burwash to G.C. Workman, 28 Dec. 1910, NBP 8:113. Workman appeared undeterred by the criticism, and the manuscript was published the following year. Workman, *At Onement*.

37 Cook, *The Regenerators*, 4; McKillop, *A Disciplined Intelligence*, 224–8.

38 Cf. his efforts in 1912 to collect money to assist Workman. See chap. 4, note 75.

39 Houghton, *The Victorian Frame of Mind*, esp. chap. 10, "Earnestness," 218–62.

40 McLoughlin, *Revivals, Awakenings and Reform*, 112–14.

41 Ibid., 9.

42 Ibid., 141–78.

43 Ibid., 12–23.

44 Victoria University, Minutes of the Board of Regents, 30 April 1912. At this time Burwash at his request was given "a year's rest ... with salary." In October of that year he formally tendered his resignation from Calgary while en route to Japan. However, his retirement was dated 1913.

45 William Withrow had died in 1908, John Potts and Alexander Sutherland in 1910. That year S.D. Chown was elected General Superintendent, a position he would share with Carman until the latter's death in 1917.

46 See Edward Moore Jackson Burwash Papers and Margaret Proctor Burwash Papers, UCA. For Edward's doubts about remaining in the ministry see N. Burwash to Ned, 24 Jan. 1912, NBP, box B.

47 See D.W. Snider to N. Burwash, 11 May 1908, NBP 3:35, and N. Burwash to D.W. Snider, 1 Apr. 1911, NBP 5:66. Examples of this trend cited by Burwash were George Wrong and University of Toronto President Robert Falconer. For a more comprehensive analysis of disorientation among the younger generation of Methodist ministers, see W.W. Patterson, "The Doctrine of the Ministry in the Methodist Church, Canada, 1884–1925," 138–50.

48 Morley Pettit to N. Burwash, 11 Feb. 1908, NBP 3:34.

49 For Workman's displeasure at the proposed changes see *Christian Guardian*, 26 Sept. 1906.

50 Burwash's reaction to the greater stress on catechetical instruction was favourable. See his defence of church union, "Church Union – Objections to Organic Union," *Christian Guardian*, 14 Feb. 1912.

51 Methodist Church (Canada, Nfld., Bermuda), *Journal* (1918): 318–19. At a much earlier date, Burwash had protested against what he believed to be a trend in Canadian Methodism to stress decision rather than forgiveness and the new birth. N. Burwash to the Editor of the Epworth *Era*, 15 Apr. 1907,

NBP 2:25. Burwash considered George Coe, professor of philosophy at Northwestern University, Evanston, Ill., to be a "very able and progressive man, thoroughly in sympathy with all modern ideas," though inclined "to go further" than he could follow him. N. Burwash to A.D. Miller, 10 Feb. 1909, NBP 3:44. For Coe's thought see Hutchison, *The Modernist Impulse*, 156–61.

52 See for example, Cook, *The Regenerators*, 213–23; McKillop, *A Disciplined Intelligence*, 223–4; Airhart, "The Eclipse of Revivalist Spirituality," 286–7. An assessment of J.S. Woodsworth's religious views similar to that of the present study is Benjamin Smillie, "The Woodsworths: James and J.S. – Father and Son," in Butcher, et al., ed., *Prairie Spirit*, 100–21. See also McNaught, *A Prophet in Politics*, 20–60.

53 J.S. Woodsworth to N. Burwash, 24 Jan. 1902, NBP 1:14.

54 Ibid.

55 Woodsworth, *Following the Gleam*, 7.

56 J.S. Woodsworth to N. Burwash, 14 Jan. 1902, NBP 1:14.

57 J.S. Woodsworth to N. Burwash, 5 Mar. 1906, NBP 2:21.

58 J.S. Woodswroth, "Heterodoxy or Hypocrisy – A Minister's Dilemma," *Acta Victoriana* 37, no. 4 (Jan. 1913): 204–5.

59 Cook, *The Regenerators*, 219.

60 Airhart, "The Eclipse of Revivalist Spirituality," esp. 237–74.

61 Allen, *The Social Passion*, 5, 16; Emery, "The Origins of Canadian Methodist Involvement in the Social Gospel Movement," 105. The extent of Methodist commitment is, however, questioned in Airhart, "The Eclipse of Revivalist Spirituality," 262–4.

62 Allen, *The Social Passion*, 4–17; Fraser, " 'The Christianization of our Civilization,' " 35–44.

63 See for example Helmstadter, "The Non-Conformist Conscience," 158–62.

64 See for example S. Bland, *The New Christianty*, esp. 80–9. S.D. Chown in "The Influence of Wesley Upon Canada," stressed different aspects of Wesley's teaching: his influence on the temperance movement, on charity, publishing, education, and work among the Indians, as well as his "catholicity of spirit."

65 J.S. Woodsworth, "Heterodoxy or Hypocrisy," *Acta Victoriana* 37:4 (Jan. 1913): 205.

66 H. Richard Niebuhr, *Christ and Culture* (New York: Harper and Row, 1975), esp. 190–229, and Welch and Dillenberger, *Protestant Christianity*, 343–60.

67 Cook, *The Regenerators*, 230; W. Hutchison, *The Modernist Impulse*, 2–8; Mark A. Noll, "Christian Thinking and the Rise of the American University"; McKillop, *A Disciplined Intelligence*, 205–32.

68 Turner, *Without God, Without Creed*, 266–7.

69 Playter, *The History of Methodism in Canada*, 368.

70 *Globe*, 1 Apr. 1918.

71 The 1887 allocation of college and university subjects was terminated in 1983 when the colleges agreed to provide accommodation for courses and programs organized by the departments of the Faculty of Arts. See "A Memorandum of Agreement Regarding the Institutional Relationships of the University of Toronto and the Federated Universities in the Faculty of Arts and Science," May 1984; and Victoria University, "Report to the Board of Regents by the President for the Session 1983–84." I am indebted to Bill Whelen, member of the Victoria Board of Regents, for his generous assistance in obtaining this documentation.

72 Zuckerman, "Dreams that Men Dare to Dream," 341.

Bibliography

MANUSCRIPT COLLECTIONS

*Archives of the United Church of Canada
Toronto, Ontario*

Addison, Margaret. Personal Papers.
Biographical Files.
Bland, Henry Flesher. Personal Papers.
Burwash, Edward Moore Jackson. Personal Papers.
Burwash, Margaret Proctor. Personal Papers.
Burwash, Nathanael. Personal Papers.
Carman, Albert. Personal Papers.
Chown, Samuel Dwight. Personal Papers.
Church Union Collection (Methodist).
Craig, John. Personal Papers.
English, William. Personal Papers.
Hill, Joseph. Personal Papers.
Hincks, William. Personal Papers.
Jackson, George. Personal Papers.
Nelles, Samuel S. Personal Papers.
Shannon, William. Personal Papers.
Taylor, Lachlin. Personal Papers.
Victoria University. Minutes of the Board of Regents. Vols. 1–3.
– Minutes of the Faculty, 1884–1917.
Wallace, Francis H. Personal Papers.
Wesleyan Methodist Church. Minutes of Annual Conference, 1860–73.
Workman, George Coulson. Personal Papers.

Nātional Archives of Canada
Ottawa, Ontario

Grant, George Monro. Personal Papers.
Laurier, Sir Wilfrid. Personal Papers.

Weldon Library, University of
Western Ontario
London, Ontario

Morgan, Henry James. Papers relating to his *Canadian Men and Women of the Time* (microfilm).

JOURNALS AND NEWSPAPERS OF THE PERIOD

Acta Victoriana, 1878–1918.
Canadian Methodist Magazine, 1875–88.
Canadian Methodist Quarterly, 1889–95.
Christian Guardian, 1829–1918.
Globe, 1867–1918.
Methodist Magazine, 1889–95.
Methodist Magazine and Review, 1896–1906.
Missionary Outlook, 1913–14.
Victoria College Bulletin, 1908–18.

OTHER SOURCES

Abraham, William J. "The Wesleyan Quadrilateral." Paper presented at the conference "Wesleyan Theology and the Next Century," August 1983, Emory University, Atlanta.

Ahlstrom, Sydney E. *A Religious History of the American People*. 2 vols. New Haven: Yale Univ. Press, 1972.

– "The Scottish Philosophy and American Theology." *Church History* 24 (1955): 257–72.

– , ed. *Theology in America: The Major Protestant Voices from Puritanism to Neo-Orthodoxy*. Indianapolis, NY: Bobbs-Merrill, 1967.

Airhart, Phyllis. "The Eclipse of Revivalist Spirituality: The Transformation of Canadian Methodist Piety 1884–1925." PHD diss., Faculty of the Divinity School, Univ. of Chicago, 1985.

Allen, James. *Facts Concerning Federation*. n.p.: [Victoria University] Alumni Association, [1889].

Allen, Richard. "Providence to Progress: The Migration of an Idea in English Canadian Thought." *Association for Canadian Studies/Association des études canadiennes* 7 (1985): 33–46.

- "Salem Bland: The Young Preacher," *The Bulletin* (Committee on Archives of the United Church of Canada) 26 (1977): 75–93.
- *The Social Passion: Religion and Reform in Canada, 1914–28.* Toronto: Univ. of Toronto Press, 1971.

Aries, Philippe. *Centuries of Childhood: A Social History of Family Life.* Trans. Robert Baldick. London: Jonathan Cape, 1962.

Armour, Leslie, and Elizabeth Trott. *The Faces of Reason: An Essay on Philosophy and Culture in English Canada 1850–1950.* Waterloo: Wilfrid Laurier Univ. Press, 1981.

Arnold, Matthew. *Higher Schools and Universities in Germany.* London: Macmillan, 1874.

Avery, Donald. *"Dangerous Foreigners": European Immigrant Workers and Labour Radicalism in Canada, 1896–1932.* Toronto: McClelland and Stewart, 1979.

Ayre, David John. "Universities and the Legislature: Political Aspects of the Ontario University Question 1868–1906." PHD diss., Univ. of Toronto, 1981.

Bailyn, Bernard. *Education in the Forming of American Society.* New York: Vintage, 1960.
- *The Ideological Origins of the American Revolution.* Cambridge, Mass.: Belknap, 1967.

Baker, Frank. *John Wesley and the Church of England.* London: Epworth, 1970.
- "The Trans-Atlantic Triangle: Relations between British, Canadian, and American Methodism during Wesley's lifetime," *The Bulletin* (Commitee on Archives of the United Church of Canada) 28 (1979): 5–21.

Ballard, Paul. "Evangelical Experience: Notes on the History of a Tradition," *Journal of Ecumenical Studies* 13 (1976): 51–68.

Bassett, Paul Merritt. "North American Methodist Biblical Scholarship and the Authority of the Scripture." Paper presented at the conference "Wesleyan Theology and the Next Century," August 1983, Atlanta.

Bauman, Mark A. *Warren Akin Candler: The Conservative as Idealist.* Metuchen, NJ: Scarecrow, 1981.

Berger, Carl. "Race and Liberty: The Historical Ideas of Sir John George Bourinot," *Canadian Historical Association Report* (1965), 87–105.
- *Science, God, and Nature in Victoria Canada.* The 1982 Joanne Goodman Lectures. Toronto: Univ. of Toronto Press, 1983.
- *A Sense of Power: Studies in the Ideas of Canadian Imperialism, 1867–1914.* Toronto: Univ. of Toronto Press, 1970.
- *The Writing of Canadian History: Aspects of English-Canadian Historical Writing, 1900–1970.* Toronto: Oxford Univ. Press, 1976.

Bland, Henry Flesher. *Student; Preacher; Pastor; Soul-Winner (Being the sixth annual sermon and lecture before the Theological Union of Victoria College in 1883).* Toronto: William Briggs, 1883.

– *Universal childhood drawn to Christ [sermon] with an appendix containing remarks on Dr. Burwash's "Moral Condition of Childhood."* Toronto: William Briggs, 1882.

Bland, Salem. *The New Christianity; or, The Religion of the New Age.* Toronto: McClelland and Stewart, 1920. 2d ed., edited by Richard Allen. Toronto: Univ. of Toronto Press, 1977.

Bliss, J. Michael. *A Canadian Millionaire: The Life and Times of Sir Joseph Flavelle, Bart. 1858–1939.* Toronto: Macmillan, 1978.

– *A Living Profit: Studies in the Social History of Canadian Business, 1883–1911.* Toronto: McClelland and Stewart, 1974.

– "The Methodist Church and World War I," *Canadian Historical Review* 47 (1966): 227–48.

– "Pure Books on Avoided Subjects: Pre-Freudian Sexual Ideas in Canada," *Historical Papers of the Canadian Historical Association* (1970), 89–108.

Bloch, Ruth H. "American Feminine Ideals in Transition: The Rise of the Moral Mother, 1785–1815," *Feminist Studies* 4, no. 2 (June 1978): 101–27.

Bowden, H.W. *Church History in the Age of Science: Historiographical Patterns in the United States 1876–1918.* Chapel Hill: Univ. of North Carolina Press, 1971.

Bowmer, John C. *Pastor and People: a Study of Church and Ministry in Wesleyan Methodism from the Death of John Wesley (1791) to the Death of Jabez Bunting (1858).* London: Epworth, 1975.

Boyle, George Alfred. "Higher Criticism and the Struggle for Academic Freedom in Canadian Methodism." THD diss., Emmanuel College, Victoria Univ., 1965.

Bozeman, Theodore Dwight. *Protestants in an Age of Science: the Baconian Ideal and Antebellum American Religious Thought.* Chapel Hill: Univ. of North Carolina Press, 1977.

Bradley, Ian C. *The Call to Seriousness: The Evangelical Impact on the Victorians.* New York: Macmillan, 1969.

– *The Optimists: Themes and Personalities in Victorian Liberalism.* London: Faber and Faber, 1980.

Brauer, Jerald C. "Conversion: From Puritanism to Revivalism," *Journal of Religion* 58 (1978): 227–43.

Brown, Robert Craig, and Ramsay Cook. *Canada 1896–1921: A Nation Transformed.* Toronto: McClelland and Stewart, 1974.

Brown, Thomas Brush. *The Autobiography of Thomas Brush Brown.* Repr. 1967 by Isabel Grace Uren with additional notes.

Brown, W.L. "The Sunday School Movement in the Methodist Church in Canada, 1875–1925." THM thesis, Univ. of Toronto, 1959.

Bucke, Emory Stevens, ed. *The History of American Methodism.* 3 vols. New York: Abingdon, 1964.

Buckle, Henry T. *History of the Civilization of the English.* New ed. 2 vols. New York: Appleton, 1894.

Burkholder, Lawrence. "Canadian Methodism and Higher Criticism, 1860–1910." Course paper, Univ. of Toronto, 1976.

Burnside, Albert. "The Contribution of the Rev. Albert Carman to Albert College, Belleville and to the Methodist Episcopal Church in Canada." THM thesis, Toronto Graduate School of Theological Studies, 1962.

Burwash, Edward Moore J. *The New Theology.* Toronto: William Briggs, 1910.

Burwash, Nathanael. *Egerton Ryerson.* Toronto: Morang, 1910.

– *The Genesis, Nature and Results of Sin. First annual lecture and sermon. Victoria Theological Union.* Toronto: William Briggs, 1878.

– *A Handbook of the Epistle of St. Paul to the Romans.* Toronto: William Briggs, 1887.

– *The History of Victoria College.* Toronto: Victoria College Press, 1927.

– *Inaugural Introduction to Section II, Royal Society of Canada, 1907. Transactions of the Royal Society of Canada.* 3d series – 1907–8. Vol. 1, Sec. 2. Ottawa: Nathanael Burwash, 1908.

– *Inductive Studies in Theology: Sin and the Atonement.* Toronto: William Briggs, 1896.

– *Manual of Christian Theology on the Inductive Method.* 2 vols. London: Horace Marshall and Son, 1900.

– *Memorials of the Life of Edward and Lydia Ann Jackson.* Toronto: S. Rose, 1876.

– *The Relation of Children to the Fall, the Atonement, and the Church.* Toronto: William Briggs, 1882.

– *Some Further Facts Concerning Federation.* [Pamphlet.] Reprinted from the *Methodist Magazine* of February 1890.

– , ed. *Wesley's Doctrinal Standards. Part I: The Sermons.* Toronto: William Briggs, 1881.

Bush, Peter George. "James Caughey, Phoebe and Walter Palmer and the Methodist Revival Experience in Canada West, 1850–1858." MA thesis, Queen's Univ., 1985.

Butcher, Dennis L., Catherine Macdonald, Margaret E. McPherson, et al., eds. *Prairie Spirit: Perspectives on the Heritage of the United Church of Canada in the West.* Winnipeg: Univ. of Manitoba Press, 1985.

Caldwell, J. Warren. "The Unification of Methodism in Canada, 1865–1884." *The Bulletin* (Committee on Archives of the United Church of Canada) 19 (1967): 3–61.

Cameron, Richard M. *Methodism and Society in Historical Perspective.* Vol. 1, *Methodism and Society.* New York: Abingdon, 1961.

Carlisle, John. *An Expose of and a Red Hot Protest against a Damnable Heresy, Smuggled into Methodism and Taught by Rev. Professor Workman of Vic-*

toria University, and Approved by Rev. Professor Burwash. Peterborough: Examiner Print, [1891].

Carroll, John. *Case and His Cotemporaries; or, The Canadian Itinerants' Memorial*. 5 vols. Toronto: S. Rose, 1866–77.

- *My Boy Life*. Toronto: William Briggs, 1882.

- *Reasons for Methodist Belief and Practice Relative to Water Baptism*. Toronto: Wesleyan Conference Office, 1872.

- *The School of the Prophets*. Toronto: Burrage and Magurn, 1876.

- *The Stripling Preacher*. Toronto: Anson Green, 1852.

Carwardine, Richard. *Trans-atlantic Revivalism: Popular Evangelism in Britian and America, 1790–1865*. Westport, Conn.: Greenwood, 1978.

Chadwick, Owen. *The Secularization of the European Mind in the Nineteenth Century*. The Gifford Lectures in the University of Edinburgh for 1973–4. Cambridge: Cambridge Univ. Press, 1975.

- *The Victorian Church*. 2 vols. New York: Oxford Univ. Press, 1966–70.

Chalmers, Randolph C. *See the Christ Stand!* Toronto: Ryerson, 1945.

Chambers, Steven. "The *Canadian Methodist Magazine*: A Victorian Forum for New Scientific and Theological Ideas." *The Bulletin* (Committee on Archives of the United Church of Canada) 30 (1983–4): 61–80.

Champion, Thomas E. *The Methodist Churches of Toronto*. Toronto: G.M. Rose, 1899.

Chiles, Robert E. *Theological Transition in American Methodism: 1790–1935*. New York: Abingdon, 1965.

Chown, S.D. *Some Causes for the Decline of the Earlier Typical Evangelism*. Toronto: Ryerson, 1930.

- *The Story of Church Union in Canada*. Toronto: Ryerson, 1930.

Clark, S.D. *Church and Sect in Canada*. Toronto: Univ. of Toronto Press, 1948.

Clifford, N. Keith. "His Dominion: A Vision in Crisis." *Studies in Religion* 2 (1973): 315–26.

- "The Interpreters of the United Church of Canada." *Church History* 46 (1977): 203–14.

- "Religion and the Development of Canadian Society: An Historiographical Analysis." *Church History* 38 (1969): 506–23.

- *The Resistance to Church Union in Canada, 1904–1939*. Vancouver: Univ. of British Columbia Press, 1985.

- "The United Church of Canada and Doctrinal Confession." *Touchstone* 2 (1984): 6–21.

Cockshut, A.O.J. *Truth to Life: The Art of Biography in the Nineteenth Century*. New York: Harcourt Brace Jovanovich, 1974.

Cook, Ramsay. *The Regenerators: Social Criticism in Late Victorian English Canada*. Toronto: Univ. of Toronto Press, 1985.

Cornish, George, ed. *Cyclopaedia of Methodism*. 2 vols. Toronto: Methodist Book Room, 1881, 1903.

Cousland, Kenneth H. *The Founding of Emmanuel College of Victoria University in the University of Toronto*. n.p., 1978.

Cowan, Kathleen. *It's Late, and All the Girls Have Gone: An Annesley Diary, 1907–1910*. Ed. Aida Farrag Graff and David Knight. Toronto: Childe Thursday, 1984.

Cragg, Gerald R. "The European Wellsprings of Canadian Christianity." McMaster Divinity College, *Theological Bulletin* 3 (Jan. 1968): 4–14.

Craig, G.M. *Upper Canada: The Formative Years, 1784–1841*. Toronto: McClelland and Stewart, 1963.

Cremin, Lawrence A. *American Education: The National Experience, 1783–1876*. New York: Harper and Row, 1980.

Cross, Whitney R. *The Burned-over District: The Social and Intellectual History of Enthusiastic Religion in Western New York, 1800–1850*. Ithaca, NY: Cornell Univ. Press, 1950.

Davies, Rupert E. *Methodism*. London: Epworth, 1963.

Davies, Rupert, A. Raymond George, and Gordon Rupp, eds. *A History of the Methodist Church in Great Britain*. 3 vols. London: Epworth, 1978–83.

Dayton, Donald W. "Whither Evangelicalism?" In *Sanctification and Liberation*, ed. Theodore Runyon, 42–63. Nashville: Abingdon, 1981.

Dewart, Edward H. *The Bible Under Higher Criticism: A View of the Current Evolution Theories about the Old Testament*. Toronto: William Briggs, 1900.

– *Broken Reeds; or the Heresies of the Plymouth Brethren Shown to be Contrary to Scripture and Reason*. Toronto: Wesleyan Conference Office, 1869.

– *Jesus the Messiah in Prophecy and Fulfilment: A Review and Refutation of the Negative theory of Messianic Prophecy*. Toronto: William Briggs, 1891.

– *University Federation Considered in its Relation to the Educational Interests of the Methodist Church*. [Pamphlet.] [Toronto]: n.p., n.d.

Dieter, Melvin Easterday. *The Holiness Revival of the Nineteenth Century*. Metuchen, NJ: Scarecrow, 1980.

Douglas, Ann. *The Feminization of American Culture*. New York: Avon, 1978.

Dreyer, Frederick. "Faith and Experience in the Thought of John Wesley." *American Historical Review* 88 (1983): 12–30.

– "'A 'Religious Society Under Heaven': John Wesley and the Identity of Methodism." *Journal of British Studies* 25 (Jan. 1986): 62–84.

Drummond, Henry. *Natural Law in the Spiritual World*. 6th ed. London: Hodder and Stoughton, 1883.

Eby, Charles S. *Christianity and Humanity: A Course of Lectures Delivered in Meiji Kuaido, Tokio, Japan*. Yokohama: R. Meiklejohn, 1883.

Emery, George. "Methodism on the Canadian Prairies, 1896–1914." PHD diss., Univ. of British Columbia, 1970.

– "The Origins of the Canadian Methodist Involvement in the Social Gospel Movement." *The Bulletin* (Committee on Archives of the United Church) 26 (1977): 104–19.

Evangelical Alliance. *Vital Questions: The Discussions of the General Christian Conference held in Montreal, Que., Canada, October 22nd to 25th, 1888.* Montreal: William Drysdale, 1889.

Evans, Margaret A. "Oliver Mowat: Nineteenth Century Liberal." In *Oliver Mowat's Ontario*, ed. Donald Swainson, 34–51. Toronto: Macmillan, 1972.

Falconer, Robert. *University Federation in Toronto.* Transactions of the Royal Society of Canada. 3d series. Sect. 2, vol. 34, 1940. Ottawa.

Farrar, Frederick William. *The History of Interpretation. Eight Lectures Preached Before the University of Oxford ... 1885.* London: Macmillan, 1886.

Farris, Allan L. "The Fathers of 1925." In *The Tide of Time. Historical Essays by the late Allan L. Farris*, ed. John S. Moir, 95–124. Toronto: Knox College, 1978.

Findlay, James. "Agency, Denominations and the Western Colleges, 1830–1860: Some Connections between Evangelicalism and American Higher Education." *Church History* 50 (Mar. 1981): 64–80.

Finney, Charles G. *Memoirs of Rev. Charles G. Finney.* New York: Fleming H. Revell, 1876.

Fiorino, Albert S. "The Moral Foundation of Egerton Ryerson's Idea of Education." In *Egerton Ryerson and His Times*, ed. Neil McDonald and Alf Chaiton, 45–58. Toronto: Macmillan, 1978.

Fraser, Brian J. " 'The Christianization of Our Civilization': Presbyterian Reformers and Their Defence of a Protestant Canada, 1875–1914." PHD diss., York Univ., 1982.

– "Theology and the Social Gospel among Canadian Presbyterians: A Case Study." *Studies in Religion* 8 (1979): 35–46.

Frei, Hans W. *The Eclipse of Biblical Narrative: A Study in Eighteenth and Nineteenth-Century Hermeneutics.* New Haven: Yale Univ. Press, 1974.

French, Goldwin S. "Egerton Ryerson and the Methodist Model for Upper Canada." In *Egerton Ryerson and His Times*, ed. Neil MacDonald and Alf Chaiton, 45–58. Toronto: Macmillan, 1978.

– "The Evangelical Creed in Canada." In *The Shield of Achilles: Aspects of Canada in the Victorian Age*, ed. W.L. Morton, 15–35. Toronto: McClelland and Stewart, 1968.

– "A History of the Christian Church in Canada." *Acadiensis* 2 (1973): 91–8.

– "The Impact of Christianity on Canadian Culture and Society to 1867." McMaster Divinity College *Theological Bulletin* 3 (Jan. 1968): 15–39.

– *Parsons and Politics: The Role of the Wesleyan Methodists in Upper Canada and the Maritimes from 1850 to 1855.* Toronto: Ryerson, 1962.

– "The People Called Methodists in Canada." In *The Churches and the*

Canadian Experience, ed. John Webster Grant, 69–80. Toronto: Ryerson, 1963.

Frye, Northrop. *By Liberal Things*. Toronto: Clarke, 1962.

Gauvreau, Michael. "The Taming of History: Reflections on the Canadian Methodist Encounter with Biblical Criticism, 1830–1900." *Canadian Historical Review* 65 (1984): 315–46.

Geertz, Clifford. "Religion as a Cultural System." In *The Interpretation of Cultures*, 87–125. New York: Basic, 1973.

Gillen, Mollie. *The Masseys: Founding Family*. Toronto: Ryerson, 1965.

Goen, C.C. "The 'Methodist Age' in American Church History." *Religion in Life* 34 (1965): 562–72.

Goheen, Peter G. *Victorian Toronto, 1850 to 1900: Pattern and Process of Growth*. Univ. of Chicago Dept. of Geography Research Paper no. 127, 1970.

Grant, John Webster. "Asking Questions of the Canadian Past." *Canadian Journal of Theology* 1 (1955): 98–104.

– " 'At Least You Knew Where You Stood with Them': Reflections on Religious Pluralism in Canada and the United States." *Studies in Religion* 2, no. 4 (1973): 340–51.

– "Blending Traditions: The United Church of Canada." *Canadian Journal of Theology*, no. 1 (1963): 30–59.

– "Canadian Confederation and the Protestant Churches," *Church History* 38 (1969): 1–11.

– *The Canadian Experience of Church Union*. London: Lutterworth, 1967.

– *The Church in the Canadian Era*. Toronto: McGraw-Hill Ryerson, 1972.

– *George Pidgeon*. Toronto: Ryerson, 1962.

– "The Impact of Christianity on Canadian Culture and Society, 1867–1967." McMaster Divinity College *Theological Bulletin* 3 (Jan. 1968): 40–50.

– "The United Church and Its Heritage in Evangelism." *Touchstone* 1 (Oct. 1983): 6–13.

– , ed. *The Churches and the Canadian Experience*. Toronto: Ryerson, 1963.

Grant, William Lawson, and Frederick Hamilton. *Principal Grant*. Toronto: Morang, 1904.

Grave, S.A. *The Scottish Philosophy of Common Sense*. Oxford: Clarendon, 1960.

Green, Anson. *The Life and Times of the Rev. Anson Green, D.D.* Toronto: Methodist Book Room, 1877.

Greenlee, James G. *Sir Robert Falconer: A Biography*. Toronto: Univ. of Toronto Press, 1988.

Greven, Philip J. *The Protestant Temperament: Patterns of Child-Rearing, Religious Experience and the Self in Early America*. New York: Alfred A. Knopf, 1977.

– , ed. *Child-Rearing Concepts, 1628–1861*. Itasca, Ill.: F.E. Peacock, 1973.

Hallas, Ted. "A Christian Businessman: William Briggs and the Methodist Book and Publishing House, 1879–1918." Course paper, McMaster Univ., 1980.

Handy, Robert T. *A Christian America: Protestant Hopes and Historical Realities*. New York: Oxford Univ. Press, 1971.

– *A History of the Churches in the United States and Canada*. New York: Oxford Univ. Press, 1977.

Harris, Robin S. "The Establishment of a Provincial University in Ontario." In *On Higher Education*, ed. D.F. Dadson, 3–35. Toronto: Univ. of Toronto Press, 1966.

– *A History of Higher Education in Canada 1663–1960*. Toronto: Univ. of Toronto Press, 1976.

Headon, Christopher. "Women and Organized Religion in Mid- and Late-Nineteenth-Century Canada," *Journal of the Canadian Church Historical Society* 20 (1978): 3–18.

Helmstadter, Richard. "The Nonconformist Conference." In *The Conscience of the Victorian State*, ed. Peter Marsh, 135–73. Syracuse, NY: Syracuse Univ. Press, 1979.

Heyck, T.W. *The Transformation of Intellectual Life in Victorian England*. London: Croom Helm, 1982.

Hibbard, F.G. *A Treatise on Infant Baptism*. New York: G. Lane and P.P. Sandford, 1843.

Hill, Patricia R. *The World Their Household: The American Woman's Foreign Mission Movement and Cultural Transformation, 1870–1920*. Ann Arbor: Univ. of Michigan Press, 1985.

Hiller, Harry. "Continentalism and the Third Force in Religion." *Canadian Journal of Sociology* 3 (1978): 183–207.

Hindley, J. Clifford. "The Philosophy of Enthusiasm: A Study in the Origins of 'Experimental Theology,' " *London Quarterly and Holborn Review* 1957 (April and July): 99–109, 199–210.

Hodgetts, J.E. "Where Victoria Evermore Shall Stand." In *Victorian Cobourg: A Nineteenth Century Profile*, ed. J. Petryshyn, 221–35. Belleville: Mika, 1976.

Hodgins, J.G., ed. *The Establishment of Schools and Colleges in Ontario, 1792–1910*. 3 vols. Toronto: L.K. Cameron, 1910.

Hoeveler, J. David. *James McCosh and the Scottish Intellectual Tradition*. Princeton: Princeton Univ. Press, 1981.

Hofstadter, Richard. *Academic Freedom in the Age of the College*. New York: Columbia Univ. Press, 1955.

– *Anti-Intellectualism in American Life*. New York: Knopf, 1964.

Hofstadter, Richard, and Walter P. Metzger. *The Development of Academic Freedom in the United States*. New York: Columbia Univ. Press, 1955.

Hofstadter, Richard, and Wilson Smith, eds. *American Higher Education: A Documentary History*. Chicago: Univ. of Chicago Press, 1961.

Houghton, Walter E. *The Victorian Frame of Mind, 1830–1870*. New Haven: Yale Univ. Press, 1957.

Hovenkamp, Herbert. *Science and Religion in America, 1800–1860*. Philadelphia: Univ. of Pennsylvania Press, 1978.

Hudson, Winthrop S. "The Methodist Age in America," *Methodist History* 3 (1974): 3–15.

– *Religion in America*. 3rd. ed. New York: Charles Scribner, 1981.

Hughes, Norah L. "A History of the Development of Ministerial Education in Canada from Its Inception until 1925 In Those Churches Which Were Tributary to the United Church of Canada in Ontario, Quebec, and the Maritime Provinces." PHD diss., Univ. of Chicago, 1945.

Hunter, Jane. *The Gospel of Gentility: American Women Missionaries in Turn-of-the-Century China*. New Haven: Yale Univ. Press, 1984.

Hutchison, William R. *The Modernist Impulse in American Protestantism*. Cambridge, Mass.: Harvard Univ. Press, 1976.

Irving, John A. "The Development of Philosophy in Central Canada from 1850 to 1900." *Canadian Historical Review* 31 (1950): 252–87.

Jackson, George. *The Old Methodism and the New*. London: Hodder and Stoughton, 1903.

– *Studies in the Old Testament*. London: Robert Culley, n.d. [1910].

James, Peter. "The Historical Imagination: Peter Brown and the Evangelical Creed." MA thesis, Carleton Univ. 1981.

Johnson, Dale A. "The Methodist Quest for an Educated Ministry." *Church History* 51 (1982): 304–20.

Johnson, Henry C., Jr. " 'Down from the Mountain': Secularization and the American Public University." Paper presented April 1983 at the American Society of Church History, Holland, Mich.

Johnston, Charles M. *McMaster University*. Vol. 1, *The Toronto Years*. Toronto: Univ. of Toronto Press for McMaster Univ., 1976.

Jones, Charles E. *Perfectionist Persuasion: The Holiness Movement and American Methodism, 1867–1936*. Metuchen, NJ: Scarecrow 1974.

Keane, David Ross. "Rediscovering Ontario University Students of the Mid Nineteenth Century." PHD diss., Univ. of Toronto, 1981.

Kewley, Arthur. "Mass Evangelism in Upper Canada before 1830." 2 vols. THD diss., Emmanuel College, Victoria Univ., 1960.

– "Ordination in a Decade of Transition, 1823–1833." *The Bulletin* (Committee on Archives of the United Church of Canada) 18 (1965): 26–34.

Kiesekamp, Burkhard. "Community and Faith: the Intellectual and Ideological Bases of the Church Union Movement in Victoria Canada." PHD diss., Univ. of Toronto, 1974.

– "Presbyterian and Methodist Divines: their case for a National Church in

Canada, 1875–1900." *Studies in Religion* 2 (1973): 289–302.

Kilpatrick, T.B. *Our Common Faith*. Toronto: Ryerson, 1928.

Kincheloe, Joe L., Jr. "European Roots of Evangelical Revivalism: Methodist Transmission of the Pietistic Socio-Religious Tradition." *Methodist History* 18 (1980): 262–71.

Kleinstuber, R. Wayne. *More Than a Memory: The Renewal of Methodism in Canada*. Mississauga: Living Light and Life Press, 1984.

Lanceley, John Ellis. *The Devil of Names, and other lectures and sermons ... with a biographical sketch by the Rev. N. Burwash*. Toronto: William Briggs, 1900.

Langford, Thomas A. "John Wesley's Doctrine of Justification by Faith"; Wesley's Doctrine of Sanctification"; "Wesley's Doctrine of the Church, the Ministry and the Sacraments." Papers of the Canadian Methodist Historical Society, vol. 2, 1977–80.

– *Practical Divinity: Theology in the Wesleyan Tradition*. Nashville: Abingdon, 1983.

– comp. *Wesleyan Theology: A Sourcebook*. Durham, NC: Labyrinth, 1984.

Langton, H.H. *Sir Daniel Wilson: A Memoir*. Toronto: Thomas Nelson, 1929.

Loetscher, Lefferts A. *A Brief History of the Presbyterians*. 4th ed. Philadelphia: Westminster, 1983.

– *The Broadening Church: A Study of Theological Issues in the Presbyterian Church Since 1869*. Philadelphia: Univ. of Pennsylvania Press, 1954.

Loudon, William James. *Sir William Mulock: A Short Biography*. Toronto: Thomas Nelson, 1929.

Lovin, Robin W. "The Physics of True Virtue." Paper presented at the conference "Wesleyan Theology and the Next Century," Aug. 1983, Emory Univ., Atlanta.

Lucas, Glenn. "Wesley Heritage in the United Church of Canada." In *Dig or Die*, ed. James S. Udy and Eric G. Clancy, 140–76. Sydney: World Methodist Historical Society, 1981.

Magney, William H. "The Methodist Church and the National Gospel." *The Bulletin* (Committee on Archives of the United Church of Canada) 20 (1968): 3–95.

Manning, Harry. "Changes in Evangelism within the Methodist Church in Canada during the time of Carman and Chown, 1884–1925: A Study of the Causes for and Shifts in Evangelism." MA thesis, Univ. of Toronto, 1975.

– "The Changing Mind-Set of Canadian Methodism." Papers of the Canadian Methodist Historical Society, vol. 2, 1977–80.

Marsden, George M. *Fundamentalism and American Culture: The Shaping of Twentieth-Century Evangelicalism 1870–1925*. Oxford: Oxford Univ. Press, 1980.

– "Fundamentalism as an American Phenomenon: A Comparison with English Evangelicalism." *Church History* 46 (1977): 215–32.

– ed. *Evangelicalism and Modern America*. Grand Rapids: Eerdmans, 1984.

Massey, Vincent. *What's Past is Prologue: The Memoirs of the Right Honourable Vincent Massey*. Toronto: Macmillan, 1963.

Masters, Donald C. "Patterns of Thought in Anglican Colleges in the Nineteenth Century." *Journal of the Canadian Church Historical Society* 6 (1964): 54–69.

– *Protestant Church Colleges in Canada*. Toronto: Univ. of Toronto Press, 1966.

Mathews, Donald G. "The Second Great Awakening as an Organizing Process, 1780–1830: A Hypothesis." *American Quarterly* 21 (1969): 23–44.

May, Henry F. *The Enlightenment in America*. New York: Oxford Univ. Press, 1976.

McColloh, Gerald O. *Ministerial Education in the American Methodist Movement*. Nashville: United Methodist Board of Higher Education and Ministry, 1980.

McCullough, Robert. "The Relations Between the English and Canadian Methodist Churches in Canada from 1833 to 1840." BD thesis, Emmanuel College, Victoria Univ. 1963.

McDonald, Neil. "Egerton Ryerson and the School as an Agent of Political Socialization." In *Egerton Ryerson and His Times*, ed. Neil McDonald and Alf Chaiton, 81–106. Toronto: Macmillan, 1978.

McKillop, A.B. "Canadian Methodism in 1884." Papers of the Canadian Methodist Historical Society, vol. 4, 1984.

– *Contours of Canadian Thought*. Toronto: Univ. of Toronto Press, 1987.

– *A Disciplined Intelligence: Critical Inquiry and Canadian Thought in the Victorian Era*. Montreal: McGill-Queen's Univ. Press, 1979.

– "John Watson and the Idealist Legacy." *Journal of Canadian Literature* 83 (1979): 72–88.

– "Nationalism, Identity and Canadian Intellectual History." *Queen's Quarterly* 81 (1974): 533–50.

McLoughlin, William G. *Modern Revivalism: Charles Grandison Finney to Billy Graham*. New York: Ronald 1959.

– *Revivals, Awakenings, and Reform: An Essay on Religion and Social Change in America, 1607–1977*. Chicago: Univ. of Chicago Press, 1978.

McNairn, Norman Alexander. "The American Contribution to Early Methodism in Canada, 1790–1840." PHD diss., Iliff School of Theology, 1969.

McNaught, Kenneth W. *A Prophet in Politics: A Biography of J.S. Woodsworth*. Toronto: Univ. of Toronto Press, 1959.

Mead, Sidney E. "The Rise of the Evangelical Conception of the Ministry in America: 1607–1850." In *The Ministry in Historical Perspectives*, ed. H. Richard Niebuhr and Daniel Day Williams, 207–49. New York: Harper and Row, 1956.

Methodist Church (Canada, Nfld., Bermuda). *Address of the General Super-*

intendent. Toronto: n.p., 1910.

– *Annual Report of the Missionary Society*. Toronto: Methodist Mission Rooms, 1913, 1914.

– *Catechism, containing a summary of Christian doctrine*. Published under the authority of the General Conference [of 1894]. Toronto: William Briggs, 1897.

– *Centennial of Canadian Methodism*. Toronto: William Briggs, 1891.

– *The Doctrine and Discipline of the Methodist Church*. Toronto: William Briggs, 1886, 1906.

– Joint Committee on Church Union Representing the Presbyterian, Methodist and Congregational Churches. *Proceedings of the Third Conference of the Joint Committee on Church Union*. 1907.

– *Journal of Proceedings of the General Conference*. Toronto: William Briggs, 1883, 1886, 1890, 1894, 1898, 1902, 1906, 1910, 1914, 1918.

– *Methodist Catechisms, nos. 1–3*. Toronto: William Briggs, 1883.

– *Proceedings of the Fourth Ecumenical Methodist Conference, held in Metropolitan Methodist Church, Toronto, Canada, October 4–17, 1911*. Toronto: Methodist Book and Publishing House, n.d.

Methodist Church of Canada. *Journal of Proceedings of the General Conference*. 13 vols. Toronto: 1874–82.

Meyer, Donald H. "American Intellectuals and the Victorian Crisis of Faith." *American Quarterly* 27 (1975): 585–603.

– *The Instructed Conscience: The Shaping of the American National Ethic*. Philadelphia: Univ. of Pennsylvania Press, 1972.

Mika, Nick. *Historic Belleville*. Belleville: Mika, 1977.

Miley, John. *Systematic Theology*. 2 vols. New York: Hunt and Eaton, 1893–4.

Miller, Perry. *The Life of the Mind in America from the Revolution to the Civil War*. Bks. 1–3. New York: Harcourt, Brace and World, 1965.

Millman, Thomas R. "The Conference on Christian Unity," *Canadian Journal of Theology* 3 (1957): 165–74.

– "The Study of Canadian Church History." *Canadian Journal of Theology* 1 (1955): 28–34.

Moir, John S. "American Influences on Canadian Churches Before Confederation." *Church History* 36 (1967): 440–55.

– "The Canadianization of the Protestant Churches." *Canadian Historical Association Report* 37 (1956): 46–62.

– *Church and State in Canada West*. Toronto: Univ. of Toronto Press, 1959.

– *The Church in the British Era*. Toronto: McGraw-Hill Ryerson, 1972.

– *A History of Biblical Studies in Canada: A Sense of Proportion*. Chico, Calif.: Scholars Press, 1982.

– "Methodism and Higher Education, 1943–1849: A Qualification." *Ontario History* 44 (1952): 109–28.

Moore, James R. *The Post-Darwinian Controversies: A Study of the Protestant*

Struggle to Come to Terms with Darwin in Great Britain and America, 1860-1900. Cambridge: Cambridge Univ. Press, 1979.

Morrow, E. Lloyd. *Church Union in Canada: Its History, Motives, Doctrine and Government.* Toronto: Thomas Allen, 1923.

Morton, Arthur S. *The Way to Union.* Toronto: William Briggs, 1912.

Neatby, Hilda "The Challenge of Education to the Christian Church." *Canadian Journal of Theology* 1, no. 1 (1955): 35–43.

– *Queen's University.* Vol. 1, *1841-1917. To strive, to seek, to find and not to yield.* Montreal: McGill-Queen's Univ. Press, 1978.

Niebuhr, H. Richard. *Christ and Culture.* New York: Harper and Row, 1951.

– *The Kingdom of God in America.* New York: Harper and Row, 1937.

– *The Social Sources of Denominationalism.* Cleveland: World Publishing, 1929.

Noll, Mark A. "Christian Thinking and the Rise of the American University." *Christian Scholar's Review* 9 (1979): 3–16.

–, ed. and comp. *The Princeton Theology, 1821-1921: Scripture, Science and Theological Method from Archibald Alexander to Benjamin Breckinridge Warfield.* Phillipsburg, NJ: Presbyterian and Reformed Publishing Co., 1983.

Norwood, Frederick A. "Methodist Historical Studies 1930-1959." *Church History* 28-9 (1959, 1960): 391–417, 74–88.

Outler, Albert C., ed. *John Wesley.* New York: Oxford Univ. Press, 1964.

Paley, William. *View of the Evidences of Christianity.* 11th ed. London: Faulder, 1805.

Paterson, Morton. "The Mind of a Methodist: The Personalist Theology of George John Blewett in Its Historical Context." *The Bulletin* (Committee on Archives of the United Church of Canada) 27 (1978): 94–103.

Patterson, William W. "The Doctrine of the Ministry in the Methodist Church, Canada, 1884-1925." THM thesis, Emmanuel College, Victoria Univ. 1966.

Persons, Stow. *American Minds.* New York: Knopf, 1958.

Peters, John Leland. *Christian Perfection and American Methodism.* Nashville: Abingdon, 1956.

Peterson, George E. *The New England College in the Age of the University.* Amherst: Univ. of Massachusetts Press, 1964.

Phillips, Alfred Moore. *"My Message," being extracts from the pulpit and platform: addresses of the late Rev. A.M. Phillips ... With an introduction by Rev. Chancellor Burwash.* Toronto: William Briggs, 1897.

Phillips, Samuel G. *The Methodist Pulpit: A Collection of Original Sermons from Living Ministers of the United Methodist Church in Canada.* Toronto: William Briggs, 1884.

–, ed. *The Canadian Methodist Pulpit: A Collection of Original Sermons, from Living Ministers of the Wesleyan Methodist Church in Canada.* Toronto: Hunter, Rose, 1875.

Pidgeon, George C. *The United Church of Canada: The Story of the Union.* Toronto: Ryerson 1950.

Pierce, Lorne. *The House of Ryerson.* Toronto: Ryerson, 1954.

Playter, George F. *The History of Methodism in Canada.* Toronto: A. Green, 1862.

Polanyi, Michael. *Personal Knowledge: Towards a Post-Critical Philosophy.* London: Routledge and Kegan Paul, 1962.

Porter, Noah. *The American Colleges and the American Public.* New ed. New York: C. Scribner's Sons, 1878.

Prang, Margaret. *N.W. Rowell: Ontario Nationalist.* Toronto: Univ. of Toronto Press, 1975.

Prentice, Alison. *The School Promoters: Education and Social Class in Mid-Nineteenth Century Upper Canada.* Toronto: McClelland and Stewart, 1977.

Rawlyk, G.A. *Ravished by the Spirit: Religious Revivals, Baptists, and Henry Alline.* Montreal: McGill-Queen's Univ. Press, 1984.

Rawlyk, George, and Kevin Quinn. *The Redeemed of the Lord Say So: A History of Queen's Theological College 1912–1972.* [Kingston: Queen's Theological College 1980.]

Reid, John G. *Mount Allison University: A History, to 1963.* 2 vols. Toronto: Univ. Toronto Press for Mount Allison Univ., 1984.

Reynar, Alfred Henry. *Ebenezer; Address on Methodism, its Significance and its History.* Delivered at the closing service of the Methodist Church, Cobourg, 18 July 1900. Toronto: William Briggs, 1900.

Rose, S.P. *The Genius of Methodism.* Toronto: Ryerson, 1923.

Ross, Brian R. "Ralph Cecil Horner: A Methodist Sectarian Deposed, 1887–1895." *The Bulletin* (Committee on Archives of the United Church of Canada) 26 (1977): 94–103.

Rothblatt, Sheldon. *The Revolution of the Dons.* London: Faber and Faber, 1968.

Rowe, Kenneth E. *The Place of Wesley in the Christian Tradition.* Metuchen, NJ: Scarecrow, 1976.

Roy, James. *Catholicity and Methodism; or, The Relation of John Wesley to Modern Thought.* Montreal: Burland-Desbarats, 1877.

Ryerson, Egerton. *Canadian Methodism; its Epochs and Characteristics.* Toronto: William Briggs, 1882.

– *The Story of My Life.* Toronto: William Briggs, 1883.

Sandeen, Ernest R. *The Roots of Fundamentalism. British and American Millenarianism, 1800–1930.* Chicago: Univ. of Chicago Press, 1970.

– "Toward a Historical Interpretation of the Origins of Fundamentalism." *Church History* 36 (1967): 66–83.

Sanders, Paul S. "The Sacraments in Early American Methodism." *Church History* 26 (1957): 355–71.

Sanderson, J.E. *The First Century of Methodism in Canada*. 2 vols. Toronto: William Briggs, 1908.

Schmidt, George Paul. *The Liberal Arts College: A Chapter in American Cultural History*. New Brunswick, NJ: Rutgers Univ. Press, 1957.

Schroeder, Gordon. "The Role of Theology in Church Union: Discussion and Controversy." Course paper, Univ. of Toronto, 1978.

Schwarz, Edward Richard. "Samuel Dwight Chown: An Architect of Canadian Church Union." PHD diss., Boston Univ. Graduate School, 1961.

– "Samuel Dwight Chown and the Methodist Contribution to Canadian Church Union." *Canadian Journal of Theology* 11 (1965): 134–8.

Scott, Ephraim. *"Church Union" and the Presbyterian Church in Canada*. Montreal: John Lovell and Son, 1928.

Scott, Leland H. "Methodist Theology in America in the Nineteenth Century." *Religion in Life* 25 (1955–56): 87–99.

Semple, Neil. "The Decline of Revival in Nineteenth Century Central-Canadian Methodism: The Extraordinary Means of Grace." Papers of the Canadian Methodist Historical Society, vol. 2, 1977–80.

– "The Impact of Urbanization on the Methodist Church in Central Canada, 1854–1884." PHD diss., Univ. of Toronto, 1979.

– " 'The Nurture and Admonition of the Lord': Nineteenth-Century Canadian Methodism's Response to 'Childhood.' " *Histoire sociale – Social History* 14 (1981): 157–75.

Shaw, William I. *Digest of the Doctrinal Standards of the Methodist Church*. Toronto: William Briggs, 1895.

Shortt, S.E.D. *The Search for an Ideal: Six Canadian Intellectuals and Their Convictions in an Age of Transition 1890–1930*. Toronto: Univ. of Toronto Press, 1976.

Silcox, Claris Edwin. *Church Union in Canada: Its Causes and Consequences*. New York: Institute of Social and Religious Research, 1933.

Sinclair-Faulkner, Tom. "Theory Divided from Practice: The Introduction of the Higher Criticism into Canadian Protestant Seminaries." *Studies in Religion* 10 (1981): 321–43.

Sissons, C.B. *Church and State in Canadian Education*. Toronto: 1959.

– *A History of Victoria University*. Toronto: Univ. of Toronto Press, 1952.

–, ed. *Egerton Ryerson: His Life and Letters*. 2 vols. Toronto: Clarke, Irwin, 1947.

Sizer, Sandra S. *Gospel Hymns and Social Religion: The Rhetoric of Nineteenth Century Revivalism*. Philadelphia: Temple Univ. Press, 1978.

Slater, Peter Gregg. *Children in the New England Mind*. Hamden, Conn.: Archon, 1977.

Slatterly, P. "The Cobourg-Peterborough Railway: Destiny Denied." In *Victorian Cobourg: A Nineteenth-Century Profile*, ed. J. Petryshyn, 85–107. Belleville: Mika, 1976.

Sloan, Douglas. *The Scottish Enlightenment and the American College Ideal.* New York: Teachers College Press, 1971.

Sloan, Douglas, comp. *The Great Awakening and American Education. A Documentary History.* New York: Teachers College Press, 1973.

Smith, Allan. "The Myth of the Self-made Man in English Canada, 1850–1914." *Canadian Historical Review* 59 (1978): 189–219.

Smith, L.E. "Nineteenth Century Canadian Preaching." THD diss., Emmanuel College, Victoria Univ., 1953.

Smith, Neil. "Nationalism in the Canadian Churches." *Canadian Journal of Theology* 9 (1963): 114–25.

Smith, Timothy L. *The History of Education in the Middle West.* Indianapolis: Indiana Historical Society, 1978.

– "Holiness and Radicalism in Nineteenth-Century America" in *Sanctification and Liberation,* ed. T. Runyon, 116–42. Nashville: Abingdon, 1981.

– *Revivalism and Social Reform: American Protestantism on the Eve of the Civil War.* New York: Abingdon, 1957.

– "Righteousness and Hope: Christian Holiness and the Millennial Vision in America, 1800–1900." *American Quarterly* 31 (1979): 21–45.

Smyth, Elizabeth M. "Centenary Methodist Church: A Study of the Congregation and Lay Membership, 1899." Papers of the Canadian Methodist Historical Society, vol. 2, 1978–80.

Stevenson, Louise L. "Between the Old Time College and the Modern University: Noah Porter and the New Haven Scholars." *History of Higher Education Annual* 3 (1983): 39–55.

– "The New Means to the Millennium: Noah Porter's College Reforms." Paper presented April 1983, at the American Society of Church History, Holland, Mich.

Stokes, Mack B. *The Holy Spirit in the Wesleyan Heritage.* Nashville: Graded Press/Abingdon Press, 1985.

Sutherland, Alexander. *Methodism in Canada: Its Work and Its Story.* Toronto: Methodist Mission Rooms, 1904.

– *The Moral Status of Children and their Relation to Christ and His Church.* Toronto: Alexander Sutherland, 1876.

– *The Proposed Plan of College Confederation.* Toronto: Alexander Sutherland, 1885.

Sutherland, Neil. *Children in English-Canadian Society.* Toronto: Univ. of Toronto Press, 1976.

Sweet, Leonard I., ed., *The Evangelical Tradition in America.* Macon, Ga.: Mercer Univ. Press, 1984.

Taylor, Robert John. "The Darwinian Revolution: The Responses of Four Canadian Scholars." PHD diss., McMaster Univ., 1976.

Thomas, Ernest. "Church Union in Canada." *American Journal of Theology* 23 (1919): 257–73.

Thomas, Hilah F., and Rosemary Keller, eds. *Women in New Worlds: Historical Perspectives on the Wesleyan Tradition*. Vol. 1. Nashville: Abingdon, 1981.

Thompson, E.P. *The Making of the English Working Class*. New York: Penguin, 1966.

Troeltsch, Ernst. *The Social Teaching of the Christian Churches*. Trans. by Olive Wyon. 2 vols. London: George Allen and Unwin, 1931.

Turner, James. *Without God, Without Creed: The Origins of Unbelief in America*. Baltimore: Johns Hopkins Univ. Press, 1985.

Upham, Thomas. *Mental Philosophy*. New York: Harper Brothers, 1875.

Veysey, Laurence R. *The Emergence of the American University*. Chicago: Univ. of Chicago Press, 1965.

Victoria University. *On the Old Ontario Strand: Victoria's Hundred Years*. Addresses at the Centenary of Victoria University and the Burwash Memorial Lectures of the Centennial Year. Toronto: Victoria Univ. 1936.

Wallace, W. Stewart, ed., *A History of the University of Toronto, 1827–1927*. Toronto: Univ. of Toronto Press, 1927.

- *The Ryerson Imprint*. Toronto: Ryerson 1956.

Walsh, Henry H. "Canada and the Church: A Job for the Historians." *Queen's Quarterly* 61 (1954): 71–9.

- *The Christian Church in Canada*. Toronto: Ryerson, 1956.

- "Trends in Canadian Church History." *Church History* 23 (1954): 236–47.

Wayland, Francis. *Elements of Moral Science*. London: Religious Tract Society, n.d.

Welch, Claude, and John Dillenberger. *Protestant Christianity Interpreted through Its Development*. 2d ed. New York: Macmillan, 1988.

Welter, Barbara. "The Cult of True Womanhood." *American Quarterly* 18 (1966): 151–74.

[Wesley, John]. *Minutes of the Methodist Conferences, from the first, held in London, by the late Rev. John Wesley, A.M. in the year 1744*. Vol. 1, 1744–98. London: John Mason, 1862.

Wesley, John. *Notes on the New Testament*. Wakefield: William Nicholson, n.d.

- *The Works of John Wesley*, ed. Thomas Jackson. 4th ed. 14 vols. London: Wesleyan Methodist Book Room, 1840.

Wesleyan Methodist Church in Canada. *The Catechisms*. Toronto: Samuel Rose, 1868.

- *Course of Study for Candidates for Membership in the Canada Conference*. Toronto: G.R. Sanderson, 1857.

- *Course of Study for Candidates for the Ministry*. Toronto: Anson Green, 1844.

- *The Doctrine and Discipline*. Toronto: M. Lang, 1836. Toronto: A. Green, 1850, 1859, 1864.

- *Minutes of the Annual Conferences from 1824 to 1845.* Toronto: Anson Green, 1846.
- *Minutes of Twelve Annual Conferences from 1846 to 1857 inclusive.* Toronto: Anson Green, 1863.
Westfall, William. "The Dominion of the Lord: An Introduction to the Cultural History of Protestant Ontario in the Victorian Period." *Queen's Quarterly* 83 (1976): 47–71.
- "Order and Experience: Patterns of Religious Metaphor in Early Nineteenth Century Upper Canada." *Journal of Canadian Studies* 20 (1985): 5–38.
- "The Sacred and the Secular: Studies in the Cultural History of Protestant Ontario in the Victorian Period." PHD diss., Univ. of Toronto, 1976.
Wiebe, Robert. *The Search for Order, 1877–1920.* New York: Hill and Wang, 1967.
Willey, Basil. *More Nineteenth Century Studies: A Group of Honest Doubters* London: Chatto and Windus, 1956; Cambridge: Cambridge Univ. Press, 1980.
- *Nineteenth Century Studies: Coleridge to Matthew Arnold.* London: Chatto and Windus, 1949. Cambridge: Cambridge Univ. Press, 1980.
Wilson, J. Donald, Robert M. Stamp, and Louis-Philippe Audet, eds. *Canadian Education: A History.* Scarborough: Prentice-Hall, 1970.
Wilson, R.J. *Church Union in Canada After Three Years.* Toronto: Ryerson Press, 1929.
Windsor, Kenneth N. "Historical Writing in Canada (to 1920)." In *A Literary History of Canada: Canadian Literature in English,* ed. Carl F. Klinck, 225–34. Toronto: Univ. of Toronto Press, 1965.
Wise, S.F. "God's Peculiar Peoples." In *The Shield of Achilles: Aspects of Canada in the Victorian Age,* ed. W.L. Morton, 36–61. Toronto: McClelland and Stewart, 1968.
Withrow, W.H. *Makers of Methodism.* Toronto: William Briggs, 1898.
- *Religious Progress of the Nineteenth Century.* Toronto: Linscott, 1906.
[Withrow, W.H.?] *Spurious Catholicity; or, Socinianism Unmasked; a review of the Rev. James Roy's recent pamphlet, in which he assails the authority of the Bible and the truth of the orthodox doctrines of religion.* Montreal: Montreal Book Room, 1877.
Workman, George Coulson. *At Onement; or Reconciliation with God.* New York: Revell, 1911.
- *Messianic Prophecy Vindicated.* Toronto: George Coulson Workman, 1899.
- *The Old Testament Vindicated as Christianity's Foundation Stone.* Toronto: William Briggs, 1897.
Woodsworth, J.S. *Following the Gleam: A Modern Pilgrim's Progress to Date.* Ottawa: n.p., 1926.
Wycliffe College. *The Jubilee Volume of Wycliffe College.* Toronto: Wycliffe College, 1927.

Zuckerman, Michael. "Dreams that Men Dare to Dream: The Role of Ideas in Western Modernization." *Social Science History* 2 (1978): 332–45.

Index